The Creativity Research Handbook Volume One

Perspectives on Creativity
Mark A. Runco (ed.)

Reclaiming the Wasteland: TV & Gifted Children
Bob Abelman

The Motives for Creative Work
Jock Abra

Remarkable Women: Perspectives on Female Talent Development
Karen Arnold, Kathleen Noble, and Rena Subotnik (eds.)

No Rootless Flower: An Ecology of Creativity
Frank Barron

Flexible Thinking: An Explanation for Individual Differences in Ability
Norbert Jausovec

Unusual Associates: Essays in Honor of Frank Barron
Alfonso Montuori (ed.)

Creativity Research Handbook, Volume One
Mark A. Runco (ed.)

forthcoming

Transgressive Discourse
Stephanie Dudek

Creativity and Giftedness in Culturally Diverse Students
Giselle B. Esquivel and John Houtz (eds.)

Investigating Creativity in Youth: A Book of Readings on
Research and Methods
Anne S. Fishkin, Bonnie Cramond, and Paula Olszewski-Kubilius (eds.)

Style and Psyche
Pavel Machotka

Critical Creative Processes
Mark A. Runco (ed.)

Theories of Creativity, Revised Edition
Mark A. Runco and Robert S. Albert (eds.)

Divergent and Creative Thinking
Mark A. Runco and Joni Radio Gaynor

The Young Gifted Child: Potential and Promise—An Anthology
Joan F. Smutny

The Creativity Research Handbook Volume One

Mark A. Runco

California State University-Fullerton

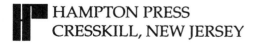

HAMPTON PRESS
CRESSKILL, NEW JERSEY

Printed in the United States of America

Library of Congress Cataloging-in-Publication Data

Runco, Mark A.
　　The creativity research handbook / Mark A. Runco
　　　　p.　cm. -- (Perspectives on creativity)
　　Includes bibliographical references and indexes
　　　ISBN 1-881303-73-X (cloth : v. 1). -- ISBN 1-881303-74-8 (pbk. : v. 1)
　　　1. Creative ability. 2. Creative ability--research. 3. Creative
　　thinking.　I. Title.　II. Series.
BF408.R78　1997
153.3'5--dc20　　　　　　　　　　　　　　　　　　　　96-31262
　　　　　　　　　　　　　　　　　　　　　　　　　　　　　CIP

Hampton Press, Inc.
23 Broadway
Cresskill, NJ 07626

This volume is dedicated to Chelsea Brooke Meilani Runco,
my favorite pianist, martial artist, and poet.

Contents

Introduction

For years the research on creativity has been divided alliteratively into person, process, product, and press (environment) foci. This structure has worked remarkably well, but it is time to put it behind us. The field is now much more extensive and diverse than it was when the alliterative scheme was proposed, and those four categories no longer capture the essence of the field. The current and subsequent volumes of the *Creativity Research Handbook* will show how extensive and diverse the field has become.

The *Handbook* is divided into two parts, the first disciplinary and the second topical. The disciplinary structure used for Part 1 is larger than the person, process, product, and press scheme, and for this reason it allows a more sensitive and accurate placement of research. At the same time it is not so large as to be unwieldy. The disciplinary framework also has an advantage in its facilitating exchanges with the wider scholarly community. Research on creative thinking, for example, shares assumptions with the cognitive sciences, and the disciplinary assignment can help individuals studying creativity to benefit from those sciences. Several of the contributions to the *Handbook* demonstrate how creativity research has benefited from such disciplinary connections. Most chapters imply that the advantage is mutual and that those studying other areas can benefit from research on creativity.

Part 2 of this *Handbook* contains six topical chapters. Several of these rely on one discipline; others are interdisciplinary. Each of them focuses on one critical topic. Bachelor and Michael, for example, prepared a psychometric chapter, but it is focused on the structure-of-intellect model. Katz's chapter describes biology but focuses on hemispheric specialization. The interdisciplinary approach is especially clear in the chapters on problem finding and humor. Jay and Perkins, for example, cite cognitive and dispositional theories, and O'Quin and Derks use both social and cognitive theories.

Recognizing that creativity research aspires to the scientific method, and with the scientific method in turn requiring integrations with previous research, the *Handbook* was conceived as an archive containing extensive reviews. It is intended to give a comprehensive view of creativity research. This comprehensiveness is apparent in two ways: first, by the breadth of coverage of the chapters (especially taking both Volume 1 and the forthcoming Volume 2 into account), and second, by the depth and coverage within each chapter.

Bachelor and Michael (Chapter 7) give an up-to-date overview of the Structure of Intellect (SOI). This approach to the intellect is significant for students of creativity, given the role played by J. P. Guilford's model in the early days of the field. Bachelor and Michael pay special attention to the major criticisms of that model and review the most recent SOI research. The recent analyses are noteworthy because many individuals look to Guilford's findings from the 1960s as indicative of SOI research. Guilford modified his model until his death in 1987—proposing 180 cells, for example, and exploring higher order factors. Clearly, that recent research should be used rather than the SOI work from the 1950s and 1960s. The reanalyses of Guilford's data should similarly be given serious consideration. Consider, for instance, the demonstration that creativity is best described in terms of a mixed or hierarchical model, with both first order and higher order factors, and that creativity is associated with several SOI cells, in addition to divergent production, such as transformation and even convergent production.

Simonton's chapter also describes methodology but the focus is on historiometry. The beauty of historiometry is clear in Simonton's definition of Historiometry as "a method that seeks out general laws or statistical regularities that transcend the names, dates, and places of history." Historiometry, therefore, allows very trustworthy generalizations about creativity. Simonton describes research on artists, scientists, politicians, and a variety of other eminent individuals, and he demonstrates how historiometry can be applied to studies of development, personality, education, and political and social presses and processes. Note that we thus have coverage of something not promised by the Table of Contents—a discussion of social factors. Teresa Amabile has contributed a chapter on social theories to Volume 2 of the *Creativity Research Handbook*.

Gedo (Chapter 2), Eysenck (Chapter 3) and Smith and Amnér (Chapter 4), each have a great deal to say about the creative personality. Smith and Amnér argue that "perception is subsumed under the broader frame of personality." They discuss the role of analogies and metaphors in perception and the workings of the unconscious. (An entire chapter is devoted to metaphor in Volume 2.) The processes that underlie creativity may very well be highly subjective and at least partly preconscious (Barron, 1995), and the empirical work of Smith and Amnér shows how we can recognize important subjective processes, and, at the same time, conduct controlled research. Implicit here is the view that creativity research must adapt its method to fit the subject matter; we cannot be scientific in the same sense as many of the harder sciences, nor even like research on other topics within psychology.

Gedo (Chapter 2) deals with the unconscious in his overview of psychoanalytic theory. He begins with the Freudian view of libido and id and then gives context for concepts which are more well-known in creativity research, such as *regression in the service of the ego*. Interestingly, some psychoanalytic concepts, such as those involving the manipulation of percepts, parallel ideas in cognitive psychology. In fact, there is much of interest in Gedo's chapter for cognitivists and developmentalists, as well as for those interested in perception, personality, and motivation. Gedo is explicit about the value of psychoanalytic work for understanding the motivation for creativity, a topic that is explored further in Volume 2 of the *Handbook* (also see Gedo & Gedo, 1990).

In his chapter on personality, Eysenck (Chapter 3) describes the theory that psychosis differs from psychoticism; the former is actually psychopathological, whereas the latter is "a dispositional trait underlying susceptibility to the development of psychotic symptoms." Psychoticism is correlated with creativity, which Eysenck explains in terms of the selective and evaluative skills that represent "the ability to weed out unsuitable and unusable associations." This ability is "the distinguishing mark between the word salad of the schizophrenic and the utterances of the poet."

Eisenman (Chapter 4) further discusses the significance of the relatively low inhibition and overinclusivensss of creative individuals, but he argues for the explanatory power of the concept of *deviance*. He writes, "perhaps whatever produces the creative deviance also produces, in some instances, mental illness or disorder." This view parallels Eysenck's on psychoticism, but Eisenman points to various virtues of deviance, including independence of judgment, healthy nonconformity, and, of course, creativity. Most notable is Eisenman's argument that "deviance can be good."

Cropley (Chapter 5) focuses on educational research. He reviews existing educational technologies and then carefully refutes the misconception that a concern for creativity leads to an unstructured and careless curriculum. He gives precise objectives for educators, some fundamental (e.g., knowledge base, imagination) and some less intuitive but clearly supported by empirical research (e.g., bisociation and janusian thinking). He also reviews available assessments, including some of the newer tests using qualitative scoring and stringent and nonstringent criteria. Thus the *Creativity Research Handbook* has more psychometric theory to go along with that of Bachelor and Michael, though the principal virtue of Cropley's work is its translation of solid creativity research into specific educational practice.

The developmental chapter of Runco and Charles has educational implications; however, their primary intent is to explore developmental trends and trajectories. Like Simonton, Runco and Charles describe the changes and transformations that occur during the lifespan. Like Smith and Amnér, Runco and Charles attend to creative potential rather than just actual performance. Also like Smith and Amnér, Runco and Charles argue that development is, in part, driven by the individual. The active role of individual as seen in Smith and Amnér's argument is that "the bored mind escapes and explores alternative ways of perceiving by 'dissolution of the whole,' or the transformation of gestalten." Runco and Charles use the fairly well-known developmental postulate that individuals do not merely react to their environments but instead seek out certain experiences and make many important choices that in turn influence their creative potentials. Runco and Charles conclude that more attention needs to be directed at conative, voluntary, judgmental processes that support creative potential and its expression.

In this sense the developmental research supports the conclusion of Jay and Perkins (Chapter 11), about problem finding. Contextual and dispositional factors and cognitive abilities and processes are all covered by Jay and Perkins. What may be most important in this chapter is the distinction between factors that *enable* and factors that actually *promote* creative behavior. Certain cognitive tendencies are conducive to problem finding, allowing it to occur, while doing little to actively facilitate or promote it. Enabling factors are necessary but not sufficient for actual performance. This is why dispositions are so important. Individuals can be capable of doing something but choose not to act. Hence, we must study their inclinations and dispositions.

Finke (Chapter 8) focuses on cognition and gives great weight to perceptual processes. He specifically relates mental images to "the exploration or anticipation of perceptual features that are often useful in solving problems or planning actions." He likewise discusses mental transformations in which a representation is cognitively manipulated and can allow "creative exploration." (Recall here that transformational skills are emphasized by Bachelor and Michael in Chapter 7.) Finke describes the research on mental synthesis, image generation, image reinterpretation, invention, and conceptual discoveries. Each of these has potential ties with creative thinking.

Much of the research reviewed by Finke helps to explain literal creations or mental constructions. *Representational momentum*, for instance, allows individuals to "to keep track of actions that momentarily pass out of view. It can also be useful in carrying out mental simulations of imagined events."[1] Finke gives other examples of mental constructions, but the point is that his chapter focuses on a fundamental aspect of creativity—the mental creation. In this way Finke's chapter reminds us of the meaning of the concept *create*. Creativity connotes originality and value, but the literal definition of *creation* is simply "bringing something new into existence" (cf. Euster, 1987; Hausman, 1979; Runco, in press; Stein, 1984).

Katz (Chapter 9) gives a detailed review of the work on hemispheric specialization. Certainly what is most important is the clear dismissal of the "simplistic argument that creativity resides in the right hemisphere." Katz also reviews chemical research (e.g., marijuana), and his comparisons of the different assessment options will be useful to anyone wishing to conduct or evaluate research in this area. The acknowledgment a tie between hemispheric asymmetries and *creative style* suggests a biological base for certain developmental trends, many of which reflect changes in style (see Chapter 6). Several of the chapters in the present volume address other aspects of the biological bases of creativity, including and Gedo (Chapter 2), Eysenck (Chapter 3), and Smith and Amnér (Chapter 4).

O'Quin and Derks (Chapter 10) distinguish between humor *appreciation* and humor *production* and argue that is the latter that seems to be most closely related to creativity. As they put it, "One can be an appreciator of humor without also being a producer, but the reverse does not seem at all likely". The distinction between appreciation and production is especially interesting given the paradox noted in the creativity literature that most individuals can judge creativity better than they can produce it (Perkins, 1981; Runco & Chand, 1994). It is one thing to be able to recognize creativity, but quite another to be able to do something creative for one's self. The production of humor or a creative product requires more than recognition, and whatever that is—cognitive, motivational, or something else—may point us to something which can be done to fulfill creative potentials. Practically speaking, the work on humor might be useful for those scoring creativity tests with humor as an index (e.g., Urban, 1991), and the differences found between groups of judges (e.g., teachers' ratings of humor vs. peer ratings) might be recognized when consensual assessments are used. The findings of O'Quin and Derks about age differences in the creativity-humor relationship fit nicely with the developmental research (Chapter 6).

---

[1]Representational momentum may be particularly useful to creators in nontraditional domains such as sports. These activities are only recently gaining attention as potentially creative, thanks in part to the convincing work on domain specificity. Representational momentum could easily contribute to athletic talent and "bodily intelligence."

The axiom "you cannot tell a book by its cover" should have the footnote, "nor can you infer all that much from a Table of Contents." Obviously this is in part true simply because a Table of Contents is always shorter than the volume itself. It is a sample, and because of its size it cannot be all that detailed. Granted, this idea about Tables of Contents does not have the same metaphorical beauty as the traditional message about the covers of books, but it does allow me to be explicit about something I have been hinting at—namely, that the Table of Contents for this *Handbook* may contain only 12 chapters, but those chapters cover everything from artists to *Zeitgeist*. Many of the topics are not listed in the Table of Contents, but they are discussed in the chapters themselves. Recall here my mention of biological, social, cognitive, and psychometric research within the various chapters.

The 12 chapters of the *Handbook* do give a fairly comprehensive overview of the field of creativity, though admittedly one reason for optimism about the comprehensiveness of the *Creativity Research Handbook* is suggested by the subtitle. This is Volume 1, Volume 2 is in production, and Volume 3 is well under way. There is every reason to believe that creativity research will continue to accelerate and grow and reason also to believe that the *Creativity Research Handbook* will allow us to follow that growth.

REFERENCES

Barron, F. (1995). *No rootless flower.* Cresskill, NJ: Hampton Press.

Euster, J. (1987) Guest editorial. *College and Research Libraries, 48,* 287-287.

Gedo, J., & Gedo, M. (1990). *Perspectives on creativity.* Norwood, NJ: Ablex.

Hausman, C. (1979). Criteria of creativity. *Philosophy and Phenomenological Research, 40,* 237-249

Perkins, D. (1981). *The mind's best work.* Cambridge, MA: Harvard University Press.

Runco, M.A. (in press) Creativity need not be social. In A. Montuori & R. Purser (Eds.), *Social creativity* (vol. 1). Cresskill, NJ: Hampton

Runco, M.A., & Chand, I. (1994). Problem finding, evaluative thinking, and creativity. In M.A. Runco (Ed.), *Problem finding, problem solving, and creativity* (pp. 40-76). Norwood, NJ: Ablex.

Stein, M. (1984, July-September). Creative: The adjective. *Creativity and Innovation Network,* pp. 115-117.

Urban, K. (1991). On the development of creativity in children. *Creativity Research Journal, 4,* 177-192.

Mark A. Runco
December 1996

I THEORETICAL APPROACHES

1 Historiometric Studies of Creative Genius

Dean Keith Simonton
University of California, Davis

What comes to mind when someone uses the term *creative genius*? Do we normally think of a person who gained a stratospheric score on some intelligence test? Probably not. Do we imagine an individual who performed exceptionally well on some instrument that purports to measure creativity? Again, likely not. Instead, many will first conjure up a great name from the annals of intellectual or aesthetic history. To count as a creative genius means to rub shoulders with the likes of Archimedes, Newton, and Einstein; Aristotle, Descartes, and Kant; Homer, Dante, and Shakespeare; Phidias, Michelangelo, and Picasso; Beethoven, Verdi, and Stravinsky—just to cite a few instances drawn from European civilization.

To be sure, some might argue that some "creative geniuses" have been overlooked in the history books. This argument is especially strong when considering all the women and minorities whose talents were either neglected or crushed by the prejudices of their times. Nevertheless, the fact that some potential genius is never realized owing to such unjust circumstances cannot discredit those who did manage to make creative contributions to human culture. Newton's *Mathematica Principia*, Kant's *Kritik der reinen Vernunft*, Dante's *La Commedia*, Picasso's *Guernica*, and Beethoven's Fifth Symphony still represent monumental achievements no matter how long is the list of overlooked talents. Therefore, at the very least these luminaries can be accepted as true exemplars of the phenomenon called *creativity*. To deny this ascription is to deny that the term has any real meaning. After all, any alternative gauge of creativity, such as a psychometric test, must undergo validation against this very criterion. To create necessarily means to produce something that many others deem creative. The consensus must be strongest when contemporaries and posterity concur that someone has conceived genuine masterworks (Simonton, 1991c).

If this line of reasoning is accepted, then the psychologist who wishes to study creativity should seriously ponder how best to investigate geniuses whose creative accomplishments have become historic. Is there any scientific way to examine subjects who happened to have been named Copernicus, Darwin, Spinoza, Nietzsche, Tolstoy, Moliere, Goya, or Debussy? Can we formulate and test hypotheses about the creative process and personality using individuals whose qualifications are unquestioned but who often have the inconvenient habit of being deceased? In short, can we construct a science of creative genius based on the scrutiny of the highest caliber exemplars?

My answer is yes. And I have a particular methodology in mind: *historiometry*. To establish the case for this approach, I do three main things. First, I offer a brief history of this technique. Next, I provide an overview of the central research topics. And last I close with a brief appraisal of the technique's key assets and liabilities. Before I can do any of these things, I first must define what we mean by historiometric research.

DEFINITION

I defined *historiometry* as "a scientific discipline in which nomothetic hypotheses about human behavior are tested by applying quantitative analyses to data concerning historical individuals" (Simonton, 1990e, p. 3). Because this is quite a mouthful, let me break up the definition into three components.

First, historiometry is dedicated to testing nomothetic hypotheses about human behavior. It is a method that seeks out general laws or statistical regularities that transcend the names, dates, and places of history. Thus, when applied to the study of creative genius, historiometric research might evaluate conjectures or predictions about what personality traits, developmental experiences, or contextual factors might contribute to exceptional achievement. This orientation must be distinguished from the idiographic approach, which places special emphasis on the principles that guide the behavior of singular persons, without worrying about whether these guidelines can be generalized (Runyan, 1982).

Second, quantitative analyses are absolutely essential to the business of conducting historiometric research. To begin with, investigators must strive to assess the central variables on some quantitative scale, whether ordinal, interval, or ratio. For example, the researcher might evaluate intelligence, personality traits, or childhood trauma along some kind of dimension. Once these measures are obtained, the historiometrician subjects these data to often complex statistical analyses. Among the methods available are multiple regression, factor analysis, linear structural models, time series analysis, and cluster analysis. These techniques allow the hypotheses that inspire the study to be confirmed or rejected with the maximum possible scientific rigor.

Third, historiometric studies examine historic individuals—people who have made history in a particular human endeavor. Often this means that the subject pool consists of deceased luminaries, but this is not essential. It is certainly possible for contemporary individuals to have achieved sufficient greatness so that their place in history is unquestionable. Someone such as Albert Einstein, for instance, became a legend in his own lifetime. Nonetheless, there are many advantages to narrowing the samples to historic personalities who are no longer living.

In any case, I cannot overemphasize the plural in the phrase "historical individuals." Historiometric inquiries are almost invariably multiple-case studies. There must be a large N to apply the elaborate statistical techniques. And there must be a respectable N to make a convincing argument that the findings are truly nomothetic in nature. The only exceptions to this rule are those occasional historiometric inquiries that take a single notable, such as Shakespeare or Beethoven, as prototypical exemplars of a particular kind of creative activity (e.g., Derks, 1989; Sears, Lapidus, & Cozzens, 1978; Simonton, 1986e, 1987a, 1989b, 1990c).

It will help clarify the nature of historiometry if it is compared with some closely related enterprises. Some possible comparisons are graphed in Figure 1.1.

According to this Venn diagram, historiometrics lies at the intersection of three broad domains—psychology, science, and history. Other activities with which it has a close affinity reside at the intersection of only two of these domains. Thus, econometrics, cliometrics, and the philosophy of history, albeit in different ways, represent the confluence of science and history. The philosophy of history, for example, aims at qualitative generalizations that go beyond the particulars of history. I would place Kuhn's (1970) analysis of scientific revolutions in this category. By comparison, cliometrics applies mathematical analyses to historical data, yet does so only to verify idiographic statements (e.g., whether slavery was profitable in the antebellum South). Psychometrics, in contrast, represents the confluence of scientific methods and psychological content. Although more engaged in the assessment of nomothetic propositions, psychometrics tends to obtains its raw data from contemporary rather than historical sources. Finally, psychohistory and psychobiography emerged from a welding of psychological theory and historical materials, but do so without the scientific commitment to quantitative analyses and nomothetic results (Simonton, 1983e). Such investigations favor qualitative discussions of single cases. Moreover, rather than test nomothetic propositions, most psychohistorians and psychobiographers are content to apply theoretical positions (usually psychoanalytic) to a particular historic personality or period (cf. deMause, 1981).

Although distinct, historiometrics shares something with all the kindred disciplines. In particular, it can be said that historiometrics embodies the convergence of certain aspects of psychometrics, psychohistory and psychobiography, and the philosophy of history, cliometrics, and even econometrics.

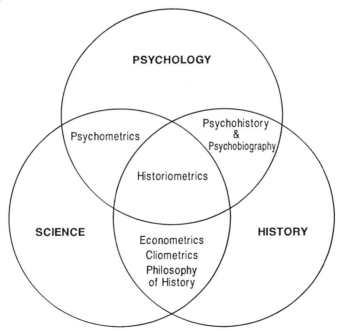

Figure 1.1. Venn diagram showing how historiometry compares with closely related subdisciplines within psychology, science, and history. Because many portions of psychology are not yet broadly accepted as "scientific" (parapsychology, psychoanalysis, humanistic psychology, etc.), the discipline of psychology is not shown as a proper subset of science in general.

HISTORY

Psychohistory and psychobiography are usually said to have begun with Sigmund Freud, whose 1910 *Leonardo da Vinci and a Memory of his Childhood* is considered one of the classics in this genre (Elms, 1988). Yet, by this date, historiometrics was already three quarters of a century old! Hence, historiometric research constitutes one of the oldest research traditions in the behavioral sciences. Moreover, this tradition has attracted contributions from some of the central figures in the development of psychological science. So I briefly narrate the history of historiometry. By narrating the discipline's origins, it can be better appreciated as to why historiometrics offers a unique perspective on the psychology of creative genius.

So far as I have been able to determine, the first published historiometric inquiry can be found in the classic *Sur l'homme* (Treatise on Man) by Adolphe Quetelet. This Belgian astronomer, meteorologist, mathematician, sociologist, and poet is perhaps best known for his introduction of statistics in the analysis of behavioral data. Although the bulk of his 1835 monograph is devoted to delineating the "average man" and establishing the "normal distribution," wedged among the pages is the first quantitative study of the relation between personal age and creative achievement. Almost 40 years later, this same substantive question was granted systematic treatment by George M. Beard (1874), thereby making this issue easily the oldest topic treated by historiometric methods. However, neither of these contributions inspired any follow-up studies until nearly a century later (Simonton, 1988a).

Accordingly, Francis Galton may be considered to be the real instigator of this distinctive practice. This English scientist, explorer, and anthropologist was a tremendous innovator. And among his more monumental achievements was his 1869 volume *Hereditary Genius*. The basic thesis of this book was that genius-grade accomplishments tend to run in families because of the genetic transmission of natural ability. Even if his core conclusions must undergo considerable qualifications (Bramwell, 1948; Kroeber, 1944; Simonton, 1988b), *Hereditary Genius* became a classic in psychology and the first truly important historiometric study of creative genius.

Many followed in Galton's footsteps. Just four years later, the Swiss botanist Alphonse de Candolle (1873) published an inquiry into the environmental conditions that produce notable creators in science. In 1904, the English sexologist Havelock Ellis published *A Study of British Genius*, which described the personal and social factors that encourage the emergence of eminent individuals (Ellis, 1926). On the other side of the Atlantic, historiometry found a proponent in James McKeen Cattell (e.g., 1903, 1910). In 1894, Cattell acquired *Science* and edited it for a half century. During that time this periodical became a major vehicle for the dissemination of many historiometric inquiries, a status it retained until the 1950s (e.g., Dennis, 1956b; Lehman, 1958).

Among the many items that appeared in *Science* were two papers by Woods (1909, 1911) that finally christened the discipline. The November 19, 1909 issue contained a note on "A New Name for a New Science," in which Woods defined historiometry as an investigation in which "the facts of history of a personal nature have been subjected to statistical analysis by some more or less objective method" (p. 703). According to Woods, "Historiometry bears the same relation to history that biometry does to biology" (p. 703). He appended to this paper a list of a dozen studies that he considered good exemplars of this new approach. In the April 14, 1911 issue of *Science*, Woods once more advertised this new field in an article on "Historiometry as an Exact Science." Here he argued that this technique would immensely enhance understanding regarding the "psychology of genius."

Unfortunately, Woods himself was more fascinated by illustrious leadership than creativity. So most of his own applications of historiometric methods looked at historic leaders, especially monarchs (Woods, 1906, 1913). Although this work did motivate many follow-up inquiries, including one by Thorndike (1936), this research tradition does not concern us here. More germane are the subsequent studies of creative geniuses that explicitly billed themselves as historiometric investigations. Among these diverse studies, the most significant by far is an ambitious study done by Cox (1926). To appreciate the place of this study in the history of historiometry, it needs to be placed in context.

As is well known, Lewis M. Terman is one of the pioneers in the early development of the intelligence test. His adaptation of the original Binet-Simon instrument—the famed Stanford-Binet test—helped make IQ one of the most discussed concepts in psychology. To validate his ideas about the importance of intelligence, Terman (1925) initiated his well-known longitudinal study of children whom he had identified as intellectually gifted. Terman hoped to show that kids with high IQs grew up to become accomplished adults. The outcome was his series of books entitled *Genetic Studies of Genius*, the last volume of which came out posthumously (Terman & Oden, 1959). However, Terman's interests went beyond psychometrics. Stimulated by Woods, Terman wondered whether it would be possible to estimate IQ scores for historic figures. Answering the affirmative, Terman (1917) published a paper on "The Intelligence Quotient of Francis Galton in Childhood." Using the definition of IQ as a ratio of mental to chronological age, Galton got a score close to 200.

As a single-case inquiry, this 1917 paper would not seem to have much importance. Still, about the time that Terman launched his longitudinal investigation he had a graduate student, Catharine Cox, searching around for a dissertation topic. What she decided to do was to apply the same method by which Terman calculated Galton's IQ to obtain scores for 301 historic personalities. Almost two-thirds of these were creative geniuses in the arts and sciences, including famous names such as Mozart, Leonardo da Vinci, Goethe, Cervantes, Rousseau, Harvey, and Huygens. Her goal was to show that those who make the big time as adults would have been identified as intellectually gifted children and adolescents. Because this demonstration complemented so well what Terman was trying to accomplish in his longitudinal study, Terman made Cox's study the second volume of *Genetic Studies of Genius* (Cox, 1926). In addition, Cox set aside a group of 100 subjects for special treatment, estimating their scores on 67 traits of character. To pull this off, Cox had again to adapt psychometric measures for historiometric purposes. The result was a product that represented the state of the art in historiometric research at that time.

Although Cox herself did not pursue further this line of inquiry, many other psychologists did do so (e.g., Albert, 1971; McCurdy, 1960; Raskin, 1936; Simonton, 1976a; Walberg, Rasher, & Parkerson, 1980; White, 1931). Moreover, some psychologists introduced research questions and techniques that appreciably broadened the scope of inquiry (e.g., R. B. Cattell, 1963; Dennis, 1955, 1966; Farnsworth, 1969; Lehman, 1953; Martindale, 1975, 1990; McClelland, 1961; Suedfeld, 1985; Thorndike, 1950). Finally, researchers outside psychology also developed various aspects of historiometric methodology (e.g., Brannigan & Wanner, 1983a, 1983b; Cerulo, 1988, 1989; Gray, 1958, 1961, 1966; Kroeber, 1944; Merton, 1961; Naroll et al., 1971; Richardson & Kroeber, 1940; Sorokin, 1937-41). Historiometry has thus become an extremely rich approach to the study of creative genius. This is manifest in the range of issues addressed by this method.

RESEARCH TOPICS

Creative genius is a phenomenon so complex that it can only be understood from multiple perspectives. Historiometric methods permit examination of the phenomenon from the viewpoints of three main subdisciplines: (a) developmental and educational psychology, (b) differential and personality psychology, and (c) social and political psychology.

Developmental and Educational Psychology

Historiometric studies of genius are truly lifespan developmental in scope (Simonton, 1987b, 1988a). The eminent creator can be studied from the moment of birth to the instant of death—and everything that happens in between. Research may begin by examining the genetic foundations of genius, usually through the examination of family pedigrees (Bramwell, 1948; Cox, 1926; Galton, 1869; Simonton, 1983d; Woods, 1906). Some investigators have also examined how the timing of one's birth in the annual cycle may affect the type and magnitude of achievement (Huntington, 1938; Kaulins, 1979). A much larger quantity of studies concentrated on yet another early event in development, namely, the child's ordinal position in the family (Albert, 1980; Bliss, 1970; Clark & Rice, 1982; Goertzel, Goertzel, & Goertzel, 1978; Schachter, 1963; Schubert, Wagner, & Schubert, 1977; Sulloway, 1990; Terry, 1989; cf. Galton, 1874). Another group of investigations examined the impact of parental loss or orphanhood (Albert, 1971; Eisenstadt, 1978; Eisenstadt, Haynal, Rentchnick, & De Senarclens, 1989; Illingworth & Illingworth, 1969; Martindale, 1972; Silverman, 1974; Woodward, 1974). And still other studies concentrated on additional family background factors, such as religion, socioeconomic class, and familial relationships (Arieti, 1976; Berry, 1981; Lehman & Witty, 1931; McCurdy, 1960; Moulin, 1955; Raskin, 1936; Simonton, 1986b; Veblen, 1919; Walberg et al., 1980).

Investigations may also move beyond the immediate family setting, looking at the impact of formal education (Goertzel et al., 1978; Hudson, 1958; Pressey & Combs, 1943; Simonton, 1983c) and professional training (Gieryn & Hirsh, 1983; Hayes, 1989; Simonton, 1984e, 1991b, 1992b). A large number of studies have focused on the consequences of role models—whether mentors or masters—on creative development (Sheldon, 1979, 1980; Simonton, 1975d, 1976f, 1977b, 1978b, 1984a, 1988b, 1992c; Walberg et al., 1980). Also worth mentioning is an examination of the place of specific "crystallizing experiences" in the emergence of talent (Walters & Gardner, 1986). For example, creative geniuses such as Galois and Ramanujan were originally inspired to enter mathematics by chance encounters with textbooks that pinpointed their true interests and talents.

Once the career commences, how the probability of making a creative contribution varies with an individual's age can be studied. As noted earlier, this probably constitutes the oldest topic in the field (Beard, 1874; Quetelet, 1835/1968). Nevertheless, the first research program devoted almost exclusively to this subject is found in the life work of Harvey C. Lehman (e.g., 1953, 1956, 1958, 1962, 1963, 1966a, 1966b). This impressive body of studies has inspired many follow-up inquiries, some critical but most supportive (Bullough, Bullough, & Mauro, 1978; Dennis,

1954d, 1956a, 1956b, 1966; Diemer, 1974; Han, 1989; Simonton, 1977a, 1984b, 1989a; Zhao & Jiang, 1985). Some of these studies concentrated on the relation between quantity and quality across the career (Davis, 1987; Lehman, 1953; Quetelet, 1935/1968; Over, 1988, 1989; Simonton, 1977a, 1985), others investigated changes in the content or impact of productive output (Inhaber & Przednowek, 1976; Root-Bernstein, 1989; Simonton, 1992b), whereas still other studies scrutinized the ages at which creators produce their landmark creations (Abt, 1983; Adams, 1946; Albert, 1975; Hermann, 1988; Lyons, 1968; Manniche & Falk, 1957; Pressey & Combs, 1943; Raskin, 1936; Simonton, 1975a, 1977b, 1991a, 1991b, 1992b, 1992c; Visher, 1947; Zhao, 1984; Zusne, 1976). Several investigations, in addition, assessed the relationships among creative precocity, career longevity, and rate of creative output (Dennis, 1954b; Simonton, 1977b, 1991a, 1991b, 1992b; Zhao & Jiang, 1986; Zusne, 1976). Relevant to the longevity question, there has been a handful of studies probing the dramatic changes in creativity that can occur in the final years before death (Haefele, 1962; Simonton, 1989c, 1990a). Finally, I should mention the many inquiries that concern the onset of death, including the specific timing (Harrison & Kroll, 1985-86, 1989-90; Harrison & Moore, 1982-83; Zusne, 1986-89), the signature lifespan that results (Cox, 1926; Ellis, 1926; Raskin, 1936; Simonton, 1975a, 1977b, 1991a, 1991b, 1992b), and the consequences of a particular lifespan for productivity and eminence (Lehman, 1943; Mills, 1942; Simonton, 1976a, 1977b, 1984d).

Over the life course one can expect more than mere transformations in creative output. A creator's basic values, interests, and preoccupations may undergo profound alternations as well, as indicated by several historiometric inquiries (Mackavey, Malley, & Stewart, 1991; Sears et al., 1978; Simonton, 1977a, 1980b, 1983a, 1986e). For example, some studies showed how the complexity of information processing may shift across the lifespan, especially in the last few years of the creator's life (Porter & Suedfeld, 1981; Suedfeld, 1985; Suedfeld & Piedrahita, 1984). These changes fit in with other empirical findings that provide qualified support for Planck's hypothesis. This is the conjecture that older scientists have lower likelihoods of accepting innovative ideas in science (Diamond, 1980; Hull, Tessner, & Diamond, 1978; Messerli, 1988; Oromaner, 1977; Stewart, 1986; Whaples, 1991).

Differential and Personality Psychology

The pioneers of historiometric methodology—such as Quetelet, Galton, Cattell, Thorndike, and Cox—were all fascinated with individual differences. They all wanted to learn how that cross-sectional variation correlated with critical outcome variables, such as creative achievement. This fascination continues to the present day. Some concentrate on intelligence, others on various personality traits, and still others on intellectual and character attributes combined (Cox, 1926; Knapp, 1962; Simonton, 1976a, 1991d; Thorndike, 1950; Walberg et al., 1980). Among these diverse investigations, perhaps the most daring are those that adapt standard psychometric measures to historiometric data. For example, R. B. Cattell (1963) applied his 16-Factor Personality Inventory to biographical data in order to tease out the typical profile of the great scientist. And several investigators have adapted the Thematic Apperception Test in order to gauge motives from literary and artistic products (Bradburn & Berlew, 1961; Cortés, 1960; Davies, 1969; McClelland, 1961, 1975).

If one wants to use individual differences to predict creativity, then there must be a suitable criterion. Therefore, many investigators have concentrated on the properties of the two principal criteria available to the historiometrician. Some have scrutinized lifetime creative output. Besides showing that this behavioral measure represents a highly reliable indicator with considerable face validity (Simonton, 1984g, 1991a, 1991b, 1992b), this work has teased out some theoretically intriguing distributional characteristics (Dennis, 1954a, 1954c; Lotka, 1926; Price, 1963; Simon, 1954; Simonton, 1988c; cf. Zusne, 1985; Zusne & Dailey, 1982). Others have analyzed the psychological significance of posthumous reputation or eminence, thereby establishing the transhistorical and cross-cultural stability and reliability of the consensus (Helmreich, Spence, & Thorbecke, 1981; Ludwig, 1992b; Over, 1982; Rosengren, 1985; Simonton, 1984g, 1991c; Zusne, 1987; Zusne & Dailey, 1982; cf. Cattell, 1903; Galton, 1869). In addition, these two criteria of differential creativity have been repeatedly shown to be strongly associated, thereby validating them both (Albert, 1975; Davis, 1987; Dennis, 1954a, 1954c; Price, 1963; Simonton, 1984g, 1992b). Indeed, usually a small percentage of creators dominate the output and the eminence achieved in any intellectual or artistic activity (see, e.g., Cole & Cole, 1972; Green, 1981; Oromaner, 1985).

I conclude this section by mentioning two topics that have received special attention in recent years. First, some investigators are beginning to look at creative achievement in women, an area sadly neglected in earlier work (Hayes, 1989; Over, 1990; Simonton, 1992a). Second, several researchers have tried to address the age-old question about how genius might be linked with psychopathology and behavior disorders (Davis, 1986; Karlson, 1970; Lester, 1991; Ludwig, 1990, 1992a; Martindale, 1972).

Social and Political Psychology

Creativity does not take place in complete isolation. The creative genius, no matter how grand, operates in a social milieu. At the simplest level, creators must successfully communicate their ideas to others—colleagues, audiences, appreciators, and so on—before mere originality becomes certified as genuine creativity. It should not be surprising, therefore, that many historiometric studies have tried to discern the qualities of creative products that grant them so much impact on others. Almost all of this work targets aesthetic products, usually by applying objective content analysis to masterworks in literature (Derks, 1989; Simonton, 1989b, 1990c) or music (Simonton, 1983b, 1986a, 1987a, 1995), albeit initial forays have been made into such domains as cinematic creativity (Boor, 1990, 1992). Moreover, lately some have ventured that scientific ideas might be susceptible to historiometric analysis as well (Donovan, Laudan, & Laudan, 1988; Faust & Meehl, 1992; Meehl, 1992; Simonton, 1992b). Today it is actually possible to program a computer to discriminate the bases for creative success among contributions to fields as diverse as poetry, music, and psychology (Simonton, 1980b, 1980c, 1984f, 1989b, 1990c, 1992b).

But communication is a two-way process. Hence, several studies have inspected how creativity might be facilitated or hindered by various social interactions, such as collaborations or rivalries (Jackson & Padgett, 1982; Price, 1965; Simonton, 1984a, 1992b, 1992c; Suls & Fletcher, 1983). Just as important are the more massive and impersonal forces that may shape the course of creativity. Broad zeitgeist factors may be roughly grouped into four categories: (a) *cultural* (Hasenfus, Martindale, & Birnbaum, 1983; Martindale, 1975; Schneider, 1937; Simonton, 1975b, 1975c, 1976c, 1976d, 1976f, 1992a, 1992b), (b) *economic* (Inhaber, 1977; Kavolis, 1964; Kuo, 1988; Padgett & Jorgenson, 1982; Rainoff, 1929; Schmookler, 1966; Simon & Sullivan, 1989); (c) *social* (Dressler & Robbins, 1975; Kavolis, 1966; Kuo, 1986, 1988; Lehman, 1947; McGuire, 1976; Yuasa, 1974), and (d) *political* (Kavolis, 1966; Kuo, 1986, 1988; Price, 1978; Richardson & Kroeber, 1940; Martindale, 1975; Simonton, 1990d). Of these, the political milieu has perhaps received the most attention, with a great many studies examining how war affects both quantity and quality of creative activity (Cerulo, 1984; Kavolis, 1966; Price, 1978; Simonton, 1976b, 1976e, 1976g, 1980a, 1986a, 1986e, 1987a). Still, another area that has attracted much empirical attention is the phenomenon of multiple discovery and invention (Brannigan & Wanner, 1983a, 1983b; Merton, 1961; Ogburn & Thomas, 1922; Price, 1963; Schmookler, 1966; Simonton, 1978a, 1979, 1986c, 1986d, 1986f, 1987c). This is the curious event when two or more creators, working independently, arrive at the same basic idea. Although many have interpreted multiple discovery in terms of zeitgeist, the actual story is much more complex than that (Simonton, 1988c).

Cyclical theories of cultural creativity have also gotten much empirical scrutiny over the past several decades (Gray, 1958, 1961, 1966; Kavolis, 1966; Klingemann, Mohler, & Weber, 1982; Kroeber, 1944; Lowe & Lowe, 1982; Marchetti, 1980; Peterson & Berger, 1975; Rainoff, 1929; Sheldon, 1979, 1980; Sorokin, 1937-41; Sorokin & Merton, 1935). Among such developments perhaps the most outstanding is Martindale's (1975, 1990) extensive research on changes in artistic styles. Besides providing a rich theory of stylistic creativity that integrates both cyclical and progressive models (Martindale, 1984b, 1986a), Martindale has tested his theory's distinctive predictions using some rather sophisticated tools (e.g., Martindale, 1984a, 1986b; Martindale & Uemura, 1983). This is one of the most fruitful historiometric research programs still active today.

Finally, there is ample evidence that many of these sociocultural factors impress themselves on the person as developmental factors (Simonton, 1984c). In other words, the cultural, economic, social, and political surroundings affect the course of creative development, including both the magnitude and the nature of the accomplishments that the creator will display as an adult.

APPRAISAL

Our speedy spin through the foregoing topics has not allowed providing an inventory of the central findings. It would take a whole book to review even the most significant results (see Simonton, 1984d, 1988c, 1994). It may suffice here just to say that historiometric research has taught a great deal about how creative genius operates. We have learned about how creativity emerges and manifests itself during the course of a human lifespan. We have discerned some of the intellectual, motivational, and dispositional attributes that differentiate the most highly acclaimed figures from the also-rans and nonentities. And we have identified some of the more social facets of creativity, including the successful communication of artistic ideas, the interpersonal relationships that support creativity, and the cultural, economic, social, and political environments that underlie exceptional creative activity. No doubt much more remains unknown. But at least historiometric methods have removed some of the mystery surrounding creative genius.

Of course, I would be remiss not to acknowledge the many objections that can be raised about this work. Certainly the raw data are not always adequate to permit a truly scientific response to prominent questions. And even if good historical information is available, often the measurement problems are insurmountable. Finally, once we obtain reasonable measures of key variables, historiometric research frequently demands extremely complex statistical methods—such as structural equation models or time-series analysis—to separate valid relationships from those sadly spurious. In all likelihood, these niceties discourage many investigators from applying historiometry to research questions for which the method may be ideally suited. Historiometric research may not be for everyone (Simonton, 1990b). Many may find single- case, qualitative analyses more to their liking, such as classic psychobiography or the more current evolving-systems approach (Wallace & Gruber, 1989).

Nevertheless, to encourage the possibly discouraged, I have recently published a monograph that deals with all the most critical issues in historiometric research (Simonton, 1990e). There I have also outlined some of the many methodological advantages of this approach. For example, no other approach enables the investigator so readily to examine creators from such a diversity of disciplines, nationalities, ethnic groups, and historical periods. No other method allows the researcher to easily scrutinize the phenomenon over a such wide range of variation—such as birth until death, from near obscurity to worldwide celebrity, from peacetime to wartime conditions.

Perhaps the most important asset of the technique is that it is really the only act in town—if one wishes to divulge the laws of creative genius. That is, if one wants to comprehend the personal, developmental, and social forces that produce individuals of the caliber of a Newton, Descartes, Dante, Picasso, or Stravinsky, there is no alternative procedure at one's disposal. Historiometry is the sole approach that attempts to extract precise and verifiable generalizations by gazing directly at the creative stars themselves. In a sense, if psychometrics is the physics of creativity research, then historiometrics is the discipline's astronomy.

REFERENCES

Abt, H.A. (1983). At what ages do outstanding American astronomers publish their most cited papers. *Publications of the Astronomical Society of the Pacific, 95,* 113-116.

Adams, C.W. (1946). The age at which scientists do their best work. *Isis, 36,* 166-169.

Albert, R.S. (1971). Cognitive development and parental loss among the gifted, the exceptionally gifted and the creative. *Psychological Reports, 29,* 19-26.

Albert, R.S. (1975). Toward a behavioral definition of genius. *American Psychologist, 30,* 140-151.

Albert, R.S. (1980). Family positions and the attainment of eminence: A study of special family positions and special family experiences. *Gifted Child Quarterly, 24*, 87-85.

Arieti, S. (1976). *Creativity: The magic synthesis.* New York: Basic Books.

Beard, G.M. (1874). *Legal responsibility in old age.* New York: Russell.

Berry, C. (1981). The Nobel scientists and the origins of scientific achievement. *British Journal of Sociology, 32*, 381-391.

Bliss, W.D. (1970). Birth order of creative writers. *Journal of Individual Psychology, 26*, 200-202.

Boor, M. (1990). Reliability of ratings of movies by professional movie critics. *Psychological Reports, 67*, 243-257.

Boor, M. (1992). Relationships among ratings of motion pictures by viewers and six professional movie critics. *Psychological Reports, 70*, 1011-1021.

Bradburn, N.M., & Breleau, D.E. (1961). Need for achievement and English economic growth. *Economic Development and Cultural Change, 10*, 8-20.

Bramwell, B.S. (1948). Galton's "Hereditary Genius" and the three following generations since 1869. *Eugenics Review, 39*, 146-153.

Brannigan, A., & Wanner, R.A. (1983a). Historical distributions of multiple discoveries and theories of scientific change. *Social Studies of Science, 13*, 417-435.

Brannigan, A., & Wanner, R.A. (1983b). Multiple discoveries in science: A test of the communication theory. *Canadian Journal of Sociology, 8*, 135-151.

Bullough, V., Bullough, B., & Mauro, M. (1978). Age and achievement: A dissenting view. *Gerontologist, 18*, 584-587.

Candolle, A. de (1873). *Histoire des sciences et des savants depuis deux siecles* [History of science and scientists after two centuries]. Geneve: Georg.

Cattell, J.M. (1903). A statistical study of eminent men. *Popular Science Monthly, 62*, 359-377.

Cattell, J.M. (1910). A further study of American men of science. *Science, 32*, 633-648.

Cattell, R.B. (1963). The personality and motivation of the researcher from measurements of contemporaries and from biography. In C.W. Taylor & F. Barron (Eds.), *Scientific creativity: Its recognition and development* (pp. 119-131). New York: Wiley.

Cerulo, K.A. (1984). Social disruption and its effects on music: An empirical analysis. *Social Forces, 62*, 885-904.

Cerulo, K.A. (1988). Analyzing cultural products: A new method of measurement. *Social Science Research, 17*, 317-352.

Cerulo, K.A. (1989). Variations in musical syntax: Patterns of measurement. *Communication Research, 16*, 204-235.

Clark, R.D., & Rice, G.A. (1982). Family constellations and eminence: The birth orders of Nobel Prize winners. *Journal of Psychology, 110*, 281-287.

Cole, J.R., & Cole, S. (1972). The Ortega hypothesis. *Science, 178,* 368-375.
Cortés, J.B. (1960). The achievement motive in the Spanish economy between the 13th and 18th centuries. *Economic Development and Cultural Change, 9,* 144-163.
Cox, C. (1926). *The early mental traits of three hundred geniuses.* Stanford, CA: Stanford University Press.
Davies, E. (1969, November). This is the way Crete went—Not with a bang but a simper. *Psychology Today,* pp. 43-47.
Davis, R.A. (1987). Creativity in neurological publications. *Neurosurgery, 20,* 652-663
Davis, W.M. (1986). Premature mortality among prominent American authors noted for alcohol abuse. *Drug and Alcohol Dependence, 18,* 133-138.
deMause, L. (1981). What is psychohistory? *Journal of Psychohistory, 9,* 179-184.
Dennis, W. (1954a). Bibliographies of eminent scientists. *Scientific Monthly, 79,* 180-183.
Dennis, W. (1954b). Predicting scientific productivity in later maturity from records of earlier decades. *Journal of Gerontology, 9,* 465-467.
Dennis, W. (1954c). Productivity among American psychologists. *American Psychologist, 9,* 191-194.
Dennis, W. (1954d). Review of Age and Achievement. *Psychological Bulletin, 51,* 306-308.
Dennis, W. (1955). Variations in productivity among creative workers. *Scientific Monthly, 80,* 277-278.
Dennis, W. (1956a). Age and Achievement: A critique. *Journal of Gerontology, 9,* 465-467.
Dennis, W. (1956b). Age and productivity among scientists. *Science, 123,* 724-725.
Dennis, W. (1966). Creative productivity between the ages of 20 and 80 years. *Journal of Gerontology, 21,* 1-8.
Derks, P.L. (1989). Pun frequency and popularity of Shakespeare's plays. *Empirical Studies of the Arts, 7,* 23-31.
Diamond, A.M., Jr. (1980). Age and the acceptance of cliometrics. *Journal of Economic History, 40,* 838-841.
Diemer, G. (1974). *Creativity versus age. Physics Today, 27,* 9.
Donovan, A., Laudan, L., & Laudan, R. (Eds.). (1988). *Scrutinizing science: Empirical studies of scientific change.* Dordrecht: Kluwer.
Dressler, W.W., & Robbins, M.C. (1975). Art styles, social stratification, and cognition: An analysis of Greek vase painting. *American Ethnologist, 2,* 427-434.
Eisenstadt, J.M. (1978). Parental loss and genius. *American Psychologist, 33,* 211-223.
Eisenstadt, J.M., Haynal, A., Rentchnick, P., & De Senarclens, P. (1989). *Parental loss and achievement.* Madison, CT: International Universities Press.
Ellis, H. (1926). *A study of British genius* (rev. ed.). Boston: Houghton Mifflin.

Elms, A. (1988). Freud as Leonardo: Why the first psychobiography went wrong. *Journal of Personality, 56,* 19-40.

Farnsworth, P.R. (1969). *The social psychology of music* (2nd ed.). Ames: Iowa State University Press.

Faust, D., & Meehl, P.E. (1992). Using scientific methods to resolve questions in the history and philosophy of science: Some illustrations. *Behavior Therapy, 23,* 195-211.

Freud, S. (1964). *Leonardo da Vinci and a memory of his childhood* (A. Tyson, Trans.). New York: Norton. (Original work published 1910)

Galton, F. (1869). *Hereditary genius: An inquiry into its laws and consequences.* London: Macmillan.

Galton, F. (1874). *English men of science: Their nature and nurture.* London: Macmillan.

Gieryn, T.F., & Hirsh, R.F. (1983). Marginality and innovation in science. *Social Studies of Science, 13,* 87-106.

Goertzel, M.G., Goertzel, V. & Goertzel, T.G. (1978). *300 eminent personalities: A psychosocial analysis of the famous.* San Francisco: Jossey-Bass.

Gray, C.E. (1958). An analysis of Graeco-Roman development: The epicyclical evolution of Graeco-Roman civilization. *American Anthropologist, 60,* 13-31.

Gray, C.E. (1961). An epicyclical model for Western civilization. *American Anthropologist, 63,* 1014-1037.

Gray, C.E. (1966). A measurement of creativity in Western civilization. *American Anthropologist, 68,* 1384-1417

Green, G.S. (1981). A test of the Ortega hypothesis in criminology. *Criminology, 19,* 45-52.

Haefele, J.W. (1962). *Creativity and innovation.* New York: Reinhold.

Han, H. (1989). Linear increase law of optimum age of scientific creativity. *Scientometrics, 15,* 309-312.

Harrison, A.A., & Kroll, N.E.A. (1985-86). Variations in death rates in the proximity of Christmas: An opponent process interpretation. *Omega, 16,* 181-192.

Harrison, A.A., & Kroll, N.E.A. (1989-90). Birth dates and death dates: An examination of two baseline procedures and age at time of death. *Omega, 20,* 127-137.

Harrison, A.A., & Moore, M. (1982-83). Birth dates and death dates: A closer look. *Omega, 13,* 117-125.

Hasenfus, N., Martindale, C., & Birnbaum, D. (1983). Psychological reality of cross-media artistic styles. *Journal of Experimental Psychology: Human Perception and Performance, 9,* 841-863.

Hayes, J.R. (1989). *The complete problem solver* (2nd ed.). Hillsdale, NJ: Erlbaum.

Helmreich, R.L., Spence, J.T., & Thorbecke, W.L. (1981). On the stability of productivity and recognition. *Personality and Social Psychology Bulletin, 7,* 516-522.

Hermann, D.B. (1988). How old were the authors of significant research in twentieth century astronomy at the time of their greatest achievements? *Scientometrics, 13,* 135-138.

Hudson, L. (1958). Undergraduate academic record of Fellows of the Royal Society. *Nature, 182,* 1326.

Hull, D.L., Tessner, P.D., & Diamond, A.M. (1978). Planck's principle: Do younger scientists accept new scientific ideas with greater alacrity than older scientists? *Science, 202,* 717-723.

Huntington, E. (1938). *Season of birth: Its relation to human abilities.* New York: Wiley.

Illingworth, R.S., & Illingworth, C.M. (1969). *Lessons from childhood.* Edinburgh: Livingston.

Inhaber, H. (1977). Scientists and economic growth. *Social Studies of Science, 7,* 514-526.

Inhaber, H., & Przednowek, K. (1976). Quality of research and the Nobel prizes. *Social Studies of Science, 6,* 33-50.

Jackson, J.M., & Padgett, V.R. (1982). With a little help from my friend: Social loafing and the Lennon-McCartney songs. *Personality and Social Psychology Bulletin, 8,* 672-677.

Karlson, J.I. (1970). Genetic association of giftedness and creativity with schizophrenia. *Hereditas, 66,* 177-182.

Kaulins, A. (1979). Cycles in the birth of eminent humans. *Cycles, 30,* 9-15.

Kavolis, V. (1964). Economic correlates of artistic creativity. *American Journal of Sociology, 70,* 332-341.

Kavolis, V. (1966). Community dynamics and artistic creativity. *American Sociological Review, 31,* 208-217

Klingemann, H.-D., Mohler, P.P., & Weber, R.P. (1982). Cultural indicators based on content analysis: A secondary analysis of Sorokin's data on fluctuations of systems of truth. *Quality and Quantity, 16,* 1-18.

Knapp, R.H. (1962). A factor analysis of Thorndike's ratings of eminent men. *Journal of Social Psychology, 56,* 67-71.

Kroeber, A.L. (1944). *Configurations of culture growth.* Berkeley: University of California Press.

Kuhn, T.S. (1970). *The structure of scientific revolutions* (2nd ed.). Chicago: University of Chicago Press.

Kuo, Y. (1986). The growth and decline of Chinese philosophical genius. *Chinese Journal of Psychology, 28,* 81-91.

Kuo, Y. (1988). The social psychology of Chinese philosophical creativity: A critical synthesis. *Social Epistemology, 2,* 283-295.

Lehman, H.C. (1943). The longevity of the eminent. *Science, 98,* 270-273.

Lehman, H.C. (1947). The exponential increase of man's cultural output. *Social Forces, 25,* 281-290.

Lehman, H.C. (1953). *Age and achievement.* Princeton, NJ: Princeton University Press.

Lehman, H.C. (1956). Reply to Dennis' critique of Age and Achievement. *Journal of Gerontology, 11,* 128-134.

Lehman, H.C. (1958). The chemist's most creative years. *Science, 127,* 1213-1222.

Lehman, H.C. (1962). More about age and achievement. *Gerontologist, 2,* 141-148.

Lehman, H.C. (1963). Chronological age versus present-day contributions to medical progress. *Gerontologist, 3,* 71-75.

Lehman, H.C. (1966a). The most creative years of engineers and other technologists. *Journal of Genetic Psychology, 108,* 263-270.

Lehman, H.C. (1966b). The psychologist's most creative years. *American Psychologist, 21,* 363-369.

Lehman, H.C., & Witty, P.A. (1931). Scientific eminence and church membership. *Scientific Monthly, 33,* 544-549.

Lester, D. (1991). Premature mortality associated with alcoholism and suicide in American writers. *Perceptual and Motor Skills, 73,* 162.

Lotka, A.J. (1926). The frequency distribution of scientific productivity. *Journal of the Washington Academy of Sciences, 16,* 317-323.

Lowe, J.W.G., & Lowe, E.D. (1982). Cultural pattern and process: A study of stylistic change in women's dress. *American Anthropologist, 84,* 521-544.

Ludwig, A.M. (1990). Alcohol input and creative output. *British Journal of Addiction, 85,* 953-963.

Ludwig, A.M. (1992a). Creative achievement and psychopathology: Comparison among professions. *American Journal of Psychotherapy, 46,* 330-356.

Ludwig, A.M. (1992b). The Creative Achievement Scale. *Creativity Research Journal, 5,* 109-124.

Lyons, J. (1968). Chronological age, professional age, and eminence in psychology. *American Psychologist, 23,* 371-374.

Mackavey, W.R., Malley, J.E., & Stewart, A.J. (1991). Remembering autobiographically consequential experiences: Content analysis of psychologists' accounts of their lives. *Psychology and Aging, 6,* 50-59.

Manniche, E., & Falk, G. (1957). Age and the Nobel prize. *Behavioral Science, 2,* 301-307.

Marchetti, C. (1980). Society as a learning system: Discovery, invention, and innovation cycles. *Technological Forecasting and Social Change, 18,* 267-282.

Martindale, C. (1972). Father absence, psychopathology, and poetic eminence. *Psychological Reports, 31,* 843-847.

Martindale, C. (1975). *Romantic progression: The psychology of literary history.* Washington, DC: Hemisphere.

Martindale, C. (1984a). Evolutionary trends in poetic style: The case of English metaphysical poetry. *Computers and the Humanities, 18,* 3-21.

Martindale, C. (1984b). The evolution of aesthetic taste. In K.J. Gergen & M.M. Gergen (Eds.), *Historical social psychology* (pp. 347-370). Hillsdale, NJ: Erlbaum.

Martindale, C. (1986a). Aesthetic evolution. *Poetics, 15,* 439-473.

Martindale, C. (1986b). The evolution of Italian painting: A quantitative investigation of trends in style and content from late Gothic to the Rococo period. *Leonardo, 19,* 217-222.

Martindale, C. (1990). *The clockwork muse: The predictability of artistic styles.* New York: Basic Books.

Martindale, C., & Uemura, A. (1983). Stylistic evolution in European music. *Leonardo, 16,* 225-228.

McClelland, D.C. (1961). *The achieving society.* New York: Van Nostrand.

McClelland, D.C. (1975). *Power: The inner experience.* New York: Irvington.

McCurdy, H.G. (1960). The childhood pattern of genius. *Horizon, 2,* 33-38.

McGuire, W.J. (1976). Historical comparisons: Testing psychological hypotheses with cross-era data. *International Journal of Psychology, 11,* 161-183.

Meehl, P.E. (1992). Cliometric metatheory: The actuarial approach to empirical, history-based philosophy of science. *Psychological Reports: Monograph Supplement, 71,* 339-467.

Merton, R.K. (1961). Singletons and multiples in scientific discovery: A chapter in the sociology of science. *Proceedings of the American Philosophical Society, 105,* 470-486.

Messerli, P. (1988). Age differences in the reception of new scientific theories: The case of plate tectonics theory. *Social Studies of Science, 18,* 91-112.

Mills, C.A. (1942). What price glory? *Science, 96,* 380-387.

Moulin, L. (1955). The Nobel Prizes for the sciences from 1901-1950: An essay in sociological analysis. *British Journal of Sociology, 6,* 246-263.

Naroll, R., Benjamin, E.C., Fohl, F.K., Fried, M.J., Hildreth, R.E., & Schaefer, J.M. (1971). Creativity: A cross-historical pilot survey. *Journal of Cross-Cultural Psychology, 2,* 181-188.

Ogburn, W.K., & Thomas, D. (1922). Are inventions inevitable? A note on social evolution. *Political Science Quarterly, 37,* 83-93.

Oromaner, M. (1977). Professional age and the reception of sociological publications: A test of the Zuckerman-Merton hypothesis. *Social Studies of Science, 7,* 381-388.

Oromaner, M. (1985). The Ortega hypothesis and influential articles in American sociology. *Scientometrics, 7,* 3-10.

Over, R. (1982). The durability of scientific reputation. *Journal of the History of the Behavioral Sciences, 18,* 53-61.

Over, R. (1988). Does scholarly impact decline with age? *Scientometrics, 13,* 215-223.

Over, R. (1989). Age and scholarly impact. *Psychology and Aging, 4,* 222-225.

Over, R. (1990). The scholarly impact of articles published by men and women in psychology journals. *Scientometrics, 18,* 71-80.

Padgett, V., & Jorgenson, D.O. (1982). Superstition and economic threat: Germany 1918-1940. *Personality and Social Psychology Bulletin, 8,* 736-741.

Peterson, R.A., & Berger, D.G. (1975). Cycles in symbol production: The case of popular music. *American Sociological Review, 40,* 158-173.

Over, R. (1989). Age and scholarly impact. *Psychology and Aging, 4,* 222-225.

Over, R. 1990). The scholarly impact of articles published by men and women in psychology journals. *Scientometrics, 18,* 71-80.

Padgett, V. , & Jorgenson, D.O. (1982). Superstition and economic threat: Germany 1918-1940. *Personality and Social Psychology Bulletin, 8,* 736-741

Peterson, R.A , & Berger, D.G. (1975). Cycles in symbol production: The case of popular music. *American Sociological Review, 40,* 158-173.

Porter, C.A., & Suedfeld, P. (1981). Integrative complexity in the correspondence of literary figures: Effects of personal and societal stress. *Journal of Personality and Social Psychology, 40,* 321-330.

Pressey, S.L., & Combs, A. (1943). Acceleration and age of productivity. *Educational Research Bulletin, 22,* 191-196.

Price, D. (1963). *Little science, big science.* New York: Columbia University Press.

Price, D. (1965). Networks of scientific papers. *Science, 149,* 510-515.

Price, D. (1978). Ups and downs in the pulse of science and technology. In J. Gaston (Ed.), *The sociology of science* (pp. 162-171). San Francisco: Jossey-Bass.

Quetelet, A. (1968). *A treatise on man and the development of his faculties.* New York: Franklin. (Reprint of 1842 Edinburgh translation of 1835 French original)

Rainoff, T.J. (1929). Wave-like fluctuations of creative productivity in the development of West-European physics in the eighteenth and nineteenth centuries. *Isis, 12,* 287-319.

Raskin, E.A. (1936). Comparison of scientific and literary ability: A biographical study of eminent scientists and men of letters of the nineteenth century. *Journal of Abnormal and Social Psychology, 31,* 20-35.

Richardson, J., & Kroeber, A.L. (1940). Three centuries of women's dress fashion: A quantitative analysis. *Anthropological Records, 5,* 111-150.

Root-Bernstein, R.S. (1989). *Discovering.* Cambridge, MA: Harvard University Press.

Rosengren, R.E. (1985). Time and literary fame. *Poetics, 14,* 157-172.

Runyan, W.M. (1982). *Life histories and psychobiography.* New York: Oxford University Press.

Schachter, S. (1963). Birth order, eminence, and higher education. *American Sociological Review, 28,* 757-768.

Schmookler, J. (1966). *Invention and economic growth.* Cambridge, MA: Harvard University Press.

Schneider, J. (1937). The cultural situation as a condition for the achievement of fame. *American Sociological Review, 2,* 480-491.

Schubert, D.S.P., Wagner, M.E., & Schubert, H.J.P. (1977). Family constellation and creativity: Firstborn predominance among classical music composers. *Journal of Psychology, 95,* 147-149.

Sears, R.R., Lapidus, D., & Cozzens, C. (1978). Content analysis of Mark Twain's novels and letters as a biographical method. *Poetics, 7,* 155-175.

Sheldon, J.C. (1979). Hierarchical cybernets: A model for the dynamics of high level learning and cultural change. *Cybernetica, 22,* 179-202.

Sheldon, J.C. (1980). A cybernetic theory of physical science professions: The causes of periodic normal and revolutionary science between 1000 and 1870 AD. *Scientometrics, 2,* 147-167.

Silverman, S.M. (1974). Parental loss and scientists. *Science Studies, 4,* 259-264.

Simon, H.A (1954). Productivity among American psychologists: An explanation. *American Psychologist, 9,* 804-805.

Simon, J.L., & Sullivan, R.J. (1989). Population size, knowledge stock, and other determinants of agricultural publication and patenting: England, 1541-1850. *Explorations in Economic History, 26,* 21-44.

Simonton, D.K. (1975a). Age and literary creativity: A cross-cultural and transhistorical survey. *Journal of Cross-Cultural Psychology, 6,* 259-277.

Simonton, D.K. (1975b). Interdisciplinary creativity over historical time: A correlational analysis of generational fluctuations. *Social Behavior and Personality, 3,* 181-188.

Simonton, D.K. (1975c). Invention and discovery among the sciences: A p-technique factor analysis. *Journal of Vocational Behavior, 7,* 275-281.

Simonton, D.K. (1975d). Sociocultural context of individual creativity. A transhistorical time-series analysis. *Journal of Personality and Social Psychology, 32,* 1119-1133.

Simonton, D.K. (1976a). Biographical determinants of achieved eminence: A multivariate approach to the Cox data. *Journal of Personality and Social Psychology, 33,* 218-226.

Simonton, D.K. (1976b). The causal relation between war and scientific discovery: An exploratory cross-national analysis. *Journal of Cross-Cultural Psychology, 7,* 133-144.

Simonton, D.K. (1976c). Do Sorokin's data support his theory?: A study of generational fluctuations in philosophical beliefs. *Journal for the Scientific Study of Religion, 15,* 187-198.

Simonton, D.K. (1976d). Ideological diversity and creativity: A re-evaluation of a hypothesis. *Social Behavior and Personality, 4,* 203-207.

Simonton, D.K. (1976e). Interdisciplinary and military determinants of scientific productivity: A cross-lagged correlation analysis. *Journal of Vocational Behavior, 9,* 53-62.

Simonton, D. K. (1976f). Philosophical eminence, beliefs, and zeitgeist: An individual-generational analysis. *Journal of Personality and Social Psychology, 34,* 630-640.

Simonton, D.K. (1976g). The sociopolitical context of philosophical beliefs: A transhistorical causal analysis. *Social Forces, 54,* 513-523.

Simonton, D.K. (1977a) Creative productivity, age, and stress: A biographical time-series analysis of 10 classical composers. *Journal of Personality and Social Psychology, 35,* 791-804.

Simonton, D.K. (1977b). Eminence, creativity, and geographic marginality: A recursive structural equation model. *Journal of Personality and Social Psychology, 35,* 805-816.

Simonton, D.K. (1978a). Independent discovery in science and technology: A closer look at the Poisson distribution. *Social Studies of Science, 8*, 521-532.

Simonton, D.K. (1978b). Intergenerational stimulation, reaction, and polarization: A causal analysis of intellectual history. *Social Behavior and Personality, 6*, 247-251.

Simonton, D.K. (1979). Multiple discovery and invention: Zeitgeist, genius, or chance? *Journal of Personality and Social Psychology, 37*, 1603-1616.

Simonton, D.K. (1980a). Techno-scientific activity and war: A yearly time-series analysis, 1500-1903 A.D. *Scientometrics, 2*, 251-255.

Simonton, D.K. (1980b). Thematic fame and melodic originality in classical music: A multivariate computer-content analysis. *Journal of Personality, 48*, 206-219.

Simonton, D.K. (1980c). Thematic fame, melodic originality, and musical zeitgeist: A biographical and transhistorical content analysis. *Journal of Personality and Social Psychology, 38*, 972-983.

Simonton, D.K. (1983a). Dramatic greatness and content: A quantitative study of Eighty-One Athenian and Shakespearean plays. *Empirical Studies of the Arts, 1*, 109-123.

Simonton, D.K. (1983b). Esthetics, biography, and history in musical creativity. In *Documentary report of the Ann Arbor Symposium* (Session 3, pp. 41-48). Reston, VA: Music Educators National Conference.

Simonton, D.K. (1983c). Formal education, eminence, and dogmatism: The curvilinear relationship. *Journal of Creative Behavior, 17*, 149-162.

Simonton, D.K. (1983d). Intergenerational transfer of individual differences in hereditary monarchs: Genes, role-modeling, cohort, or sociocultural effects? *Journal of Personality and Social Psychology, 44*, 354-364.

Simonton, D.K. (1983e). Psychohistory. In R. Harré & R. Lamb (Eds.), *The encyclopedic dictionary of psychology* (pp. 499-500). Oxford: Blackwell.

Simonton, D.K. (1984a). Artistic creativity and interpersonal relationships across and within generations. *Journal of Personality and Social Psychology, 46*, 1273-1286.

Simonton, D.K. (1984b). Creative productivity and age: A mathematical model based on a two-step cognitive process. *Developmental Review, 4*, 77-111.

Simonton, D.K. (1984c). Generational time-series analysis: A paradigm for studying sociocultural influences. In K. Gergen & M. Gergen (Eds.), *Historical social psychology* (pp.141-155). Hillsdale, NJ: Erlbaum.

Simonton, D.K. (1984d). *Genius, creativity, and leadership: Historiometric inquiries*. Cambridge, MA: Harvard University Press.

Simonton, D.K. (1984e). Is the marginality effect all that marginal? *Social Studies of Science, 14*, 621-622.

Simonton, D.K. (1984f). Melodic structure and note transition probabilities: A content analysis of 15,618 classical themes. *Psychology of Music, 12,* 3-16.

Simonton, D.K. (1984g). Scientific eminence historical and contemporary: A measurement assessment. *Scientometrics, 6,* 169-182.

Simonton, D.K. (1985). Quality, quantity, and age: The careers of 10 distinguished psychologists. *International Journal of Aging and Human Development, 21,* 241-254.

Simonton, D.K. (1986a). Aesthetic success in classical music: A computer analysis of 1935 compositions. *Empirical Studies of the Arts, 4,* 1-17.

Simonton, D.K. (1986b). Biographical typicality, eminence, and achievement style. *Journal of Creative Behavior, 20,* 14-22.

Simonton, D.K. (1986c). Multiple discovery: Some Monte Carlo simulations and Gedanken experiments. *Scientometrics, 9,* 269-280.

Simonton, D.K. (1986d). Multiples, Poisson distributions, and chance: An analysis of the Brannigan-Wanner model. *Scientometrics, 9,* 127-137.

Simonton, D.K. (1986e). Popularity, content, and context in 37 Shakespeare plays. *Poetics, 15,* 493-510.

Simonton, D.K. (1986f). Stochastic models of multiple discovery. *Czechoslovak Journal of Physics, B 36,* 138-141.

Simonton, D.K. (1987a). Musical aesthetics and creativity in Beethoven: A computer analysis of 105 compositions. *Empirical Studies of the Arts, 5,* 87-104.

Simonton, D.K. (1987b). Developmental antecedents of achieved eminence. *Annals of Child Development, 5,* 131-169.

Simonton, D.K. (1987c). Multiples, chance, genius, creativity, and zeitgeist. In D.N. Jackson & J.P. Rushton (Eds.), *Scientific excellence: Origins and assessment* (pp. 98-128). Beverly Hills, CA: Sage.

Simonton, D.K. (1988a). Age and outstanding achievement: What do we know after a century of research? *Psychological Bulletin, 104,* 251-267.

Simonton, D.K. (1988b). Galtonian genius, Kroeberian configurations, and emulation: A generational time-series analysis of Chinese civilization. *Journal of Personality and Social Psychology, 55,* 230-238.

Simonton, D.K. (1988c). *Scientific genius: A psychology of science.* Cambridge: Cambridge University Press

Simonton, D.K. (1989a). Age and creative productivity: Nonlinear estimation of an information-processing model. *International Journal of Aging and Human Development, 29,* 23-37.

Simonton, D.K. (1989b). Shakespeare's sonnets: A case of and for single-case historiometry. *Journal of Personality, 57,* 695-721.

Simonton, D.K. (1989c). The swan-song phenomenon: Last-works effects for 172 classical composers. *Psychology and Aging, 4,* 42-47.

Simonton, D.K. (1990a). Creativity in the later years: Optimistic prospects for achievement. *Gerontologist, 30,* 626-631.

Simonton, D.K. (1990b). History, chemistry, psychology, and genius. An intellectual autobiography of historiometry. In M. Runco & R. Albert (Eds.), *Theories of creativity* (pp. 92-115). Newbury Park, CA: Sage.

Simonton, D.K. (1990c). Lexical choices and aesthetic success: A computer content analysis of 154 Shakespeare sonnets. *Computers and the Humanities, 24*, 251-264.

Simonton, D.K. (1990d). Political pathology and societal creativity. *Creativity Research Journal, 3*, 85-99.

Simonton, D.K. (1990e). *Psychology, science, and history: An introduction to historiometry.* New Haven, CT: Yale University Press.

Simonton, D.K. (1991a). Career landmarks in science: Individual differences and interdisciplinary contrasts. *Developmental Psychology, 27*, 119-130.

Simonton, D.K. (1991b). Emergence and realization of genius: The lives and works of 120 classical composers. *Journal of Personality and Social Psychology, 61*, 829-840.

Simonton, D.K. (1991c). Latent-variable models of posthumous reputation: A quest for Galton's G. *Journal of Personality and Social Psychology, 60*, 607-619.

Simonton, D.K. (1991d). Personality correlates of exceptional personal influence: A note on Thorndike's (1950) creators and leaders. *Creativity Research Journal, 4*, 67-78.

Simonton, D.K. (1992a). Gender and genius in Japan: Feminine eminence in masculine culture. *Sex Roles, 27*, 101-119.

Simonton, D.K. (1992b). Leaders of American psychology, 1879-1967: Career development, creative output, and professional achievement. *Journal of Personality and Social Psychology, 62*, 5-17.

Simonton, D.K. (1992c). The social context of career success and course for 2,026 scientists and inventors. *Personality and Social Psychology Bulletin, 18*, 452-463.

Simonton, D.K. (1994). *Greatness: Who makes history and why.* New York: Guilford.

Simonton, D.K. (1995). Drawing inferences from symphonic programs: Musical attributes versus listener attributions. *Music Perception.*

Sorokin, P.A. (1937-41). *Social and cultural dynamics* (4 vols.). New York: American Book.

Sorokin, P.A., & Merton, R.K. (1935). The course of Arabian intellectual development, 700-1300 A.D. *Isis, 22*, 516-524.

Stewart, J.A. (1986). Drifting continents and colliding interests: A quantitative application of the interests perspective. *Social Studies of Science, 16*, 261-279.

Suedfeld, P. (1985). APA presidential addresses: The relation of integrative complexity to historical, professional, and personal factors. *Journal of Personality and Social Psychology, 47*, 848-852.

Suedfeld, P., & Piedrahita, L.E. (1984). Intimations of mortality: Integrative simplification as a predictor of death. *Journal of Personality and Social Psychology, 47*, 848-852.

Sulloway, F.J. (1990). *Orthodoxy and innovation in sciences: The role of the family.* Unpublished manuscript, Harvard University, Cambridge, MA.

Suls, J., & Fletcher, B. (1983). Social comparison in the social and physical sciences: An archival study. *Journal of Personality and Social Psychology, 44*, 575-580.

Terman, L.M. (1917). The intelligence quotient of Francis Galton in childhood. *American Journal of Psychology, 28*, 209-215.

Terman, L.M. (1925). *Mental and physical traits of a thousand gifted children.* Stanford, CA: Stanford University Press.

Terman, L.N., & Oden, M.H. (1959). *The gifted group at mid-life.* Stanford, CA: Stanford University Press.

Terry, W.S. (1989). Birth order and prominence in the history of psychology. *Psychological Record, 39*, 333-337.

Thorndike, E.L. (1936). The relation between intellect and morality in rulers. *American Journal of Sociology, 42*, 321-334.

Thorndike, E.L. (1950). Traits of personality and their intercorrelations as shown in biography. *Journal of Educational Psychology, 41*, 193-216.

Veblen, T. (1919). The intellectual preeminence of Jews in modern Europe. *Political Science Quarterly, 34*, 33-42.

Visher, S.S. (1947). Starred scientists: A study of their ages. *American Scientist, 35*, 543, 570, 572, 574, 576, 578, 580.

Walberg, H.J., Rasher, S.P., & Parkerson, J. (1980). Childhood and eminence. *Journal of Creative Behavior, 13*, 225-231.

Wallace, D.B., & Gruber, H.E. (Eds.). (1989). *Creative people at work: Twelve cognitive case studies.* New York: Oxford University Press.

Walters, J., & Gardner, H. (1986). The crystallizing experience: Discovering an intellectual gift. In R.J. Sternberg & J.E. Davidson (Eds.), *Conceptions of giftedness* (pp. 306-331). New York: Cambridge University Press.

Whaples, R. (1991). A quantitative history of the Journal of Economic History and the cliometric revolution. *Journal of Economic History, 51*, 289-301.

White, R.R. (1931). The versatility of genius. *Journal of Social Psychology, 2*, 460-489.

Woods, F.A. (1906). *Mental and moral heredity in royalty.* New York: Holt.

Woods, F.A. (1909). A new name for a new science. *Science, 30*, 703-704.

Woods, F.A (1911). Historiometry as an exact science: *Science, 33*, 568-574.

Woods, F.A. (1913). *The influence of monarchs.* New York: Macmillan.

Woodward, W.R. (1974). Scientific genius and loss of a parent. *Science Studies, 4*, 265-277.

Yuasa, M. (1974). The shifting center of scientific activity in the West: From the sixteenth to the twentieth century. In N. Shigeru, D.L. Swain, & Y. Eri (Eds.), *Science and society in modern Japan* (pp. 81-103). Tokyo: University of Tokyo Press.

Zhao, H. (1984). An intelligence constant of scientific work. *Scientometrics, 6*, 9-17.

Zhao, H., & Jiang, G. (1985). Shifting of world's scientific center and scientists' social ages. *Scientometrics, 8*, 59-80.

Zhao, H., & Jiang, G. (1986). Life-span and precocity of scientists. *Scientometrics, 9*, 27-36.

Zusne, L. (1976). Age and achievement in psychology: The harmonic mean as a model. *American Psychologist, 31*, 805-807.

Zusne, L. (1985). Contributions to the history of psychology: XXXVIII. The hyperbolic structure of eminence. *Psychological Reports, 57*, 1213-1214.

Zusne, L. (1986-89). Some factors affecting the birthday-deathday phenomenon. *Omega: Journal of Death and Dying,17*, 9-26.

Zusne, L. (1987). Contributions to the history of psychology: XLIV. Coverage of contributors in histories of psychology. *Psychological Reports, 61*, 343-350.

Zusne, L., & Dailey, D.P. (1982). History of psychology texts as measuring instruments of eminence in psychology. *Revista de Historia de la Psychología, 3*, 7-42.

2 Psychoanalytic Theories of Creativity

John E. Gedo

In essence, psychoanalysis is a psychology of motivation; consequently, most of the psychoanalytic literature on creativity has concerned itself with the nature of the motivational impetus for creative activities. Of necessity, specific hypotheses about this issue have reflected their proponents' views on the wider issue of the sources of all human motives. From the early 1890s, when Freud first postulated a theory of mentation fueled by psychic energies,[1] until well beyond his death almost a half century later, within psychoanalysis there was no serious alternative for his view that all human behavior is motivated by instinctual drives. Freud periodically revised his proposals for classifying the relevant dri-

---

[1]Freud initially postulated such a hypothesis in a letter to his scientific mentor, Josef Breuer (published in 1893/1966a). This hypothesis was elaborated in a draft of 1895, unpublished in Freud's lifetime, known as the "Project for a Scientific Psychology" (Freud, 1895/1966b). Perhaps the clearest statements of the hypothesis were in *The Unconscious* (Freud, 1915/1957b) and Part IV of *The Ego and the Id* (Freud, 1923/1961a). The last restatement of the hypothesis occurred in a posthumous publication (Freud, 1940/1961b; see especially. p. 163).

ves,[2] but all versions of his drive theory consistently maintained that creative activities did not make use of sexuality (or aggression) in raw form—that, in the service of creativity, the drives are somehow *sublimated*.[3] In Freud's lifetime, therefore, all psychoanalysts explained the ability to be creative as a function of a putative capacity for sublimation. Freud's own pronouncement, that the artist seeks fame, fortune, and sexual love, was merely a restatement in operational terms of the assumption that creativity amounts to the discharge of a sublimated libido, in the realm of narcissistic aims as well as that of object seeking (Freud, 1908/1959).

The foregoing viewpoint was essentially sterile because there is no way to detect sublimatory capacities *before* the success of the creative act. Retreat from this blind alley was a by-product of the advent of "ego psychology." This was a theoretical trend ushered in by Freud's last revision of his views of mental function, in the mid-1920s, a change that gave equal weight to the drives and to the regulatory functions that inhibit their immediate gratification. The new conceptualization was definitively articulated in *The Ego and the Id* (Freud, 1923/1961a). This change also sanctioned a fresh look at creativity, a research program pioneered by the art historian-turned-psychoanalyst Ernst Kris, whose work on this topic earned him a leadership role within ego psychology.

The cumulative impact of Kris's (1952) contributions on creativity did not make itself felt until their publication in book form. Before the appearance of *Psychoanalytic Explorations in Art*, much of his work had only been available in German. His familiarity with the lives of numerous artists and his interest in the creative activities of psychotics cast doubt on Freud's facile assumptions about artistic motives. As Kris (1950) gained greater expertise in the realm of psychoanalytic theorizing, he began to assert that the mental processes crucial for creativity were not those of the id but preconscious aspects of the ego.[4]

Large segments of the psychoanalytic community remained unconvinced by the arguments of ego psychology and continued to elab-

---

[2]The first restatement occurred in response to a searching critique by Jung (Freud, 1914/1957a). Freud (1920/1955) proposed a more radical revision in *Beyond the Pleasure Principle*. For the ultimate elaboration of drive theory, see Hartmann (1952/1964a).

[3]Freud (1905/1953) introduced the concept of sublimation in *Three Essays on the Theory of Sexuality* and gave it a more precise definition in *The Ego and the Id* (1923/1961a). The definitive statement of the hypothesis was made by Hartmann (1955/1964b).

[4]Gedo's survey covers work within psychoanalysis. With his permission, several additional sources are cited in editorial footnotes. See, for example, Dudek and Verreault (1989) for recent work on regression in the service of the ego—Editor.

orate further psychological drive theories. Even today, the heirs of Melanie Klein (mainly in England and Latin America) and those of Jacques Lacan (in France) remain loyal to the "early Freud." It may be no coincidence that these schools of psychoanalysis have had relatively little to say on the subject of creativity. Lacan, in a seminar during 1959-60, did give a critique on the theory of sublimation (see Lacan, 1986), but he never explicitly addressed the topic of creativity. Some of Melanie Klein's students, notably Segal (1957) and the critic Stokes (1957, 1963), managed to coin a new hypothesis to account for creativity on the basis of drive psychology. They postulated that in creative activities libido may be used to overcome aggression (either past aggressive behaviors or future potentials for aggression) through activities they called *reparation*.

By contrast, the ego psychologist Greenacre (1971a) pointed out that creative activities are far from lacking in passion, as the theory of sublimation would require; on the contrary, they seem to involve as much intensity as human beings can muster (see also Kubie, 1962; Levey (Lee), 1949). To account for this fact as well as the supreme control required in carrying out the creative act, Kris devised an ingenious theoretical oxymoron, the notion of "regression in the service of the ego."[5] By this he meant that creativity requires the ability to use ego functions at their best while allowing "regression" to primitive modes of drive organization.[6]

Although the ability for such selective regression is as inexplicable as is that for sublimation, from a scientific point of view the new hypothesis represented a major advance because it opened the door within psychoanalysis for detailed examination of the nature of specific talents. These were now dealt with in terms of the manner in which preconscious ego functions of various kinds are exercised in the process of creative work. I return to the question of the cognitive operations involved in creativity in a later section of this chapter. Here I merely note that, through his theoretical *tour de force*, Kris succeeded in preserving for another generation the Freudian hypothesis that all motivations have their sources in instinctual drives.

Probably the most fruitful ideas on creativity produced by the ego psychological school were those published by Greenacre (1971a). Based on extensive clinical experience with a range of creative persons, Greenacre concluded that children destined to become artists were relatively protected from the expectable unfortunate consequences of difficult vicissitudes in life by what she called a "love affair with the

---

[5]Kris (1952) stated this most explicitly in the section on "Creation and Re-creation" (pp. 55-63).
[6]See Krystal and Krystal (1994), Rothenberg (1990), and Smith and van de Meer (1990) for additional discussion of the preconscious and creativity—Editor.

world"—a lessened reliance on good relations with the caretakers. She also noted that creative endowments seem to involve constitutional differences from expectable norms in terms of various physiological criteria. But the best exposition of the over-all ego psychological view of creativity was that of Eissler (1967). As this era in psychoanalysis was drawing to a close, Coltrera (1965) stated that the focus of study should shift to the "autonomous functions" involved in conflict-free thought processes, particularly those of perception and consciousness. Coltrera's prescient article forms a bridge to more recent conceptual innovations in the psychoanalytic study of creativity.

RECENT DEVELOPMENTS

About 20 years ago, Freud's original paradigm for motivation gradually collapsed, in parallel with the realization that mental functioning cannot be analogized to the operation of a machine driven by some form of energy.[7] The statement of a new conception most directly relevant for the study of creativity was made by Klein (1976), who proposed a list of "vital pleasures" that motivate everyone: one of these is the pleasure of *effectance*—the joy to be had through the sheer exercise of competence. Among others, I soon applied this concept to the problem of creativity (Gedo, 1989a), for I had previously made clinical observations (Gedo, 1972) suggesting that the self-esteem born of great accomplishments irresistibly pulls persons with major talent into a ceaseless exercise of their gifts. In my clinical experience, children destined for greatness are frequently misperceived by their caretakers, precisely because of the physiological peculiarities that are harbingers of their unusual talents, as defective (rather than outstanding). As a result of such childhood vicissitudes, creative persons often suffer from vulnerabilities in self-esteem and need the kind of affirmation provided by success in creative endeavors.

However, it was Klein's (1976) abandonment of the equation of motivation with instinctual drive that made it clear that the crux of the matter in creative activity was not the need to overcome narcissistic injury, as some authors have continued to insist. These students of creativity have been so impressed by the anecdotal evidence encountered in clinical work that they postulate that preexisting injuries to self-esteem constitute the universal driving forces of creative endeavors. In

---

[7]The exciting debates that led to this result culminated in a volume (Gill & Holzman, 1976) including contributions from Gill, Holt, Rubinstein, and Wallerstein, and espousing both the older viewpoint and the need for its replacement.

particular, Niederland (1967, 1976) has stressed the frequency of physical handicaps underlying the self-esteem problem. In my judgment, such views are based on inadequate and biased samples of creative persons. The pleasure of effectance is also irresistible for persons who suffer from no problems of self-esteem. When, in 1983, I reviewed the psychoanalytic literature on creativity for my book, *Portraits of the Artist*, I cited the work of Klein's collaborator, Pinchas Noy (on the question of creativity in music), as the model to be followed in this domain (Noy, 1968, 1972; see also Esman, 1979).

I must emphasize at this point that I have been discussing hypotheses about creativity that were intended to be universally applicable. In particular instances, these indispensable factors may be supplemented by a variety of additional motives that are not to be found in other cases. Many of the psychoanalytic hypotheses I have dismissed as universal explanations were developed on the basis of sound clinical evidence, but they turned out to be applicable to limited segments of the creative domain. Thus, it is perfectly true that the creativity of certain individuals is enhanced by a need to counterbalance their deficient self-esteem (caused, for example, by psychological injuries inflicted by the childhood caretakers or by bodily defects). In other instances, a competitive factor is part of the motivational spectrum, and such a state of affairs may well reflect childhood competitiveness with parental figures, sometimes on the basis of awe of the mother's quasi-miraculous ability to create new life (see Greenacre 1957/1971b). Not infrequently, creative activities are stimulated by a need to make reparation for fantasied or real destructiveness (as the Kleinians believe), to substitute order for chaos (Rose, 1980), or to accomplish a work of mourning (Pollock, 1978). Even the tendentious motives Freud (1908/1959) believed to be central for creativity—money, prestige, or sexual rewards—are important in many instances. But none of these ancillary motives will suffice by itself to maintain a commitment to the creative life.

Although he never made his theoretical position on the question of creativity (or, for that matter, on most other issues) explicit, Winnicott (1967) was probably the most influential contributor to the literature to espouse the emerging consensus about the need for a new theory of creativity. Winnicott located "cultural experience" in what he called a *transitional space*, wherein the person operates playfully. In a recent paper (Gedo, 1993), I have endorsed Winnicott's position; however, in my view creativity also depends on the joy of effectance and on a preference for novelty.[8]

---

[8]Miller and Karl (1993) described certain linguistic rituals as transitional phenomena—Editor.

These novel psychoanalytic views preclude the conceptualization of creativity as a by-product of psychopathology (see Modell, 1970; Weissman, 1971). In this regard, the psychoanalytic consensus has tended to depart from the views of an influential psychiatric faction who propose correlating creative accomplishments with a propensity for depressive illness (see Andreasen, 1987; Jamison, 1989). The most cogent statement of the objections to these reductionistic views is probably that of Rothenberg (1990a). Eysenck (1993, this volume) has proposed a much more sophisticated hypothesis, linking creativity with a measurable set of personality traits he calls *psychoticism*. He has chosen this term because similar traits are also found in testing psychotic patients. However, Eysenck explicitly acknowledges that such traits may be acquired on the basis of manifold constitutional variables interacting with a great variety of infantile experiences.

Whenever the subject matter of artistic activities is focused on the artist's personal disturbances, that preoccupation is in the service of mastery (for details, see Gedo, 1996), and the creative effort itself cannot be involved in intrapsychic conflict. More often than not, the creative person primarily desires to transmit an artistic (or scientific or scholarly) message that represents his or her highest ideals in the form of a perfected offering (see Gedo, 1989a, chap. 7).

CREATIVE THINKING

A decade ago, the psychoanalytic revolution I have just summarized finally led to the conclusion that creativity can no longer be conceptualized as the outcome of manipulating sets of fantasies: It must be understood, instead, as the ability to process percepts (or abstractions concretized in terms of perceptual metaphors) in an extraordinarily flexible and sophisticated manner (Gedo, 1989a, Section I). The most extensive exposition of this new point of view can be found in the work of Ehrenzweig (1967, 1953/1975), an art educator also trained in gestalt psychology and psychoanalytic theory.

Ehrenzweig spelled out what is extraordinary about the manner in which the creative person (in Ehrenzweig's publications, exemplified by musicians and practitioners of the visual arts) manipulates the percepts relevant within a particular creative domain. In his view, this process involves the integration of two distinct modes of perception: the gestalt-free mode that characterizes the first several years of childhood, and a mode acquired later in development that makes use of gestalten. Ehrenzweig assumes that in most people the ability to perceive an accurate gestalt (that is, to apprehend a percept as one whole, rather than as an assembly of uncoordinated details) gradually suppresses gestalt-free perception. From this perspective, talent in any particular creative field implies the preservation and development of gestalt-free perception and its use in conjunction with gestalten. In music, for example, the gestalt-free elements are the interpretive variations not found in the written score, as well as the unfocused polyphony that coexists with the harmonic gestalt. Rothenberg (1971) proposed calling such an ability to think simultaneously in two disjunctive ways *Janusian* (see also Gedo, 1983, chap. 2; Noy, 1972; Rothenberg, 1990b).

Noy (1969) may have been the first to exploit Ehrenzweig's (1976, 1953/1975) conclusions within the theoretical domain of psychoanalysis proper. Noy proposed that Freud's classification of thought processes into primary and secondary varieties should no longer be understood to represent a development from a more primitive to a more mature position; rather, Noy conceived of the two modes of thought as having independent developmental lines, so that they remain available throughout life. As a result of recent advances in cognitive psychology and brain science, this conclusion has become widely accepted (Hoppe & Kyle, 1990). Bucci (1993) carried the argument even further: She pointed out that the availability of both primary and secondary process mentation does not constitute the ultimate stage in the development of thinking. Bucci looks on the integration of these distinct modes of thought, through what she calls *referential activity*, as the culmination of this line of development. In these terms, creativity depends on the availability of a maximal degree of referential activity, particularly as this involves both modes of perception. This complex set of requirements for creative thinking can only be met if superior constitutional endowments are channeled into a particular form of referential activity as a result of rich environmental input at crucial junctures.

THE PROSPECT BEFORE US

The development of the psychoanalytic theory of creativity just outlined implies that the most urgent investigative task before us does not lie within the province of clinical psychoanalysis. Priority in creativity research should go to attempts to correlate various types of early experience with the development of unusual cognitive (especially perceptual) abilities. These extraordinary skills, possessed by persons who have major creative accomplishments to their credit, have to be studied through the methods of cognitive psychology and brain science.

Psychoanalysis should be able to make its contribution to this field in making further comparative studies of the *personality types* most suited to various distinctive creative endeavors (see Gedo, 1996). The focus of such investigations should differ from that of previous psychoanalytic writings on creativity in giving priority to the fact that, whatever the sources of creative behavior may be, ultimately every human action must necessarily reflect those structured psychological dispositions called *character*. I have already attempted to survey the characterological attributes that seem to be prerequisites for significant creative accomplishments of any kind (Gedo, 1993), as well as to provide several illustrative instances of particular attributes that permit successful responses to specific creative opportunities (Gedo, 1989b, 1992, 1995). I also plan to review the manner in which unusual constitutional endowments may lead to the crystallization of special talents through fortunate nurturance. The other side of the same coin is the difficulty of raising children who are constitutionally atypical in having special endowments—a challenge that defeats many families and often leads to characterological vulnerabilities in the unusual child (see Gedo, 1989a, chap. 6).

These legacies of an atypical childhood predispose persons who possess creative gifts to an incidence of psychopathology perhaps greater than that of the general population, but this conclusion cannot be used to argue that creativity is a function of such pathology. On the contrary, creative success often makes it possible to overcome emotional difficulties (see Gedo, 1990), even if these have had their genesis in problems unconnected to the creative life (see M. Gedo, 1992). Any interference with continuing creative accomplishments can prove to be a trigger for serious deterioration in adaptation (see Gedo, 1996). At the same time, commitment to creative endeavors constitutes a challenge of real magnitude, one that may overburden a vulnerable personality and lead to acute psychopathological developments. In some cases, the creative challenge can only be met insofar as the psychopathology is walled off and kept apart from the subject matter of the creative work (see Gedo, 1989a, chap. 9).

Such hypotheses about creative personalities depart radically from the views formerly prevalent in the psychoanalytic literature. What I emphasize here is that the question of character (or of the vicissitudes of its formation in specially endowed children) was formerly largely neglected in psychoanalytic writings on this subject. I believe the foregoing survey demonstrates that psychoanalytic contributors have focused instead on, first, the issue of the motivational impetus for creative activities and, second, the cognitive operations required to succeed in them.

Understanding of both similarities and differences in personality among creative people of every sort will undergo progressive refinement as the clinical theories of psychoanalysis continue their progress. In the 100 years since Freud launched the psychoanalytic enterprise, our understanding of human psychological vicissitudes has been immensely broadened and deepened with the advent of every new generation within the discipline, and there is every reason to hope that psychoanalysis will maintain this vitality as it heads into the 21st century.

REFERENCES

Andreasen, N. (1987). Creativity and mental illness: Prevalence rates in writers and their first-degree relatives. *American Journal of Psychiatry, 144,* 1288-1292.

Bucci, W. (1993). The development of emotional meaning in free association: A multiple code theory. In A. Wilson & J. Gedo (Eds.), *Hierarchical concepts in psychoanalysis* (pp. 3-47). New York: Guilford.

Coltrera, J. (1965). On the creation of beauty and thought. *Journal of the American Psychoanalytic Association, 13,* 634-703.

Dudek, S.Z., & Verreault, R. (1989). The creative thinking and ego functioning of children. *Creativity Research Journal, 2,* 64-86

Ehrenzweig, A. (1967). *The hidden order of art.* Berkeley: University of California Press.

Ehrenzweig, A. (1975). *The psychoanalysis of artistic vision and hearing* (3rd ed.). London: Shelton. (Original work published 1953)

Eissler, K. (1967). Psychopathology and creativity. *American Imago, 24,* 35-81.

Esman, A. (1979). The nature of the artistic gift. *American Imago, 36,* 305-312.

Eysenck, H. (1993). Creativity and personality: Suggestions for a theory. *Psychological Inquiry, 4,* 147-178; 238-246.

Freud, S. (1953). Three essays on the theory of sexuality. *Standard Edition, 7,* 125-243. London: Hogarth. (Original work published 1905)

Freud, S. (1955). Beyond the pleasure principle. *Standard Edition, 18,* 3-64. London: Hogarth. (Original work published 1920)

Freud, S. (1957a). On narcissism: An introduction. *Standard Edition, 14,* 67-102. London: Hogarth. (Original work published 1914)

Freud, S. (1957b). The unconscious. *Standard Edition, 14,* 166-204. London: Hogarth. (Original work published 1915)

Freud, S. (1959). Creative writers and daydreaming. *Standard Edition, 9,* 142-156. London: Hogarth. (Original work published 1908)

Freud, S. (1961a). The ego and the id. *Standard Edition, 19,* 3-66. London: Hogarth. (Original work published 1923)

Freud, S. (1961b). An outline of psychoanalysis. *Standard Edition, 23,* 141-207. London: Hogarth. (Original work published 1940)

Freud, S. (1966a). Sketches for the 'preliminary communication' of 1893. *Standard Edition, 1,* 147-156. (Original work published 1893)

Freud, S. (1966b). Project for a scientific psychology. *Standard Edition, 1,* 283-397. London: Hogarth. (Original work published 1895)

Gedo, J. (1972). On the psychology of genius. *International Journal of Psycho-Analysis, 53,* 199-203.

Gedo, J. (1989a). *Portraits of the artist* (2nd ed.). Hillsdale, NJ: Analytic Press. (Original work published 1983)

Gedo, J. (1989b). Some differences in creativity in performers and other artists. *Medical Problems of Performing Artists, 4*(1), 15-19.

Gedo, J. (1990). More on the healing power of art: The case of James Ensor. *Creativity Research Journal, 3*(1), 33-57.

Gedo, J. (1992). Life histories within a creative cohort: The journey into abstraction. In J. Gedo & M. Gedo (Eds.), *Perspectives on creativity* (pp. 115-132). Norwood, NJ: Ablex.

Gedo, J. (1993). The creative personality: Challenge and opportunity. *Medical Problems of Performing Artists, 8*(3), 103-109.

Gedo, J. (1995). The anti-classical insurgency. *Revista Argentina de Arte y Psicoanálisis,* No. 3, 121-130.

Gedo, J. (1996). *The artist and the emotional world.* New York: Columbia University Press.

Gedo, M. (1992). Creativity and adaptation: Goya as his own physician. In J. Gedo & M. Gedo (Eds.), *Perspectives on creativity* (pp. 25-82). Norwood, NJ: Ablex.

Gill, M., & Holzman, P.(Eds). (1976). *Psychology versus metapsychology. Psychological issues* (Monograph 36). New York: International Universities Press.

Greenacre, P. (1971a). Studies in creativity. In *Emotional growth* (Vol. 2, pp. 399-615). New York: International Universities Press.

Greenacre, P. (1971b). The childhood of the artist. In *Emotional growth* (Vol. 2, pp. 479-504). New York: International Universities Press.

Hartmann, H. (1964a). Comments on the psychoanalytic theory of instinctual drives. In *Essays in ego psychology* (pp.69-89). New York: International Universities Press. (Original work published 1952)

Hartmann, H. (1964b). Notes on the theory of sublimation. In *Essays in ego psychology* (pp. 215-240). New York: International Universities Press.

Hoppe, K., & Kyle, N. (1990). Dual brain, creativity, and health. *Creativity Research Journal, 3,* 150-157.

Jamison, K. (1989). Mood disorders and patterns of creativity in British writers and artists. *Psychiatry, 52,* 125-34.

Klein, G. (1976). *Psychoanalytic theory.* New York: International Universities Press.

Kris, E. (1950). On preconscious mental processes. In *Psychoanalytic explorations in art* (pp. 303-318). New York: International Universities Press.

Kris, E. (1952). *Psychoanalytic explorations in art.* New York: International Universities Press.

Krystal, H., & Krystal, A.D. (1994). Psychoanalysis and neuroscience in relationship to dreams and creativity. In M.P. Shaw and M.A. Runco (Eds.), *Creativity and affect.* Norwood, NJ: Ablex

Kubie, L. (1962). The fallacious misuse of the concept of sublimation. *Psychoanalytic Quarterly, 31,* 73-79.

Lacan, J. (1986). *L'ethique de la psychanalyse*. Paris: Seuil.

Levey (Lee), H. (1949). A critique of the theory of sublimation. *Psychiatry, 2*, 239-270.

Miller, N., & Karl, N. (1993). Religious language as a transitional phenomenon: Lubbabies in times of danger. *Creativity Research Journal, 6*, 99-110.

Modell, A. (1970). The transitional object and the creative act. *Psychoanalytic Quarterly, 39*, 240-250.

Niederland, W. (1967). Clinical aspects of creativity. *American Imago, 24*, 6-34.

Niederland, W. (1976). Psychoanalytic approaches to artistic creativity. *Psychoanalytic Quarterly, 45*, 185-212.

Noy, P. (1968). The development of musical ability. *The Psychoanalytic Study of the Child, 23*, 332-347.

Noy, P. (1969). A revision of the psychoanalytic theory of the primary process. *International Journal of Psycho-Analysis, 50*, 155-178.

Noy, P. (1972). About art and artistic talent. *International Journal of Psycho-Analysis, 53*, 243-249.

Pollock, G. (1978). On siblings, childhood sibling loss, and creativity. *Annual of Psychoanalysis, 6*, 443-481.

Rose, G. (1980). *The power of form. Psychological Issues* (Monograph 49). New York: International Universities Press.

Rothenberg, A. (1971). The process of Janusian thinking in creativity. *Archives of General Psychiatry, 24*, 195-205.

Rothenberg, A. (1990a). *Creativity and madness*. Baltimore: Johns Hopkins University Press.

Rothenberg, A. (1990b). Creativity, mental health, and alcoholism. *Creativity Research Journal, 3*, 179-201.

Segal, H. (1957). A psycho-analytic approach to aesthetics. In M. Klein, P. Heiman, & R. Money-Kyrle (Eds.), *New directions in psychoanalysis* (pp. 384-405). New York: Basic Books.

Smith, G.J.W., & Van der Meer, G. (1990). Creativity in old age. *Creativity Research Journal, 3*, 249-264.

Stokes, A. (1957). Form in art. In M. Klein, P. Heiman, & R. Money-Kyrle (Eds.), *New directions in psychoanalysis* (pp. 406-420). New York: Basic Books.

Stokes, A. (1963). *Painting and the inner world*. London: Tavistock Publications.

Weissman, P. (1971). *Creativity in the theater*. New York: Basic Books.

Winnicott, D. (1967). The location of cultural experience. *International Journal of Psycho-Analysis, 48*, 368-372.

3 Creativity and Personality

H.J. Eysenck

Institute of Psychiatry, University of London

Theories of creativity march on two legs, which are usually treated separately by theorists. One is concerned with the nature of creative thought; the questions asked relate to such matters as the distinctive character of creativity (e.g., wide associative horizons, intuition, unconscious processing, primordial modes of thought). The other is concerned with the kind of person who is creative; the questions asked relate to such matters as the influence of psychopathology or of ego strength, extraverted or introverted personality, and the like. Ideally a good theory of creativity would find some biological substratum to join these two concepts and add a body to the two legs; several attempts to do this are noted in this chapter (Eysenck, 1993, 1994, 1995; Martindale, 1990, 1991; Simonton, 1980). Studies implicating genetic factors in creativity (Waller, Bouchard, Lykken, Tellegen, & Blacker, 1993) strongly suggest the existence and importance of such biological intermediaries between DNA and behavior, and it seems that their discovery could bring the appearance of unity to a sadly divided field.

In looking at the problems created by the postulation of creativity, the very definition of the term presents some difficulties. There are two major ways of using the term. Behavior can be called *creative* if the outcome is novel, original, surprising, and unusual or unique, and a *trait* of creativity can be postulated as a dispositional construct making possible such behavior and differentiating people who show much, a modicum, or little creativity. Normally one would insist that creativity also implies some degree of social usefulness, or at least conformity to meaningful expectation; the word salad of the schizophrenic is novel, unique, and original, but it is not creative in this sense. The *creative person* can be described as the person who frequently shows creative behavior as defined, even though such creativity may only be on a small scale.

In contrast, creativity is often spoken of in terms of great achievements or the outcome of the workings of genius. Creativity writ large presupposes trait creativity, but it also requires much else. It demands high intelligence, persistence and hard work, strong motivation, special musical, artistic, verbal or mathematical abilities; it demands proper background and teaching, social support, and much else (Amabile, 1983). Figure 3.1 shows in rough outline the relationship between trait creativity and creative achievement. Trait creativity is a *necessary* but not a *sufficient* condition of creative achievement.

Creativity in this case is assumed to be different from intelligence, at least partly. The work of Hargreaves (1927), a student of Spearman, established for the first time the existence of *divergent* thinking (imagination) as distinct from the usual convergent type of thinking characteristic of IQ test items. It is now accepted that whereas tests of creativity may show low correlations with IQ, they do measure a separate mode of thinking (Barron & Harrington, 1981), with .30 often sug-

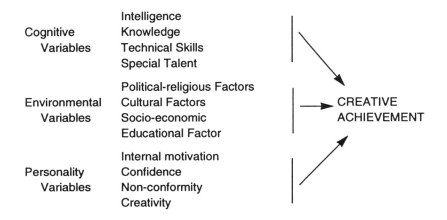

Figure 3.1. Hypothetical relation between creativity as a trait and creative achievement

gested as a typical correlation, depending on such factors of the actual tests employed, the sample tested, the instructions given, and so on. It is often said that the correlation is stronger in the lower levels of IQ, and weaker above IQs of 120, but Runco and Albert (1986) have shown that this is probably untrue in many cases; in others, heteroscedasticity has been found, so that no final decision on this point is possible.

THE ASSOCIATIVE GRADIENT

What underlies successful performance on tests of divergent thinking, assuming for the moment that they are appropriate measures of creativity? Barron and Harrington (1981), Eysenck (1994), and Glover, Ronning, and Reynolds (1989) have surveyed the literature that shows reasonable validity for at least some of the many tests used in this field. The view most widely accepted is that people differ with respect to the *associative gradient*, which characterizes their thinking. Consider Figure 3.2, which shows the frequency with which certain words are given as responses to *Foot* or *Command* in a word association test. Some clearly are given much more frequently than others, presumably because in the past it has been found that *foot* was associated with *shoe* more frequently than *soldier*, or *walks*, or the words constituting the row of singles at the bottom of Figure 3.2. A person who habitually responds with high-frequency words would be said to have a *steep associative gradient* (Mednick, 1962; Simonton, 1980), as opposed to someone who habitually produces low-frequency responses. There is good evidence that such steepness of gradient in word association tests correlates with rated or demonstrated creativity quite highly (approximately .50) in well-organized studies (MacKinnon, 1962a, 1962b)—the flatter the gradient, the more creative the person.

 The concept of a steep or flat associative gradient is fundamental to all tests of divergent thinking; it implies less adherence to the usual, habitual type of thinking, a certain imaginative freedom, and a lack of cognitive inhibition (Mednick, 1962; Mednick & Mednick, 1964). When kept within bounds, this is clearly a valuable property; it can offer solutions for difficult problems when the narrow range of associations fails to generate such a solution. One does have to take into account, of course, another component—namely, the total number of possible associations, ideas, or words a person possesses; this is conceived as independent of the flatness of the associative gradient. The genius (creative achievement) will have a large background of cognitive elements, the ordinary person only a few. Simonton (1980) contrasted the intuitive genius, who in addition has a flat gradient of association, with the analytical genius, who has a steep gradient, just as the ordinary person can

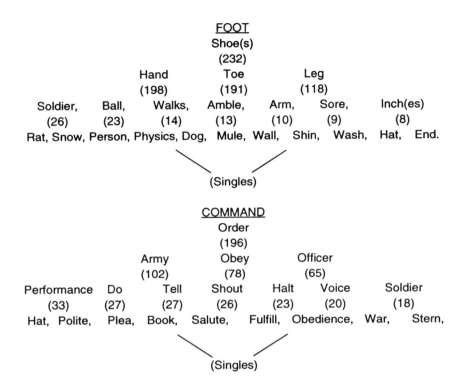

Figure 3.2. Width of associative horizons illustrated in
terms of the word associative test

have a flat or steep gradient for his or her much smaller number of
ideas. Much more could be said about the nature of the creative process,
but this is not the main purpose of this chapter, and I have only mentioned the nature of the creative process in order to link it with personality and with possible biological mechanisms underlying it later on
(Eysenck, 1995).

THE CREATIVE PERSON—EGO STRENGTH

Much work has been done over the years trying to correlate creativity
(measured, rated, or demonstrated in actual achievement) with personality. Given that the attempt here is to correlate one fuzzy concept with
another, there has been some considerable amount of agreement. Dellas

and Gaier (1970) gave an early summary of such studies; they argued that their evidence pointed to a common pattern of personality traits among creative persons, regardless of the field in which they were engaged. They also found that the personalities of young creative people were similar to those of creative adults. They concluded that these characteristics were probably determinants of creative performance, rather than traits developed in response to recognition of creative behavior. Such a conclusion would correlate well with the genetic determination of creativity suggested by the work of Waller et al. (1993).

Dellas and Gaier (1970) gave a list of 13 personality traits that they consider characteristic of the creative person. Such people show: (a) independence of attitude and social behavior, (b) dominance, (c) introversion, (d) openness to stimuli, (e) wide interests, (f) self-acceptance, (g) intuitiveness, (h) flexibility, (i) social presence and poise, (j) an antisocial attitude, and (k) unconcern for social norms. Two additional traits seemed to be more closely related to aesthetic rather than scientific creativity: (l) radicalism, and (m) rejection of external constraints.

It is not uncharacteristic of the literature that some of these traits are contradictory. The gifted person is apparently introverted, but also dominant; usually dominance is found to be a leading extraverted trait. It is not impossible to be introverted and dominant, the correlation is only about -.50 to -.60, but it is perhaps unusual (Eysenck & Eysenck, 1985). Other examples can be found of such incongruity; perhaps the incongruity itself is the sign of a creative person, combining traits in an unusual manner.

A more recent summary by Barron and Harrington (1981) produced a similar set of descriptive traits. They listed broad interests, attraction to complexity, high energy, independence of judgment, autonomy, inhibition, self-confidence, high valuation of aesthetic qualities, and an ability to resolve antinomies or to accommodate apparently opposite or conflicting traits in one's self-concept. Agreement between different authors was strong enough to give rise to several empirically keyed creative personality scales that typically correlate around .75. Typical items are, in alphabetical order: active, alert, ambitious, argumentative, artistic, assertive, capable, clear thinking, clever, complicated, confident, curious, cynical, demanding, egotistical, energetic, enthusiastic, hurried, idealistic, imaginative, impulsive, independent, individualistic, ingenious, insightful, intelligent, interests wide, inventive, original, practical, quick, rebellious, reflective, resourceful, self-confident, sensitive, sharp-witted, spontaneous, unconventional, versatile, and *not* inhibited. These terms give a good sense of what Barron (1969) referred to as a factor of *ego strength* (i.e., strong, self-determining, dominant ego, self-reliant, and independent). There is good evidence to support this view.

Yet, there is also good evidence for *introversion* as an important aspect of creativity. Well-known studies of acknowledged leading scientists and artists have shown that introversion is indeed a leading characteristic (Cattell & Drevdahl, 1955; Drevdahl & Cattell, 1958; Götz & Götz, 1979a, 1979b; Roe, 1951, 1952, 1953). The importance of this finding will become apparent when the theory that creativity is associated with low cortical arousalis considered; introversion is empirically associated with high cortical arousal (Eysenck & Eysenck, 1985).

Neuroticism and anxiety have also been found to be associated with creativity (Götz & Götz, 1979a, 1979b), but mostly in artists; for scientists emotional stability seems more prominent (Klingman, 1950; Sternberg, 1956, Wankowski, 1973). If that is true, and the evidence is not strong enough to be certain, then neuroticism is not relevant to creativity as such, but rather to the *direction* of creativity. This view may deserve a more detailed study and analysis. So far our survey has strongly agreed with views of the creative person, such as those of Maslow (1976), in which the creative person is self-actualizing and autonomous, or, as Barron (1969, 1972) put it, characterized by ego strength. However, there is also a darker side to the picture.

THE CREATIVE PERSON: PSYCHOPATHOLOGY

Creativity has from the earliest times been thought to be related to psychosis or *madness* (Hyslop, 1925; Lange-Eichbaum, 1956; Lombroso, 1901; Nisbet, 1900), with some researchers (Ellis, 1926; Juda, 1949) actually bringing forward evidence from controlled studies to supplement these mostly anecdotal accounts (Hasenfus & Magaro, 1976). Other researchers have found evidence of high creativity in close relatives or descendants of psychotic parents; this evidence has been surveyed by Richards (1981) and Eysenck (1983), who suggested that it was not *psychosis* (i.e., a psychopathological state) that was related to creativity genius, but *psychoticism* (i.e., a dispositional trait underlying susceptibility to the development of psychotic symptoms; Eysenck & Eysenck, 1976). It was postulated that high scores on measures of the trait *psychoticism* (P) were positively correlated with creativity, both as a trait and in terms of achievement (Eysenck, 1993, 1994, 1995).

It may be useful to digress and explain a little further what precisely is meant by *psychoticism*. It is postulated (and found) that certain traits frequently found in psychotics and their relatives are correlated to form a continuum ranging from psychotic through average to highly socialized, conventional, and altruistic. The continuum in question is shown in Figure 3.3; in the figure the curved line P_A, indicates the prob-

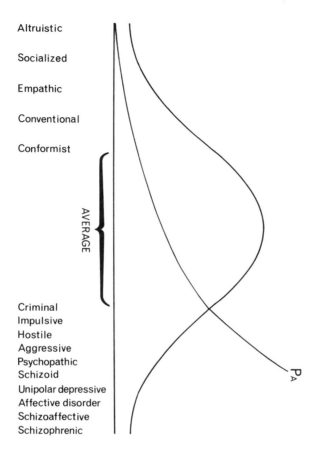

Figure 3.3. Diagrammatic representation of the psychoticism continuum

ability that an individual on any given part of the abscissa will develop a psychotic illness. The further to the right, the greater is the probability. This theory, and the empirical evidence supporting it, has been described in great detail elsewhere (Eysenck, 1992), and I will not go into it again here.

A rather similar connection to that postulated here was already contained in Bleuler's description of the *schizoid personality*, a concept in some ways similar to psychoticism and first used by him around 1911. The following is his description, based, of course, on careful observation rather than on formal correlational study:

He is taciturn or has little regard for the effect on others of what he says. Sometimes he appears tense and becomes irritated by senseless provocation. He appears as insincere and indirect in communication. His behaviour is aloof and devoid of human warmth; yet he does have a rich inner life. In this sense he is introverted. Ambivalent moods are more pronounced in the schizoid than in others, just as he distorts the meanings of, and introduces excessive doubts into, his own concepts. But on the other hand, the schizoid is also capable of pursuing his own thoughts and of following his own interests and drives, without giving enough consideration to other people and to the actual realities of life. He is autistic. The better side of this autism reveals a sturdiness of character, and inflexibility of purpose, an independence and a *predisposition to creativity*. The worse side of it becomes manifest in a lack of consideration for others, unsociability, a world-alien attitude, stubbornness, egocentricity, and occasionally even cruelty. (Bleuler, 1978, p. 185; emphasis added).

It is certainly a frequent finding in studies of genuinely creative people (i.e., those identified with an achievement criterion) that they show evidence of what is often called *psychopathology*. Thus, Barron (1969), comparing creative groups (writers, mathematicians, architects) with representative (average, noncreative) groups, stated that "the creative groups consistently emerge as having *more* psychopathology than do more representative members of the same profession. The *average* creative writer, in fact, is in the upper 15 per cent of the general population on *all* measures of psychopathology furnished by this test (the MMPI)" (p. 72). Thus, creative writers have average MMPI scores of 63 (for Hypochondriasis), 65 (for Depression), 68 (for Hysteria), 65 (for Psychopathic Deviate), 61 (for Paranoia), 64 (for Psychasthenia), 67 (for Schizophrenia), and 61 (for Hypomania)—as compared with a score of 50 for the general population.

Andreasen (1987) looked at the rate of mental illness in 30 creative writers, 30 matched control subjects, and the first-degree relatives of both groups. The writers had a substantially higher rate of mental illness, a predominantly affective disorder, with a tendency toward the bipolar type. There was also a higher prevalence of affective disorder and creativity in the writers' first-degree relatives, suggesting that these traits run together in families and could be genetically mediated. Writers and controls had IQs in the superior range, with the writers only excelling on the WAIS vocabulary subtest, confirming the view that intelligence and creativity are independent variables.

MacKinnon (1962a, 1962b) found correlations with creativity in his sample of architects of MMPI *psychopathic deviate* ($r = .22$) and schizophrenia ($r = .19$). As he pointed out, the meanings of these correlations for such an effective reality-correlating sample as our 124 architects, are not those which would apply in psychopathological groups. In the present context they are indicative of greater unusualness of thought processes and mental content and less inhibition and freer expression of impulse and imagery. (1962a, p. 34)

This may be so, but comparing creative with noncreative architects, MacKinnon (1962b) found the former lower than the latter on sense of well-being, responsibility, socialization, self-control, good impression, communality, achievement via conformance, and sociability, as shown by the California Psychological Inventory (Gough, 1957)—all are signs of failure in social integration.

Barron (1969) found that his creative writers and architects showed not only considerable psychopathology, but also superior ego strength (score of 58 for writers, 61 for architects on the MMPI), a pattern that as he pointed out is quite unusual; the ego-strength scale usually correlates *negatively* with the psychopathological scales (between -.50 and -.60). A similar pattern was found for the CPI scores, linking psychopathology in creative subjects with personal effectiveness. Barron contrasted psychosis and the "divine madness" of the artist by saying that the latter is not, like psychosis, something subtracted from normality; rather, it was something added. "Genuine psychosis is stifling and imprisoning, the divine madness is a liberation from the consensus (p. 73). All this may be true, but it does not furnish a criterion of *genuine psychosis* as contrasted with *divine madness*, other than creative achievement—but, of course, that is needs explanation!

PSYCHOTICISM AND CREATIVITY

Given the hypothesis that P, as a measure of predisposition to the development of psychotic illness, is causally related to creativity, how can one test this hypothesis? There are several directions that such tests can take, and these will be enumerated and the available evidence discussed. First in line is evidence of creativity in persons who are not psychotic, but closely related to psychotics, and hence genetically likely to be high on psychoticism. A number of genetic studies have indeed supported such a view. Heston (1966) studied offspring of schizophrenic mothers raised by foster parents, and found that although about half showed psychosocial disability, the remaining half were notably successful adults, possessing artistic talents and demonstrating imaginative adaptations to life to a degree not found in the control group. Karlsson (1968, 1970) in

Iceland found that among relatives of schizophrenics there was a high incidence of individuals of great creative achievement. McNeil (1971) studied the occurrence of mental illness in highly creative adopted children and their biological parents, discovering that the mental illness rates in the adoptees and in their biological parents were positively and significantly related to the creativity level of the adoptees.

A second line of investigation would suggest a significant correlation between P and creativity as measured by current creativity (trait) tests, such as the Wallach and Kogan (1965) and Torrance (1974) tests. Several such studies have been reviewed elsewhere (Eysenck & Eysenck, 1976); here I concentrate on what is perhaps the most impressive study done so far, namely, the work of Woody and Claridge (1977).

The subjects of their study were 100 university students at Oxford, both undergraduate and graduate. The students constituted a wide sampling of the various fields of specialization at the university. Woody and Claridge chose students as their subjects because of evidence that creativity is significantly related to IQ up to about IQ 120, but that it becomes independent of IQ above this level (Canter, 1973; Heansley & Reynolds, 1989). The tests used by them were the EPQ (Eysenck & Eysenck, 1975) and the Wallach-Kogan Creativity Tests, although somewhat modified and making up five different tasks (Instances, Pattern Meanings, Uses, Similarities, and Line Meanings). Each task was evaluated in terms of two related variables: the number of unique responses produced by the subject (originality), and the total number of responses produced by the subject (fluency).

The Pearson product-moment correlation coefficients between psychoticism and creativity scores for the five tests are as follows—P with the *number of responses* scores: Instances = .32, Pattern Meanings = .37, Uses = .45, Similarities = .36, and Line Meanings = .38; and P with *uniqueness* scores: .61, .64, .68, and .65. It will be shown that all the correlations are positive and significant, and those with the uniqueness scores (which is, of course, the more relevant of the two) are all between .6 and .7. These values are exceptionally high for correlations between what is supposed to be a cognitive measure and a test of a personality trait, particularly when general intelligence has effectively been partialled out from the correlations through the selection of subjects. There were no significant correlations between E and N, on the one hand, and creativity on the other. It is interesting to note, however, that the L score of the personality questionnaire, which up to a point is a measure of social conformity, showed throughout *negative* correlations with creativity scores, 7 out of 10 being statistically significant. L is known to correlate negatively with P (Eysenck & Eysenck, 1976). Other confirmatory studies have been reviewed by Eysenck (1993). Other creativity tests (e.g., word uniqueness and preference for complex drawings, have also been found to correlate with P (Eysenck, 1994b; Merten, 1992, 1993).

A third line of research is suggested by the theory, namely, that P correlates with creative achievement of a high order. The only study of what most persons would consider genuine creativity has been reported by Götz and Götz (1979a, 1979b). Götz and Götz administered the EPQ to 337 professional artists living in West Germany, of whom 147 male and 110 female artists returned the questionnaire; their mean age was 47 years. Regarding their scores on psychoticism, the results are very clear: Male artists had much higher P scores than male nonartists, and female artists had much higher P scores than female nonartists. As Götz and Götz pointed out, "these results suggest that certainly many artists may be more tough-minded than non-artists. Some traits mentioned by Eysenck and Eysenck (1985) may also be typical for artists, as for instance they are often solitary, troublesome and aggressive, and they like odd and unusual things." (p. 332).

It can be concluded that creative people combine personality traits usually negatively correlated—namely, ego strength and psychopathology. Given that the usual correlation between these two traits would be -.50 to -.60, they only share a quarter to a third of a common variance. This gives ample room for a relatively small portion of the population to share both traits; there is no statistical obstacle. I next turn to a consideration of the possibility that personality traits might lead to causal mechanisms of creativity.

THE AROUSAL THEORY OF CREATIVITY

The arousal theory of creativity is mostly detailed in Martindale (1990, 1991; Martindale & Armstrong, 1974) and Simonton (1980). Simonton argued as follows: Associations between events or ideas are formed through experience—learning—conditioning, producing conditional probability functions that give rise to four probability thresholds. The threshold of attention basically determines if an association between two events has a high enough conditional probability to be worth further examination. Such associations are weak and *nonconscious*. Next there is the threshold of behavior, when a conditional probability is large enough to have behavioral consequences; such associations are *infraconscious*. Third is the threshold of cognition; this determines if a conditional probability is strong enough to become consciously embodied as a symbol. And fourth, there is the threshold of habituation, in which a particular conditional probability is so high that it can be acted on without any further deliberation. These are *ultraconscious*.

For Simonton, creative people have flat association gradients, as already explained; such associations are likely to be found in the nonconscious and the infraconscious, these containing the less strongly conditional association. This brings Simonton into contact with the rich body of psychoanalytic speculation, including Kris (1952) and Kubie (1958), although he went well beyond the arid psychoanalytic theories, which, as even Freud (1925/1973) admitted, "can do nothing toward elucidating the nature of an artistic gift, nor can it explain the means by which the artist works" (p. 65).

Simonton made use of the concept of *arousal*, relying on the well-documented fact that an increase in arousal raises the likelihood that the more dominant responses will be performed (Eysenck, 1973; Spence, 1956). Thus, more remote associations would become accessible in a state of low arousal (i.e., in the nonconscious or infraconscious state. High arousal would strengthen the more dominant associations and, hence, lead to a steep association gradient. The argument presented by Simonton is very detailed, but, in essence, it marks the creative person as the person with a low arousal pattern. What of the evidence? Martindale has experimented extensively in this field and provides much evidence.

Martindale (1977a, 1977b, 1991) put forward a somewhat different theory that nevertheless agrees in many particulars with Simonton's just outlined. Beginning with theories such as Kris's (1952) on the ability of creative people to alternate between primary process and secondary process modes of thought, and Mendelsohn's (1976) contention that differences in focus of attention are the causes of differences in creativity, he argued that defocused attention is a property of primary process cognition. He used a neural network model to illustrate the phenomena I have subsumed under the label of *over-inclusiveness* (Eysenck, 1993), and he went on to use the concept of cortical arousal to explain creativity, making use, very much like Simonton, of Hull's (1943) *behavioral law*, which states that increases in Drive (arousal) make the dominant response to a stimulus even more dominant, because $P = D \times H$ (i.e., performance is the product of drive and habit). Thus, high drive arousal makes performance scores stereotyped, and low drive arousal makes creative and original behavior more likely. Indeed, virtually anything that increases arousal seems to impair performance on tests of creativity. This has been shown to be true of stress (Dentler & Mackler, 1964), a mere presence of other people (Lindgren & Lindgren, 1965), noise (Martindale & Greenough, 1973; Toplyn & Maguire, 1991), extremes of temperature (Lombroso, 1901), and even reward (Amabile, 1983). This seems true in spite of the fact that creative people may be *habitually* somewhat more anxious than noncreative people and have slightly higher levels of basic arousal on physiological measures (Martindale,

1994). Martindale suggested that creative people may be more variable in their levels of arousal than are uncreative people (i.e., show more extreme fluctuation).

An alternative hypothesis would be that although high on arousal, creative people practice *withdrawal* in order to escape overstimulation. There is much evidence for oversensitivity in creative people (e.g., Martindale & Armstrong, 1974; Nardi & Martindale, 1981). On all these points creative individuals behave exactly like introverts (Eysenck, 1967; Eysenck & Eysenck, 1985), showing both high arousal and withdrawal in order to lower their level of arousal.

Martindale (1994) himself appears to accept this as the more likely interpretation when he said: "Although creative people do not seem in general to have low levels of arousal, their over-sensitivity may drive them to withdraw or to restrict sensory input. This in turn would put them in the low-arousal state necessary for creative inspiration" (p. 161). The findings about oversensitivity strongly agree with the widespread finding that creativity is found more frequently in introverts, showing precisely this combination of high arousability and withdrawal. Martindale also linked creativity with a lack of cortical inhibition: "primary process cognition can be connected with a relative lack of cortical inhibition. The disinhibition of creative people seems not to be confined to cognition but is a general trait. This is to be expected if creativity is related to low levels of cortical arousal" (p. 162). The result, Martindale (1994) said, is "a general lack of both cognitive and behavioral inhibition" (p. 162).

Autobiographical writings by well-known geniuses seem to bear out at least some aspects of this theory (Koestler, 1964), in that the moment of creation often occurs when they are in a state of low arousal (e.g., on holiday, daydreaming, not thinking about the problem in question). Perhaps this solves the paradox: Creative people are introverted, but create novel ideas when in a state of low arousal. Clearly this theory is still at an early stage, but it is sufficiently promising to elaborate and test it more closely.

THE INHIBITION OF COGNITION THEORY

There is strong evidence that psychopathology (high psychoticism, but not actual psychosis) is closely connected with creativity, both on measured (trait) creativity, and as achievement. This suggests that one may be able to discover the cognitive mechanisms underlying creativity by drawing on the rich storehouse of factual and theoretical information deriving from the study of schizophrenia and the functional psychoses generally.

Determining what is the main characteristic of schizophrenic thinking has been hotly debated, but divergent theories often refer to similar underlying reality. I begin with the concept of *overinclusive thinking*, originally formulated by Cameron (1938, 1947; Cameron & Magaret, 1951) and reviewed and extended by Payne (1960, 1973; Payne & Hewlett, 1960). Overinclusive thinking is a conceptual disorder in which the boundaries of concepts become overextensive. Associated ideas, or even distantly related ideas, become incorporated into the concepts of schizophrenics, making them broad, vague, and imprecise. A second aspect of overinclusive thinking is the *interpretation* of irrational themes. Completely irrelevant, often personal ideas intrude themselves and become mixed up with the problem-solving process. Related to this conception is Cromwell's (1968) *defective filter* hypothesis, describing the failure of schizophrenics to "filter out" any irrelevant stimuli. Payne and Hewlett (1960) have provided much empirical support for theories of this kind.

The notion of a defective filter was an early application of the information-processing paradigm in schizophrenic research, following Broadbent's (1958) model. Later work along several lines has been reviewed by Hemsley (1976, 1982), who also pointed out the weaknesses of this approach as customarily applied to schizophrenic thinking. Hemsley (1987, 1991) has published a rather different theory, drawing on the work of Schneider and Shiffrin (1977), Posner (1982), and Frith (1979, 1987). His theory postulates that it is a weakening of the influence of stored memories of regularities of previous input on current perception that is basic to the schizophrenic condition (see also Patterson, 1987). This weakening of stored memories of regularities of previous input on current cognitions is conceived to lead to a lessening in the abilities of schizophrenics to use top-down strategies in the processing of information (i.e., at interpreting incoming stimuli with reference to a model composed of stored information of past experience and knowledge). Schizophrenics thus have to rely on bottom-up processing, wherein fragments of information from the stimulus are pieced together without reference to an expected model (Hemsley, 1987).

In some ways, these models are but adaptations of Bleuler's (1978) original hypothesis that the primary problem in schizophrenics is a disturbance of the associative process (i.e., a disturbance of the cognitive organizing mechanisms that allow associations or connections between ideas, enabling the organization of single thoughts and the exclusion of irrelevant thoughts). All of the models mentioned would suggest that one deduction from the theories involved would be a *widening* of the associative horizon. This indeed appears to be an almost universal accompaniment of schizophrenia (and affective disorders frequently associated with schizophrenia; Sheldrick, Jablensky, Sartorius, & Shepherd, 1977).

A good example of the widening of the associative horizon (or the flattening of the associative gradient) of schizophrenics is the unusual nature of the word association test responses they produce. In a similar manner, normal high P scorers produce unusual responses (Merten, 1992, 1993; Upmanyu & Kaur, 1986), as do biological relatives of schizophrenics, themselves not psychotic. Several studies have shown this to be true (Cialo, Lidz & Ricci, 1967; Griffith, Mednick, Schulsinger, & Diderichsen, 1980; Mednick & Schulsinger, 1968; Zahn, 1968). As Ward, McConaghy, and Catts (1991) pointed out, this suggests that the altered associative process reflected by normal Word Association Test (WAT) responses may be linked to a constitutional vulnerability factor, rather than to schizophrenia as such. This is important evidence suggesting that psychoticism rather than psychosis is linked with the greater associative horizon. McConaghy and Clancy (1968) used the term *allusive thinking* to describe this familially transmitted conceptual style; they used "loose" sortings on an object sorting test (OST) created by Lovibond (1954) as a measure of this allusive thinking, and they found that parents of "thought-disordered" schizophrenics showed greater "loosening" on the test, as did the parents of university students with high OST scores.

Similar results have also been reported by Miller and Chapman (1983), using the Chapman and Chapman (1980) scales as measures of schizotypal behavior. Using a continuous word association test they found that subjects with high scores in Perception Aberration/Magical ideation gave a larger number of idiosyncratic responses. It is also relevant that Griffiths et al. (1980) reported more deviant associations in the children of schizophrenic parents.

Andreasen and Powers (1974) have shown that highly creative writers are overinclusive as shown by their scores on the Goldstein-Sheerer Object Sorting Test (OST). Their data suggested that the conceptual style of writers may resemble mania rather than schizophrenia, and that if overinclusiveness is an index of thought disorder, manics may have a more florid thought disorder than schizophrenics.

Along similar lines, Armstrong and McConaghy (1973) examined measures of word association in university students based on the hypothesis that the "halo" of words considered to be related in meaning to a particular stimuli word would be broader in allusive than in nonallusive thinkers, containing more words and, hence, words that are more distant in meaning from the stimulus word. Armstrong and McConaghy (1973) did indeed find significant correlations between their Word Halo Test, testing the selection of words considered by the subject to be nearly the same in meaning as nominated stimulus words, a Word Sorting Test requiring the subject to group together words similar in meaning, and the OST. Several doctoral theses quoted by Ward, McConaghy, and Catts (1991) reported the expected correlations between these tests, on a variety of samples, and also the predicted correlation with the Word Association Test, using less common responses as the score.

THE PSYCHOPHYSIOLOGY OF CREATIVITY

What underlies this general factor of over-inclusiveness? Latent inhibition (Lubow, 1989) can be considered a promising candidate. Latent inhibition is defined by an experimental paradigm that requires, as a minimum, a two-stage procedure. The first stage involves stimulus *preexposure*, with the to-be-CS (conditioned stimulus) exhibited without being followed by any UCS (unconditioned stimulus); this leads theoretically to the CS acquiring a *negative salience*, in which it signals a lack of consequences, and thus acquires inhibitory properties. The second stage is one of *acquisition*, with the CS now followed by an UCS, and acquires the property of initiating the UCS response. Latent inhibition (LI) is shown by increasing difficulties of acquiring this property, as compared with a lack of preexposure. There is usually a *masking task* during exposure to the CS; for instance, the masking task might be the presentation of a series of syllable pairs auditorially, whereas the CS would be a white noise randomly superimposed on the syllable reproduction. The LI group would be exposed to this combined recording, whereas the control group would be exposed only to the syllable pairs, without the white noise. During the test phase the white noise is reinforced, and subjects are given scores according to how soon they discovered the rule linking CS with reinforcement. LI would be indicated by the group having the reexposure of the white noise discovering the rule later than the control group. There are more complex, three-stage procedures, but these complications are not crucial to this argument (Lubow, 1989; Lubow, Ingberg-Sachs, Zalstein, & Gewirtz, 1992).

How does this relate to creativity? The cognitive elements in latent inhibition theory are emphasized by Lubow (1989) in terms of his *conditioned attention theory*. According to this theory, nonreinforced preexposure to a stimulus retards subsequent conditioning to that stimulus because during such preexposure the subject learns not to attend to it. The theory is based on the use of attention as a hypothetical construct, with the properties of a Pavlovian response, and on the specification of reinforcement conditions that modify attention.

The relevance of latent inhibition to creativity lies in the fact that it correlates negatively with both schizophrenia and psychoticism.

Baruch, Hemsley, and Gray (1988a, 1988b) found an abolition of LI in acute schizophrenics, but not in chronic schizophrenics and normals. Lubow (1989) also failed to find such abolition in chronic cases, presumably due to the fact that such patients are on a dopaminergic antagonist, neuroleptic drug regime that would normalize attentional processes. There is a large body of evidence to show that LI can be attenuated or abolished in rats by dopamine agonists such as amphetamine, and it can also be increased with dopamine antagonists such as haloperidol and chlorpromazine; see discussion by Lubow, Ingberg-Sachs, Zalstein, & Gewirtz, 1992).

Regarding their high versus low psychoticism group, Baruch et al. (1988a) found the expected negative correlation between LI and P—the greater the proneness to psychosis, the less latent is inhibition. Similar results have been reported by Lubow et al. (1992), using two different experimental procedures; again high P subjects showed an attenuated latent inhibition effect compared with low P scores. Both auditory and visual stimulus preexposure resulted in slower acquisition of new associations as compared with nonpreexposure to the test stimulus, but to a much lesser extent in high P than in normal and low P subjects. Lubow et al. (1992) argued that:

> the idea that schizophrenics fail to filter out irrelevant stimuli is congruent with the phenomenology of schizophrenics, and with a considerable variety of data on the differential effects of distractors on the behaviour of schizophrenics and normals. Frith (1979) cogently and succinctly described this type of result as "reflecting an inability to limit the contents of consciousness. (p. 570)

This, of course, is precisely what is characteristic of the mechanism needed to explain the overinclusiveness of schizophrenics and high P scorers; the failure of latent inhibition to limit associationist spreading (flat associationist gradient) would appear to account for the prominent symptoms of psychotic cognition and the major feature of creativity. Accordingly, this may be the missing link between psychopathology and genius. Of course, creativity based on a flat associative gradient produced by an absence of cognitive inhibition is not enough *by itself* to produce creative achievement; other components, such as those listed in Figure 3.1, are needed. Among these the ability to weed out unsuitable and unusable associations must be the distinguishing mark between the word *salad* of the schizophrenic and the utterances of the poet.

Latent inhibition, of course, has a biological basis, and this seems firmly related to dopamine levels. As reported, dopamine agonists such as amphetamine attenuate or abolish LI, whereas dopamine antagonists (heloperidol and chlorpromazine) increase LI, just as they weaken psychotic behavior. As Lubow et al. (1992) pointed out, these data are in accord with the premise that schizophrenia has a major attentional deficit component and that the disorder is mediated by a dopamine system dysfunction. Although other neurotransmitter involvements in schizophrenia have been proposed, the dopamine hypothesis remains a leading component in understanding schizophrenia (Gray, Feldon, Rawlins, Hemsley, & Smith, 1991).

The suggested relevance of LI to creativity is based on the fact that cognitive inhibition characteristic of most people is lessened or removed in creative people, and hence the associationist gradient is flattened, criteria for "relevance" are reduced, and overinclusiveness appears. It should be emphasized that there is no *direct* evidence in favor of the theory; it is based essentially on the strong association between creativity and psychoticism, the finding that psychoticism (like schizophrenia) is characterized by low degrees of LI, and that LI and negative priming account for the lack of cognitive inhibition apparent in schizophrenia and high P scorers. Direct evidence is therefore needed before the theory can be accepted as a true, rather than a possible, account of the observed relation between personality and creativity. Figure 3.4 shows in diagrammatic form the postulated path from DNA to creativity.

SUMMARY AND CONCLUSIONS

It is not to be expected that the conjunction of two "fuzzy" concepts, such as creativity and personality, would generate a clear-cut, testable, and predictive theory. Nevertheless, research has provided promising material that may in due course lead to such a theory. Personality descriptions of creative people—young and old—showing creativity as a trait and showing high creative achievement—male and female—have demonstrated remarkable agreement over the years. Creative people show apparently contradictory behavior patterns; they combine traits characteristic of ego strength, but also of psychopathology. These two sets of traits usually correlate between -.50 and -.60, suggesting that the combination of traits shown by creative people is unusual but not impossible. Similarly, creative people are introverted, but also show extraverted traits like dominance.

The major cognitive characteristic of creative people is the possession of a *flat associative gradient* (i.e., the tendency to extend widely and unusually their associative horizon). Concepts from schizophrenic research (over-inclusiveness or a lack of cognitive inhibition) suggest the

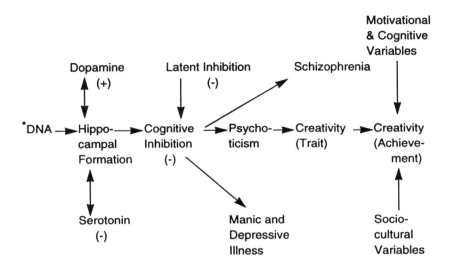

Figure 3.4. Path diagram from DNA to creative achievement

possibility of explaining the flat associative gradient of the creative person by means of concepts borrowed from clinical psychology, such as latent inhibition. The failure of the schizophrenic, or the normal high-psychoticism scorer, to limit his or her associations along the lines of latent inhibition may demonstrate the relevance of this mechanism to the study of creativity, particularly when it is realized that latent inhibition is linked through the effects of dopamine agonists and antagonists to the general theory of schizophrenia. This may be the kernel of truth in the old adage that "great wits are sure to madness near alli'd, and thin partitions do their bounds divide." It may also solve the paradox that geniuses may often be considered psychotic, but that psychosis seems to be completely antagonistic to creativity; the "thin partitions" may be all important.

The alternative theory linking creativity with unconscious association and low arousal also embodies a paradox in that the type of persons genuinely creative in the arts and in science tends to be *introverted*, which means having a cortex in a state of high arousal. A possible way out of this dilemma postulates that external conditions (e.g., rest, drowsiness, holiday atmosphere) may inhibit arousal and that creative ideas arise in precisely such conditions. Although relying more on anecdote than experiment, one should perhaps not reject entirely the accumulated wisdom and experience of the most creative men and women who have spoken about the circumstances accompanying their great "Aha!" experiences (see Ghiselin, 1952; Koestler, 1964; Vernon, 1970).

Certain theories linking personality and creativity have been neglected in this brief account. Psychoanalytic theories, for example, are largely untestable, and hence beyond science. Theories relating to masculinity, femininity, and androgyny have given such contradictory results that no conclusions can be reached. Theories concerning lateralization (brain hemispheric differences) have been tested, but the studies so far reported are weak methodologically and do not on the whole support the theory (Eysenck & Barrett, 1993; Katz, this volume). Lack of space have necessitates concentration on what seems the most promising theories in the field.

It will be clear from the descriptive accounts of creative people that they may not fit in too well into the context of their noncreative fellows' lives. Creativity, by its nature, is nonconformist, independent, different; nothing annoys mediocrity as much as this combination. We may not be able to produce or encourage creativity—the personality traits accompanying it are strongly determined genetically (Eaves, Eysenck, & Martin, 1989)—but perhaps having gained some knowledge of this combination of traits, we may learn to live with creativity without stamping it into the ground.

REFERENCES

Amabile, T.M. (1983). *The social psychology of creativity*. New York: Springer-Verlag.

Andreasen, N.C. (1987). Creativity and mental illness: Prevalence rates in writers and their first-degree relatives. *American Journal of Psychiatry, 144*, 1288-1292.

Andreasen, N.J.C., & Powers, P.S. (1974). Over-inclusive thinking in mania and schizophrenia. *British Journal of Psychiatry, 125*, 452-456.

Armstrong, M.S., & McConaghy, N. (1973). Allusive thinking, the word halo and verbosity. *Psychological Medicine, 7*, 439-445.

Barron, F. (1969). *Creative person and creative process*. New York: Holt, Rinehart & Winston.

Barron, F. (1972). *Artists in the making*. New York: Seminar Press.

Barron, F., & Harrington, D.M. (1981). Creativity, intelligence and personality. *Annual Review of Psychology, 32*, 439-476.

Baruch, I., Hemsley, D.R., & Gray, J. (1988a). Differential performance of acute and chronic schizophrenics in a latent inhibition task. *Journal of Nervous and Mental Disease, 176*, 598-606.

Baruch, I., Hemsley, D.R., & Gray, J. (1988b). Latent inhibition and "psychotic proneness" in normal subjects. *Personality and Individual Differences, 9*, 777-783.

Bleuler, M. (1978). *The schizophrenic disorders.* New Haven, CT: Yale University Press.

Broadbent, D., (1958). *Perception and communication.* Cambridge: Cambridge University Press.

Cameron, N. (1938). Reasoning, repression and communication in schizophrenics. *Psychological Monographs, 50*, 1-33.

Cameron, N. (1947). *The psychology of behavior disorders.* Boston: Houghton Mifflin.

Cameron, N., & Magaret, A. (1951). *Behavior pathology.* Boston: Houghton Mifflin.

Canter, S. (1973). Some aspects of cognitive function in twins. In G. Claridge, S. Canter, & W.I. Hume (Eds.), *Personality differences and biological variation: A study of twins* (pp. 115-138). Oxford: Pergamon Press.

Cattell, R.B., & Drevdahl, J.E. (1955). A comparison of the personality profile (16 P.F.) of eminent researchers with that of eminent teachers and administrators, and of the general population. *British Journal of Psychology, 46*, 248-261.

Chapman, L.J., & Chapman, J.P. (1980). Scales for rating psychotic and psychotic-like experiences as continua. *Schizophrenia Bulletin, 6*, 476-489.

Cialo, D.P., Lidz, T., & Ricci, J. (1967). Word meaning in parents of schizophrenics. *Archives of General Psychiatry, 17*, 470-477.

Cromwell, R.L. (1968). Stimulus redundancy and schizophrenia. *Journal of Nervous and Mental Diseases, 146*, 360-375.

Dellas, M., & Gaier, E.L. (1970). Identification of creativity: The individuals. *Psychological Bulletin, 73*, 55-73.

Dentler, R.A., & Mackler, B. (1964). Originality: Some social and personal determinants. *Behavioural Science, 9*, 1-7.

Drevdahl, J.E., & Cattell, R.B. (1958). Personality and creativity—artists and writers. *Journal of Clinical Psychology, 14*, 107-111.

Eaves, L., Eysenck, H.J., & Martin, N. (1989). *Genes, culture and personality: An empirical approach.* New York: Plenum Press.

Ellis, H. (1926). *A study of British genius.* New York: Houghton Mifflin.

Eysenck, H.J. (1967). *The biological basis of personality.* Springfield, Il.: C.C. Thomas.

Eysenck, H.J. (1973). Personality, learning and "anxiety". In H.J. Eysenck (Ed.), *Handbook of abnormal psychology* (2nd. ed., pp. 390-419). London: Pitman.

Eysenck, H.J. (1983). The roots of creativity: Cognitive ability or personality trait? *Roeper Review, 5*, 10-12.

Eysenck, H.J. (1992). The definition and measurement of psychoticism. *Personality and Individual Differences, 13*, 757-785.

Eysenck, H.J. (1993). Creativity and personality: Suggestions for a theory. *Psychological Inquiry, 4*, 147-246.

Eysenck, H.J. (1994a). The measurement of creativity. In M. Boden (Ed.), *Dimensions of creativity* (pp. 199-242). Cambridge, MA: MIT Press.

Eysenck, H.J. (1994b). Creativity and personality: Word association, origence, and psychoticism. *Creativity Research Journal, 7,* 209-216.

Eysenck, H.J. (1995). *Genius: The natural history of creativity.* Cambridge: Cambridge University Press.

Eysenck, H.J., & Barrett, P. (1993). Brain research related to giftedness. In K.A. Heller, F.J. Monks, & A.H. Pursue (Eds.), *The international handbook for research on giftedness and talent* (pp. 249-273). London: Pergamon Press.

Eysenck, H.J., & Eysenck, M.W. (1985). *Personality and individual differences: A natural science approach.* New York: Plenum.

Eysenck, H.J., & Eysenck, S.B.G. (1975). *Manual of the Eysenck personality questionnaire.* London: Hodder & Stoughton.

Eysenck, H.J., & Eysenck, S.B.G. (1976). *Psychoticism as a dimension of personality.* London: University of London Press.

Freud, S. (1973). *An autobiographical study.* London: Hogarth Press. (Original work published 1925)

Frith, C.D. (1979). Consciousness, information processing and schizophrenia. *British Journal of Psychiatry, 134,* 225-235.

Frith, C.D. (1987). The positive and negative symptoms of schizophrenia reflect impairments in the perception and inhibition of action. *Psychological Medicine, 17,* 631-648.

Ghiselin, B. (1952). *The creative process.* Berkeley: University of California Press.

Glover, J.A., Ronning, R.R., & Reynolds, C.R. (Eds.). (1989). *Handbook of creativity.* New York: Plenum Press.

Götz, K.O., & Götz, K. (1979a). Personality characteristics of successful artists. *Perceptual and Motor Skills, 49,* 919-924.

Götz, K.O., & Götz, K. (1979b). Personality characteristics of professional artists. *Perceptual & Motor Skills, 49,* 327-334.

Gough, H.G. (1957). *California psychological inventory manual.* Palo Alto: Consulting Psychologists Press.

Gray, A., Feldon, J., Rawlins, J.P., Hemsley, D.R.,& Smith, A.D. (1991). The neuropsychology of schizophrenia. *Behavioral and Brain Sciences, 14,* 1-84.

Griffith, J.J., Mednick, S., Schulsinger, F., & Diderichsen, B. (1980). Verbal associative disturbances in children at high risk for schizophrenia. *Journal of Abnormal Psychology, 89,* 125-131.

Hargreaves, H.L. (1927). The "faculty" of imagination. *British Journal of Psychology,* Monograph Suppl. 10.

Hasenfus, N., & Magaro, P. (1976). Creativity of schizophrenia: An equality of empirical constructs. *British Journal of Psychiatry, 129,* 346-349.

Heansley, P., & Reynolds, C.R. (1989). Creativity and intelligence, In J.A. Glover, R.R. Ronning, & C.R. Reynolds (Eds.), *Handbook of creativity* (pp. 111-132). New York: Plenum Press.

Hemsley, D.R. (1976). Attention and information processing in schizophrenia. *British Journal of Social and Clinical Psychology, 19*, 199-209.

Hemsley, D.R. (1982). Cognitive impairment in schizophrenia. In A. Burton (Ed.), *The pathology and psychology of cognition* (pp. 169-203). London: Methuen.

Hemsley, D.R. (1987). An experimental psychological model for schizophrenia. In R. Hafner, W.F. Gattaz, & W. Janzarik (Eds.), *Search for the causes of schizophrenia* (pp. 179-188). Heidelberg: Springer Verlag.

Hemsley, D.R. (1991). What have cognitive defects to do with schizophrenia? In G. Huber (Ed.), *Idiopathische psychosen* [Idiopathic psychoses] (pp. 138-146). Stuttgart: Schattover.

Heston, I.I. (1966). Psychiatric disorders in foster home reared children of schizophrenic mothers. *British Journal of Psychiatry, 112*, 819-825.

Hull, C.L. (1943). *Principles of behavior.* New York: Appleton-Century-Crofts.

Hyslop, T.B. (1925). *The great abnormals.* New York: G.H. Doran.

Juda, A. (1949). The relationship between highest mental capacity and psychic abnormalities. *American Journal of Psychiatry, 106*, 296-307.

Karlsson, J.I. (1968). Genealogic studies of schizophrenia. In D. Rosenthal & S. Kety, (Eds.), *The transmission of schizophrenia.* Oxford: Pergamon Press.

Karlsson, J.I. (1970). Genetic association of giftedness and creativity with schizophrenia. *Heredity, 66*, 177-182.

Klingman, S.F. (1950). Speed of vocational interest and general adjustment. *Journal of Counseling Psychology, 34*, 108-114.

Koestler, A. (1964). *The art of creation.* New York: Macmillan.

Kris, E. (1952). *Psychoanalytic explorations in art.* New York: International University Press.

Kubie, L.S. (1958). *Neurotic distortion of the creative process.* Kansas City: Kansas University Press.

Lange-Eichbaum, W. (1956). *Genie, Irrsin und Ruhm* [Genius, madness and fame]. Munich: Reinhardt Verlag.

Lindgren, H.C., & Lindgren, F. (1965). Brainstorming and orneriness as facilitators of creativity. *Psychological Reports, 16*, 577-583.

Lombroso, C. (1901). *The man of genius.* London: Walter Scott.

Lovibond, S.N. (1954). The Object Sorting Test and conceptual thinking in schizophrenia. *Australian Journal of Psychology, 6*, 52-70.

Lubow, R.E. (1989). *Latent inhibition and conditioned attention theory.* New York: Cambridge University Press.

Lubow, R.E., Ingberg-Sachs, Y., Zalstein, N., & Gewirtz, J. (1992). Latent inhibition in low and high "psychotic-prone" normal subjects. *Personality and Individual Differences, 13*, 563-572.

MacKinnon, D.W. (1962a). The nature and nurture of creative talent. *American Psychologist, 17*, 484-495.

MacKinnon, D.W. (1962b). The personality correlates of creativity. A study of American architects. In G.S. Nielsen (Ed.), *Proceedings of the XIV International Congress of Applied Psychology* (pp. 11-39). Copenhagen: Munksgaard.

Martindale, C. (1977a). *Cognitive consciousness*. Homewood, Il: Dorsey.

Martindale, C. (1977b). Creativity, unconsciousness and cortical arousal. *Journal of Altered States of Consciousness, 3*, 69-87.

Martindale, C. (1988). *Cognition and consciousness*. Homewood, IL: Dorsey.

Martindale, C. (1990). *The clockwork muse*. New York: Basic Books.

Martindale, C. (1991). Personality, situation and creativity. In J.C.A. Glover, R.R. Ronning, & C.R. Reynolds (Eds.), *Handbook of creativity* (pp. 211-231). New York: Plenum.

Martindale, C. (1993). How can we measure a society's creativity? In M. Boden (Ed.), *Dimensions of creativity*. Cambridge, MA: MIT Press.

Martindale, C., & Armstrong, J. (1974). The relationship of creativity to cortical activation and its operant control. *Journal of Genetic Psychology, 124*, 311-320.

Martindale, C., & Greenough, J. (1973). The differential effect of increased arousal on creative and intellectual performance. *Journal of Genetic Psychology, 123*, 329-335.

Maslow, A. (1976). Creativity in self-actualizing people. In A. Rothenberg & C.R. Hausman (Eds.), *The creative question* (pp. 86-92). Durham, NC: Duke University Press.

McConaghy, N., & Clancy, M. (1908). Familial relationships of allusive thinking in university students and their parents. *British Journal of Psychiatry, 114*, 1079-1087.

McNeil, T.F. (1971). Rebirth and postbirth influence on the relationship between creative ability and recorded mental illness. *Journal of Personality, 39*, 391-4406.

Mednick, S.A. (1962). The associative basis of the creative process. *Psychological Review, 69*, 220-232.

Mednick, S.A., & Mednick, M.T. (1964). An associative interpretation of the creative process. In L.W. Taylor (Ed.), *Widening horizons in creativity* (pp. 54-68). New York: Wiley.

Mednick, S.A., & Schulsinger, F. (1968). Some premorbid characteristics related to breakdown in disorder with schizophrenic mothers. *Journal of Psychiatric Research, 6*(Suppl. 1), 267-291.

Mendelsohn, G.A. (1976). Associative and attentional processes in creative performance. *Journal of Personality, 44*, 341-369.

Merten, T. (1992). Wortassoziation und schizophrenie: Eine empirische Studie [Word association and schizophrenia: An empirical study]. *Der Nervenarzt, 63*, 401-408.

Merten, T. (1993). Word association responses and psychoticism. *Personality and Individual Differences, 4*, 837-839.

Miller, E.N., & Chapman, L.J. (1983). Continued word association in hypothetically psychosis-prone college students. *Journal of Abnormal Psychology, 92*, 468-478

Nardi, K., & Martindale, C. (1981). *Creativity and preference for tones varying in dissonance and intensity*. Paper presented at Eastern Psychological Association Convention, New York.

Nisbet, J.F. (1900). *The insanity of genius*. London: Grant Richards.

Patterson, T. (1987). Studies towards the subcortical pathogenesis of schizophrenia. *Schizophrenia Bulletin, 13*, 555-576.

Payne, R.W. (1960). Cognitive abnormalities. In H.J. Eysenck (Ed.), *Handbook of abnormal psychology* (pp. 193-261). London: Pitman.

Payne, R.W. (1973). Cognitive abnormalities. In H.J. Eysenck (Ed.), *Handbook of abnormal psychology* (2nd ed., pp. 420-486). London: Pitman.

Payne, R.W., & Hewlett, J.H.G. (1960). Thought disorder in psychotic patients. In H.J. Eysenck (Ed.), *Experiments in personality* (pp. 3-104). London: Routledge & Kegan Paul.

Posner, M.I. (1982). Cumulative development of attentional theory *American Psychologist, 37*, 168-179

Richards, R.L. (1981). Relationship between creativity and psychopathology: An evaluation and interpretation of the evidence. *Genetic Psychological Monographs, 103*, 261-324.

Roe, A. (1951). A psychological study of physical scientists. *Genetic Psychology, 43*, 121-239

Roe, A. (1952). *The making of a scientist*. New York: Dodd, Mead.

Roe, A. (1953). A psychological study of eminent psychologists and anthropologists, and a comparison with biological and physical scientists. *Psychological Monograph: General and Applied, 67* (Whole No. 352).

Runco, M.A., & Albert, R.S. (1986). The threshold theory regarding creativity and intelligence: An empirical test with gifted and non-gifted children. *Creative Child and Adult Quarterly, 11*, 212-218.

Schneider, W., & Shiffrin, R.M. (1977). Controlled and automatic human information processing. I. Detection, search and attention. *Psychological Review, 84*, 1-66.

Sheldrick, C., Jablensky, A., Sartorius, N., & Shepherd, M. (1977). Schizophrenia succeeded by affective illness: catamnestic study and statistical enquiry. *Psychological Medicine, 7*, 619-627.

Simonton, D.K. (1980). Intuition and analysis: A predictive and explanatory model. *Genetic Psychology Monograph, 102*, 3-60.

Spence, K.W. (1956). *Behavior theory and conditioning*. New Haven, CT: Yale University Press.

Sternberg, C. (1956). Interests and tendencies toward maladjustment in a normal population. *Personnel and Guidance Journal, 35*, 94-99.

Toplyn, G., & MacGwire, W. (1991). The differential effect of noise on creative task performance. *Creativity Research Journal, 4*, 337-347.

Torrance, E.P. (1974). *Torrance Tests of Creative Thinking: Norms— Technical Manual*. Lexington, MA: Ginn.

Upmanyu, V.V., & Kaur, K. (1986). Diagnostic utility of word association emotional indicators. *Psychological Studies, 32*, 71-78.

Vernon, P.E. (Ed.). (1970). *Creativity*. New York: Penguin.

Wallach, M.A., & Kogan, N. (1965). *Modes of thinking in young children*. New York: Holt, Rinehart & Winston.

Waller, N.G., Bouchard, T.J., Lykken, D.T., Tellegen, A., & Blacker, D.M. (1993). Creativity, heritability, familiality: Which word does not belong? *Psychological Inquiry.*

Wankowski, J.A. (1973). *Temperament, motivation and academic achievement.* Birmingham: University of Birmingham Educational Survey and Counselling Unit.

Ward, P.B., McConaghy, N., & Catts, S.P. (1991). Word association and measures of psychosis-proneness in university students. *Personality and Individual Differences, 12,* 473-480.

Woody, E., & Claridge, G. (1977). Psychoticism and thinking. *British Journal of Social and Clinical Psychology, 16,* 241-248.

Zahn, T.P. (1968). Word association in adoptive and biological parents of schizophrenics. *Archives of General Psychiatry, 19,* 501-503.

4 Creativity and Perception

Gudmund J.W. Smith
Gunilla Amnér
Lund University, Sweden

There is no uniform theory of creative perception. Many of the various studies collected in the present chapter apparently have no theoretical aspirations at all. In others, Witkin's (1949) theory of field dependence seems to have been the major source of inspiration. The percept-genetic theory of creative functioning underlies our own work, an outline of which is offered when the Creative Functioning Test is described. Without such an outline the test could hardly be comprehended. Before reviewing the theories and the field we must clarify the two key concepts, namely, *perception* and *creativity*.

Perception, particularly in its relation to creativity, cannot be conceived of as a purely reproductive activity. Indeed, it has become a commonplace assumption that a considerable part of information processing via perceptual channels takes place outside immediate awareness. The support for this is almost overwhelming. Let it suffice in the present context to refer to the pioneering work by Dixon (1971, 1981), an exhaustive survey of cognitive research by Reber (1992), and a penetrating review by Greenwald (1992). But there is still no unambiguous description of what Spence, Klein, and Fernandez (1986) termed the size and shape of *the subliminal window*. Although Reber and others seem to be mainly concerned with the efficiency or smartness (Loftus, 1992) of subliminal activity, Dixon emphasized the qualitative difference between the non-conscious and conscious perceptual systems. The work by Silverman (e.g., Silverman & Geisler, 1986) on subliminal priming would hardly have been successful, but for the fact that subliminal processing is particularly sensitive to emotional influence, and Westerlundh (1986) demonstrated that subliminal verbal messages act more via their emotional content than their syntactic structure. This makes the relation between conscious and nonconscious aspects of perception a crucial issue in the present context, bringing along with it the role of motivation and early experiences for the construction of our perceptual world. For Arnheim (1966) a just understanding of perception is not possible unless it is considered in its biological context, in which it has evolved as a means of detection and orientation in a changing environment to find food and avoid threats and dangers.

The inclusion of perception in the broader frame of personality is admittedly not new. It was included in some of the European psychology before World War II (e.g., Stern, 1938) and, indeed, in what came to be known as the New Look of perception (e.g., Blake & Ramsey, 1951). Presently, we have a more secure empirical base for maintaining that perception cannot be regarded in isolation from personality and its antecedents, the possible exception being highly habituated acts of notation. Without such an assumption any research on perception and creativity would be meaningless.

Creativity is a very difficult concept to define. In a perceptual context it often implies readiness to accept new information or to view old information from new vantage points. Flexibility has been regarded as a key concept in research on creative perception. It can be defined as the ability to shift points of view and to avoid a one-sided, stereotyped perspective (McKim, 1972). The creative individual is flexible in the sense that he or she is open to change and ready to bring about such change. The roots of change are to be found in one's personal world. The individual is, of necessity, autonomous, not bound by the stimulus situation. Jung (1959) discussed flexibility in "human beings who reach the heights of creativity"; he pertained the term to how freely the creative person moves among what he called the four perceptual types: thinking, feeling, sensation, and intuition.

In the studies to be reviewed here, creativity has been defined in many different ways. Among operational definitions, scores in self-report inventories are traditional. But there is a great variety of other tests, including some that could be termed perceptual. To some researchers creativity should be defined by (valuable) creative products, to others it is more or entirely existential. Both views are represented in this chapter. The emphasis on cognition is obvious in most studies. The psychodynamic-emotional aspects are more remote.

THE PERCEPTUAL WORLD OF CREATIVE PEOPLE

McWhinnie (1967) studied the association between the creativity in 136 sixth-grade children, on the one hand, and performance on such perceptual tasks as the so-called Embedded Figures Test (EFT)—an adaptation by Thurstone (1943) of the original Gottschaldt (1926) figures—and the Welsh Figure Preference Test (Barron & Welsh, 1952), on the other. Creativity was defined by means of the nonverbal measures of creative thinking developed by Torrance (1966; see also later). No association was detected in this study or in a later one (McWhinnie, 1969), in which roughly the same basic design was used, but the subjects were 95 fourth-grade children. When subjecting data from 95 fourth-and fifth-grade children to a factor analysis, McWhinnie (1970) did extract a factor loaded with fluency, flexibility, originality, and elaboration—scores from the Torrance (1966) tests originally defined as measures of creativity—but no other mixing could be detected. In none of these studies were any controls used for intelligence (cf. Schulman, 1966).

The three more successful studies listed later tested older subjects and defined creativity by means of other assessments. Among the early studies with positive outcomes, Spotts and Mackler's (1967) seems to be one of the most noteworthy. Subjects were 138 male undergraduates and the criteria a battery of creativity tests. The study confirmed a positive association between field independence and creativity.

Noppe and Gallagher (1977) tested 62 education majors with the Group Embedded Figures Test and Mednick's Remote Associates Test (RAT). Self-report measures of conformity and creativity were also administered. Field independence was significantly related to creativity as measured with the RAT. The self-report correlations were not significant, but in the expected direction. Given that a field-independent person is able to move freely among possible solutions, and because creative insight has to build on systematic search of the material, the results were expected. Noppe and Gallagher discussed their positive findings in relation to Piaget's notion of *decentration*.

Grundlach and Gesell (1979) viewed the Embedded Figures Test as a test of differentiation. They measured eight creativity traits covered by Guilford's (1967) Creative Potential Tests and also included a biographical inventory derived from Schaefer and Anastasi (1968). Subjects were 100 boys 16-19 years old. Field-independent subjects achieved higher means on Guilford's Match Problems (visualization), Paper Folding (adaptive flexibility), and Alternative Uses (spontaneous flexibility). Grundlach and Gesell regarded these as transformation skills. The differentiation measured by the EFT is apparently associated with correlates of creativity in the scientific area, not in the arts.

Bergum and Flamm (1975) studied the relation between figure-ground reversals and creativity. Subjects fixated on Necker cubes, monocularly and binocularly, and answered a 33-item checklist. The correlation was positive. Most reversals occurred when the cube faces were small. Mono- or binocularity had no effect. In an extension by Bergum and Bergum (1979), students of architecture and business administration served as subjects. The perceptual tasks were again Necker cubes as well as the Rubin profile vase and several others. On the creativity side biographical and checklist forms were used. The architectural students saw themselves as more creative and original and also reported more reversals than the business students.

Bergum and Bergum (1979) concluded that individuals associated with activities that rely heavily on visual manipulative display have higher reversal rates and perceive themselves to be more creative. However, when Simpson, Landry, Senter, and Peterson (1983) repeated the Bergum and Bergum (1979) experiment, they found no correlation between reversal rates and creativity. One reason could be that creative ability was judged in a slightly different way, via self-ranking and ranking by others, and that the subjects were not specifically attuned to work with visual displays. But in a later study by Klintman (1984), the positive relationship between Necker cube reversals and creativity reappeared. Here creativity was defined by the Alternative Uses Test in the Guilford (1967) tradition. Differences in the operational definitions of creativity were thus most likely to be responsible for the different outcomes in these studies.

What these studies were concerned with was perceptual style or strategy, which was assumed to be different for creative and noncreative individuals. Schrot (1990) touched on this problem in his study of concept formation strategies in pattern recognition tasks. He explored the effects of two kinds of strategies—nonanalytic and analytic—and used as stimuli nonsense shapes and highly recognizable patterns. Subjects were better able to classify stimuli correctly by relying on memory rather than rule learning (analytic strategy). Schrot's conclusion was that nonanalytic processes may be the source of creativity and discovery of exceptions. Well-defined stimuli are likely to favor analytic strategies and thus hamper creative solutions. Actually, this insight has been the basis for the construction of projective tests (e.g., Rorschach) since the 1920s and 1930s.

The much earlier study by Maini (1973) focused on an analogous problem (see also Jern & Maini, 1971). Subjects were 66 high school students. They were presented with an abbreviated version of the Gestalt Completion Test, originally a series of 15 relatively unorganized and mutilated figures, and were requested to make communicable interpretations. The degree of agreement with the original stimulus motif was accredited with points, but so were fluency and originality. As a test of fantasy the classical film by Heider and Simmel was introduced. Creativity was operationally defined by the Utility Test (similar to the Unusual Uses test of Guilford). A high score on this test was, above all, a measure of originality. The more original the subject, the less likely he or she was to be stimulus bound (i.e., the more likely he or she was to offer interpretations having little correspondence with the picture).

Torrance's nonverbal tests of creative thinking have been used to identify the tendency to produce unusual visual perspectives (Torrance, 1972). If the individual approaches a stimulus repeatedly, can he or she produce new images? This represents a novel development of the original test. Quality and quantity of creative achievement were rated by judges 12 years later. The correlations were modest. Although McWhinnie (1967, 1969, 1970) failed to obtain any positive results in his analogous studies using conventional scoring of creative ability, Torrance's more penetrating and reliable assessment was obviously rewarding.

The classic study by Barron and Welsh (1952) should also be mentioned. They used the Welsh Figure Preference Test and found that an artist sample preferred complex asymmetrical figures and rejected simple symmetrical ones. Analogous results were later reported by Gilchrist (1982). Her group of creative architectural students were more inclined to reject conventions and conformity than less creative students.

Schulman (1966) hypothesized that openness of perception was a sine qua non for creativity. His starting point was Schachtel's (1959) classic volume, *Metamorphosis*. Subjects were 89 fourth graders. Creativity was assessed by means of a Drawing Completion Task, adapted from Franck and Rosen (1949), but basically reminiscent of the German Wartegg Test. Both tests were meant to measure conventionality, theme variability, constriction, and playfulness. The Drawing Completion Task had an acceptable correlation with teachers' assessments. Perceptual openness was measured by Changing Figures Test, adapted from Frenkel-Brunswik (1949), and the Finding of Enclosed Areas Test. This promising enterprise yielded only modest and low correlations, partly due to skewed distribution of data from the Drawing Completion Task. An interesting side result was the absence of IQ correlations.

Carlsson's (1990) study, also concerned with hemisphericity, had creativity as one of its main foci. Eighty-four undergraduate students, randomly divided into two groups, were tested with a percept-genetic test (the Meta-Contrast Technique) of anxiety and defense in either the right or the left visual half-field. They also took the Creative Functioning Test (see later). Subjects low in creativity were significantly lateralized on defenses typical for the right visual half-field group (isolation and repression), and they tended to differ on a left visual half-field defense (regression). For highly creative subjects no differences were found between the visual half-field groups. Moreover, highly creative persons more often responded with non-hemispheric-specific defenses than low creative ones. Carlsson interpreted the results as due to differing levels of transmission of information between the hemispheres. Related work on hemispheric specialization is reviewed by Hassler (1990) and Katz (this volume).

STIMULATING CREATIVITY BY MEANS OF PERCEPTUAL MANIPULATION

Homospatial thinking and imagery, together with Janusian thinking, play a crucial role in Rothenberg's (1976, 1979) creativity research. It might be described as the graphic side of creative cognitive processing. Rothenberg and Sobel (1981) defined *homospatial thinking* as the inclination to visualize simultaneously or conceive in some other way two or more discrete entities occupying the same space. Typically, these entities do not belong together, neither logically nor conventionally.

This way of functioning does not only apply to artistic creative work. It leads to the articulation of new and unusual visual combinations in poetry, science, and the field of invention. The elements of an inventor's new machine, for instance, may come together in his or her inner (preconscious) eye, although the combination, on closer inspection, appears improbable, abstruse, or even silly. But it ignites an irrevocable process of creation.

Encouraged by these observations, richly exemplified in Rothenberg (1979), Rothenberg and Sobel (1980, 1981) tried to manipulate the homospatial process experimentally. A detailed account of the technique is presented in Sobel and Rothenberg (1980). The research compares situations with separated versus superimposed stimuli. The subjects—40 students—were asked to produce drawings afterward. Professional artists judged the degree of creativity reflected in these products. This was obviously an attempt to "externalize" homospatiality.

The interrater reliabilities were modest, which is a not uncommon consequence of using professional artists as judges (cf. Smith & Carlsson, 1990, reviewed later). Drawings containing intermingled elements from each component image were judged as higher in creative potential when they were stimulated by the superimposed presentation. The reverse was true of drawings in which elements from only one picture could be detected. The implications of these results were, however, not quite obvious.

A later study by Rothenberg (1986) employed a variation of this design. Thirty-nine art students were referred to either of two conditions: two stimuli superimposed or presented as a background-foreground arrangement. Professional raters were asked to use the following rating dimensions: originality, value, overall creative potential, technical proficiency, and realism/abstractedness. Creativity potential differed significantly between the groups or, in Rothenberg's own words, in that a "complex bringing together of visual elements, rather than additive combining in a figure-ground configuration, leads to creative products" (p. 380). The implicit assumption must be that artists create these conditions for themselves and that creativity is not just "reactive."

A related attempt to influence the creative behavior of children was made by Tegano and Moran (1989). It had been known previously that the quantity and quality of responses to three-dimensional objects could be increased if young subjects were given the opportunity to handle them. Tegano and Moran assessed 188 children aged 4-9 years. The test was Pattern Meanings from the Multidimensional Stimulus Fluency Measure. Scores on this test did not correlate with IQ, but the most interesting result was that the opportunity to handle two- or three-dimensional objects indeed facilitated original responses in the youngest children. The handling, apparently, helped these children to overcome their cognitive egocentricity and make them less stimulus fixated.

Different methods to manipulate perception for the stimulation of the creative process are often mentioned in the art literature. Gombrich (1960) referred to Alexander Cozens, who in his teaching advocated a method he called *blotting*, which was the use of accidental inkblots to suggest landscape motifs. Cozens was at the time rather controversial, but his thoughts were well founded in, for instance, Leonardo da Vinci's writings, in which the power of "confused shapes," such as clouds or muddy water, are suggested to rouse the mind to new inventions.

Numerous examples also confirm how scientists have let themselves be stimulated in their creative endeavors by seeing analogies and metaphors for their scientific problems in the smallest things surrounding them. Gordon (1971), for instance, reported that Einstein used muscular and visual "signs" and "images" in his work. Moreover, the way buzzards kept their balance in flight served as an analogy for the Wright brothers when maneuvering and stabilizing an airplane. The idea that the solar system is continually restored came to Laplace when he considered the body's self-healing processes.

An experiment by Smith and Danielsson (1979; see also Smith & Carlsson, 1990) was less concerned with perceptual manipulation than with changing the inner state of the subject. The hypothesis was that a modest increase of anxiety would facilitate creativity. To accomplish this a drawing of a threatening face was flashed subliminally five times together with the stimulus used in the Creative Functioning Test (CFT) and just before the test series started. Subjects were 43 adults, some of them with creative inclinations. Half of the group received the threatening stimulation, the other half a formally analogous neutral stimulation. When comparing the results, subjects in the groups were equalized with respect to artistic-creative interests and a number of other dimensions supposedly associated with creativity. The anxiety *injection* increased the results in the CFT, particularly in the middle ranges of ability. The highly creative subjects had already reached their ceiling, with or without the extra stimulation; the totally uncreative ones could not be helped. A later study of psychiatric patients (Smith & Carlsson, 1983; see also Smith & Carlsson, 1990) showed that extreme anxiety was detrimental to creative functioning (see also Toplyn and Maguire, 1991).

When thinking of creativity and optimization of the flow of material from within, one usually associates with fresh impressions; habituation is considered as the worst enemy of creativity and its very opposite. But there is more to it than that. When considering the studies from 1953 by the Japanese psychologist Hitoshi Sakurabayashi (Arnheim, 1966), one can think of habituation as something potentially useful. He found that when the kind of pattern on which Gestalt studies based their conclusions was subjected to prolonged inspection, fundamental structural changes occurred. The figure spontaneously abandoned its "good Gestalt" and produced other configurations. This shows that lacking excitation can be supplemented from inner resources. The bored mind escapes and explores alternative ways of perceiving by "dissolution of the whole."

In the early steps of the process the effects of these changes remain below the level of awareness. After a while they penetrate consciousness. Sakurabayashi did, of course, make the connection between prolonged inspection and the creative process. It is known that some great artists, such as Cézanne and Rodin, often spent a long time looking at their objects instead of immediately putting them down as finished. Maybe they did profit from the Gestalt disintegration brought about by prolonged inspection.

The consequent phenomena of prolonged inspection can be related to creativity, either just as a method to further the creative process, or as an explanatory model for the whole creative process. In the latter case the model is used to show what happens when the creative person faces the world. The prolonged inspection is not passive, but essentially active because the transformations are the result of the mind's defensive or manipulative operations when confronted with too monotonous surroundings. This kind of transformation brought about in confrontation with the world could thus be considered as identical to what is known as creativity (Arnheim, 1966). These phenomena might also be a way to explain the fact that creative activity, for instance, much of the great world literature, often blossoms in the most barren environments.

PERCEPTION AS A GATEWAY TO CREATIVITY

Most of the perceptual creativity tests have already been mentioned. The basic idea of entering the world of creative fantasy via perception is relatively old as evidenced by the Rorschach test and various drawing completion tasks (e.g., Franck & Rosen, 1949) and the publications of the New Look I researchers (see Loftus, 1992), even if reference to the concept of creativity was rarely explicit.

The Welsh Figure Preference Test (WFPT) is a classic in the field (Barron & Welsh, 1952). Preference for complexity-asymmetry was shown to be typical of artists. Eisenman (1992) used preference for complex polygons as a test of creativity in a group of prisoners. Although prisoners were generally low in creativity, those diagnosed as conduct disordered were more creative than those diagnosed as psychotic.

The Multidimensional Stimulus-Fluency Measure (MSFM) was adapted from the earlier divergent thinking test battery of Wallach and Kogan (1965). The test consists of three subtests (Instances, Pattern Meanings, and Alternate Uses) with three items per subtest. Only the middle subtest is primarily perceptual. This test was presented by Moran, Milgram, Sawyers, and Fu (1983) in their study of original thinking in 47 preschool children. Each test response was scored as popular or original (unique). Original thinking proved to be distinct from intelligence in its conventional meaning. The findings were taken as a support for the idea that Guilford's (1967) and Mednick's (1962) conceptualization of original thinking is applicable to very young children. The MSFM was administered to adults by Sawyers and Canestaro (1989); they found a positive association between MSFM and achievement in design coursework. The research of Tegano and Moran (1989), reviewed earlier, should also be considered as a contribution to the validation of the test.

We can now turn to the Creative Functioning Test (CFT). It was developed within the framework of a micro- or percept-genetic, theoretical model (Smith & Carlsson, 1990), in which percepts are viewed as the end result of ultrashort processes, most often outside awareness. These processes can, however, be experimentally reconstructed using tachistoscopic presentations, which are close to threshold values to begin with, but are gradually prolonged until full recognition is accomplished.

If outside reality is thus shaped by means of constructive microprocesses, what happens if a process is reversed? How would the viewer respond if, once the final and correct conception of the stimulus has been established, the perceptual basis is gradually eroded by systematic abbreviation of exposure times? This was done in the CFT using still lifes as stimuli (one for the main test, another for a parallel version). The less the viewer feels tempted to cling to the established interpretation of the stimulus picture and the more explicit alternative interpretations the individual offers in the inverted series of exposures, the more creative he or she is supposed to be.

Because CFT scores, particularly in the middle range of the scale, are sensitive to suggestive instructions, it is important to use a strictly neutral wording (Smith & Danielsson. 1976). In this standardized setting Smith and Danielsson (1978) found a substantial correlation between CFT and richness in ideas in a group of 20-30-year-old researchers. It was typical of creative researchers to entertain subjective and correct interpretations simultaneously. A similar result was reported by Schoon (1992), who studied creative achievement in architects using the same test. In a study of professional artists (Smith, Carlsson, & Sandström, 1985) the product-moment correlation between CFT and quality of artistic output (see earlier) was also high. The study of amateur artists, described previously, in which anxiety was induced, had a significant correlation in the control group with the special scale used there.

In studies of children (Smith & Carlsson, 1990) (4-6 years old, N = 47), the youngest and cognitively most egocentric ones had difficulties taking the test: Instead of reporting their own impressions they borrowed themes from what they saw in the test room. In the older and more mature children it was possible to get a significant test-criterion correlation, the criterion being the interview scale that also correlated with the artistic evaluations.

Creativity was lowest in the beginning and at the end of the early and middle school years (ages 7-11, N = 86). The trend was similar in children from academic and nonacademic homes; the amplitude of the drops being more marked in the former. Correlations (G indexes) with the interview scales were significant in all age and maturity subgroups. Correlations with artistic criteria were in the expected direction, but more often than not insignificant; these children were obviously less motivated than younger children to apply their creative energies to artistic products. On the other hand, the judges reacted positively to artistic products of children with signs of anxiety in the Meta-Contrast Technique (MCT). As demonstrated in the experiment with threatening subliminal stimulation just reviewed, anxiety appears to be a constituent part of creative processing.

Among school children aged 12-16 (N = 142), there was a low tide of creativity at age 12 (cf. Ayman-Nolley, 1992), an age when the MCT characterized them as compulsive and lacking anxiety. Correlations between CFT and the interview scales were low to begin with. When the children had left mid puberty behind them and became more reliable interview objects (the 16-year-old girls), the high correlation reappeared.

In a study of the life-time development of creativity (Smith & van der Meer, 1990), 171 youngsters aged 10-16 years were compared with 59 middle-aged individuals (M = 34 years) and 60 elderly ones (M = 72 years). Although the youngsters were relatively more creative than the others, many elderly people still scored high on the CFT. The most marked decline seemed to occur early in middle age.

Because a group of children was followed from the age of 5-6 years to the age of 10-11—both periods shown to be high creativity peaks—it was possible to make predictions using a parallel CFT version at the older age. The early CFT results correlated with the later ones. Evaluations of early artistic products were also predictive, particularly if a combination of CFT values and the interview scale was used on the second occasion.

When creative persons as defined by the CFT were confronted with brief tachistoscopic flashes of an ambiguous face and thus forced to project something of themselves in their description of it, they reported, more often than their noncreative counterparts, childish or adolescent faces alternately with adult ones (Smith, Carlsson, & Andersson, 1989; Smith & van der Meer, 1990). The creative person is not a child, but apparently can reestablish contact with his or her childish past.

A special study of gender differences in 171 youngsters (Carlsson & Smith, 1987) revealed no association between gender and CFT scores (cf. Harris, 1989).

CONCLUDING COMMENTS

The empirical landscape appears fragmented. One reason is the diversity of criteria and a fundamental dissonance about the concept of creativity (e.g., Schuldberg, French, Stone, & Heberle, 1988). Moreover, too many studies have not been followed up and remain abortive and inconclusive.

There is, however, some association between creativity as generally understood, on the one hand, and perceptual style, on the other. Creative people have a more flexible view of the world, are less bound by the immediate stimulus context, and are more fascinated by unusual perspectives. Arnheim (1966) concluded, "Faced with the pregnant sight of reality the truly creative person does not move away from it but toward and into it" (p. 295). The creative individual is not afraid, or is less afraid, than uncreative persons of novelty and more easily deviates from consensus interpretations of a stimulus (Hentschel & Schneider, 1986).

According to Hentschel (1987; Hentschel & Schneider, 1986), perception is particularly well suited to serve as a focal center for a theory of creativity. But the picture of perceptual processing in creative endeavors is rather formal and abstract in most contemporary studies, referred to as flexible, fluent, and the like. There are too few attempts at integrating meaning, motivation, and emotional coloring in the experimental designs. One exception to this is Rothenberg (1979, 1986), particularly when he aims at unveiling homospatial imagery. His and his coworker's experiments are very directly concerned with the contextual side of creative perceptual processing.

The focusing on visual perception may seem rather one sided. But although the emphasis on visual perception is dominant in research about creativity and many researchers, even early ones (see Arnheim, 1954, pp. 165 ff.) argued that the tactile channel has a greater and more penetrative power than the visual one. Others strongly claimed that sight had to be considered the most primary because infants take hold of the world with their eyes long before they do so with their hands (cf. Bower, 1971; Gesell, 1950).

Another argument, offered by Stern (1985, pp. 165 ff.), that might reduce the skepticism about too much reliance on visual perception is the thought of "the unity of senses." Psychologists have been drawn to this by the phenomena of *synesthesia*, in which the stimulation of one sense elicits sensations in another modality. A sound might, for instance, produce a picture of a certain color alongside the auditory perception. Artists, and poets in particular, have taken the unity of senses for granted. Hardly any poetry would permeate an audience if there did not exist an implied assumption of analogies between and common metaphors among the senses. In fact, the association between synesthesia and creativity was recently corroborated by Domino (1989) in his study of 358 fine-arts students.

The most serious criticism of current research in creativity and perception is perhaps that the creative person has no clear profile. Sensitive historians of art and architecture appear more interested in this theme than many psychologists. The neglect is particularly obvious when creativity is handled as something apart from the individual, something exclusively defined by a creative product, not by a more general existential dimension. Smith and Carlsson (1990) tried to remedy this by including anxiety and closeness to an inner world of dreams and childhood memories in their definitions.

What is particularly needed in the study of creativity and perception is not continued experimentation relating abortive perceptual variables to superficial shorthand definitions of "creative ability," but rather a serious effort to formulate a more explicit theory of perception in its relation to personality (cf. Schoon, 1992). Contact with both historical and contemporary attempts at understanding the perceiving person, attempts defined as the New Looks 1, 2, and 3 (Loftus, 1992), may be rewarding in this regard.

REFERENCES

Arnheim, R. (1954). *Art and visual perception.* Berkeley: University of California Press.

Arnheim, R. (1966). *Toward a psychology of art: Collected essays.* Berkeley: University of California Press.

Ayman-Nolley, S. (1992). Vygotsky's perspective on the development of imagination and creativity. *Creativity Research Journal, 5,* 77-85.

Barron, F., & Welsh, G.S. (1952). Artistic perception as a factor in personality style. *Journal of Psychology, 33,* 199-203.

Bergum, B.O., & Bergum, J.E. (1979). Creativity, perceptual stability, and self-perception. *Bulletin of the Psychonomic Society, 14,* 61-63.

Bergum, B.O., & Flamm, L.E. (1975). Perceptual stability, image size, binocularity, and creativity. *Perceptual and Motor Skills, 41,* 667-671.

Blake, R.R., & Ramsey, G.V. (Eds.). (1950). *Perception: An approach to personality.* New York: Ronald Press.

Bower, T.G.R. (1971). The object in the world of the infant. *Scientific American, 223,* 30-38.

Carlsson, I. (1990). Lateralization of defence mechanisms related to creative functioning. *Scandinavian Journal of Psychology, 31,* 241-247.

Carlsson, I., & Smith, G.J.W. (1987). Gender differences in defence mechanisms compared with creativity in a group of youngsters. *Psychological Research Bulletin, Lund University, 27*(1).

Dixon, N.F. (1971). *Subliminal perception: The nature of a controversy.* New York: McGraw-Hill.

Dixon, N.F. (1981). *Preconscious processing.* New York: Wiley.

Domino, G. (1989). Synesthesia and creativity: An empirical look. *Creativity Research Journal, 2,* 17-29.

Eisenman, R. (1992). Creativity in prisoners: Conduct disorders and psychotics. *Creativity Research Journal, 5,* 175-181.

Franck, K., & Rosen, E. (1949). A projective test of masculinity-femininity. *Journal of Consulting Psychology, 13,* 247-256.

Frenkel-Brunswik, E. (1949). Intolerance of ambiguity as an emotional and perceptual variable. *Journal of Personality, 18,* 108-143.

Gesell, A. (1950). Infant vision. *Scientific American, 182,* 20-22.

Gilchrist, M.B. (1982). Creative talent and academic competence. *Genetic Psychology Monographs, 106,* 261-318.

Gombrich, E.H. (1960). *Art and illusion. A study in psychology of pictorial representation.* New York: Pantheon.

Gordon, W.J.J. (1971). *The metaphorical way.* Cambridge, MA: Books.

Gottschaldt, K. (1926). Uber den Einfluss der Erfahrung auf die Wahrnehmung von Figuren, I [The influence of experience on the perception of figures]. *Psychologische Forschung, 8,* 261-317.

Greenwald, A.G. (1992). Unconscious recognition reclaimed. *American Psychologist, 47,* 766-779.

Grundlach, R.H., & Gesell, G.P. (1979). Extent of psychological differentiation and creativity. *Perceptual and Motor Skills, 48,* 319-333.

Guilford, J.P. (1967). *The nature of human intelligence.* New York: McGraw-Hill.

Harris, L.H. (1989). Two sexes in the mind: Perceptual and creative differences between women and men. *Journal of Creative Behavior, 23,* 14-25.

Hassler, M. (1990). Functional cerebral asymmetries and cognitive abilities in musicians, painters, and controls. *Brain and Cognition, 13,* 1-17.

Hentschel, U. (1987). *Creativity as a personality variable.* Leiden: University of Leiden.

Hentschel, U., & Schneider, U. (1986). Psychodynamic personality correlates of creativity. In U. Hentschel, G.J.W. Smith, & J.G. Draguns (Eds.), *The roots of perception* (pp. 249-275). Amsterdam: North-Holland.

Jern, S., & Maini, S.M. (1971). An interpretation of utility, Gestalt completion, and personality variables on the continuum of objectivity-subjectivity. *Psychological Research Bulletin, Lund University, 11*(12).

Jung, C.G. (1959). *The structure and dynamics of the psyche.* New York: Pantheon.

Klintman, H. (1984). Original thinking and ambiguous figure reversal rates. *Bulletin of the Psychonomic Society, 22,* 129-131.

Loftus, E.F. (1992). Is the unconscious smart or dumb? *American Psychologist, 47,* 761-765.

Maini, S.M. (1973). Personality and cognitive differences between an original and a non-original group. *Perceptual and Motor Skills, 37,* 555-563.

McKim, R. (1972). *Experiences in visual thinking.* Monterey, CA: Brooks, Cole.

McWhinnie, H.J. (1967). Some relationships between creativity and perception in sixth grade children. *Perceptual and Motor Skills, 25,* 979-980.

McWhinnie, H.J. (1969). Some relationships between creativity and perception in fourth grade children. *Acta Psychologica, 31,* 169-175.

McWhinnie, H.J. (1970). A factor analytic study of perceptual behavior in 4th and 5th grade children. *Acta Psychologica, 34,* 89-97.

Mednick, S.A. (1962). The associative basis of the creative process. *Psychological Review, 69,* 220-232.

Moran, J.D. III, Milgram, R.M., Sawyers, J.R., & Fu, V.R. (1983). Original thinking in preschool children. *Child Development, 54,* 921-926.

Noppe, L.D., & Gallagher, J.M. (1977). A cognitive style approach to creative thought. *Journal of Personality Assessment, 42,* 85-90.

Reber, A.S. (1992). The cognitive unconscious: An evolutionary perspective. *Consciousness and Cognition: An International Journal, 1,* 93-133.

Rothenberg, A. (1976). Homospatial thinking in creativity. *Archives of General Psychiatry, 33,* 17-26.

Rothenberg, A. (1979). *The emerging goddess: The creative process in art, science, and other fields.* Chicago: University of Chicago Press.

Rothenberg, A. (1986). Artistic creation as stimulated by superimposed versus combined-composite visual images. *Journal of Personality and Social Psychology, 50,* 370-381.

Rothenberg, A., & Sobel, R.S. (1980). Adaptation and cognition: An experimental study of creative thinking. *Journal of Nervous and Mental Disease, 168,* 370-374.

Rothenberg, A., & Sobel, R.S. (1981). Adaptation and cognition. II. Experimental study of the homospatial process in artistic creativity. *Journal of Nervous and Mental Disease, 169,* 417-423.

Sawyers, J.K., & Canestaro, N. (1989). Creativity and achievement in design coursework. *Creativity Research Journal, 2,* 126-133.

Schachtel, E.G. (1959). *Metamorphosis.* New York: Basic Books.

Schaefer, C.E., & Anastasi, A. (1968). A biographical inventory for identifying creativity in adolescent boys. *Journal of Applied Psychology, 52,* 42-48.

Schoon, I. (1992). *On the psychology of creative achievement in architecture.* Leiden: University of Leiden.

Schrot, M.L. (1990). A comparison of concept formation strategies in pattern recognition tasks. *Journal of General Psychology, 117,* 303-309.

Schuldberg, D., French, C., Stone, B.L., & Heberle, J. (1988). Creativity test scores and perceptual aberration, magical ideation, and impulsive nonconformity. *Journal of Nervous and Mental Disease, 176,* 648-657.

Schulman, D. (1966). Openness of perception as a condition for creativity. *Exceptional Children, 33,* 89-94.

Silverman, L.H., & Geisler, C.J. (1986). The subliminal psychodynamic activation method: Comprehensive listing update, individual differences and other considerations. In U. Hentschel, G.J.W. Smith, & J.G. Draguns (Eds.), *The roots of perception* (pp. 49-74). Amsterdam: North-Holland.

Simpson, M.T., Landry, L.M., Senter, R.J., & Peterson, J.M. (1983). Figure reversals and creativity. *Perceptual and Motor Skills, 57,* 582.

Smith, G.J.W., & Carlsson, I. (1983). Creativity and anxiety: An experimental study. *Scandinavian Journal of Psychology, 24,* 107-115.

Smith, G.J.W., & Carlsson, I. (1990). The creative process. *Psychological Issues* (Monograph 57). New York: International Universities Press.

Smith, G.J.W., Carlsson, I., & Andersson, G. (1989). Creativity and subliminal manipulation of projected self-images. *Creativity Research Journal, 2,* 1-16.

Smith, G.J.W., Carlsson, I., & Sandström, S. (1985). Artists and artistic creativity. *Psychological Research Bulletin, Lund University, 25*(9-10).

Smith, G.J.W., & Danielsson, A. (1976). A new type of instrument constructed to explore the generative qualities of perception. *Psychological Research Bulletin, Lund University, 16*(5).

Smith, G.J.W., & Danielsson, A. (1978). Richness in ideas, ego-involvement and efficiency in a group of scientists and humanists: A study of creativity using a process-oriented technique. *Psychological Research Bulletin, Lund University, 18*(4-5).

Smith, G.J.W., & Danielsson, A. (1979). The influence of anxiety on the urge for aesthetic creation: An experimental study utilizing subliminal stimulation and a percept-genetic technique. *Psychological Research Bulletin, Lund University, 19*(3-4).

Smith, G.J.W., & van der Meer, G. (1990). Creativity in old age. *Creativity Research Journal, 3,* 249-264.

Sobel, R.S., & Rothenberg, A. (1980). Artistic creation as stimulated by superimposed versus separated visual images. *Journal of Personality and Social Psychology, 39,* 953-961.

Spence, D.P., Klein, L., & Fernandez, R.J. (1986). Size and shape of the subliminal window. In U. Hentschel, G.J.W. Smith, & J.G. Draguns (Eds.), *The roots of perception* (pp. 103-142). Amsterdam: North-Holland.

Spotts, J.V., & Mackler, B. (1967). Relationship of field-dependent and field-independent cognitive styles to creative test performance. *Perceptual and Motor Skills, 24,* 239-268.

Stern, D.N. (1985). *The interpersonal world of the infant: A view from psychoanalysis and developmental psychology.* New York: Basic Books.

Stern, W. (1938). *General psychology.* New York: McMillan.

Tegano, D.W., & Moran, J.D. (1989). Developmental study of dimensionality and presentation mode on original thinking in children. *Perceptual and Motor Skills, 68,* 1275-1281.

Thurstone, L.L. (1943). *A factorial study of perception.* Chicago: University of Chicago Press.

Toplyn, G., & Maguire, N. (1991). The differential effect of noise on creative task performance. *Creativity Research Journal, 4,* 337-348.

Torrance, E.P. (1966). *Torrance tests of creative thinking: Norms—technical manual.* Princeton, NJ: Personnel Press.

Torrance, E.P. (1972). Tendency to produce unusual visual perspective as a predictor of creative achievement. *Perceptual and Motor Skills, 34,* 911-915.

Wallach, M.A., & Kogan, N. (1965). *Modes of thinking in young children: A study of creativity-intelligence distinction.* New York: Holt, Rinehart, & Winston.

Westerlundh, B. (1986). On reading subliminal sentences: A psychodynamic activation study. *Psychological Research Bulletin, Lund University, 26*(10).

Witkin, H.A. (1949). Perception of body position and of position of the visual field. *Psychological Monographs, 63*(302).

5 Fostering Creativity in the Classroom: General Principles

A.J. Cropley

University of Hamburg

The upsurge of interest in creativity following the Sputnik shock in the 1950s was initially driven by educational issues. These centered on the view that schools and universities were producing large numbers of graduates, but that most of them were trained simply to apply the already known in conventional ways. The call was for forms of education that encourage creativity. This call initially aroused a controversy centering on the argument advanced by some thinkers that creativity is a special property found in only a few individuals, and that it cannot be promoted or fostered. Most educators reject this view, concentrating on psychological aspects of creativity that they believe are present, at least as potentials, in everyone. Deliberately fostering creativity in schools rests on the proposition that characteristics necessary for creativity can be helped to unfold by providing appropriate learning conditions. This chapter concentrates on defining what it is that teachers should foster and on principles they can apply in order to do this.

Many teachers and parents seem to be uneasy about emphasizing creativity in school because this might mean encouraging unruly, disobedient, careless, imprecise, or just plain naughty behavior. Others see the call for creativity in the classroom as meaning that any and all behaviors would be tolerated, and that basic skills, standards, and principles such as being correct or incorrect would be abandoned. Other commentators regard talk of fostering creativity as pretentious, intimidating, or elitist because it seems to involve finding little geniuses and force feeding them until they become Michelangelos, Mozarts, or Einsteins. Such doubts make it necessary to clear up two issues right from the start. As will be shown later, it is not necessary for teachers interested in fostering creativity to set their sights on achieving scientific, technological, literary, artistic, or other revolutions (although fostering creativity in the classroom might make a modest contribution in this direction by sowing the seeds). The processes and personal properties involved in fostering creativity in the classroom are seen in all children and young people, and fostering creativity brings benefits for all students, not just the few who go on to establish reputations as famous creators.

It is also important to recognize from the start that the desire to foster creativity is part of a tradition in educational thinking going back at least to the Ancient Greeks. In this tradition, all children should be given the opportunity to develop their potentials to the fullest, and education should help prepare young people for the richest and most productive life possible. The promotion of creative potentials brings benefits to the individual in terms of better learning (e.g., Schubert, 1973) and improved mental health (e.g., Cropley, 1990), as well as benefits to the society (see Walberg & Staniha [1992] for a comprehensive review). In this context it is important to note that the purpose of creativity is not self- aggrandizement or domination of other people, but the making of contributions to the common good. For this reason, any discussion of the fostering of creativity should have an ethical element (Gruber, 1993).

EXISTING CREATIVITY TECHNOLOGY

Over 20 years ago, Treffinger and Gowan (1971) identified more than 50 procedures for training creativity. Davis and Scott (1971) listed 20 separate creativity facilitating activities such as attribute listing, idea matrix, and creativity toolbox. Sometimes, as in the case of Endriss (1982), such activities are presented as games: bridge building, idea production, or creative productions. In contrast to some degree with such discrete activities (often referred to as "techniques") are creativity training programs—packages of materials that are meant to be used regularly for creativity training, according to a schedule. (These programs often make systematic use of various techniques.) It has become common to refer to such materials (both the discrete activities and the packages) as involving the *technology* of creativity training, in much the same way as the machines in a gymnasium constitute the technology of bodybuilding. The basic idea is that it is possible, with the help of this technology, to do mental workouts, just as athletes do physical workouts.

Among the techniques that have become relatively well known are synectics, bionics, brainstorming, morphological methods, imagery training, the KJ Method, the NM Method, and mind maps. Several of these were described by Torrance (1992). The U.S. Patent and Trademark Office (1990) compiled an extensive overview of relevant techniques and materials. They listed about 25 packages aimed at promoting creative thinking—several hundred separate activities in all. About a dozen sets of materials they listed were concerned with fostering critical thinking, once again encompassing hundreds of individual activities. Also listed were materials on fostering decision making, higher order thinking skills, and problem solving. This publication is an invaluable source of information on creativity technology.

Some of the better known programs for fostering creativity are listed in Table 5.1. Particularly important for the present discussion are the psychological characteristics that the programs aim at promoting. As can be seen from Table 5.1, most programs give greatest weight to the *cognitive aspects* of creativity (getting ideas, combining elements of information, and the like), even those that do not specifically see themselves as focusing on creative thinking. Only one program focuses on *aspirations and feelings*, and another gives some weight to *attitudes* to problem solving.

There is only limited evidence that such approaches actually increase creativity. Torrance (1972) acknowledged that many researchers would be likely to discredit his evaluation of some 142 studies of attempts to enhance creativity. However, he still maintained that many procedures really do have a positive effect, especially those that emphasize not only cognitive but also affective aspects (e.g., the courage to try something new, positive feelings about creativity). Franklin and Richards (1977) demonstrated that deliberate attempts to increase creativity via formal training are more effective than simply reducing the level of formality in the classroom or exposing children to a wider variety of experience (i.e., systematic promotion is superior to mere openness or tolerance). However, Cropley and Feuring (1971) showed that the results of such training are mediated by other factors: What was effective with girls did not necessarily work with boys, and the effects of training depended on the conditions under which the criterion data were obtained.

Many creativity training procedures seem to improve performance only on activities that closely resemble the training procedures. In a detailed review of evidence, Rump (1979) came to the conclusion

Table 5.1. Main Characteristics of Well-Known Creativity Programs.

Program	Age Level	Material	Aimed at Promoting
Imagi/Craft	Elementary School	Dramatized recordings of great moments in the lives of famous inventors and discoverers	• The feeling that their own ideas are important • Widened horizons • Career aspirations of a creative kind
Creative Problem Solving	All levels	No special material—makes great use of brainstorming	• Problem finding • Data collection • Idea finding • Solution finding • Implementing of solutions
Talents Unlimited	All levels	Workbooks based on idea of "inventive thinking," aimed at problem solving—emphasis on brainstorming	• Productive thinking • Communication • Planning • Decision making • Forecasting
Productive Thinking Program	Fifth- and Sixth-grade pupils	Booklets containing cartoons	• Problem-solving abilities • Attitudes toward problem solving
Purdue Creative Thinking Program	Fourth-grade pupils	Audiotapes and accompanying printed exercises	Verbal and figural fluency, flexibility, originality, and elaboration

Table 5.1. Main Characteristics of Well-Known Creativity Programs (cont.).

Osborne-Parnes Program	High school and college students	No special materials	• Getting many ideas • Primary emphasis on brainstorming, with separation of idea generation and idea evaluation
Myers-Torrance Workbooks	Elementary school pupils	Workbooks containing exercises	Perceptual and cognitive abilities needed for creativity
Khatena Training Method	Adults and children	No special materials; simple teacher-made aids are employed	• Ability to break away from the obvious • Transposing ideas • Seeing analogies • Restructuring information • Synthesis of idea

that the effects of training are strongest when the criterion closely resembles the training procedure, and weakest when this similarity is weak. In the case of personality, interests, and preferences (as against thinking skills), only limited effects are obtained. Consequently, it is possible to conclude that training procedures have little effect on attitudes, values, self-image, or motivation. There is even a danger that creativity training may have the opposite effect from the desired one. For instance, children could become aware that certain kinds of behavior are preferred by the teacher and could alter their own approach to problems accordingly, thus engaging in conformist, not original, behavior. Although children may be encouraged by the training to work hard on a variety of tasks, they may learn that it is easy to give "original" answers by engaging in hairsplitting, giving rambling answers without regard to accuracy or relevance, or offering unexpected banalities. Commenting on brainstorming, Parloff and Handlon (1964) suggested that instead of becoming more creative as a result of offering ideas freely and without evaluation, people may simply become less self-critical.

The idea of deliberately encouraging creativity is clearly very attractive to teachers. However, many training procedures seem to be too specific: To adapt an analogy suggested by Wallach (1985), teaching sprinters how to hammer down their starting blocks might well lead to better times, but it can hardly be regarded as teaching them how to run faster. To take a concrete example he mentioned, students in a creative writing program practiced for two years by working on creativity tests. At the end of this time they were noticeably better on such tests, but their writing had hardly become more creative at all. The basic weakness of techniques and programs aimed at facilitating creativity is that they are too narrow in their psychological content, and are usually confined to brief periods in the school week, often linked with a particular discipline. The creative process does not depend on a few specific skills that can be learned like tables in arithmetic, in much the same way as specific muscles can be developed via specialized bodybuilding. What is required is facilitating creativity by means of special teaching and learning methods diffused throughout the whole curriculum.

WHAT SHOULD TEACHERS FOSTER?

Early studies of creativity focused primarily on creative thinking (see specifics later). However, it has become increasingly apparent that children only display creativity when they *want* to and when they *feel able to*. In addition, children need appropriate skills and abilities, such as the capacity to recognize inconsistencies and to get ideas. These aspects of creativity will be discussed in more detail in later sections. I have described creativity as arising from a constellation of psychological characteristics including expertise (knowledge of a field), creativity-related skills and abilities, motivation, and personal properties such as self-confidence (see Cropley, 1992a). Some of these are—at least in theory—easy to promote in schools, although school traditions and conventional classroom practice often make this more difficult than theory suggests. It is necessary at this point to outline the main aspects of this constellation, for these are the processes and properties teachers need to foster in the classroom in order to promote the emergence of creativity.

Achieving Effective Surprise

In an early study summarizing research up to his time, Morgan (1953) concluded that the central element of creativity is *novelty*. Bruner (1962) referred to novelty's capacity to evoke surprise, but pointed out that *relevance* and *effectiveness* are also important; otherwise, every crazy idea, irrational behavior, or absurd product that surprised people would be creative. The first thing that students need to learn is how to achieve effective surprise. For Perkins (1981), the surprise can be effective for a single individual alone (usually the creator), whereas others (earlier, Stein, 1963; later, Csikszentmihalyi, 1988) emphasized that recognition by the society (validation) is necessary for surprise to be effective. Otherwise, the less a person knew, the greater the creativity: Any idea would be surprising to somebody who knew nothing! This in turn implies that creativity requires *communication*; if it lies hidden within the individual it cannot be validated by the society. In view of the strongly positive connotations of the term *creativity*, it is unlikely that a society would recognize and acknowledge evil, criminal, or otherwise socially proscribed acts as creative, so that an element of creativity as a social phenomenon is *ethicality* (see Eisenman 1991; Grudin, 1990). To Wallas's (1926) well-known cognitive approach to creating effective surprise, which involves *preparation* (obtaining information), *incubation* (processing it internally), *inspiration* (hitting on a solution), and *verification* (evaluating the solution), I would add *communication* and *validation*. These principles offer important guidelines to teachers seeking to foster their students' creativity. Teachers should consider information, special ways of thinking about it, inventiveness in finding solutions, ability to evaluate ideas, ability and willingness to communicate solutions to others, and evaluation of solutions in the context of the real world.

Heinelt (1974) made a distinction that helps to differentiate effective from ineffective novelty by distinguishing between pseudocreativity and quasicreativity. The former involves mere unconventionality (such as wearing a large ring through the nose to a high society ball), whereas the latter involves fantasy and the like—properties of genuine creativity, it must be admitted, but of a kind more characteristic of day-dreaming or children's play. Taylor (1975) also offered insights into the distinction between the genuinely creative (the effectively surprising) and other forms of novelty. He described five levels of creativity: (a) *expressive spontaneity* manifests itself in the uninhibited production of ideas; (b) *technical creativity* is seen in exceptional skill with language, tools of a trade, instruments, and the like; (c) *inventive creativity* involves using the already known in a novel way; (d) *innovative creativity* occurs when known principles or paradigms are used to develop new ideas; and (e) *emergent creativity* results in the development of new principles or paradigms. Expressive spontaneity and technical creativity are every-day phenomena that can easily be fostered in schools. However, teach-ers should set their sights on encouraging inventive creativity and at least elements of innovative and emergent creativity.

Other researchers have also drawn a distinction between novel-ty achieved via new applications of the already known and via the working out of new principles: Ghiselin (1963), for instance, distin-guished between *secondary* and *primary* creativity (primary requires development of new principles), whereas Mumford and Gustafson (1988) differentiated between *minor* and *major* creativity. Rejskind, Rapagna, and Gold (1992) emphasized the practical usefulness of distin-guishing between *assimilative* and *accommodative* creativity, these two terms being used in the Piagetian sense. This distinction is important for educators, as it emphasizes that fostering creativity involves both broad-ening and deepening the existing organization of knowledge in a process of enrichment (i.e., promoting assimilative creativity), as well as fostering the building of novel ways of seeing the world (accommoda-tive creativity).

Fostering Creative Thinking

In an early study by Platt and Baker (1931), 83% of a group of people publicly acclaimed as highly creative attributed their creativity to sud-den inspiration. On the other hand, Edison ("genius is 1% inspiration, 99% perspiration"), Pasteur, Disraeli, and Land emphasized the impor-tance of hard work and knowledge of a field. Campbell (1963) proposed that creativity is the result of logical thinking carried through to its logi-cal conclusion. In their review, Tardif and Sternberg (1988) identified a group of researchers who favor sudden inspiration (Feldman, Ghiselin, Taylor, Wallas), a group who take a middle position (Gardner, Sternberg, Torrance), and a group who reject inspiration as a source of creativity

(Gruber, Weisberg, Simonton). The sudden inspiration view is explicitly rejected in this chapter on the grounds that it does not provide a basis for systematic, purposeful broadening of students' intellectual activity.

A related question is whether or not creativity can result from chance or sheer good fortune. Both Beveridge (1980) and Rosenman (1988) gave many examples of famous chance discoveries in the work of Pasteur, Fleming, Röntgen, Becquerel, Edison, Galvani, and Nobel, to name a few. According to Austin (1978), there are four forms of luck that can lead to "accidental" creativity: pure chance (the creative person is irrelevant), serendipity (anyone who is very active in an area may have a lucky break), the luck of the well informed (anyone who knows a great deal about an area may stumble on something novel), and self-made luck (a combination of knowledge and skill, hard work, and the like, creates fertile ground for creativity). Austin's view was that the highest levels of creativity occur when all aspects of luck are simultaneously present. The important point for educators is that, apart from sheer chance-which cannot be harnessed by any classroom procedures because its essence is that it is blind and random—even accidental creativity requires a strong base involving activity in a field, a rich stock of information, and possession of appropriate attitudes, values, skills, and the like. Promotion of all of these lies within the teacher's province.

Simonton (1988) and Langley, Simon, Bradshaw, and Zytkow (1986) documented empirically the role of thorough knowledge of a field for creativity. Snow (1986) supported this view and discussed its consequences for the fostering of creativity in schools. To take several simple examples, a child would be greatly aided in displaying musical creativity if it could play a musical instrument, literary creativity requires knowledge of language, scientific creativity knowledge of mathematics or other areas. A large number of researchers have argued that, in addition to knowledge, creativity is the result of systematic cognitive processes. Without these, luck, as it was defined earlier (except blind chance), would lead to nothing. Among these processes is *problem finding*. This involves recognizing that a problem exists, producing a large number of relevant ideas, evaluating these ideas, and drawing appropriate conclusions. Tardif and Sternberg (1988) and Runco and Okuda (1988) stressed the importance of finding "good" problems, and Getzels and Csikszentmihalyi (1978) showed that this also applies to practical, artistic creativity. According to Dillon (1982), there are three levels of problem finding: (a) identifying obvious problems on the basis of knowledge of the field, (b) discovering hidden problems on the basis of concentrated work in an area, and (c) inventing problems as a result of reorganizing existing knowledge. Teachers are accustomed to specifying the problems on which students are to work and evaluating the extent to which students' solutions coincide with the correct answer, which is usually known in advance to the teacher. However, an instructional approach that emphasizes making the students responsible for finding problems, showing them how to distinguish between good problems and mundane ones, and teaching them to go beyond obvious problems to discover hidden ones is a major aspect of teaching to foster creativity.

Other writers have emphasized surprising associations as the core of creative thinking. Mednick's (1962) concept of remote associates is well known: Each person develops a hierarchy of associations to any stimulus, with commonly occurring associations standing high in the hierarchy, unusual associations low. Creative individuals are able to bypass obvious associations and find those low in the hierarchy (hence, surprising). Koestler (1964) adopted a somewhat different approach by emphasizing *bisociation*. According to this view, ideas exist in matrices: Conventional associations involve linking ideas from the same matrix and surprising associations ideas from two different matrices (i.e., bisociation). Simonton (1988) proposed the chance configuration model: Creativity requires a basic stock of mental elements (information, ideas, memories, concepts, beliefs, feelings, emotions, etc.). Now and then combinations (*configurations*) pop up that offer solutions to problems. Weisberg (1986) emphasized that such creative configurations do not occur by chance, but are the result of strictly logical chains of associations.

Perhaps the best known definition of creative thinking is Guilford's (1950) distinction between convergent and divergent thinking. *Convergent thinking* involves applying conventional logic to a number of elements of information in order to home in on the one and only best answer implied by the available information—the answer that would be arrived at by everyone who possessed the same stock of information and applied the rules of conventional logic. Because the answer is unique and arises more or less inevitably from the available information, in a certain sense it already exists and must only be discovered. By contrast, divergent thinking involves making up answers by branching out from the available information (diverging), for instance, by seeing unexpected aspects that others might not notice. There are as many answers implied by a given set of information as human ingenuity can invent. Many of them may be of equal value, and different thinkers may come up with drastically different sets of solutions.

This cognitive approach has more recently been further extended, for instance, by the psychoanalyst Rothenberg (1988), who introduced the idea of *Janusian* thinking. The term derives from the Roman God Janus, after whom the month of January is named. Janus could look ahead and backward simultaneously, and was thus aware of information coming from two directions at the same time. This approach emphasizes the bringing together of apparently contradictory ideas; such ideas are then combined into a new whole by means of homospatial thinking. In contrast to Weisberg (1986), Rothenberg regarded Janusian thinking as essentially illogical, because the ideas that are brought together are contradictory.

The idea of a kind of thinking that permits irrational linking of ideas is also found in traditional psychoanalytic explanations of creativity (e.g., Kris, 1950; Kubie, 1958). Primary process thinking is dominated by the unconscious and is not bound by the rules of reality. Anything can be combined with anything, an advantageous condition for creativity. However, the ego is dominated by the reality principle, engages in secondary process thinking, and does not allow primary process thinking into consciousness. In order to think creatively, a person must be willing to "regress in the service of the ego" and admit primary process material into consciousness (see Suler [1980] for a summary). A related view is that creativity requires *biphasic* thinking or *tertiary process* thinking (Arieti, 1976), through which primary and secondary thinking are combined. Gestalt psychology distinguishes between reproductive thinking, as a result of which groups of elements are brought together to form a familiar gestalt, and *productive* thinking, which leads to surprising (creative) gestalts. Such novel gestalts are necessary to deal with "dynamic gaps" (Henle, 1974) in conventional gestalts (contradictions, unexpected similarities, strange forms, inadequacies of the gestalt). The ability to recognize such gaps derives from knowledge of the field (Birch, 1975).

What these findings on the cognitive aspects of creativity mean for teachers can now be summarized in the following way. They should strive to promote in their students:

1. Possession of a fund of general knowledge
2. Knowledge of one or more special fields
3. An active imagination
4. Ability to recognize, discover, or invent problems
5. Skill at seeing connections, overlaps, similarities, and logical implications (convergent thinking)
6. Skill at making remote associations, bisociating, accepting primary process material, forming new gestalts, etc (divergent thinking)
7. Ability to think up many ways to solve problems
8. A preference for accommodating rather than assimilating
9. Ability and willingness to evaluate their own work
10. Ability to communicate their results to other people.

Personal Properties Favorable for Creativity

McLeod and Cropley (1989) summarized research findings on special properties of creative individuals: They can, among other things, break boundaries easily and build broad categories. They are field independent, build more complex cognitive structures, and generate ideas more rapidly, as well as express them more fluently. Mehlhorn and Mehlhorn (1985) showed that the variance of such characteristics was low in groups selected for high creativity and increased steadily in groups displaying successively lower levels of creativity.

Eysenck (1983) went so far as to argue that creativity is the result of a particular pattern of personality. Many studies have investigated this area by studying people already acknowledged as creative (see Hocevar & Bachelor [1989] for a recent review and Dellas and Gaier [1970] for an earlier one). These studies showed that properties such as flexibility, sensitivity, tolerance, responsibility, autonomy, and positive self-image are strongly related to creativity. Albert and Runco (1989) showed that independence is significantly correlated with creativity: Creative people are marked by greater autonomy and nonconformity and less willingness to conform, lower self-control, and less desire to make a good impression. Both Maslow (1959) and Rogers (1959) regarded openness to the new as crucial for creativity. McCrae and Costa (1985) defined openness as an interest in novelty for its own sake; the open person simply likes to go beyond the conventional, is spurred on by the unexpected, and seeks alternative explanations for everything. McCrae (1987) demonstrated the relationship between openness and creativity in an empirical study. I have emphasized the importance of "openness to the spark of inspiration" (Cropley, 1992b).

Fromm (1980) and Helson (1983) drew attention to the fact that descriptions of the creative personality cross the boundaries of gender stereotypes: Inspiration is thought to be stereotypically female, for instance, and elaboration stereotypically male. In a similar way, sensitivity and responsibility are regarded as female, autonomy and positive self-image as male. Thus, the creative personality is said to involve a mixture of stereotypically male and stereotypically female characteristics. Shaughnessy and Manz (1991) summarized studies that supported this view empirically, especially regarding creative women. However, evidence on gender differences in creativity is equivocal. Nonetheless, in a review of studies on this topic, Bramwell Rejskind (1988) concluded that there is probably an advantage in favor of girls. According to McMullan (1978), creativity results from a *paradoxical personality*, which requires an integration of seven polarities: (a) openness versus the forming of good gestalts; (b) acceptance of the unconscious into the conscious; (c) a distanced attitude versus being strongly engaged; (d) a critical, questioning attitude versus constructive problem solving; (e) ego centeredness versus altruism and empathy; (f) self-criticism and self-doubt versus self-confidence; and (g) relaxedness versus concentration. According to Block (1984), gender differences arise from the different socialization of girls and boys—boys being trained to be, in Piagetian terms, more accommodative, and girls more assimilative.

Creative individuals differ from less creative in *motivational patterns* as well. Dynamic gaps (Henle, 1974) motivate them to create new order out of chaos (to accommodate), whereas less creative people seek to return things to the way they were before (to assimilate). A further motivational characteristic of highly creative individuals is their obsession with a task. They are usually entirely willing to strive to their mental and physical limits (Mehlhorn, 1988). This requires a fascination with the field and a sense of invincibility, which is only possible when the drive comes from within, that is, when motivation is intrinsic (Amabile, 1983). Empirical studies of mathematicians (Biermann, 1985) and musicians (Csikszentmihalyi, 1988) have demonstrated the importance of motivation. According to Tardif and Sternberg (1988), the motivational prerequisites for creativity are curiosity, willingness to take risks, tolerance for ambiguity, dedication, stamina, and fascination for the task. Briggs (1988) concluded that of these, dedication and tolerance for ambiguity are most crucial. Tolerance for ambiguity is so highly developed that it does not involve simple tolerance for two alternatives (ambivalence), but a willingness to see that anything could be combined with anything else (omnivalence).

Shaw (1989) offered a further vital point when he complained that creativity research has scarcely been concerned with the role of *feelings and emotions* in the process of finding effective novel solutions. In a study with creative engineers and physicists, he demonstrated the importance of a number of feelings: fascination for the task, self-confidence, frustration when progress was blocked, excitement at the moment of illumination, and satisfaction upon successful verification. These are all aspects of what might be called "the joy of creating." Interestingly, Shaw's respondents made little mention of competitiveness or aggressiveness, perhaps because these feelings are socially undesirable. Shaw concluded that aspects of creativity are positively affected by feelings such as fascination or excitement, and negatively by the feeling of stress.

Finally, it is important to bear in mind that the personal disposition to be creative has a *social aspect*. As Moustakis (1977) put it, being creative means living your life your own way. Barron (1969) postulated a connection between creativity and "resistance to socialization," and this was confirmed empirically by Aviram and Milgram (1977) in studies conducted in Israel, the Soviet Union (as it then was), and the United States. Harrington, Block, and Block (1987) reviewed the relevant literature and concluded that—under appropriate circumstances—a low level of family control facilitates creativity. Low levels of control must, however, be accompanied by warmth and support, as they may otherwise be interpreted by the child as aloofness and lack of concern for his or her well-being.

Several authors have emphasized the role of social factors such as norms and conformity pressure in inhibiting creativity. According to Anderson and Cropley (1966), this involves "stop rules." Children learn that certain things are simply not done and thus acquire general rules forbidding certain lines of action (e.g., "You shouldn't question what the teacher tells you.") As a result, whole classes of theoretically possible solutions are banned *en masse*. Fromm (1980) argued that society has "filters" with which certain behaviors, even certain thoughts, are blocked. To take a concrete example, a grade-two class was given the task of drawing a person's head. They worked away at their places for some time, and then one boy went to the teacher's desk, explaining that he had a problem. When he explained his problem to the teacher, she realized that he was drawing the *inside* of a head! Her reaction was to fly into a rage. She made him hold up his drawing so that all the others could see it, then said, "Everybody look at what Mr. Clever has drawn. He couldn't draw a *proper* head, could he? Oh no. He had to be different from everybody else and draw the inside." She then had all the other children hold up their drawings for the offending boy to see. "There, Mr. Clever, you see what a proper head looks like. Everybody else got it right, all except you!" The other children took their lead from the teacher and looked shocked or pointed their fingers and jeered. The offender sat down with a red face. What this boy had learned was far more than how a proper head looks: He had been taught that unusual viewpoints are not wanted, that the right way is the way everybody else does things, and that it is very dangerous to reveal in public that you have (in this case, probability unwittingly) looked at something from a novel perspective.

A more positive aspect of the effect of social factors on creative achievement was demonstrated by Bloom (1985). His studies of the factors that led to the emergence of creative potential in young people showed that in many cases a single significant person played a crucial role, for instance, by making the young person aware of his or her own potential. This was often done by a person in a fairly humble position, such as a grade school teacher who demonstrated passionate interest in a topic and awakened it in the child, showed a creative youngster that he or she was not alone, or helped the student make contact with peers, experts, or other supportive adults. Despite this, a major aspect of social factors seems to be their powerful role as inhibitors. Thus, in fostering creativity teachers must seek not only to provide releasers, but also to eliminate blockers.

Combining summaries such as those of Cropley (1992a) and Torrance (1992), the findings just presented suggest that teachers should value and promote in their students properties such as:

1. Task commitment, persistence, and determination
2. Curiosity, adventurousness, and tolerance for ambiguity
3. Independence and nonconformity
4. Self-confidence and willingness to risk being wrong
5. Drive to experiment and willingness to try difficult tasks.

This might prove to be sooner said than done, given that teachers often frown on traits associated with creativity. Research has shown that many teachers actually dislike such characteristics. Torrance's (1970) early findings to this effect have been supported by more recent studies in the United States (e.g., Bachtold, 1974), as well as in other countries (Howieson, 1984; Obuche, 1986; Raina, 1972). Stone (1980) found that Grade Two students who scored highest on tests of creativity were rated by their classmates as the ones most often in trouble with teachers. It might be asked what feedback teachers give creative students if their behavior is seen as undisciplined, disruptive, defiant, or even an attempt to humiliate the teacher. Nonetheless, there is evidence that teachers overwhelmingly state their support of creativity as something that should be fostered in the classroom—Feldhusen and Treffinger (1975) reported that 96% of teachers expressed this view. The problem seems to be that of recognizing "immature" creativity or creative potential; undoubtedly many teachers are often confronted by genuinely disruptive behavior, and such behavior cannot simply be excused and tolerated in the hope that it is a sign of creativity. Once again, the issue of recognizing indicators of creative potential and distinguishing between these and misbehavior is emphasized here.

An interesting finding in this regard is that creative teachers tend to be more supportive of creative students. Milgram (1979) showed that there were correlations between teacher creativity and that of students. McLeod and Cropley (1989, p. 245) referred to "creativity fostering" teachers, who seem to get along particularly well with creative students. As Cropley (1982) pointed out, such teachers provide a model of creative behavior, reinforce such behavior when students display it, protect creative students from conformity pressure from their peers, provide a safe refuge for the students when they are subjected to ridicule or criticism from peers, parents, or other teachers, and establish a class-room atmosphere that is supportive of creativity. According to Cropley (1982), creativity fostering teachers are those who:

1. Encourage students to learn independently
2. Have a cooperative, socially integrative style of teaching
3. Motivate their students to master factual knowledge, so that they have a solid base for divergent thinking
4. Delay judging students' ideas until they have been thoroughly worked out and clearly formulated
5. Encourage flexible thinking in students
6. Promote self-evaluation in students
7. Take students' suggestions and questions seriously
8. Offer students opportunities to work with a wide variety of materials and under many different conditions
9. Help students to learn to cope with frustration and failure, so that they have the courage to try the new and unusual.

A HOLISTIC MODEL OF CREATIVITY

In modern discussions, creativity was initially conceived of as primarily a matter of thinking, especially divergent thinking. This approach was particularly attractive to educators because it provided an explanation of many behaviors seen in the classroom (it was plausible), and it generated simple suggestions for fostering creativity (it was practical). However, as has just been shown, an approach to creativity focusing on divergent thinking is too simple, although far better than nothing. The discussion of affective, motivational, personal, and social factors in creative behavior outlined earlier has implied and supported a holistic approach, holistic both with regard to the psychological elements of creativity and also with regard to the stages of the creative process. The question now arises as to how thinking, motivation, and personality combine to yield information, incubation, communication, and so on.

In a seminal study of Romanian engineering students, Facaoaru (1985) showed that successful creative work in practical settings required a combination of psychological elements. In the case of cognition, this meant a combination of convergent and divergent thinking. However, motivation and personal characteristics were also important in distinguishing between highly and less creative students. According to Perkins (1981), creativity arises out of a combination of six elements: (a) the drive to create order out of chaos, (b) the ability to ask unexpected questions and to tolerate criticism, (c) mental mobility, (d) willingness to take risks, (e) openness for the new, and (f) the feeling of being challenged. Necka (1986) suggested that the particular combination of elements constitutes a profile for each individual. He regarded these profiles as dynamic in nature, in the sense that they can change with experience. Gruber and Davis (1988) developed this point further. For them, a creative product is not an isolated event but the result of a developmental process that may stretch over many years. In their "evolving systems" model, knowledge, attitudes, values, and the like are constantly not only acquired, but also reorganized, to yield changing and developing cognitions, emotions, and goals.

The creation of effective surprise was described by Shaw (1989) as involving "loops" between the stages of the creative process. He called this the Eureka Process. For instance, there is a loop between information and incubation because incubation occurs on the basis of information. Shaw called this interaction the *Arieti loop*. The loop between incubation and illumination was labeled the *Vinacke* loop, that between illumination and verification the *Lalas* loop, between verification and communication the *Communication* loop, and between communication and validation the *Rossman* loop. (Except for the communication loop, these labels all derive from the names of eminent researchers on creativity.) Shaw made the point that these loops are not confined to interactions between two stages: In all probability there are loops involving three or more stages—for instance, validation (or lack thereof) is itself a piece of information, which would be expected to have consequences for subsequent incubation.

The crux of the arguments just spelled out is that creativity results from the interaction of cognitive, affective, motivational, and social/personal factors. Figure 5.1 shows schematically how this interaction could occur. The left-hand column in Figure 5.1 divides the process of producing a creative product into stages (Wallas's stages supplemented by the stages of communication and social validation discussed earlier). In each stage, certain cognitive processes are dominant (e.g., convergent thinking in the stage of incubation, divergent thinking in the stage of illumination). The results of each particular stage (shown in the third column) form the contents of the following stage. In the stage of illumination, for example, divergent thinking is applied to cognitive elements formed in the stage of incubation to yield configurations. At the same time, the configurations (which are the result of divergent thinking in the stage of illumination) are the subject matter of the stage of verification. These steps in the creative process are accompanied by feelings and emotions. If the process is to continue, these need to be positive—for instance, confrontation with a complex mass of cognitive elements must excite not frighten the individual. In Figure 5.1, the whole process was successful in

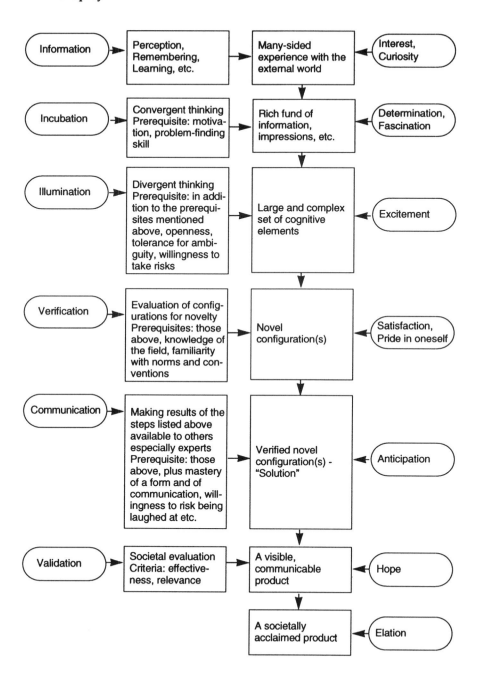

Figure 5.1. The production of a creative product

that a societally acclaimed (validated) product resulted. However, it is possible for the production sequence to cease in an earlier stage: Obviously, not all products are validated. It is also possible that the divergent thinking in the stage of illumination might not yield a configuration, or that the creator might not possess sufficient information about the field for appropriate cognitive elements to be formed, and so on.

This analysis of the emergence of creative products is easy to apply in practical settings. Reduced for simplicity's sake to its basic elements, the process of achieving a creative solution could be specified in the following paradigm: Exposure to a rich variety of information leads not to anxiety and avoidance, but to increased interest and desire for more information; information is not blindly accepted (assimilated) and later regurgitated, but causes a reevaluation of the situation in question and the formation of expanded or enriched configurations (i.e., accommodation). Fascination, openness, and a "nose" for the incongruous lead to ways of coming to grips with the situation that are marked by attention to peripheral aspects of the information in question, willingness to try the unexpected, search for the novel, and so on. Possession of a fund of knowledge in the area allows the individual to "feel" that a solution is near, to recognize a good solution, and to experience the satisfaction of solving a problem (the problem might be technical, scientific, philosophical, artistic, commercial, or whatever, depending on the area in which creativity is occurring). Self-confidence yields the courage to present the solution in a form understandable to the teacher and classmates in the hope of convincing them and receiving recognition. Ultimately, in the ideal case, the whole process culminates in the creator experiencing the satisfaction of creative achievement.

The sequence of events just described requires possession of the basic skills necessary for obtaining information: the three Rs, library and computer literacy, and the like. People also need a basic fund of knowledge of how the world around them is structured and how it functions (i.e., conventional schoolhouse knowledge of literature, history, science, and so on). In addition, however, and of central importance to this chapter, they need skill in other processes closely related to creativity: making remote associations, seeing the world without censorship, admitting unconscious material into consciousness, dealing with information in a playful way, seeing gaps (in the gestalt sense), experiencing fascination with a subject area, feeling the joy of creating, evaluating their own work, and so on. Helping students to acquire the knowledge and skills just specified and to experience the emotions related to them provides a set of tenable goals for educators in the classroom.

RECOGNIZING CREATIVE POTENTIAL

Capturing the essence of creativity and defining behavioral indicators that give evidence of creative potential has proved difficult. Obviously, no indicators are needed in the case of individuals already recognized by virtue of their creative achievements, but very few schoolchildren belong to this group. Furthermore, the concern here is not so much with certifying acknowledged creativity after the fact but with fostering its development and emergence in cases in which this might otherwise not happen. Educators already have at their disposal a substantial armory of tests of ability, particularly intelligence tests. The question that now arises is whether these tests (and the IQ scores they yield) are capable of detecting creative potential. Over 30 years ago, Torrance (1962) pointed out that defining the highly able on the basis of an IQ score alone overlooked about 30% of students with high creative potential. Early research in Canada (Cropley, 1967b) and Great Britain (Hudson, 1966) confirmed that assuming that a high IQ indicates high creativity involves missing a substantial proportion of the most creative youngsters. Thus, there is a need for identification procedures that go beyond the measurement of conventional intelligence. This task lies somewhere beyond the boundaries of conventional standardized tests, given that creative thinking requires innovation and novelty (which are inherently difficult to express in standardized forms), as well as combining cognitive, affective, and social components. Despite this, a variety of procedures for assessing creativity as a psychological trait has been developed, some of them quite strongly resembling conventional abilities tests in certain respects, although there are also striking differences, as is shown in the next section.

Creativity Tests

As might be expected, increasing interest in creativity saw the emergence of a new kind of test, a test of creativity. Strictly speaking, such tests had already existed for many years. Binet himself had suggested that interpretations of inkblots could be used to assess creativity and, as Barron and Harrington (1981) pointed out, there had already been "a proliferation of studies" by creativity investigators prior to 1915, adopting Binet's open ended multiple solution format. A substantial number of creativity tests also appeared between the world wars, including tests of "imagination," "recreative imagination," "ideational fluency," and "idea combinations" (see McLeod & Cropley, 1989, for a review). Such tests had largely fallen into disuse and were exerting little influence by the time Guilford (1950) reopened discussions in a seminal address to the American Psychological Association. Some psychologists (including Guilford himself) thus began to construct tests of divergent thinking— usually called creativity tests, although the appropriateness of this label is discussed later. The best known among this flood of tests in the 1950s and 1960s were the *Alternative Uses* test, the *Product Improvement* test, and a revived *Consequences* test, seen in their most highly developed form in the work of Torrance and associates. All of these tests were later incorporated into the battery of creativity tests published by Torrance in 1966 and recently revised (Torrance, 1990), and referred to today as the *Torrance Tests of Creative Thinking* (TTCT). An often cited creativity test of the same period was the *Remote Associates* test (Mednick, 1962), although this has since been criticized on the grounds that it is really a test of convergent thinking. The other influential set of creativity tests to appear during this period was that of Wallach and Kogan (1965), whose major contribution was perhaps their emphasis on a gamelike atmosphere and the absence of time limits in the testing procedure.

The crucial aspect of these tests is that they concentrate on measuring kinds of thinking that branch out from the conventional and seek unusual answers, in other words, divergent thinking. The prototypical tests of this kind are those of Torrance. People taking the tests are confronted with simple situations and asked to generate unusual or unexpected ideas, for instance, "Write down as many uses as you can think of for a tin can" (*Uses*), or "What would the consequences be if the clouds all had strings hanging down from them?" (*Consequences*). The nonverbal test, *Product Improvement*, presents children with a toy (e.g., a stuffed monkey) and asks them to suggest as many ways as possible to change the toy to make it more fun to play with. Scoring of such tests involves ascertaining the sheer quantity of responses by counting their number (*Fluency*) or focusing on their unusualness. This is done by ascertaining the number of separate categories to which responses belong (*Flexibility*) or the number of novel responses (*Originality*). To take an example, "Use a tin can as a saucepan," "Use it as a jug," and "Make it into a suit of armor for a mouse," would yield three points for Fluency (total number of responses), two for Flexibility (one point for the category "container of fluids" [saucepan and jug] and one for the category impenetrable object [suit of armor]), but only one point for Originality (saucepan and jug are commonplace, only suit of armor is unusual). Extraordinarily uncommon answers may be given several points for Originality (see for instance Torrance, 1990, and Cropley, 1967a).

Similar tests appeared in Europe, including the *Test zum divergenten Denken* [Divergent Thinking Test] (Meinberger, 1977), the *Verbaler Kreativitätstest* [Test of Verbal Creativity] (Schoppe, 1975), and the

Kreativitätstest für Vorschul-und Schulkinder [Creativity Test for Preschool and School Children] (Krampen, Freilinger, & Wilmes, 1988) in Germany and the *Espressioni* test [Expressing Ideas] in Italy (Calvi, 1966). However, despite their widespread acceptance, it has repeatedly been pointed out that such tests have only low face validity (they do not resemble what common sense suggests creativity is like) because they seem to have little in common with the kind of mental activities involved in painting the Mona Lisa or writing, for example, *Gone with the Wind* (see Schubert, Wagner, & Schubert, 1988, for a recent discussion). Bachtold and Werner (1973) reported that more than half of a group of acknowledged creative women refused to fill out creativity tests sent to them by mail on the grounds that the tests were stupid, banal, or boring.

Newer Tests

An important advance in creativity testing in recent years derives from increasing recognition of the fact that creative production depends not only on divergent thinking, but also on convergent thinking. This point of view has already been emphasized in several places and in earlier sections. Facaoaru (1985) called for a "two-track" testing procedure, which assesses the "area of overlap" between the two kinds of thinking. The *Divergent-Convergent Problem Solving Processes Scale* (Facaoaru & Bittner, 1987) assesses, among others, "goal-directed divergent thinking," "flexibility," and "task commitment." A somewhat different, although still essentially cognitive approach, is that of Rothenberg (1988). His test of Janusian thinking is based on the idea that creative people are particularly good at bringing apparently incompatible ideas into a state of harmony via *homospatial* thinking. In one version of his test stimulus words are exposed to subjects for very short periods; the subjects are required to make verbal associations to these words, and scoring is based on the number of associations opposite in meaning to the original stimulus word to which they were offered. Schubert's (1973) *Creative Imagination Test* requires subjects to suggest solutions to real-life problems presented in the test. Responses are evaluated according to number and quality of problem-solving suggestions.

Other tests have attempted to measure creativity in terms of specific, noncognitive models of psychological processes. Urban (1991) designed the *Test for Creative Thinking-Drawing Production*, which differs from the tests listed in the previous section in that scores are derived not from the statistical uncommonness of verbal or figural associations, but from what Urban called "image production." Although respondents are asked to complete incomplete figures, as in several other tests, scoring is based not on the unusualness of the figures created, but on nine psychological aspects of creativity derived from Gestalt psychology. These include "boundary breaking," "proportion of new elements," and "humor."

Adopting a psychoanalytic approach, the Swedish psychologist Smith (Smith & Carlsson, 1989) developed the *Creative Functioning Test*. This test regards creativity as dependent on the ability to communicate with one's own subconscious and involves gradually prolonged tachistoscopic exposure of a still-life painting. Subjects who quickly "recognize" the painting and identify it as an object with subconscious overtones (in the Freudian sense) are adjudged to be more willing to admit unconscious material into consciousness, and thus be potentially more creative. The *Myers-Briggs Type Indicator* (Myers & McCaulley, 1985), which is based on Jungian concepts, has recently enjoyed a new lease of life, in the course of which it is frequently used as an indicator of creativity. Based in Jungian personality theory, the scale measures four bipolar dimensions: Thinking-Feeling, Sensing-Intuiting, Judging-Perceiving, and Extroversion-Introversion. The combination Feeling/Intuiting/Perceiving/Introversion is regarded as indicative of creativity.

Reliability and Validity of Creativity Tests

Early studies such as those of Mackler (1962) and Wodtke (1964) concluded that the reliabilities of the Guilford and Torrance tests were unsatisfactorily low. Nonetheless, Dewing (1970), who administered the *Circles* and *Uses* tests on two occasions six weeks apart, reported reliabilities of .68 for fluency and .54 for originality on the *Circles* test, and .51 and .39, respectively, for the *Uses* test. Cropley and Clapson (1971) calculated reliabilities over several years for boys and girls separately, for the same tests, and obtained coefficients ranging from .33 to .58. In a 10-year longitudinal study, Howieson (1981) reported reliabilities for the TTCT ranging from .15 to .37, according to sex and method of scoring. A tally of the test-retest reliabilities quoted in the manual for the TTCT is more optimistic, yielding a median value of .68. Wallach and Kogan (1965) reported reliabilities in excess of .90 for their tests, and this was confirmed by Cropley and Maslany (1969) and Kogan and Pankove (1972). Reliabilities between about .50 and .90 compare favorably with the reliabilities of the subtests of, for instance, the WISC, so that it can be said that individual creativity tests display levels of reliability that are, at the very least, high enough to justify further work.

Probably more interesting for practitioners is the question of the validity of creativity tests—do they really measure creativity? The construct validity of tests based on divergent thinking has largely been investigated by comparing creativity scores with IQs. Early studies indicated that correlations *among* creativity tests were usually lower than correlations *between* creativity and intelligence tests (McLeod & Cropley, 1989). These findings have been extended by studies of correlations of creativity scores with school grades. Hocevar and Bachelor (1989) reviewed the results of a large number of studies of the construct validity of creativity tests and showed that it is not possible to draw unequivocal conclusions. Nonetheless, both early (e.g., Gibson & Light, 1967) and more recent (e.g., Sierwald, 1989) studies have shown that IQs alone do not distinguish adequately between high and low achievers in academic settings: Sierwald confirmed in Germany much earlier findings in Australia (Cropley, 1967a) and Canada (Cropley, 1967b) that students who obtain high scores on *both* intelligence and creativity tests surpass others in school achievement. Zarnegar, Hocevar, and Michael (1988), Milgram (1990), and Runco (1991) each concluded that creativity test scores yield information over and above that provided by conventional intelligence tests.

Barron and Harrington (1981) reviewed over 70 studies of the predictive validity of creativity tests and showed that correlations with creative performances in real life were often significant. One especially relevant approach in this area has involved what Wallach and Wing (1969) called *nonacademic talented accomplishments*. They showed that high scorers on creativity tests obtained significantly higher scores in life areas such as leadership, art, and music than low scorers. Sierwald (1989) reported low but significant correlations ($r = .20$) between out of school accomplishments and creativity test scores in German high school students, and Okuda, Runco, and Berger (1990) reported coefficients of approximately .50, using creativity tests based on solving real-life problems. Torrance (1981) conducted several longitudinal studies covering periods of 6, 7, and even 22 years. He concluded that the creativity tests had measured aspects of ability not covered by intelligence tests. A 10-year study by Howieson (1981) came to the conclusion that creativity tests predicted creative achievements 10 years later for boys, but not for girls, a finding supported by a 5-year longitudinal study by Cropley (1972a) in Canada. A longitudinal study by Harrington, Block, and Block (1983) also found a significant relationship between creativity scores and creativity in life. In a cross-cultural study in Brazil, Israel, Japan, and the United States, Milgram (1990) demonstrated that creativity scores are related to creative activity in real life. In addition to satisfying psychometric concerns, this reinforces the argument that creativity is a worthwhile educational objective.

Conditions of Administration

Part of the lack of unanimity in findings about the reliability and validity of creativity tests may well result from differences in test content, variability in conditions of administration, and differences in methods of evaluation. Wallach (1985) pointed out that creativity tests are highly reliable when they concentrate on ideational fluency. This also seems to be the case when they focus on a narrow set of contents—the more general the contents, the lower the reliability and validity (much like a bandwidth-fidelity dilemma). There is already something of a literature on conditions of administration (group vs. individual testing, presence or absence of time limits, etc.). Hattie (1977, 1980) showed that administering tests under different conditions led to substantial differences in performance. He concluded that conventional test conditions are best. Wallach and Kogan (1965) emphasized absence of time limits, individual administration, and game-like atmosphere. Cropley (1972b) showed that time limits affected children's scores: Some respondents gave original answers quickly, but others only after a warm-up period. These latter children obtained low creativity scores under timed conditions and high scores under untimed conditions. Milgram (1990) made an important distinction here between *stringent* and *nonstringent* test administration and scoring: The more test contents are specific and concrete, and the more scoring emphasizes practical usefulness (i.e., the more they are stringent), the higher are reliability and validity.

CLOSING REMARKS

If all children's creativity is to be fostered effectively in the classroom, it seems unlikely that narrow, limited exposure to cookbook creativity-facilitating exercises will achieve the desired effects. Although limitations of space preclude a detailed discussion here, this is especially the case with children from disadvantaged groups and children of low intellectual ability. What is needed is an approach in which all aspects of teaching and learning adhere to basic principles for fostering creativity. These involve, as has been pointed out in this chapter, not only intellectual, but also personal, motivational, emotional, and social aspects of creativity. As Runco and Albert (1986) put it, children need contact with complexity, ambiguity, puzzling experiences, uncertainty, and imperfection. Scott (1988) listed three central tasks for parents (which can be transferred to teachers): Challenge children to be open for the novel; give them courage to think for themselves and to seek the new; and show respect for children and their achievements in order to foster in them self-confidence and high expectations. What is needed is to infuse all aspects of educational experiences with such contacts and such actions.

REFERENCES

Albert, R.S., & Runco, M.A. (1989). Independence and the creative potential of gifted and exceptionally gifted boys. *Journal of Youth and Adolescence, 18,* 221-230.

Amabile, T.M. (1983). *The social psychology of creativity.* New York: Springer.

Anderson, C.C., & Cropley, A.J. (1966). Some correlates of originality. *Australian Journal of Psychology, 18,* 218-227.

Arieti, S. (1976). *Creativity: The magic synthesis.* New York: Basic Books.

Austin, J.H. (1978). *Chase, chance, and creativity.* New York: Columbia University Press.

Aviram, A., & Milgram, R. (1977). Dogmatism, locus of control and creativity. *Psychological Reports, 40,* 27-34.

Bachtold, L.M. (1974). The creative personality and the ideal pupil revisited. *Journal of Creative Behavior, 8,* 47-54.

Bachtold, L.M., & Werner, E.E. (1973). Personality characteristics of creative women. *Perceptual and Motor Skills, 36,* 311-319.

Barron, F.X. (1969). *Creative person and creative process.* New York: Holt, Rinehart & Winston.

Barron, F.X., & Harrington, D.M. (1981). Creativity, intelligence and personality. *Annual Review of Psychology, 32,* 439-476.

Beveridge, W.I.B. (1980). *Seeds of discovery.* New York: Norton.

Biermann, K.R. (1985). Über Stigmata der Kreativität bei Mathematikern des 17. bis 19. Jahrhunderts [Characteristics of creative mathematicians of the 17th to 19th centuries]. *Rostocker Mathematik Kolloquium, 27,* 5-22.

Birch, H. (1975). The relation of previous experience to insightful problem solving. *Journal of Comparative Psychology, 38,* 367-383.

Block, J.H. (1984). *Sex role identity and ego development.* San Francisco: Jossey-Bass.

Bloom, B.S. (1985). *Developing talent in young people.* New York: Ballantine.

Bramwell Rejskind, F.G. (1988). *Sex differences and specialization in the divergent thinking styles of gifted children.* Unpublished doctoral dissertation, McGill University, Montreal, Canada.

Briggs, J. (1988). *Fire in the crucible: The alchemy of creative genius.* New York: St. Martin's Press.

Bruner, J.S. (1962). The conditions of creativity. In H. Gruber, G. Terrell, & M. Wertheimer (Eds.), *Contemporary approaches to creative thinking* (pp. 1-30). New York: Atherton.

Calvi, G. (1966). *Il problemo psicologico della creativita* [The psychological problem of creativity]. Milan: Ceschina.

Campbell, D.T. (1963). Blind variation and selective retention in creative thought as in other knowledge processes. *Psychological Review, 67,* 380-400.

Cropley, A.J. (1967a). Divergent thinking and science specialists. *Nature, 215,* 671-672.

Cropley, A.J. (1967b). Creativity, intelligence and achievement. *Alberta Journal of Educational Research, 13,* 51-58.

Cropley, A.J. (1972a). A five year longitudinal study of the validity of creativity tests. *Developmental Psychology, 6,* 119-124.

Cropley, A.J. (1972b). Originality scores under timed and untimed conditions. *Australian Journal of Psychology, 24,* 21-36.

Cropley, A.J. (1982). *Kreativitäet und Erziehung* [Creativity and childrearing]. Munich: Reinhardt.

Cropley, A.J. (1990). Creativity and mental health. *Creativity Research Journal, 3,* 167-178.

Cropley, A.J. (1992a). *More ways than one. Fostering creativity in the classroom.* Norwood, NJ: Ablex.

Cropley, A.J. (1992b). Glück und Kreativität: Förderung von Aufgeschlossenheit für den zündenden Gedanken [Luck and creativity: Fostering openness to the spark of inspiration]. In K.K. Urban (Ed.), *Begabungen entwickeln erkennen und fördern* [Developing, recognizing and fostering ability] (pp. 216- 222). Hanover: Faculty of Education, University of Hanover.

Cropley, A.J., & Clapson, L.G. (1971). Long term test-retest reliability of creativity tests. *British Journal of Educational Psychology, 41,* 206-208.

Cropley, A.J., & Feuring, E. (1971). Training creativity in young children. *Developmental Psychology, 4,* 105.

Cropley, A.J., & Maslany, G.W. (1969). Reliability and factorial validity of the Wallach-Kogan creativity tests. *British Journal of Psychology, 60,* 395-398.

Csikszentmihalyi, M. (1988). Society, culture, and person: A system view of creativity. In R.J. Sternberg (Ed.), *The nature of creativity* (pp. 325-339). New York: Cambridge University Press.

Davis, G.A., & Scott, J.A. (1971). *Training creative thinking.* New York: Holt, Rinehart & Winston.

Dellas, H., & Gaier, E.L. (1970). Identification of creativity: The individual. *Psychological Bulletin, 73,* 55-73.

Dewing, E. (1970). The reliability and validity of selected tests of creative thinking in a sample of seventh grade West Australian children. *British Journal of Educational Psychology, 40,* 35-42.

Dillon, J.T. (1982). Problem finding and solving. *Journal of Creative Behavior, 16,* 97-111.

Eisenman, R. (1991). *From crime to creativity: Psychological and social factors in deviance.* Dubuque, IA: Kendall Hunt.

Endriss, L. (1982). *Entwicklung und Auswirkung eines Kreativitäetsrainings —Fäerderung des spielerischen Denkens bei jungen Erwachsenen* [Development and evaluation of a procedure for fostering creativity—Facilitating playful thinking in young adults.] Unpublished master's thesis, University of Hamburg.

Eysenck, H.J. (1983, May). The roots of creativity: Cognitive ability or personality trait? *Roeper Review,* pp. 10-12.

Facaoaru, C. (1985). *Kreativität in Wissenschaft und Technik* [Creativity in science and technology]. Bern: Huber.

Facaoaru, C., & Bittner, R. (1987). Kognitionspychologische Ansätze der Hochbegabungsdiagnostik [Cognitive approaches to assessing giftedness]. *Zeitschrift für Differentielle und Diagnostische Psychologie* [Journal of Personality and Assessment], *8*(3), 193-205.

Feldhusen, J.F., & Treffinger, D.J. (1975). Teachers' attitudes and practices in teaching creativity and problem solving to economically disadvantaged and minority children. *Psychological Reports, 37,* 1161-1162.

Franklin, B.S., & Richards, P.N. (1977). Effects on children's divergent thinking abilities of a period of direct teaching for divergent production. *British Journal of Educational Psychology, 47,* 66-70.

Fromm, E. (1980). *Greatness and limitations of Freud's thought.* New York: New American Library.

Getzels, J.W., & Csikszentmihalyi, M. (1978). *The creative vision: A longitudinal study of problem finding in art.* New York: Wiley.

Ghiselin, B. (1963). Ultimate criteria for two levels of creativity. In C.W. Taylor & F. Barron (Eds.), *Scientific creativity: Its development and validation* (pp. 30-43). New York: Wiley.

Gibson, J., & Light, P. (1967). Intelligence among university scientists. *Nature, 213,* 441-443.

Gruber, H.E. (1993). Creativity in the moral domain: Ought implies can implies create. *Creativity Research Journal, 6,* 3-15.

Gruber, H.E., & Davis, S.N. (1988). Inching our way up Mount Olympus: The evolving-systems approach to creative thinking. In R.J. Sternberg (Ed.), *The nature of creativity* (pp. 243-270). New York: Cambridge University Press.

Grudin, R. (1990). *The grace of great things.* New York: Tichnor and Fields.

Guilford, J.P. (1950). Creativity. *American Psychologist, 5,* 444-454.

Harrington, D.M., Block, J., & Block, J.H. (1983). Predicting creativity in preadolescence from divergent thinking in early childhood. *Journal of Personality and Social Psychology, 45,* 609-623.

Harrington, D.M., Block, J.H. & Block, J. (1987). Testing aspects of Carl Rogers's theory of creative environments: Child-rearing antecedents of creative potential in young adolescents. *Journal of Personality and Social Psychology, 52,* 851-856.

Hattie, J.A. (1977). Conditions for administering creativity tests. *Psychological Bulletin, 84,* 1249-1260.

Hattie, J.A. (1980). Should creativity tests be administered under test like conditions? *Journal of Educational Psychology, 72,* 87-98.

Heinelt, G. (1974). *Kreative Lehrer—kreative Schüler* [Creative teachers—creative students]. Freiburg: Herder.

Helson, R. (1983). Creative mathematicians. In R.S. Albert (Ed.), *Genius and eminence: The social psychology of creativity and exceptional achievement* (pp. 311-330). Elmsford, NY: Pergamon.

Henle, M. (1974). The cognitive approach: The snail beneath the shell. In S. Rosner & L.E. Aber (Eds.), *Essays in creativity* (pp. 23-44). Croton on Hudson, NY: North River Press.

Hocevar, D., & Bachelor, P. (1989). A taxonomy and critique of measurements used in the study of creativity. In J.A. Glover, R.R. Ronning, & C.R. Reynolds (Eds.), *Handbook of creativity* (pp. 53-76). New York: Plenum.

Howieson, N. (1981). A longitudinal study of creativity—1965-1975. *Journal of Creative Behavior, 15*, 117-134.

Howieson, N. (1984, August). *Is Western Australia neglecting the creative potential of its youth?* Paper presented at the 1984 Annual Conference of the Australian Psychological Society, Perth, Australia.

Hudson, L. (1966). *Contrary imaginations*. London: Methuen.

Koestler, A. (1964). *The act of creation*. London: Hutchinson.

Kogan, N., & Pankove, E. (1972). Creative ability over a five year span. *Child Development, 43*, 427-442.

Krampen, G., Freilinger, J., & Wilmes, L. (1988). Kreativitätstest für Vorschul- und Schulkinder (KVS): Testentwicklung, Handanweisung, Testheft [Creativity test for preschool and schoolchildren: Test development, instructions for administration, manual]. *Trierer Psychologische Berichte, 15*, Heft 7.

Kris, E. (1950). On preconscious mental processes. *Psychoanalytic Quarterly, 19*, 539-552.

Kubie, L. (1958). *Neurotic distortion of the creative process*. Lawrence: University of Kansas Press.

Langley, P.W., Simon, H.A., Bradshaw, G.R., & Zytkow, J.M. (1986). *Scientific discovery: Computational exploration of the creative process*. Cambridge, MA: MIT Press.

Mackler, B. (1962). *Creativity and lifestyles*. Unpublished doctoral dissertation, University of Kansas.

Maslow, A.H. (1959). Creativity in self-actualizing people. In H.H. Anderson (Ed.), *Creativity and its cultivation* (pp. 83-95). New York: Harper & Row.

McCrae, R.R. (1987). Creativity, divergent thinking and openness to experience. *Journal of Personality and Social Psychology, 52*, 1258-1265.

McCrae, R.R., & Costa, P.T. (1985). Openness to experience. In R.R. Hogan & W.H. Jones (Eds.), *Perspectives in personality* (Vol.1, pp.145-172). Greenwich, CT: JAI Press

McLeod, J., & Cropley, A.J. (1989). *Fostering academic excellence*. Oxford: Pergamon.

McMullan,W.E. (1978). Creative individuals: Paradoxical personages. *Journal of Creative Behavior, 10*, 265-275.

Mednick, S.A. (1962). The associative basis of creativity. *Psychological Review, 69*, 220-232.

Mehlhorn, H.-G. (1988). *Persönlichkeitsentwicklung Hochbegabter* [Personality development in the gifted]. Berlin: Volk und Wissen Volkseigener Verlag.

Mehlhorn, G., & Mehlhorn, H.-G. (1985). *Begabung, Schöpfertum, Persönlichkeit* [Giftedness, creativity and personality]. Berlin: Volk und Wissen Volkseigener Verlag.

Meinberger, U. (1977). *Test zum divergenten Denken (Kreativität) für 4. bis 6. Klassen (TDK 4-6)* [Test of divergent thinking (creativity) for the 4th to 6th grades (TDK 4-6)]. Weinheim: Beltz.

Milgram, R.M. (1990). Creativity: An idea whose time has come and gone? In M.A. Runco & R.S. Albert (Eds.), *Theories of creativity* (pp. 215-233). Newbury Park, CA: Sage.

Morgan, D.N. (1953). Creativity today. *Journal of Aesthetics, 12*, 1-24.

Moustakis, C.E. (1977). *Creative life*. New York: Van Nostrand.

Mumford, M.D., & Gustafson, S.B. (1988). Creativity syndrome: Integration, application, and innovation. *Psychological Bulletin, 103*, 27-43.

Myers, I.B., & McCaulley, M.H. (1985). *Manual: A guide to the development and use of the Myers-Briggs Type Indicator*. Palo Alto, CA: Consulting Psychologists Press.

Necka, E. (1986). On the nature of creative talent. In A.J. Cropley, K.K. Urban, H. Wagner, & W.H. Wieczerkowski, (Eds.), *Giftedness: A continuing worldwide challenge* (pp. 131-140). New York: Trillium.

Obuche, N.M. (1986). The ideal pupil as perceived by Nigerian (Igbo) teachers and Torrance's creative personality. *International Review of Education, 32*, 191-196.

Okuda, S.M., Runco, M.A., & Berger, D.E. (1990). Creativity and the finding and solving of real world problems. *Journal of Psychoeducational Assessment, 9*, 45-53.

Parloff, M.D., & Handlon, D.H. (1964). The influence of criticalness on creative problem solving. *Psychiatry, 27*, 17-27.

Perkins, D.N. (1981). *The mind's best work*. Cambridge, MA.: Harvard University Press.

Platt, W., & Baker, R.A. (1931). The relation of the scientific "hunch" to research. *Journal of Chemical Education, 8*, 1969-2002.

Rejskind, F.G., Rapagna, S.O., & Gold, D. (1992). Gender differences in children's divergent thinking. *Creativity Research Journal, 5*, 165-174.

Rogers, C.R. (1959). Toward a theory of creativity. In H.H. Anderson (Ed.), *Creativity and its cultivation* (pp. 25-42). New York: Harper and Row.

Rosenman, M.F. (1988). Serendipity and scientific discovery. *Journal of Creative Behavior, 22*, 132-138.

Rothenberg, A. (1988). Creativity and the homospatial process: Experimental studies. *Psychiatric Clinics of North America, 11*, 443-460.

Rump, E.E. (1979). *Divergent thinking, aesthetic preferences and orientation towards arts and sciences.* Unpublished doctoral dissertation, University of Adelaide.

Runco, M.A. (Ed.). (1991). *Divergent thinking.* Norwood, NJ: Ablex.

Runco, M.A., & Albert, R.S. (1986). The threshold hypothesis regarding creativity and intelligence: An empirical test with gifted and nongifted children. *Creative Child and Adult Quarterly, 11*, 212-218.

Runco, M.A., & Okuda, S.M. (1988). Problem-discovery, divergent thinking, and the creative process. *Journal of Youth and Adolescence, 17*, 213-222.

Schoppe, K.J. (1975). *Verbaler Kreativitätstest* [Test of verbal creativity]. Göttingen: Hogrefe.

Schubert, D.S. (1973). Intelligence as necessary but not sufficient for creativity. *Journal of Genetic Psychology, 112*, 45-47.

Schubert, D.S.P., Wagner, H.E., & Schubert, H.J.P. (1988). Family constellation and creativity: Increased quantity of creativity among lastborns. *Creative Child and Adult Quarterly, 13*, 97-103.

Scott, M. (1988). Gifted-talented-creative children's development. *Creative Child and Adult Quarterly, 13*, 119-132.

Shaughnessy, M.F., & Manz, A.F. (1991). Personalogical research on creativity in the performing and fine arts. *European Journal for High Ability, 2*, 91-101.

Shaw, M.P. (1989). The Eureka process: A structure for the creative experience in science and engineering. *Creativity Research Journal, 2*, 286-298.

Sierwald, W. (1989, September). *Kreative Hochbegabung—Identifikation, Entwicklung und Förderung kreativ Hochbegabter.* [Creative giftedness—identification, development and fostering of the creatively gifted]. Paper presented at the second annual meeting of the working group, Educational Psychology of the German Psychological Society, Munich.

Simonton, D.K. (1988). *Scientific genius. A psychology of science.* Cambridge: Cambridge University Press.

Smith, G., & Carlsson, I. (1989). *The creative process.* New York: International Universities Press.

Snow, R.E. (1986). Individual differences in the design of educational programs. *American Psychologist, 41*, 1029-1039.

Stein, M.I. (1963). A transactional approach to creativity. In C.W. Taylor & F.X. Barron (Eds.), *Scientific creativity: Its discovery and development* (pp. 217-227). New York: Wiley.

Stone, B.G. (1980). Relationship between creativity and classroom behavior. *Psychology in the Schools, 17*, 106-108.

Suler, J.R. (1980). Primary process thinking and creativity. *Psychological Bulletin, 88*, 144-165.

Tardif, T.Z., & Sternberg, R.J. (1988). What do we know about creativity? In R.J. Sternberg (Ed.), *The nature of creativity* (pp. 429-440). New York: Cambridge University Press.

Taylor, I.A. (1975). An emerging view of creative actions. In I.A. Taylor & J.W. Getzels (Eds.), *Perspectives in creativity* (pp. 3-12). Chicago: Aldine.

Torrance, E.P. (1967). *Education and the creative potential*. Minneapolis: University of Minnesota Press.

Torrance, E.P. (1972). Predictive validity of the Torrance Test of Creative Thinking. *Journal of Creative Behavior, 32*, 401-405.

Torrance, E.P. (1981). Predicting the creativity of elementary school children (1958-1980). *Gifted Child Quarterly, 25*, 55-62.

Torrance, E.P. (1990). *Torrance Tests of Creative Thinking*. Beaconville, IL: Scholastic Testing Services.

Torrance, E.P. (1992, January/February). A national climate for creativity and invention. *Gifted Child Today*, pp. 10-14.

Treffinger, D.J., & Gowan, I.C. (1971). An updated representative list of methods and educational materials for stimulating creativity. *Journal of Creative Behavior, 6*, 236-252.

United States Patent and Trademark Office. (1990). *The Inventive Thinking Curriculum Project*. Washington, DC: U.S. Patent and Trademark Office.

Urban, K.K. (1991). On the development of creativity in children. *Creativity Research Journal, 4*, 177-192.

Walberg, H.J., & Staniha, W.E. (1992). Productive human capital: Learning, creativity, and eminence. *Creativity Research Journal, 5*, 323-341.

Wallach, M.A. (1985). Creativity testing and giftedness. In F.D. Horowitz & M. O'Brien (Eds.), *The gifted and talented: Developmental perspectives* (pp. 99-124). Washington, DC: American Psychological Association.

Wallach, M.A., & Kogan, N. (1965). *Modes of thinking in young children*. New York: Holt, Rinehart & Winston.

Wallach, M.A., & Wing, C.W. (1969). *The talented student*. New York: Holt, Rinehart & Winston.

Wallas, G. (1926). *The art of thought*. New York: Harcourt Brace.

Weisberg, R.W. (1986). *Creativity*. New York: Freeman.

Wodtke, K.H. (1964). Some data on the reliability and validity of creativity tests at the elementary school level. *Educational and Psychological Measurement, 24*, 399-408.

Zarnegar A., Hocevar, D., & Michael, W.B. (1988). Components of original thinking in gifted children. *Educational and Psychological Measurement, 48*, 5-16.

6 Developmental Trends in Creative Potential and Creative Performance*

Mark A. Runco
Robyn E. Charles
California State University, Fullerton

One of the most important questions in the creativity literature concerns the distinction between *potential* and *performance*. Should research focus on the potential creativity of individuals, perhaps inferring it from measures such as divergent thinking tasks, personality inventories, or assessments of previous activity, or should research focus on the actual creative products of individuals, such as publications or works of art? This question leads directly to several others, including one concerning whether or not researchers should study the creativity of all individuals or just the exceptional ones. Often the creativity of gifted children is studied, the assumption being that these exceptional youths have high potential and a high probability of actually using their talents when they enter the adult world. Critics argue that the creativity of gifted children is ambiguous and uncertain, and that research should focus on unambiguously creative adults, such as Einstein or Picasso, or some other individuals who have actually performed in an unquestionably creative fashion.

*Material from this chapter was presented at the meeting of the American Psychological Association in Toronto, Ontario, Canada, August 1993. Correspondence should be directed to Mark A. Runco, EC 105, California State University, Fullerton, CA 92634. (email: MRunco@Fullerton)

115

Interestingly, developmental trends have been found in studies of creative potential *and* in studies of actual creative performance. There are, for example, documented declines in children's original thinking at various stages of development (Gardner, 1982; Smith & van der Meer, 1990; Torrance, 1968; Urban, 1991), as well as various peaks and troughs in creative productivity during adulthood (Lindauer, 1992; Simonton, 1975, 1983). Our assumption in this chapter is that if we understand the developmental patterns and trends we might be able to infer the causes and contributing factors and thereby avoid or minimize the losses. Put differently, the trends may tell us which contributing factors are the most critical for the expression of creativity, and in this sense they might explain the fulfillment of potential. On a more general level, the trends may very well be indicative of the true nature of creativity. Creativity may have inherent spurts and lulls in the lifespan, as manifested in developmental trends.

This chapter focuses on the trends that have been identified in the research.[1] Explanations for the trends are compared and contrasted, and points of agreement and disagreement are highlighted. As will be shown, there are disagreements about the trends themselves (e.g., some research has identified only one slump, and other studies suggest several), and these too will be discussed. Somewhat surprisingly, there is even more disagreement about the peaks and slumps that occur during adulthood than about those occurring during childhood. This may be because of the longer time span covered, or it may be a methodological artifact, with disagreements reflecting cross-sectional and longitudinal findings. We suggest that a great deal of the uncertainty about trends seems to reflect often overlooked individual differences in the spurts and lulls and in reactions to experience. For obvious reasons we begin the review of research with childhood trends.

CHILDHOOD TRENDS

Torrance (1962) found a decline in the creativity of children at approximately 5 years of age, which is the age children typically enter school. Torrance (1962, 1963) specifically cited the academic demands for adaptation and acceptance of authority as the cause of this early decline in creativity. A few years later Torrance called attention to a decline in creative functioning during the fourth grade, and not surprisingly referred

[1]Other developmental concerns are reviewed elsewhere, including family position (Albert, 1983; Runco & Bahleda, 1987; Simonton, 1987), family size (Gaynor & Runco, 1992; Sulloway, 1993), and socioeconomic status (Dudek, Strobel, & Runco, 1993).

to it as the "fourth-grade slump" (Torrance, 1968). This description was based on a longitudinal study in which all children enrolled in two elementary schools in Minnesota were given the Torrance Tests of Creative Thinking (TTCT) each year from 1959 to 1964. The results were based on a randomly selected sample of 100 children. Testing began in the third grade and continued in the fourth and fifth grades. (To enable comparisons across age, the raw scores were standardized based on fifth-grade comparison group norms.) Statistically significant fourth-grade slumps were found in fluency, flexibility, originality, and elaboration. Across the four indices, between 45% and 61% of the students showed a decline of five or more standard score points between the third and fourth grades, whereas only between 11% and 38% of the subjects showed growth over this time. Between the fourth and fifth grades, between 17% and 29% of the children showed a decline in their scores, whereas between 33% and 59% showed an increase. In terms of the overall trends, fluency showed a significant net slump from third to fifth grade, and flexibility showed a decreasing although nonsignificant trend. Originality showed a nonsignificant tendency for growth, and elaboration showed significant growth. Although not all subjects experienced a fourth-grade slump, approximately half of them did. Moreover, there were many children who actually scored lower in the fifth grade than they did in the third grade. In particular, 52% of the subjects showed a net slump in fluency between third and fifth grades, whereas only 17% showed a net growth.

Torrance's work is important partly because he found different trends for the various divergent thinking indices. This is noteworthy because divergent thinking tests have been criticized for their redundant indices (Hocevar, 1979). Although we cannot explore the statistical details of that issue here, the finding of different developmental trends supports the cognitive independence and discriminant validity of the indices.[2] Other research with children (Lopez, Esquivel, & Houtz, 1993) and adults (Guilford, 1967; Jaquish & Ripple, 1981, 1984-85; McCrae, Arenberg, & Costa, 1987) also supports that independence.

Torrance's (1962, 1963) theory of a decline at school entry and the fourth-grade slump is particularly important because it is the standard view that many subsequent investigations have attempted to test

---

[2]Incidentally, this developmental evidence for separate indices was described by Cyril Burt (1970) approximately 20 years before his unethical research was identified as such. Burt suggested that fluency, divergence, receptivity, and sagacity in ideation mature at different rates. Although we might be suspicious of Burt's work, his suggestion is consistent with the evidence for differential rates of development of the various indices of divergent thinking (Guilford, 1967; Torrance, 1968). Perhaps we should not throw Burt out with the bathwater.

and extend. Camp's (1994) longitudinal investigation reflects one such effort. He used the TTCT, along with relevant self-concept and motivation variables. He found that figural fluency, flexibility, and originality showed relatively high scores up to 6th grade and then a drop until 12th grade. Verbal flexibility and fluency showed similar drops between the 6th and 12th grades. Figural elaboration scores were much less consistent, with some increase between the 9th and 12th grades.

In a study of culturally and linguistically diverse first- through eighth-grade students (mostly Hispanic), Lopez et al. (1993) reported that "growth in creativity continued throughout the middle elementary years without any striking slumps" (p. 407). Their samples were, however, somewhat small (13 < ns < 23), and Lopez et al. relied on within-subject analyses, comparing scores from the beginning of the school year (October) with those at the end (May). Interestingly, they did find a significant increase in flexibility scores, at least between the fourth and eighth grades. Because they were working with linguistically and culturally diverse students, Lopez et al. inferred that "bilingualism contributes to cognitive flexibility" (p. 408). And as noted just above, the finding of increases in flexibility scores supports the idea that the various indices of divergent thinking develop at different rates.

Urban (1991) developed the Test for Creative Thinking-Drawing Production (TCT-DP) with the goal of looking beyond quantitative trends. He focused on the quality, content, gestalt, and elaboration of ideas. The TCT-DP consists of a drawing with six figural fragments that children are asked to complete. Five of the fragments are located within a large square frame; the sixth fragment is outside of the frame. Scoring is quantitative and qualitative, the latter relying on the following criteria: use of the presented elements, addition of a new element, use of the space outside of the frame, humor, unconventionality, and the addition of three-dimensional objects.[3] Time spent on the drawings was also recorded. A total score is obtained by summing the points obtained for each category.[4]

---

[3]The inclusion of humor is justified by a recent review of the literature on humor and creativity (see O'Quin & Derkes, this volume). The interesting thing is that if humor is associated with creativity, creativity might in turn be inversely related to longevity. This is because humor is negatively related to longevity (Friedman et al., 1993). This assertion is contrary to a great deal of evidence from the creativity literature (Runco & Richards, in press) and the humor-health literature (Cousins, 1988). If creativity is inversely related to longevity, we must reopen the question about creativity and health (Runco & Richards, in press).

[4]Runco (1993a) noted that an increasing amount of research on creativity is looking to qualitative research. For example, he described several content analyses of divergent thinking, each looking to emotional and affective aspects of ideation. Other recent qualitative research is presented by Murdock and Moore (in press).

Urban's general conclusion was that there is a tendency for children to become increasingly more goal- and gestalt-oriented and more aware of the kinds of products that are socially accepted and rewarded. Although statistical comparisons of the scores across all age groups were not significant, there was a drop in total scores between 5 and 6 years and a significant increase in scores between 6 and 8 years. The only statistically significant decline was in the total scores of the 5- and 6-year-old boys. An investigation of the different schools showed that the mean of all the kindergarten children (4, 5, and 6 years old) was significantly higher than that of all the first-grade children (6 and 7 years old), but there were increases with age within each classroom group. A breakdown of the total scores showed that dramatic drops in scores for the two categories related to boundary breaking (using the space outside of the frame) were responsible for the lower total scores for the 6-year-old children. These scores increased for the 7- and 8-year-old children, but even the boundary-breaking scores of the 8-year-old children were lower than those of the 5-year-old children. Qualitatively, all of the 4-year-old and 80% of the 5-year-old children were unable to produce a thematic relation/composition between the elements. Based on this finding, there may be some doubt concerning whether or not the TCT-DP is adequate for assessing the creative potential of children younger than 6 years.

Daugherty (1993) recently used qualitative indices to describe changes in the thinking of kindergarten and preschool children. She assumed an association between *private speech* and creativity, but there is substantial theoretical (mostly Vygotskian) support of this assumption (Ayman-Nolley, 1992; Daugherty, 1993; Smolucha, 1992a). Vygotsky proposed that verbal processes are distinct from other cognitive processes in early childhood, but the two join as the child matures. In his terms, private speech is internalized into verbal cognition. As Daugherty described it, overt but private speech reflects the thinking of young children as they cope with and attempt to solve problems. Daugherty argued that the transition from overt to covert verbal behavior would "provide essential information on the development of thought" (p. 288). She developed a qualitative scheme to capture the semantic content of private speech and, in turn, to explore qualities of potentially creative thought. It included task-relevant and task-irrelevant speech, nonfacilitative speech, coping/reinforcing speech, and solving speech. The Torrance Test of Creative Action and Movement (TCAM) was also administered. Results suggested a linear decline between ages 3 and 5 for fluency and originality, with a slight increase at age 6. The imagination score showed a linear drop from ages 3 to 6. Task-irrelevant private speech declined between 4 to 6 years, but the nadir of facilitative and solving speech was age 5. Although Vygotsky's ideas about internalized speech may be applicable to these trends, one cannot but wonder if the observers coded literally divergent ideas as task irrelevant. This would explain the synchronized drop in imagination and task-irrelevant speech.

Smith and Carlsson (1983) took an entirely different approach and utilized a *percept-genetic model* of creativity. In investigations using this model, Swedish subjects of various ages were presented with a stimulus, first at very short "subthreshold" exposure times and then at systematically longer times until the stimulus was correctly identified and described. Creativity was specifically defined in relation to individuals' willingness to venture into subjective impressions of the stimulus when the exposure times were again abbreviated, as opposed to holding to their original description. In Smith and Carlsson's (p. 168) own words, creativity is defined as "the individual's *inclination to transgress the confines of an established perceptual context*" (emphasis in original). Their view, with creativity allowing an individual to "free him- or herself from the correct (conventional) meanings of the stimulus and entertain subjective interpretations" (Smith & van der Meer, 1990, p. 250), is in this sense compatible with theories that look to the growth of conventionality to explain slumps in creativity (Rosenblatt & Winner, 1988; Runco, 1991).

Smith and Carlsson (1983) acknowledged that their approach to creativity cannot be adequately used with children under the age of 5 or 6 years. They suggested that young children have not yet established the necessary representational capacities and cannot clearly distinguish between outside realities and inside representations. This is a complex issue, especially given that Smith and Carlsson (1983) suggested that rather than relying on subjective material, younger and less mature children tend to rely on stimuli within their environment to construct their impressions. This seems contrary to the typical argument about the creativity of young children. The typical argument is that the thinking of young children is creative, although perhaps only in the subjective sense and not in a manner that is quantifiable or obvious to observers (Hong & Milgram, 1991; Runco, in press-a; Smolucha & Smolucha, 1985). Smith and Carlsson's idea about the use of subjective material does parallel the theory offered by Harrington, Block, and Block (1983), in which only ideas (or more specifically responses to a divergent thinking test) that reflect things that are absent from the immediate environment reflect high-quality creative responses. Runco, Okuda, and Thurston (1991) gave a similar argument when they defined environmentally cued responses as unoriginal, as did Mednick (1962) when he defined creative insights as remote. Still, many persons question the value of the nonobjective and immature creativity.

Smith and Carlsson's (1983) results are similar to those reported by Torrance (1962) with regard to a child's transition to regular school (at 7 years of age for Swedish children). In contrast to Torrance's (1968) fourth-grade slump, Smith and Carlsson (1983) found an increase in creativity between the ages of 10 and 11 years. A comparison of 7-8-year-old children with 6-year-old children evaluated in an earlier study suggested a decline. This would at first seem to correspond to the predicted decline at the start of regular school; however, Smith and Carlsson offered an alternative explanation. They noted that a subjective contraction (i.e., a decline in the subjective impressions of children) would be expected following the subjective expansion detected in 5- to 6-year-old children, if a spiral model is used. This spiral model can also explain the subjective expansion at 10 to 11 years of age. Here the individual's impressions rely more on material drawn from the private self than on accidental impressions. Smith and Carlsson concluded that true creativity does not appear until 10 to 11 years of age.

Importantly, Smith and Carlsson (1983) had two professional artists evaluate the work of the children. These ratings did not correspond with the percept-genetic findings. Granted, artists' judgments are difficult to use (cf. Runco, 1989; Runco, McCarthy, & Svensen, 1994),[5] but these specific artists apparently had particular difficulty differentiating between the artwork of both the 7- to 8-year-old and the 10- to 11-year-old children. Smith and Carlsson felt that this occurred because the creative expression of individuals in these age groups is no longer focused on artistic expression per se, as it is in preschool children, but instead is directed into different areas, including poetry, music, and inventions. This increased diversity is itself an interesting trend, and one that should be noted in developmental theories of creativity. It may be predictive of the polymath behavior Root-Bernstein, Root-Bernstein, and Garnier (1993) found to characterize eminent scientists.

Rosenblatt and Winner (1988) also investigated age differences in artwork. They reported that drawings by the preschoolers were often spontaneous and aesthetically appealing, but as the children moved into the middle elementary school years, their artwork seemed to emphasize accuracy and realism. Rosenblatt and Winner found that 5-year-old children actually preferred drawings by 10-year-old children to their own drawings, suggesting that preschoolers have the desire to make realistic drawings but lack the necessary skills. When comparing 6-, 8-, 10-, and

[5]Ironically, this is largely because of their subjectivity (Runco & Chand, 1994). Professional artists are often poor judges of nonprofessional work, especially that of children, the reason being that they are too accustomed to professional level work (Runco, 1989; Runco et al., 1994). Their standards, criteria, and expectations are therefore probably inappropriate.

12-year-old children in their ability to complete drawings according to an existing level of realism, 6-year-old children were found to perform as well as 12-year-old children. Both the youngest and the oldest children were able to vary the level of realism they used when completing either an unrealistic "Picasso schematic" or a much more realistic drawing. The 8- and 10-year-old children, however, completed both schematics with equally high levels of realism, indicating again that the main goal of their drawing was to be as realistic as possible.

Rosenblatt and Winner referred to the middle childhood years as the *conventional* years, with the early years called the *preconventional* years, and the later years described as the *postconventional* years. Apparently, only in the postconventional phase (beginning around 12 years) do children with a special interest and skill in visual art learn to violate the rules they worked so hard to master just a few years earlier. By way of comparison, whereas the preschooler might be said to lack conventions, the postconventional artist (including the adult artist) can choose to reject those conventions. The lack of convention depicted in the artistic endeavors of children in both stages results in a similar aesthetic appeal and thus a similar evaluation of artistic creativity. This research is consistent with several lines of work—including Urban's (1991) psychometric investigation reviewed earlier—in that there is an emphasis on changes in the individual's recognition and appreciation of conventions, with increased conventionality associated with lower creativity.

Runco (1991) explained the changes in conventionality in terms of the skills and strategies that allow *evaluative* and *valuative* thinking, both of which underlie judgments about the appropriateness of ideas, solutions, or potentially creative products. Runco suggested that children become more conventional and realistic specifically because of their newly developed critical and evaluative skills. In this view, children develop the ability to discriminate conventional and unconventional ideas and behaviors. Combined with a preference for conventional and appropriate ideas, this leads to a slump. The slump is not a loss, then, but instead is a reflection of an acquisition—namely, of evaluative skills.

This theory is consistent with Gardner's (1982) description of how children between the ages of 2 and 7 begin to master the use of symbols, most notably linguistic ones. They become adept at symbolism in various ways, including hand or body movements, drawings, numbers, music, clay figures, and so on, and they can combine these symbols in striking ways. In just a few years, though, the desire for convention and conformity begins to permeate their activities. Children in this stage often limit themselves to copying pictures, or they may even stop drawing altogether. Although this *literal stage* may be seen as a detriment to creativity, Gardner suggested that the mastery of rules is critical to development. It gradually allows children to respond to the works of others in terms of style, expressiveness, balance, and composition.

The mastery of rules is therefore like other developments that offer a benefit to the individual, but that simultaneously inhibit existing abilities or capacities. It is, for example, similar to the egocentricism of adolescents (Elkind, 1981), which can cause problems in that adolescents can be extremely unrealistic—even giving more weight to "imaginary audiences" than real friends and relatives—but do so only because they have developed the very useful ability to think about hypothetical things. Again, there are benefits and drawbacks. Unfortunately, after the mastery of rules, only a minority of children resume their own creative efforts. Gardner (1982) described this as a U-shaped developmental trajectory, a position that was empirically supported by Johnson (1985). She took a Piagetian approach, comparing individuals in different cognitive stages, and found significant differences between stages in verbal fluency and originality scores. The concrete operational children in her sample (ages 9 years 4 months to 10 years 4 months) had lower scores than the preoperational and formal operational children.

Ayman-Nolley (in press), Dudek (1974), Pariser (1993), Runco (in press-a), and Smolucha and Smolucha (1985) also used the concept of stages and Piagetian terms to describe the creativity of children. Runco (in press-a), for example, commented on the Piagetian idea of development from egocentric to sociocentric thought, and how that can have an impact on the use of conventions (and in turn inhibit creativity), with more sociocentric children being more conventional and less original. He also commented on Piagetian classification skills, suggesting that they may be necessary for an individual to make decisions about what is appropriate, and what is not. This might influence decisions about creativity in that it is usually defined in terms of novelty and appropriateness or fit (Runco & Charles, 1993). Classification is, in this sense, related to evaluative skill. A third concept used by Piaget—although not initially proposed by him—is that of internalization, which describes how conventions might be acquired by children (Smith & Carlsson, 1983).

Dudek (1974) drew from Piagetian theory in her description of how "at 8 or 9 the child begins to see and integrate reality in a differentiated as opposed to global way. . . . At age 8 he becomes free of perceptual dominance. . . . He is not in the stage of concrete operations . . . [and] therefore begins to express his new cognitive mastery through a more differentiated, more realistic drawing and painting" (p. 268). Dudek also described how the egocentricism of children "stands in the way of differentiation" (p. 286), and how children's art is surprising because they are not concerned with representation. Dudek described a slump in creativity early in formal operations, at around age 12, but she felt that most of the changes we see are changes in expressiveness rather than creativity. For Dudek, creative products must have recognizable value and meaning for others.

Although there is agreement that slumps occur in creativity during childhood, there appears to be disagreement about the exact ages of these slumps. There is also some question about whether or not the slumps in creativity are inevitable. Creative tendencies, although expressions of cognitive development, are influenced by social, motivational, and maturational factors. This is why the individual differences reported by Torrance (1968) and others are so important. Recall that although between 45% and 61% of his sample experienced a fourth-grade slump on at least one measure, 38% of the subjects experienced growth in elaboration, 22% in originality, 20% in flexibility, and 11% in fluency. Not all children experience a significant drop in divergent thinking. Even if a large number do, it may be because of analogous experiences rather than inevitable maturation.[6] Children have many of the same experiences, especially in social and educational situations.

The impact of social experiences was explicitly addressed in two recent reviews of Vygotsky's theory of creativity, imagination, and play. Vygotsky's theory was first proposed in the 1930s, but has been reviewed and extended by Ayman-Nolley (1992) and Smolucha (1992a, 1992b). In this theory, creative imagination develops largely through pretend play. Creativity is in this sense experiential; but importantly, for Vygotsky, children learn pretend play by interacting with a more experienced play partner, quite often a parent. Creativity may, for example, develop as result of *object substitutions* (e.g., using a stick as a horse), but these have the most impact when shared with another person. (Object substitution arises during a child's second year and is a necessary precursor to role playing, which is demonstrated in the third year.) Smolucha (1992b) found little evidence for pretend play arising spontaneously in children. She concluded that social interactions with the parent or another more experienced partner are necessary in the initial phases of development, and that creative imagination gradually becomes internalized and can be regulated through inner speech. It is in this latter phase that Vygotsky referred to creative imagination as a higher mental function. Recall here Daugherty's (1993) research on trends in private speech.

---

[6]We use the term *analogous* in the evolutionary sense (Dobzhansky, Ayala, Stebbins, & Valentine, 1977, chap. 9), in which similarities between species do not reflect similar (homologous) origins, but instead similar demands and parallel adaptations. In behavioral terms, it is possible that many children slump at about age 9 to 10 years of age, but that might at least in part reflect common educational pressures or expectations, or similar experiences with reinforced conventions.

Smolucha and Smolucha (1985) developed a test that seems to be similar to Urban's (1991), described earlier. However, unlike all previous work, Smolucha and Smolucha administered their test to children as young as 2 years. In the preliminary report of 1985, they compared individuals between the ages of 2 and 57 years. The test contained eight plastic shapes that the examinee was to arrange. Scores were based on the fluency and flexibility of arrangements of the shapes. Smolucha and Smolucha found that adult artists between 21 and 29 years had the highest fluency and flexibility scores. They concluded, "When the results were graphed for all 46 subjects for age and fluency, and age and flexibility, a J-shaped pattern emerged with a small peak at age 6 years and a higher peak in the 20s" (p. 98). Perhaps the U-shaped distribution noted by various investigators (e.g., Gardner, 1982) is actually a J-shaped distribution, meaning that children do well, albeit not as well as adults.[7]

According to Smolucha and Smolucha (1985), adults have an advantage when they develop "an equilibrium between analogical and logical thinking . . . [this represents] a fifth Piagetian stage" (p. 90). This theory about equilibrium supports Runco's (1991; Runco & Chand, 1994) contention that both divergent and evaluative processes are necessary for creativity. In fact, long ago Vygotsky "described the tension that arises between the adolescent's increasingly self-critical attitude and the emotional vicissitudes of puberty. . . . This overly critical attitude leads many adolescents to abandon their creative efforts" (Smolucha, 1992a, p. 56). Although Vygotsky was discussing adolescence, we can see some theoretical convergence to support our theory of age differences being a reflection of evaluative tendencies.

Vygotsky suggested that although children's creativity and fantasy are unpretentious and more emotionally exciting than that of adults, children have less trust in and less control over the products of their creative activities (Ayman-Nolley, 1992). This lack of control, combined with limited life experiences, simpler interests and motivations, less complex and less diversified modes of interacting with the world, and the separation of imagination and reason apparently led Vygotsky to conclude that children's creativity is less rich than that of adults. Adolescence, in contrast, reflects the transition from immature, childhood fantasies to mature creativity, in which reasoning and imagination interact. With this in mind Vygotsky defined two distinct but interrelated areas of creativity— *subjective creativity* and *objective creativity*. The former is a private continuation of childhood fantasy that assists the adolescent's coping with the unsatisfying realities of life. It apparently functions like what others have

---

[7]To complete the alphabetical descriptions, we should mention Simonton's (1975) findings of productivity as a function of age appearing to be an *inverted* J (also see Vernon, 1989).

called *cathartic originality* (Csikszentmihalyi, 1988; Runco, 1994a). Objective creativity, on the other hand, is the process through which the adolescent creates new ideas and understandings of reality, and this of course aids the development of reasoning. This more mature form of creativity, combining reason, imagination, and a developing appreciation for aesthetics, causes adolescents to become more critical of their creative products, which often results in yet another decline in creativity.[8] As Vygotsky described it, "the fantasy of adolescence is more creative than the child and less productive than adults" (cited in Ayman-Nolley, 1992, p. 81). Thus Vygotsky, although acknowledging a decline in creative productivity during adolescence, still saw this stage of creativity as more mature and balanced, and therefore richer, than the uninhibited creativity of younger children. This view is entirely consistent with current descriptions of creativity as divergent and convergent (Bailin, 1994; Runco, 1994b). The variation during adolescence is largely consistent with findings from Smith and Carlsson (1985). In a continuation of their earlier studies, they evaluated the creativity of 12- to 16-year-old children. A significant decline in strong creativity signs was found for 12-year-old subjects followed by a gradual increase at 14 to 15 years, and a more marked increase at 16 years. Smith and Carlsson felt that only the oldest subjects (16 years) had adopted the flexible, adult strategies and self-reliance needed to achieve a balance between their inward, subjective worlds and the outside reality.

Recall that Smith and Carlsson (1983) emphasized subjective processes, whereas Harrington et al. (1983) and Runco et al. (1991) suggested that creative ideas are not dependent on the objective and immediate environment. The psychodynamic theories of Kris (1952) and Rothenberg (1990a) emphasize preconscious processes (e.g., regression in the service of the ego or Janusian thinking) and material, and they therefore support the view of creativity as personal and subjective. Vygotsky apparently believed that mature creativity was *both* subjective and objective.

This makes good sense, but there is a methodological issue. In fact, it might be viewed as a bias in the research. More and more researchers are emphasizing objective instances of creativity. Quantitative investigations are preferred, as are studies of "unambiguous cases" and eminent creative individuals. Our hope is that the subjective side of creativity, noted by Smith and Carlsson, Vygotsky, and the psychodynamic theorists, will earn greater respect. Realistically, creativity is in part subjective (Barron, 1995; Runco, in press-b), and we will not

---

[8]While on the topic of aesthetics, Bloom (1961) found that artistic interests became stable about around age 17. Frois and Eysenck (1995) found stability of aesthetic judgments between ages 10 and 15.

understand it without tolerating subjectivity in the research. This is particularly true for developmental theories. The creativity of children may only qualify as such if we acknowledge that originality and appropriateness must be defined relative to individual children rather than relative to larger, objective norms.

Surely it is reasonable to view a child's subjective creative acts as creative, but at the same time view accomplishments during adulthood, be they personal, workaday, or eminent, as creative. The difference is merely the frame of reference. For the child, the comparative standard is the child him- or herself. Many creative acts are original and useful, if only for that individual child. Adult acts are creative in the same sense of being original and useful, although the standard may differ (perhaps being the individual's ouevre, or even a movement or genre). Adults are also social and expressive, having an impact on others. What we are suggesting may sound like a kind of "sliding scale," but that should not surprise anyone, given that relative norms are already used in creativity research. Entire domains of creativity (e.g., any of the arts) are only valued, respected, appreciated, and encouraged in certain sociohistorical situations (Csikszentmihalyi, 1990), and this is a kind of relativity. Indeed, all judgments of creativity involve some relativity (Runco & Chand, 1994), and developmentalists should not therefore shy away from an age-relative scale when studying trends and slumps. In fact, we should encourage it, given the need to recognize that all creativity is at least partly subjective.

Some disagreements about the exact ages of slumps or declines in creativity during childhood may reflect the assessments used. Torrance's (1962, 1963, 1968) work was based on quantitative divergent thinking, and he found different trends for the various indices. Urban (1991) included qualitative aspects of creative thought, and he replicated the drop noted by Torrance (1962, 1963). Smith and Carlsson (1983) utilized the perceptgenesis technique, which emphasizes subjective creative processes, and they found a decline at early school entry and an increase at 10-11 years. Smith and Carlsson (1985) noted a decline at 12 years and then another significant increase at 16 years. In their work on artistic development, Rosenblatt and Winner (1988) noted a decline during the conventional years (8 to 10 years old) and an increase during the postconventional years (beginning at around 12 years old). Daugherty (1993) found mostly declines between 3 and 6 years, and Camp (1993) reported declines from 6 to 12 years. The specific aspect of creativity evaluated in these studies seems to have determined which trends were observed.

Is this true of the trends in adulthood? Is there just one peak in adulthood? Are conventions and social experiences important, as they are in childhood?

ADULTHOOD TRENDS

Creative performances in adulthood show both slumps and peaks, and like the trends during childhood, the ages of transitions seem to depend on how creativity is defined and measured. The specific ages and explanations are reviewed in this section.

In the study cited earlier, Smolucha and Smolucha (1985) concluded that the peak of creative thinking is during young adulthood, between 21 and 29 years. This is strikingly similar to the peak of *fluid intelligence*, the biologically based capacity that is thought to be involved in most intellectual functioning (Cattell & Butcher, 1968; Horn, 1979). However, if creative capacities dropped because of declines in fluid intelligence, all expressions of that capacity would be expected to drop. This apparently does not happen. Guilford (1967), for example, suggested that flexibility shows a particular loss, but that different kinds of flexibility have different rates of loss. Using terms from Guilford's own structure of intellect (SOI) model, the flexibility of classes is lost at a different rate than is the flexibility of transformations. Such differences might come as no surprise given that the different manifestations of divergent thinking develop at different ages (Jaquish & Ripple, 1984-85; Lopez et al., 1993; Torrance, 1968), but they are contrary to the earlier suggestion about a general loss. Guilford also suggested that different rates of loss may occur at different levels of ability, but that in general the peak of fluency and originality is just past age 30. The idea of levels of ability supports our argument about the importance of individual differences. Incidentally, it is also consistent with Wechsler's (1958) concept of a *deterioration quotient*. He explained deterioration in terms of education, occupation, and the loss of cells, and he suggested that losses could be calculated for each individual, much like an IQ.

Abra (1989), Chown (1961), and Rubenson and Runco (1992) also pointed to flexibility as a prime contributor to developmental changes in adulthood. Abra described the increased rigidity of older individuals and cited physiological changes, increased anxiety, and a decline in self-esteem as contributing factors. Chown (1961) found increases in flexibility until approximately age 40, and then stable flexibility scores until approximately 55 years of age. Flexibility, in his view, leads to originality, the sine qua non of creativity. We might debate the connection between flexibility and originality, with evidence in our favor (Runco, 1985; Runco & Okuda, 1991), but this does not detract from the usefulness of flexibility. On the contrary; it makes its independence more important and useful.

Abra (1989) and Guilford (1967, chap. 18) also noted memory difficulties, with Guilford specifically pointing to problems of encoding rather than retrieving. This is a difficult argument to evaluate because memory can either inhibit or facilitate creativity (Runco & Chand, 1995). It can inhibit creative thinking when the individual relies on previous experience and does not look to new and original ideas and insights. It can facilitate creative thinking if the individual uses previous experience, but as a point of departure and not to the exclusion of originality.[9] The individual might draw information from his or her experience, but at the same time consider hypothetical or analogical options.

About 10 years after Guilford's (1967) review, Alpaugh and Birren (1977; Alpaugh, Renner, & Birren, 1976) administered several SOI divergent production tests to a group of teachers between the ages of 20 and 83 years. Results showed a clear decline in performance. Significantly, Alpaugh and Birren also found a decline in scores on the Barron-Welsh Art Scale (BWAS). No decline was found in intelligence test scores, implying that divergent thinking and BWAS trends were not caused by a loss of fluid intelligence or any other general intellectual process. As just noted, if declines in divergent thinking occurred because of a drop in fluid abilities, more general declines in other intellectual areas would also be apparent. Still, Alpaugh and Birren relied on cross-sectional data. There was, then, a possibility that declines reflected differences between groups. If 30-year-old individuals were compared with 60-year-old individuals, for example, differences might reflect the average educational attainment within the two groups, in addition to or instead of changes in intellectual potential or capacity.

Ripple and Jaquish (1982) took a cross-cultural approach and compared four groups from the United States and South Africa. Two were adult groups (18-25 vs. 26-39 years of age); one was a group of 13-17-year-old adolescents, and one a group of 9-12-year-old children. The samples from the United States and South Africa had been matched in terms of age, sex, and socioeconomic status (SES). Everyone received open-ended tests with acoustic stimuli. These were scored for fluency, originality, and flexibility. Results indicated that developmental trends were similar in samples from the South Africa and the United States, with increases up to young adulthood and then a decrease. Like the findings from Smolucha and Smolucha (1985), the drop was apparent in young adults—here between the ages of 26 and 39. The drops reported by Ripple and Jaquish (1982) were not all that dramatic; mean scores for

---

[9]It is for reasons like this that we cannot equate development with increased experience, nor even accurately predict one from the other (e.g., developmental level from experience). Though experience is tied to expertise, and expertise typically contributes to creative potential (Rubenson & Runco, 1992), more experience is not always a good thing, as this discussion of memory brings out (see Martinsen, 1995).

the 26-39-year-old adults were comparable to those of the adolescents. Interestingly, the South African groups had higher fluency scores than the U.S. groups, but the U.S. groups had higher originality scores than the South African groups. The originality scores of the U.S. samples were approximately three times higher than those of the South Africans, and this held true of all four age groups.

Jaquish and Ripple (1984-85) compared scores from Chinese and U.S. samples. Auditory tests were again used. Findings indicated that the Chinese adolescents (13 to 17 years) earned higher fluency and flexibility scores than children (9 to 12 years) and other adults (18 to 60 years). Chinese adults (ages 26-39 years) had the highest originality scores. In the U.S. samples, all three scores were highest in the middle adult (ages 40-60 years) age group. Each score from the U.S. samples was higher than the corresponding score from the same-aged Chinese samples. These findings suggest that young adults do well on tests of originality, but they are difficult to interpret given the unusual acoustic test. It was acoustical in the sense that the stimuli were auditory rather than verbal or visual. Apparently, it was similar to the Sounds and Images test (Khatena & Torrance, 1973), but even this is not all that commonly used. Ripple and Jaquish were well aware of the potential limitations of their work, and they even conceded that it "might be argued that this is not a cross-cultural study at all" (p. 99). To their credit they based their conclusions more on the pattern of age differences instead of the magnitude of the differences between cultures.

It is quite possible that differences among groups reflect individual and group differences in reactions to tests and testing (Guilford, 1967, chap. 18; Kogan, 1973; Ripple & Jaquish, 1982; Romaniuk & Romaniuk, 1981). There is, for instance, a possibility older individuals think as originally or flexibly as younger individuals, but do so at a slower rate and therefore earn relatively low scores on tests with temporal constraints. Performance may also be influenced by examinees' familiarity with the test questions, topics, or stimuli, with higher familiarity leading to less original responses (Romaniuk & Romaniuk, 1981; Runco & Albert, 1985). When individuals are familiar with a task or problem, they may rely on ideas and solutions that have been suggested or discovered before—that is, by ideas that are preconceived and unoriginal. (This is what we suggested earlier when we questioned the role of memory.) Individuals undoubtedly become increasingly familiar with certain problems, situations, and stimuli as they grow older, and it would thus be very difficult to find tasks about which young and old examinees have equal familiarity. Older individuals would typically be penalized, but it is because they can rely on familiar routines, reactions, and responses rather than because of a loss of skill.

Older individuals may also be penalized because of their lack of familiarity with testing. Most younger individuals have experience with testing in education and thus know how to take tests. Some older individuals, on the other hand, may not have had much experience with tests. As Guilford (1967, chap. 18) explained it, older individuals are less likely to have the *test wiseness* and strategies for success that younger individuals often have, because of their experience with educational examinations. Test wiseness has recently gained credibility (Benson, Urman, & Hocevar, 1986), perhaps in part because of the respect now widely given to metacognitive components of intelligence and creativity (Jausovec, 1994; Runco, 1994a). In addition to its reflecting familiarity or lack thereof, metacognition represents yet another relevant individual difference variable. Additional confounding might occur as a result of age differences in perceptions of the degree to which tasks are challenging and fun, and the degree to which the testing itself is comfortable for examinees (Kogan, 1973; Romaniuk & Romaniuk, 1981). These potential issues—familiarity, speed, test wiseness, and so on—are potential confounds in all cross-sectional research.

It was for this reason that McCrae et al. (1987) examined longitudinal and sequential data, along with cross-sectional data. These were collected from 278 of 825 participants (ages 17 to 101 years) over a 6-year interval. McCrae et al. administered several SOI divergent production tests and found clear declines as a function of age. A test of word fluency showed a peak at approximately age 24, but all others had peaks between 34 and 40. McCrae et al. concluded that "there are true maturational declines in divergent thinking abilities. However, there is no support for the hypothesis that these abilities increase in early adulthood; in this sample, there were cross-sectional declines for all of the groups" (p. 133). This particular result, with a decline across adult groups, is contrary to the findings of Jaquish and Ripple (1984-1985) and Smolucha and Smolucha (1985), but is consistent with the general declines in adulthood reported by Bromley (1956), Dennis (1966), Lehman (1962, 1966), and Simonton (1975). Simonton's (1975) findings of a peak and then a decline in creative performances are especially convincing because he addressed both cross-cultural and "transhistorical invariance."

Lindauer (1992, 1993) presented a much more optimistic view of creativity during adulthood. He showed that artists—at least eminent artists—often do their best work, even producing masterpieces, late in life. He concluded that

> The relatively late time period in which creativity peaked, and its continuation over several decades . . . are encouraging signs for the life-long maintenance of cognitive abilities. Assuming that the abili-

> ties found in artists are normally distributed, then the development and expression of creative potential should be similar in other kinds of artists and in creative people in general. (Lindauer, 1993, p. 236)

He supported our contention of individual differences when he wrote that

> Generalizations about the exact ages at which creativity is at it highest point, and whether or not there are single or several points at which it declines, are not easily made. Differences between the productivity patterns for specific artists and for artists as a group, indicate that records of achievement are highly individualistic. (pp. 236-237)

Lindauer (1992, 1993) defined creativity in terms of unambiguously creative products. His results therefore refute the claim that the optimistic theories of development rely on personal and subjective assessments of potential, and that research using actual performance measures tends to find decrements (cf. Romaniuk & Romaniuk, 1981). Like Lindauer, Dudek and Hall (1991) presented optimistic results, and they too used measures of actual performance. They assessed architectural work, along with personality, and they found that talented architects often continue working productively and creatively well into the eighth and ninth decades of their lives.

Declines occur, but they are far from universal. Some individuals have steady declines; others have no apparent slumps, even late in life. Why does a decline occur, when it does occur?

As Romaniuk and Romaniuk (1981) explained it,

> The decline in creative production [may be explained in terms of] . . . reduced physical or mental energy, declining sensory capacity, illness, increased competition and changes in motivation, interest or intellectual curiosity. More specifically, changes in physical vigor or sensory processes brought on by normal biological decline or disease processes may set a limit on an individual's creative accomplishments but not affect the person's creative ability. (p. 368)

This view relies on the same distinction between capacity or potential and performance or production that we used in the introduction to this chapter. Of most importance at this point might be that a drop in productivity, when it occurs, can fairly easily be explained in terms of changes in motivation, incentives, and effort. It might be extracognitive or conative. A drop in capacity, on the other hand, suggests an actual loss of potential.

Extracognitive and Conative Influences

Some individual differences are undoubtedly more a reflection of conative changes than cognitive losses. Abra (1989) listed persistence, thoughts of mortality, selfishness, naivete, self-confidence, and insecurity as influences on changes in creativity as a function of age, and each of these is extracognitive. Persistence changes, in Abra's view, as "energy and stamina" change. It also reflects decrements in an individual's "willingness to battle frustrations," and it may reflect the tendency for adults to spread and divide their resources. A young scientist might be able to focus on research, for example, but then earns tenure and becomes more involved in personnel committees and university and community service. Each of these can detract from his or her concentration, and each can take time away from the research itself (cf. Root-Bernstein et al., 1993; Rubenson & Runco, 1992). Similar arguments might be made for an artist who teaches, writes, or judges more as he or she grows older.

An interplay between these cognitive (e.g., memory, rigidity) and conative (decisions following motives) changes is suggested by Mumford's (1984; Mumford, Olsen, & James, 1989) description of changes in an individual's responsibilities and options, with demands during early adulthood (e.g., finding a career or place of employment, raising children) allowing the individual to remain prepared for cognitive shifts and thereby insights. Mumford proposed that one result of this preparedness is the tendency for major breakthroughs to come from young researchers. It is as if young individuals are more adaptable because they respond to demands placed on them, and at the same time this adaptability influences their work and their intellectual flexibility. Rubenson and Runco (1992) explained changes in flexibility in terms of similar "active personal investments." They added that older individuals tend to have invested more of their time and energy into a given line of thought, and hence changes may cause some *depreciation* of their intellectual holdings (Rubenson & Runco, 1992). The older individual might therefore be expected to be less open to change and less flexible.

Abra (1989) described how mortality might weigh heavily on individuals as they move through adulthood, with a corresponding increase in certain motives, such as the *will to self immortalization* (Rank, 1932), *generativity* (Erikson, 1950), or simply the desire to leave something behind. Granted, these concerns may change the content of an individual's work more than its quantity. There is a great deal of evidence that artistic themes change in late adulthood, with a clear *old-age style* (Arnheim, 1990; Cohen-Shalev, 1989; Lindauer, 1992, 1993; Schwebel, 1993). Lindauer (1993) suggested that style "is one of the most intractable features of art" (p. 221), and he noted that old-age style often reflects an "abrupt shift in creative expression" (p. 211). Schwebel (1993) also described developmental patterns in style and the content of an artist's work, but his focus was specifically on fluctuations in an artist's moral concerns, and his examples were primarily from literature.

The connection between selfishness and creativity, noted by Abra (1989), is supported by Gardner's (1993) findings of *self-promotion* by eminent individuals. Still, these findings have unknown generality, and selfishness may be difficult to reconcile with common views of creative effort. Perhaps it is easier to view this association by considering selflessness rather than selfishness. We suggest this because creativity can be tied to selfless and moral acts (Gruber, 1993a; Runco, 1993c), but even more clearly because of the generativity (Erikson, 1950), alluded to earlier. The self-actualizing tendencies of creative individuals may also be pertinent (Maslow, 1971; Rogers, 1961; Runco, Ebersole, & Mraz, 1991). By definition, self-actualization requires an acceptance of one's self; and according to Rogers, it is inextricable from creativity and a function of development. This raises the possibility that developmental trends in creativity follow from specific psychological changes, with changes in self-actualization and the like actually underlying and determining changes in creative performances. If selflessness depends on self-esteem, the empirical research of Jaquish and Ripple (1980, 1981) is also supportive; they found self-esteem to be the best predictor of changes in divergent thinking. They explained it in terms of the confidence that is needed to express one's self. Self-esteem is also suggested by descriptions of creative women being highly independent and mature in their ego development (Helson, 1990, in press-a, in press-b).

Perhaps the most interesting of Abra's (1989) categories is the one labeled *naivete*. This is not indicative of a lack of experience, but rather a way of describing how creative individuals resemble children. In which specific ways are they like children? Picasso's famous remark about learning to paint like a child is relevant, as is the research cited earlier that children are unconventional in their art and ideation, and Root-Bernstein et al.'s (1993) findings that long-term, high-impact scientists systematically change their research areas. These systematic changes could easily contribute to a youthful enthusiasm and preclude rigidity. Abra (1989) cited theories of regression in the service of the ego (Kris, 1952) as evidence of immaturity, but he was quick to add that creativity is not just childlike thinking. It is not just free expression and play but instead requires a "critical detachment provided by the ego" (p. 115). Recall in this regard Vygotsky's theory about a balance of imagination and logic (Ayman-Nolley, 1992), with logic being a mature skill. Creativity may be childlike in some ways, but clearly it is not entirely that. For the most part it is merely a useful metaphor to describe the creativity of an adult as childlike.

Both cognitive and conative factors influence creativity, but to be realistic we should remember that the so-called nonintellective factors are not entirely distinct from the intellective factors. Consider flexibility: It is typically viewed as a cognitive capacity, but it is not entirely that. Flexibility and its antithesis, rigidity, both are tied to personality and personal preferences (McCrae, 1987). Or consider intrinsic motivation, which is an important affective component of creativity (Runco, 1993b), but requires a *cognitive* appraisal. An individual is not disturbed or motivated by a problem unless he or she perceives a situation that is in fact interpreted as problematic (Runco, 1994a).

The Direction of Effect

Much of the research in this area assumed one direction of effect, with creativity changing *as a result of* experience and maturation. Creativity is not, however, just a result of development; it is also a *determinant* of it. This is implied by findings about the role of intentions, preferences, and decisions, and is also supported by theories that creative activity can contribute to psychological growth (Miller & Karl, 1993; Rhodes, 1990; Wikstrom, Theorell, & Sandstrom, 1992). Simplifying the argument some, creativity can allow the individual to deal successfully with life's demands and challenges, the result being a kind of growth. As Smith and van der Meer (1990) put it, creative adults have

> less negative attitudes toward aging and do not unequivocally close the door to life after death. Their attitude to illness appears to be less defensive, probably because they are able to handle their fears in a more constructive way. . . . [They are] not only more flexible [than uncreative individuals] but also more emotional, and consequently, less marred by boredom. (pp. 263-264)

A parallel notion is implicit in the Piagetian notion of creativity as the construction of understandings (i.e., creation in the literal sense).

An alternative way to describe this direction of effect is to think of individuals as not merely reacting and passively absorbing experience, but instead bringing something to their experiences, or even using their talents to create experiences (Albert & Runco, 1989; Rubenson & Runco, 1992; Scarr & McCartney, 1983). They might bring preferences that direct them to invest in their own creative potential (Rubenson & Runco, 1992).[10] An individual might, for instance, decide to enroll in an

---

[10]This may sound like an operant approach to creativity, with returns being reinforcers, but the psychoeconomic approach gives much greater weight to the active investments an individual might make in his or her own creativity than

art class or attend a writer's workshop. This view further substantiates our ideas about the conative processes and the role of choice in creativity. For a review of supporting literature, see Runco, Johnson, and Gaynor (in press).

This direction of effect, with creativity leading to particular attitudes, perceptions, and viewpoints, is apparent in descriptions of creativity as adaptability, coping, and resilience (Flach, 1990; Gedo, this volume; Maslow, 1971; Richards, 1990; Rogers, 1961; Runco, 1994a; Runco, Ebersole, & Mraz, 1991; Wikstrom et al., 1992). Each of these assumes growth as a result of creative activity.

This issue of effects is related to the more general issue concerning the relationships between health and creativity. In late adulthood, for example, it is possible that deteriorating health inhibits the efficiency of the individual's information processing, which in turn inhibits his or her potential for creative insight. Creative thinking, on the other hand, might help minimize the stress that contributes to ill health (Mraz & Runco, 1994; Smith & van der Meer, 1990). The different possible directions of effect may explain why there is a controversy about the relationship of stress and creativity: Simonton (1977) and Kaun (1991) reported that stress can interfere with creativity, but Mumford (1984) described how responsibilities and activities, which can be stressful, can also insure that an individual continues to restructure his or her thinking and remain adaptive.

Kaun (1991) presented a very clear example of how creative work can be detrimental to one's health. He suggested that creative work can lead to certain leisure activities, which in turn can lead to certain unhealthful tendencies. This progression seems to be especially clear in the case of writers, and they are indeed the group with the lowest lifespan. In Kaun's (1991) sample, writers lived an average of 61.7 years, with cartoonists (67.9), musicians (68.9), and architects (69.4) the next youngest to die. These figures are lower than those representing composers, conductors, dancers, singers, painters, and photographers.

Year of birth may be relevant to such comparisons, given the improvements in health and economic standards, yet Kaun (1991) suggested that the benefits are offset by the increasing stress that is placed

---

does the operant approach. The individual does not necessarily respond according to the absolute potency of the benefit, but takes a variety of personal concerns into account. This is especially pertinent to present purposes because age itself also influences how an individual will respond (e.g., benefits have marginal returns, and individuals might have a greater variety of opportunity costs as they mature). This view is, then, closer to the theory of bidirectional influence (Albert & Runco, 1989; Scarr & McCartney, 1983) than it is to operant theory (see Runco, 1993b).

on artists. Kaun suggested, for instance, that writers might be frustrated by the lack of immediate gratification. Unlike performing artists, writers often work years before they have a product to show for their efforts. One might presume that most or all writers receive some gratification while they work and are thus not dependent on the product of their efforts, but Kaun suggested that writers have few significant social interactions while working and thus have little opportunity for reinforcement. He cited Andreasen and Canter's (1974) data on the dissatisfaction of writers as suggesting that they do not enjoy the actual writing. (He will no doubt appreciate Abra's [in press] quotation of the writer who said, "Sure, writing is easy. . . . Just sit at a typewriter and open an artery!") Kaun also suggested that "creative writing provides the least stimulation to all the senses save the imagination" (p. 388), the implication being that this too contributes to dissatisfaction. For developmentalists (and anyone concerned about the health of writers), the most interesting part of Kaun's argument may be that writers "come to rely heavily on leisure activity as a source of immediate satisfaction" (p. 388) and the suggestion that this often leads them to lifestyles that are "generally ill-suited to good health." Hence the high mortality rate.

Kaun's (1991) suggestions are contrary to the theories cited earlier showing a positive relationship between creativity and resilience or coping (Flach, 1990; Richards, 1990; Runco, 1994a), although he was discussing long-term lifestyle rather than short-term adaptation. We should also mention Simonton's (1983, 1985, 1988, 1990) data on the longevity of eminently creative individuals. They often live a very long time. Indeed, from his historiometric findings Simonton inferred that three things are critical for achieving eminence: starting at a young age, producing a great deal on a regular basis, and living a long time. If nothing else, when an individual lives a long time he or she has many opportunities.

Kaun's (1991) view is compatible with what was said earlier about the role of intentions and choice for creativity. Choices might lead an individual to devote his or her life to a particular area of study, and this in turn will determine what experiences he or she will have. An individual motivated to play the piano might practice and compose to the exclusion of nearly all else, just as a scientist might read everything in his or her field to the exclusion of fiction and the daily newspaper. Creative individuals are well known for such enthusiasms (Simonton, 1984, chap. 6), although some apparently read outside their disciplines (Gruber, 1993b; Skinner, 1983) and change the foci of their work from time to time (Root-Bernstein et al., 1993). Albert (1994) described how creative individuals are often totally immersed in their work, which would require a kind of enthusiasm.

Gruber (1993b) and Milgram and Hong (1994) also believed that leisure activity is critical for understanding creativity. Gruber (1993b) suggested that much can be learned by studying *binges* of interest that occur in childhood, and Milgram and Hong argued that the leisure-time activities of children and adolescents may be the best predictors of adult creative achievement. Leisure activities are by definition intrinsically motivated, and predictions using them (e.g., activity at age 15 as a predictor of achievement at age 40) should therefore be very accurate, at least if the criterion also reflects intrinsic motivation. In both of these arguments we again see that an individual's choices, preferences, and inclinations have a huge impact on developmental trends (including expected lifespan).

DISCUSSION

Various slumps of creative potential and performance occur throughout the lifespan. Torrance (1968) described a fourth-grade slump that seems to be the most commonly recognized developmental change, and that is consistent with several areas of research (e.g., on the development of art). However, like Urban (1991) and Smith and Carlsson (1990), Torrance actually saw several peaks and troughs, rather than one slump. Multiple slumps and peaks are also characteristic of adulthood. Peaks have been uncovered in the late 20s, for example, and for some individuals there is another peak in the 80s and 90s (Dudek & Hall, 1991; Lindauer, 1992, 1993). Given the variety of measures used and the lack of replication, most trends are at this point merely suggestive, or at best descriptive of certain groups.

There are certain points of consensus in the research. One is in the research on trends occurring during childhood: It is agreement about the relevance of *conventionality*. Conventions determine what is considered appropriate, for example, and they are at the heart of Gardner's (1982) theory of rule mastery and the literal stage, Smith's (Smith & Carlsson, 1983; Smith & van der Meer, 1990) theory of subjective interpretations, Runco's (1991; Runco & Smith, 1990; Runco & Vega, 1990) theory of evaluations and valuations, and, of course, Rosenblatt and Winner's (1988) theory of the movement from preconventional to postconventional thinking in the production and appreciation of art. The importance of autonomy, which is a kind of independence from conventions, is also widely recognized (e.g., Albert & Runco, 1989; Rank, 1932, 1936). With this in mind Sheldon (in press) recently reiterated Otto Rank's view that "to achieve our creative potential we must first overcome our social conditioning and develop a strong and autonomous will."

Conventions are also recognized in cross-cultural research on creativity. Jaquish and Ripple (1984-85), for example, explained significant differences in the divergent thinking of individuals from the United States and China in terms of the tendency in the United States to produce many ideas with a "willingness to depart from conventionally accepted established behavior" (p. 9). The tendency of the Chinese was to avoid mistakes. A similar conclusion was offered by Aviram and Milgram (1977) to explain differences among U.S., Soviet, and Israeli children.

Creativity is often defined in terms of originality, with originality in turn defined relative to specific norms. Conventions are also tied to norms and expectations for individuals at particular ages: A child is expected to do certain things, whereas an adolescent or adult is expected to do very different things. Expectations about everything from language to morality reflect age-appropriate norms, which is why we suggested earlier that the original behavior of children can be called *creative* even if it is not original by adult norms (cf. Dudek, 1974; Smith & van der Meer, 1990; Wolf & Larson, 1981).

An important methodological point of agreement concerns divergent thinking. Research with both children (Lopez et al., 1993; Torrance, 1962, 1963) and adults (Guilford, 1967; Jaquish & Ripple, 1981; McCrae et al., 1987) suggests that the various indices of divergent thinking develop and decline at different rates. In addition to suggesting something about cognitive growth, these differences support the discriminant validity of the various indices. Several researchers have suggested that only fluency scores be used when scoring divergent thinking tests because the indices are often highly correlated; others argue that the indices are distinct. The work reviewed herein supports the distinctiveness of the indices of thinking and suggests that they should be treated separately in research and practice. If fluency alone is used, as is often the case, important trends or products may be overlooked. The distinctiveness of the indices also has developmental significance, especially given that it is flexibility that shows the most obvious change (Guilford, 1967; Lopez et al., 1993). Flexibility may be the dimension of divergent thinking that is the most closely tied to psychological health, and with its role in adaptability (Mraz & Runco, 1994), it may be the most sensitive to experience. The point is that more attention should probably be given to flexibility. More attention might also be given to analogical thinking and associative tendencies (Finke, this volume). Not much has been done to track trends in the use of analogies and associations, although other areas of research show that both play a role in some creative insights.

The evidence for individual differences suggests that slumps in creativity are not inevitable. A useful way to think about them relies on the concept of *reaction range*. That term is often used to describe nature-nurture interactions, and on that general level it can be applied to creativity. Creative performances no doubt reflect both nature *and* nurture. Our suggestion is to turn around the typical reaction range argument. Usually it is used to explain how certain abilities or aptitudes are expressed to the degree that potentials are fulfilled—potential determining the range and nurturance determining the reaction. But slumps can be viewed as *potential slumps*. In this light, the degree of drop is the individual's reaction to his or her environment and experience. Helson (in press-a) seemed to be describing something like this in her argument about culture exaggerating the sex differences that are determined by biology and early socialization, and Gaines (1983) explicitly described individual differences in reactions to social pressures.

The theories that emphasize social experience, such as Vygotsky's (Ayman-Nolley, 1992; Smolucha, 1992a), imply that parents and teachers must assume a large responsibility for nurturing creativity, perhaps by encouraging children to persist in creative activities, even in the difficult literal stage. Given what was said earlier about balanced modes of thought, parents and teachers should focus on a balance of convergent and divergent thinking, in addition to a balance of fact and possibility and a balance of structure and flexibility (see Runco & Okuda, 1993). During adulthood, it may be the individual him- or herself who needs to make the most of his or her experience. Langer's (1988) ideas about *mindfulness*, and Skinner's (1983) ideas about what he called *managing old age* will be useful in this regard, at least for those interested in maintaining productivity and originality (also see Gott, 1992, 1993; Torrance, Clements, & Goff, 1989). In fact, Langer's and Skinner's ideas fit nicely with our suggestions about conative developmental factors and the impact of active, intentional choices for the expression of creativity. Hogg (1993) described how specific leisure activities, such as gardening, benefit individuals in the later years.

The most surprising debate in this area of research is that concerning the possibility that children's creativity is not actually creative. Dudek (1974), quoted earlier in this chapter, argued that children are refreshingly expressive, but not truly creative. Similarly, Smith and Carlsson (1990) and Rothenberg (1990b) argued that children are not creative until age 10. Arlin (1975) described problem finding as a postformal operational accomplishment, the implication being that real-world creative performance is impossible until late adolescence. Wolf and Larson (1981) suggested that the behaviors labeled *creative* by adults are simply unexpected, and perhaps even accidental. In this view children do certain things because they do not know any better, and adults label such unexpected behavior *creative*. Consider the 3-year-old child who describes a broken toy car as "badly hurt." This is incorrect in the sense that the car does not have feeling (must we really explain that?), but the child's phrase could be interpreted as creative because it does communicate the important idea, and it accomplishes it in an unusual manner. Is "badly hurt" a mistake or a creative expression? Perhaps it is both. It can be viewed as uncreative only if intentions are prerequisite for creativity. We believe that intentions are important, but we are referring to intentions to understand one's self or one's experience, not intentions to achieve or impress.

One corollary of the theory emphasizing intentionality is that children's creativity should be relegated (or at least labeled differently) until we can be certain about it. This notion underlies the suggestion that creativity research should focus on unambiguous cases, and in particular on eminent adults (reviewed by Runco, in press-b). The underlying methodological assumption is that research should focus on objective instances of creativity. This is an important point because it dictates which phenomena can be recognized as legitimate for study. If only unambiguous cases of creativity are studied, only actual performance will be studied, and potential will be ignored. Additionally, only recognized domains of performance, such as art, will be recognized.[11] If only objective instances of creativity are studied, research is pushed toward products that allow consensual assessments (Amabile, 1990; Hennessey, in press) and away from nonheroic cases and everyday creative activities (Cropley, 1990; Richards, 1990). Subjective instances of creativity, noted by Piaget and Vygotsky and characteristic of so much of children's behavior, will be ignored.

If we accept the view that children's creative acts are accidental and the premise that creativity must have purpose, we force a division between the activities of children and those of adults and preclude the possibility of developing theories that define creativity along a lifespan developmental continuum (e.g., Cohen, 1989; Korzenik, 1992; Pariser, 1991). This would be a significant setback, and one we have tried to avoid by arguing throughout this chapter that creativity can be viewed as a function of an individual's decisions, choices, inclinations, and preferences. Creativity is influenced by decisions about what to study, what to produce, what to practice, what to share, and so on (Runco et al., in

---

[11]Actually, various age trends have been studied within a variety of domains. Simonton focused on literary creativity (Simonton, 1975) and classical composition (1989); Lindauer (1992, 1993) and Crosson and Robertson-Tchabo (1983) focused on visual art; Kaun (1991) focused on writers; and numerous investigations have focused on scientists (Cole, 1979; Dennis, 1958) or even psychology in particular (Lehman, 1966; Simonton, 1985; Zusne, 1976). Rothenberg (1990b) suggested that "whereas activity in visual art may generally decline at the time of adolescence, music and literary pursuits do not" (pp. 419-420).

press). Moreover, it makes the most sense to us that the mechanisms that allow the child to behave in an original and adaptive manner may be the same that allow the adult—even the eminent creator—to discover a creative breakthrough.

Surely children's preferences and inclinations have an impact on their development and their creativity. In the simplest case, the common choice for conventional behaviors (or preference for fitting in and behaving as expected) leads many children to conform and think in literal fashion, and this probably causes changes in ideational patterns (perhaps including those described as the fourth-grade slump) and artistic expression. In the divergent thinking research such changes are typically explained in terms of changes in the generation of ideas, but it is more likely that the potential to *generate* ideas does not change with age but instead changes arise in how the ideas are *selected* and shared. These selections reflect some sort of skill or strategy (Runco, 1992) in addition to preferences and inclinations (Johnson, 1985; Runco & Chand, 1994; Runco et al., in press).

Apparently creativity during childhood or adulthood can be maximized by certain decisions, but although decisions and conative changes may help explain trends occurring across the lifespan, they are often overlooked in theories of creativity. Only the work on style as a function of age (Arnheim, 1990; Cohen-Shalev, 1986, 1989; Kogan 1973; Lindauer, 1992, 1993; Mumford, 1984) and the work of Root-Bernstein et al. (1993) on research strategies seems to explicitly acknowledge the importance of decision making and inclination. In their comparison of high- and low-impact scientists, Root-Bernstein et al. (1993) found that

> Creativity and productivity do not necessarily decline with age. Some very successful scientists retain a youthful profile of scientific research well into old age. . . . Long-term, high-impact scientists demonstrated that scientific creativity need not decline. But note the apparent reason: These men purposely placed themselves in the position of becoming a novice again every 5 or 10 years. In effect they became mentally young by starting over again. (p. 341)[12]

Surely conative processes are critical for future developmental research on creativity. Such research might even help resolve the confusion surrounding the subjective and the objective manifestations of creativity, or in the terms we started with, the potential for creativity as it is often contrasted with actual performance. Both subjective and objective creative acts reflect the individual's inclinations and decisions.

---

[12]Sadly, the benefits of starting over and diversified studies by an individual are contrary to contemporary pressures for specialization (Root-Bernstein et al., 1993).

FINAL COMMENTS

We have tried to emphasize several questions and themes throughout this review. Given its length, it might be helpful to summarize the main points here:

- Slumps and peaks have been found for both creative potential and for creative performances. The ages of those slumps and peaks vary. Trajectories are often described as multimodal, U-shaped, J-shaped, or as an inverted J.
- Various aspects of creative thinking seem to both develop and decline at different rates. Even the different kinds of flexibility ostensibly change at different rates.
- There are important individual differences in both childhood and adulthood. Not all individuals show declines, just as not all persons fulfill potential and perform in an unambiguously creative fashion. Slumps and declines are therefore themselves potentials and presumably can be understood as having ranges of reaction.
- Creativity at all ages seems to involve certain decisions, choices, and preferences. In childhood, binges of interest and preferences for activities influence the development of creative skills, and in adulthood career choice and styles reflect intentional investments in potential.
- More research is needed on decision making and conative processes. More research is also needed on the development of analogical reasoning, associative tendencies, and evaluative skills. The last of these may explain slumps—at least those in childhood—better than theories emphasizing idea generation.

This review suggests that the developmental trajectory of creativity tends to vary from person to person. Various symbols have been used to describe a typical trajectory, including a U, a J, and an inverted J; but each of these assumes that there is one trajectory that characterizes most individuals. The individual differences are , however, quite significant and should be emphasized. If a symbol is used to describe the developmental of creativity it should be <, the "less than" or inequality sign, and it should be used to describe possible trajectories rather than one typical pattern. Admittedly some persons may develop in a manner suggested by the U, the J, or the inverted J, but each of these is within the boundaries of the inequality sign. There is no one symbol or sign that can adequately describe the developmental trajectory of creativity, but at least the inequality sign captures the idea that the developmental of individuals is extremely varied.

With the focus on development, it is interesting that age is typically not the concern in this area of research. It is too general. Rather, the "concomitants of advancing age need to be studied" (Lehman, 1962, p. 416). Because those concomitants vary from individual to individual, this supports the argument about individual differences. Individual differences must be recognized in theories of development. They have been empirically demonstrated with both adults (Lindauer, 1993; McCrae et al., 1987; Schultz, Kaye, & Hoyer, 1984) and children (Harrington et al., 1983; Torrance, 1968). We may even find that individual differences are so great that group differences (e.g., adolescents vs. young adults) become relatively insignificant. The individual differences also suggest that what we need are *mini-theories*, like those used when studying behavior problems (Kazdin, 1989), but in this context they would focus on the specific contributions to decline or on particular effects. Mini-theories might focus on test wiseness, conventionality, memory, career choice, and so on.

As in many areas of developmental research, longitudinal investigations are sorely needed for a better understanding of trends. Several longitudinal studies of gifted children are currently underway (e.g., Albert & Runco, 1986, 1989; Milgram & Hong, 1994; Subotnik & Arnold, 1994), and these typically include assessments of creativity. Longitudinal studies have their problems, but these are now well recognized (Romaniuk & Romaniuk, 1981; Subotnik & Arnold, 1994). This makes them fairly manageable, and that kind of management will help us to continue making progress toward understanding developmental trends in creativity.

REFERENCES

Abra, J. (1989). Changes in creativity with age: Data, explanations, and further predictions. *International Journal of Aging and Human Development, 28*, 105-126.

Albert, R.S. (1983). Family position and the attainment of eminence. In R.S. Albert (Ed.), *Genius and eminence: The social psychology of creativity and exceptional achievement* (pp. 141-154). New York: Pergamon.

Albert, R.S. (1992, August). *Sensitive periods in a developmental model of the achievement of eminence*. Paper presented at the annual meeting of the American Psychological Association, Washington, DC.

Albert, R.S., & Runco, M.A. (1986). The achievement of eminence: A model of exceptionally gifted boys and their families. In R.J. Sternberg & J.E. Davidson (Eds.), *Conceptions of giftedness* (pp. 332-357). New York: Cambridge University Press.

Albert, R.S., & Runco, M.A. (1989). Independence and cognitive ability in gifted and exceptionally gifted boys. *Journal of Youth and Adolescence, 18,* 221-230.

Alpaugh, P.K., & Birren, J.E. (1977). Variables affecting creative contributions across the adult life span. *Human Development, 20,* 240-248.

Alpaugh, P.K., Renner, V.J., & Birren, J.E. (1976). Age and creativity: Implications for educations and teachers. *Educational Gerontology, 1,* 17-40.

Amabile, T. (1990). Within you, without you: Towards a social psychology of creativity, and beyond. In M.A. Runco & R.S. Albert (Eds.), *Theories of creativity* (pp. 61-91). Newbury Park, CA: Sage.

Andreasen, N.C., & Canter, A. (1974). The creative writer: Psychiatric symptoms and family history. *Comprehensive Psychology, 15,* 123-131.

Arlin, P. (1975). Cognitive development in adulthood: A fifth stage? *Developmental Psychology, 2,* 602-606.

Arnheim, R. (1990). On the late style. In M. Perlmutter (Ed.), *Late life potential* (pp. 113-120). Washington, DC: Gerontological Society of American.

Aviram, A., & Milgram, R.M. (1977). Dogmatism, locus of control, and creativity in children educated in the Soviet Union, the United States, and Israel. *Psychological Reports, 40,* 27-34.

Ayman-Nolley, S. (1992). Vygotsky's perspective on the development of imagination and creativity. *Creativity Research Journal, 5,* 101-109.

Ayman-Nolley, S. (in press). A Piagetian perspective of the dialectical process of creativity. *Creativity Research Journal.*

Bailin, S. (1994). *Achieving extraordinary ends.* Norwood, NJ: Ablex.

Barron, F. (1995). *No rootless flower.* Cresskill, NJ: Hampton Press.

Benson, J., Urman, H., & Hocevar, D. (1986, January). Effects of test-wiseness training and ethnicity on achievement of third- and fifth-grade students. *Measurement and Evaluation in Education,* pp. 154-162.

Bloom, B.S. (Ed.). (1961). *Stability and change in human characteristics.* New York: Wiley.

Bromley, D.B. (1956). Some experimental tests of the effects of age on creative intellectual output. *Journal of Gerontology, 11,* 74-82.

Burt, C.L. (1970). Critical note. In P.E. Vernon (Ed.), *Creativity* (pp. 203-216). New York: Penguin.

Camp, G.C. (1994). A longitudinal study of correlates of creativity. *Creativity Research Journal, 7,* 125-144.

Cattell, R.B., & Butcher, H.J. (1968). *The prediction of achievement and creativity.* New York: Bobbs Merrill.

Chown, S.M. (1961). Age and the rigidities. *Journal of Gerontology, 16,* 353-362.

Cohen, L. (1989). Continuum of adaptive creative behaviors. *Creativity Research Journal, 2,* 169-183.

Cohen-Shalev, A. (1986). Artistic creativity across the adult life span: An alternative approach. *Interchange, 17,* 1-16.

Cohen-Shalev, A. (1989). Old age style: Developmental changes in creative production from a life-span perspective. *Journal of Aging Studies, 3,* 21-37.

Cole, S. (1979). Age and scientific performance. *American Journal of Sociology, 84,* 958-977.

Cousins, N. (1988). *Head first.* New York: Dutton.

Cropley, A.J. (1990). *More ways than one: Fostering creativity.* Norwood, NJ: Ablex.

Crosson, C.W., & Robertson-Tchabo, E.A. (1983). Age and preference for complexity among manifestly creative women. *Human Development, 26,* 149-155.

Csikszentmihalyi, M. (1988). The dangers of originality: Creativity and the artistic process. In M.M. Gedo (Ed.), *Psychoanalytic perspectives on art* (pp. 213-224). Hillsdale, NJ: Analytic Press.

Csikszentmihalyi, M. (in press). The domain of creativity. In M.A. Runco & R.S. Albert (Eds.), *Theories of creativity* (rev. ed.). Cresskill, NJ: Hampton Press.

Daugherty, M. (1993). Creativity and private speech: Developmental trends. *Creativity Research Journal, 6,* 287-296.

Dennis, W. (1958). The age decrement in outstanding contributions: Fact or artifact? *American Psychologist, 13,* 457-460.

Dennis, W. (1966). Creative productivity between the ages of 20 and 80 years. *Journal of Gerontology, 21,* 1-8.

Dobzhansky, T., Ayala, F. J., Stebbins, G.L., & Valentine, J.W. (1977). *Evolution.* San Francisco: Freeman.

Dudek, S.Z. (1974). Creativity in young children: Attitude or ability? *Journal of Creative Behavior, 8,* 282-292.

Dudek, S.Z., & Hall, W. (1991). Personality consistency: Eminent architects 25 years later. *Creativity Research Journal, 4,* 213-232.

Dudek, S.Z., Strobel, M., & Runco, M.A. (1993). Cumulative and proximal influences of the social environment on creative potential. *Journal of Genetic Psychology, 154,* 487-499.

Elkind, D. (1981). *Children and adolescence.* New York: Oxford University Press.

Erikson, E. (1950). *Childhood and society.* New York: Norton.

Flach, F. (1990). Disorders of the pathways involved in the creative process. *Creativity Research Journal, 3,* 158-165.

Friedman, H.W., Tucker, J.S., Tomlinson-Keasey, C., Schwartz, J.E., Wingard, D.L., & Criqui, M.H. (1993). Does childhood personality predict longevity? *Journal of Personality and Social Psychology, 65,* 176-185.

Frois, J.P., & Eysenck, H.J. (1995). The Visual Aesthetic Sensitivity Test as applied to Portuguese children and fine arts students. *Creativity Research Journal, 8,* 277-284.

Gaines, R. (1983). Children's artistic abilities: Fact or fancy? *Journal of Genetic Psychology, 143,* 57-68.

Gardner, H. (1982). *Art, mind, and brain.* New York: Basic Books.

Gardner, H. (1993). *Creating minds.* New York: Basic Books.

Gaynor, J.L.R., & Runco, M.A. (1992). Family size, birth order, age-interval, and the creativity of children. *Journal of Creative Behavior, 26,* 108-118.

Gott, K. (1992). Enhancing creativity in older adults. *Journal of Creative Behavior, 26,* 40-49.

Gott, K. (1993). Creativity and life satisfaction of older adults. *Educational Gerontology, 19,* 241-250.

Gruber, H.E. (1993a). Creativity in the moral domain: Ought implies can implies create. *Creativity Research Journal, 6,* 3-15.

Gruber, H.E. (1993b). *Jean Piaget's ideas about creativity.* Paper presented at the annual meeting of the American Psychological Association, Toronto, Ontario, Canada.

Guilford, J.P. (1967). *The nature of human intelligence.* New York: McGraw Hill.

Harrington, D.M., Block, J., & Block, J.H. (1983). Predicting creativity in preadolescence form divergent thinking in early childhood. *Journal of Personality and Social Psychology, 45,* 609-623.

Helson, R. (in press-a). Creativity in women: Inner and outer views over time. In M.A. Runco & R.S. Albert (Eds.), *Theories of creativity* (rev. ed.). Cresskill, NJ: Hampton Press.

Helson, R. (in press-b). Ego identity and trajectories of productivity in women with creative potential. In C. Adams-Price (Ed.), *Creativity and aging.* New York: Springer.

Hennessey, B.A. (1994). The consensual assessment technique: An examination of the relationship between ratings of product and process creativity. *Creativity Research Journal, 7,* 193-208.

Hocevar, D. (1979). Ideational fluency as a confounding factor in the measurement of originality. *Journal of Educational Psychology, 71,* 191-196.

Hogg, J. (1993). Creative, personal, and social engagement in the later years: Realisation through leisure. *Irish Journal of Psychology, 14,* 204-218.

Hong, E., & Milgram, R.M. (1991). Original thinking in preschool children: A validation of ideational fluency measures. *Creativity Research Journal, 4,* 253-260.

Horn, J.L. (1979). Intelligence—why it grows, why it declines. In L. Willerman & R.G. Turner (Eds.), *Readings about individual and group differences* (pp. 20-31). San Francisco: Freeman.

Jaquish, G.A., & Ripple, R.E. (1980). Divergent thinking and self-esteem in preadolescents and adolescents. *Journal of Youth and Adolescents, 9,* 143-152.

Jaquish, G.A., & Ripple, R.E. (1981). Cognitive creative abilities and self-esteem across the adult life-span. *Human Development 24,* 110-119.

Jaquish, G.A., & Ripple, R.E. (1984-85). A life-span developmental cross-cultural study of divergent thinking abilities. *International Journal of Human Development, 20,* 1-11.

Jausovec, N. (1994). *Flexible thinking: An explanation for individual differences in ability.* Cresskill, NJ: Hampton Press.

Johnson, L.D. (1985). Creative thinking potential: Another example of U-shaped development? *Creative Child and Adult Quarterly, 10,* 146-159.

Kaun, D.E. (1991). Writers die young: The impact of work and leisure on longevity. *Journal of Economic Psychology, 12,* 381-399.

Kazdin, A.E. (1989). Developmental psychopathology: Current research, issues, and directions. *American Psychologist, 44,* 180-187.

Khatena, J., & Torrance, E.P. (1973). *Thinking creatively with sounds and images.* Bensenville, IL: Scholastic Testing Service.

Kogan, N. (1973). Creativity and cognitive style: A life-span perspective. In P.P. Baltes & K.W. Schaie (Eds.), *Life-span developmental psychology: Personality and socialization* (pp. 145-178). New York: Academic Press.

Korzenik, D. (1992). Gifted child artists. *Creativity Research Journal, 5,* 313-319.

Kris, E. (1952). *Psychoanalytic explorations in art.* New York: International Universities Press.

Langer, E. (1988). *Mindfulness.* Reading, MA: Addison-Wesley.

Lehman, H.C. (1962). The creative production rates of present versus past generations of scientists. *Journal of Gerontology, 17,* 409-417.

Lehman, H.C. (1966). The psychologist's most creative years. *Psychology, 21,* 363-369.

Lindauer, M.S. (1992). Creativity in aging artists: Contributions from the humanities to the psychology of old age. *Creativity Research Journal, 5,* 211-231.

Lindauer, M.S. (1993). The span of creativity among long-lived historical artists. *Creativity Research Journal, 6,* 221-239.

Lopez, E.C., Esquivel, G.B., & Houtz, J.C. (1993). The creative skills of culturally and linguistically gifted and diverse students. *Creativity Research Journal, 6,* 401-412.

Martinsen, O. (1995). Cognitive styles and experience in solving insight problems: A replication and extension. *Creativity Research Journal, 8,* 291-298

Maslow, A.H. (1971). *The farther reaches of human nature.* New York: Viking Press.

McCrae, R.R. (1987). Creativity, divergent thinking, and openness to experience. *Journal of Personality and Social Psychology, 52,* 1258-1265.

McCrae, R.R., Arenberg, D., & Costa, P.T., Jr. (1987). Declines in divergent thinking with age: Cross-sectional, longitudinal, and cross-sequential analyses. *Psychology and Aging, 2,* 130-137.

Mednick, S.A. (1962). The associative basis of the creative process. *Psychological Bulletin, 69,* 220-232.

Milgram, R.M., & Hong, E. (1994). Creative thinking and creative performance in adolescents as predictors of creative attainments in adulthood: A follow-up after 18 years. In R. Subotnik & K. Arnold (Eds.), *Beyond Terman: Longitudinal studies of giftedness* (212-228). Norwood, NJ: Ablex.

Miller, N., & Karl, S. (1993). Religious language as transitional phenomena: Lullabies in times of danger. *Creativity Research Journal, 6,* 99-110.

Mraz, W., & Runco, M.A. (1994). Suicide ideation and creative problem solving. *Suicide and Life Threatening Behavior, 24,* 38-47.

Mumford, M.D. (1984). Age and outstanding occupational achievement: Lehman revisited. *Journal of Vocational Behavior, 25,* 225-244.

Mumford, M.D., Olsen, K.A., & James, L.R. (1989). Age-related changes in the likelihood of major contributions. *International Aging and Human Development, 29,* 9-32.

Murdock, M., & Moore, M. (in press). Qualitative creativity research. In M.A. Runco (Ed.), *Creativity research handbook* (Vol. 2). Cresskill, NJ: Hampton Press.

Pariser, D. (1991). Normal and unusual aspects of juvenile artistic development in Klee, Lautrec, and Picasso. *Creativity Research Journal, 4,* 51-65.

Pariser, D. (1993, March). *Not under the lamppost: A review and critique of Piagetian and neo-Piagetian research in the arts.* Paper presented at the meeting of the National Association for Education of the Arts, Chicago, IL.

Rank, O. (1932). *Art and artist.* New York: Knopf.

Rank, O. (1936). *Truth and reality* (J. Taft, Trans.). New York: Knopf.

Rhodes, C. (1990). Growth from deficiency to being creativity. *Creativity Research Journal, 4,* 287-299.

Richards, R. (1990). Everyday creativity, eminent creativity, and health: Afterview for CRJ issues on creativity and health. *Creativity Research Journal, 3,* 300-326.

Ripple, R.E., & Jaquish, G.A. (1981). Fluency, flexibility, and originality in later adulthood. *Educational Gerontology, 7,* 1-10.

Ripple, R.E., & Jaquish, G.A. (1982). Developmental aspects of ideational fluency, flexibility, and originality: South Africa and the United States. *South African Journal of Psychology, 12,* 95-100.

Rogers, C.R. (1961). *On becoming a person.* Boston: Houghton Mifflin.

Romaniuk, J.G., & Romaniuk, M. (1981). Creativity along the life span: A measurement perspective. *Human Development, 24,* 366-381.

Root-Bernstein, R.S., Root-Bernstein, M., & Garnier, H. (1993). Identification of scientists making long-term, high-impact contributions, with notes on their methods of working. *Creativity Research Journal, 6,* 320-343.

Rosenblatt, E., & Winner, E. (1988). The art of children's drawings. *Journal of Aesthetic Education, 22,* 3–15.

Rothenberg, A. (1990a). Creativity, health, and alcoholism. *Creativity Research Journal, 3,* 179-201.

Rothenberg, A. (1990b). Creativity in adolescence. *Psychiatric Clinics of North America, 13,* 415-434.

Rubenson, D., & Runco, M.A. (1992). The psychoeconomic approach to creativity. *New Ideas in Psychology, 10,* 131-147.

Runco, M.A. (1985). Reliability and convergent validity of ideational flexibility as a function of academic achievement. *Perceptual and Motor Skills, 61,* 1075-1081.

Runco, M.A. (1989). The creativity of children's art. *Child Study Journal, 19,* 177-189.

Runco, M.A. (1991). The evaluative, valuative, and divergent thinking of children. *Journal of Creative Behavior, 25,* 311-319.

Runco, M.A. (1992). Children's divergent thinking and creative ideation. *Developmental Review, 12,* 233-264.

Runco, M.A. (1993a). Divergent thinking, creativity, and giftedness. *Gifted Child Quarterly, 37,* 16-22.

Runco, M.A. (1993b). Operant theories of insight, originality, and creativity. *American Behavioral Scientist, 37,* 59-74.

Runco, M.A. (1993c). Moral creativity: Intentional and unconventional. *Creativity Research Journal, 6,* 17-28.

Runco, M.A. (1994a). Creativity and its discontents. In M.P. Shaw & M.A. Runco (Eds.), *Creativity and affect* (pp. 53-65). Norwood, NJ: Ablex.

Runco, M.A. (1994b). Giftedness as critical and creative thought. In N. Colangelo (Ed.), *Proceedings of the Second Wallace National Symposium on Talent Development* (pp. 239-249). Dayton: Ohio Psychology Press.

Runco, M.A. (1996). Objectivity in creativity research. In A. Montuori (Ed.), *Unusual associates: Essays in honor of Frank Barron.* Cresskill, NJ: Hampton Press.

Runco, M.A., & Albert, R.S. (1985). The reliability and validity of ideational originality in the divergent thinking of academically gifted and nongifted children. *Educational and Psychological Measurement, 45,* 483-501.

Runco, M.A., & Bahleda, M.D. (1987). Birth order and divergent thinking. *Journal of Genetic Psychology, 148,* 119-125.

Runco, M.A., & Chand, I. (1994). Problem finding, evaluative thinking, and creativity. In M.A. Runco (Ed.). *Problem finding, problem solving, and creativity* (pp. 40-76). Norwood, NJ: Ablex.

Runco, M.A., & Chand, I. (1995). Cognition and creativity. *Educational Psychology Review, 7,* 243-267.

Runco, M.A., & Charles, R. (1993). Judgments of originality and appropriateness as predictors of creativity. *Personality and Individual Differences, 15,* 537-546.

Runco, M.A., Ebersole, P., & Mraz, W. (1991). Self-actualization and creativity. *Journal of Social Behavior and Personality, 6,* 161-167.

Runco, M.A., Johnson, D., & Gaynor, J.R. (in press). The judgmental bases of creativity and implications for the study of gifted youth. In A. Fishkin, B. Cramond, & P. Olszewski-Kubilius (Eds.), *Creativity in youth: Research and methods.* Cresskill, NJ: Hampton Press.

Runco, M.A., McCarthy, K.A., & Svensen, E. (1994). Judgments of the creativity of artwork from students and professional artists. *Journal of Psychology, 128,* 23-31.

Runco, M.A., & Okuda, S.M. (1991). The instructional enhancement of the ideational originality and flexibility scores of divergent thinking tests. *Applied Cognitive Psychology, 5,* 435-441.

Runco, M.A., & Okuda, S.M. (1993). Reaching creatively gifted children through their learning styles. In R.M. Milgram, R. Dunn, & G. Price (Eds.), *Teaching and counseling gifted and talented adolescents: An international learning style perspective* (pp. 103-115). New York: Praeger.

Runco, M.A., Okuda, S.M., & Thurston, B.J. (1991). Environmental cues and divergent thinking. In M.A. Runco (Ed.), *Divergent thinking* (pp. 79-85). Norwood, NJ: Ablex.

Runco, M.A., & Richards, R. (Eds.). (in press). *Eminent creativity, everyday creativity, and health.* Norwood, NJ: Ablex.

Runco, M.A., & Smith, W.R. (1992). Interpersonal and intrapersonal evaluations of creative ideas. *Personality and Individual Differences, 13,* 295-302.

Runco, M.A., & Vega, L. (1990). Evaluating the creativity of children's ideas. *Journal of Social Behavior and Personality, 5,* 439-452.

Scarr, S., & McCartney, K. (1983). How people make their environments: A theory of genotype-environment effects. *Child Development, 54,* 424-435.

Schultz, N.R., Kaye, D.B., & Hoyer, W.J. (1984). Intraindividual variability in divergent and convergent thinking: Adult age differences. *Educational Gerontology, 10,* 109-118.

Schwebel, M. (1993). Moral creativity as artistic transformation. *Creativity Research Journal, 6,* 65-82.

Sheldon, K.K. (in press). Creativity and self-determination in personality. *Creativity Research Journal.*

Simonton, D.K. (1975). Age and literary creativity: A cross-cultural and transhistorical survey. *Journal of Cross-Cultural Psychology, 6,* 259-277.

Simonton, D.K. (1977). Creative productivity, age, and stress: A biographical time-series analysis of 10 classical composers. *Journal of Personality and Social Psychology, 35,* 791-804.

Simonton, D.K. (1983). Creative productivity and age: A mathematical model based on a two-step cognitive process. *Developmental Review, 3,* 97-111.

Simonton, D.K. (1984). *Genius, creativity, and leadership.* Cambridge, MA: Harvard University Press.

Simonton, D.K. (1985). Quality, quantity, and age: The careers of ten distinguished psychologists. *International Aging and Human Development, 21,* 241-254.

Simonton, D.K. (1987). Developmental antecedents of achieved eminence. *Annals of Child Development, 4,* 131-169.

Simonton, D.K. (1988). Age and outstanding achievement: What do we know after a century of research? *Psychological Bulletin, 104,* 251-267.

Simonton, D.K. (1989). The swan-song phenomenon: Last-works effects for 172 classical composers. *Psychology and Aging, 4,* 42-47.

Simonton, D.K. (1990) Creativity in later years: Optimistic prospects for achievement. *Gerontologist, 30,* 626-631.

Skinner, B.F. (1983). Intellectual self-management in old age. *American Psychologist, 38,* 239-244.

Smith, G.J.W., & Carlsson, I. (1983). Creativity in early and middle school years. *International Journal of Behavioral Development, 6,* 167-195.

Smith, G.J.W., & Carlsson, I. (1985). Creativity in middle and late school years. *International Journal of Behavioral Development, 8,* 329-343.

Smith, G.J.W., & Carlsson, I. (1990). *The creative process.* Madison, CT: International Universities Press.

Smith, G.J.W., & van der Meer, G. (1990). Creativity in old age. *Creativity Research Journal, 3,* 249-264.

Smolucha, F. (1992a). A reconstruction of Vygotsky's theory of creativity. *Creativity Research Journal, 5,* 49-67.

Smolucha, F. (1992b). The relevance of Vygotsky's theory of creative imagination for contemporary research on play. *Creativity Research Journal, 5,* 69-76.

Smolucha, L., & Smolucha, F. (1985). A fifth Piagetian stage: The collaboration between analogical and logical thinking in artistic creativity. *Visual Arts Research, X,* 90-99.

Subotnik, R., & Arnold, K. (Eds.). (1994). *Beyond Terman: Longitudinal studies of giftedness.* Norwood, NJ: Ablex.

Sulloway, F. (1993). *Orthodoxy and innovation in science: Birth order.* Unpublished manuscript.

Torrance, E.P. (1962). *Guiding creative talent.* Englewood Cliffs, NJ: Prentice-Hall.

Torrance, E.P. (1963). *Education and the creative potential.* Minneapolis: University of Minnesota Press.

Torrance, E.P. (1968). A longitudinal examination of the fourth-grade slump in creativity. *Gifted Child Quarterly, 12,* 195–199.

Torrance, E.P., Clements, C.B., & Goff, K. (1989). Mind-body learning among the elderly: Arts, fitness, and incubation. *Educational Forum, 54,* 123-133.

Torrance, E.P., & Gott, K. (1991). Maintaining creativity in later years. *Creative Child and Adult Quarterly, 16,* 5-16.

Urban, K.K. (1991). On the development of creativity in children. *Creativity Research Journal, 4,* 177–191.

Vernon, P.E. (1989). The nature-nurture problem in creativity. In J.A. Glover, R.R. Ronning, & C.R. Reynolds (Eds.), *Handbook of creativity* (pp. 93-110). New York: Plenum.

Wechsler, D. (1958). *The measurement and appraisal of adult intelligence* (4th ed.). Baltimore: Williams & Wilkins.

Wikstrom, B.-M., Theorell, T., & Sandstrom, S. (1992). Psychophysiological effects of stimulation with pictures of works of art in old age. *International Journal of Psychosomatics, 39,* 68-75.

Wolf, F.M., & Larson, G.L. (1981). On why adolescent formal operators may not be creative thinkers. *Adolescence, 26,* 346-348.

Zusne, L. (1976). Age and achievement in psychology: The harmonic mean as a model. *American Psychologist, 31,* 805-807.

II TOPICS AND ISSUES

7 The Structure-of-Intellect Model Revisited

Patricia A. Bachelor
William B. Michael
University of Southern California

This chapter is divided into five main sections. First, a brief overview of factor analytic theories of intelligence is presented. Second, Guilford's Structure-of-Intellect model (SOI) is described. Third, various factor models (i.e., Spearman, Vernon, Thurstone, and Cattell) are contrasted to the SOI model. Technical and conceptual criticisms of the structure-of-intellect model are discussed next. Last, efforts into higher order SOI factors are set forth.

BRIEF HISTORY

The origin of the word *intelligence* stems from Aristotle. He distinguished *orexis*, the moral and emotional faculties, from *dianoia*, the intellectual and cognitive faculties (Burt, 1955). Cicero translated dianoia as *intelligentia* (*inter*—within, *leger*—to bring together, discriminate, choose).

Every human or animal thought about action combines cognitive and affective functioning, yet the two domains are distinct enough to permit separate critical examination. (The historical roots of the term

155

intelligence may be partially accountable for the numerous misunderstandings and dissensions.) Still, one should not be led to treat the abstraction of intelligence as a concrete material object of some kind of monolithic entity within the mind. Ryle (1949) pointed to the attempts to define intelligence as futile, as they involve "the ghost in the machine" fallacy. One cannot observe intelligence directly; all one can do is to observe that some thoughts, words, or actions are more clever, complex, efficient, or intelligent than others.

FACTOR THEORIES OF INTELLIGENCE

The notion that intelligence must be "univocal" or unitary in order to exist is itself a remnant of the historical phase in which Spearman (1927) presented a simple, clear-cut, two-factor theory of intelligence. The theory Spearman put forth emphasized *g* (general intelligence) and a number of *s* (specific) factors equal to the number of tests in the analysis. Spearman also acknowledged the existence of group factors such as verbal ability and fluency (a factor later rediscovered as *originality* or *divergent ability*).

It is important to note that Spearman delineated specific conditions for the discovery of *g*. The conditions he delineated were: (a) there should be no undue similarities between the tests used, as any such similarity may result in overlap among the functions (specific factors), which would cause correlations to be higher than those due to *g*; and (b) the tests should be administered to samples representative of the entire population. Many critics have overlooked these conditions. For example, Thurstone's (1938) early studies did not find evidence supporting the existence of *g*, but they also did not comply with Spearman's recommendation that representative samples be used. Clearly, testing only very bright (high-level) university students minimizes the differences in *g* within the population—a circumstance that denies *g* an ample opportunity to emerge.

Once Thurstone extended his samples to reflect a more representative group than that afforded by students at the University of Chicago (i.e., a broad sample of school children), he recognized the existence of a general factor because of the intercorrelations between his primary factors (Thurstone & Thurstone, 1941). Thus, eventually both Spearman and Thurstone argued for a hierarchical structure with *g* and primary abilities (group factors) playing important roles. Nevertheless, there has existed a difference in emphasis between the American and British schools. The British extracted *g* first and then confined themselves to only a few of the most important primary factors, whereas the

Americans extracted the primary factors first and then removed higher order factors from the primary-factor correlation matrixes. No principal difference between the two schools is necessarily involved.

Thurstone is also known specifically for his contributions in the area of factor analysis. In his research, he specified two main rules for rotation of axes—simple structure and orthogonality. With the university student sample, Thurstone (1938) was able to obtain a solution that generally satisfied both conditions. However, the two conditions were not met with the more broadly representative schoolchildren sample (Thurstone & Thurstone, 1941). One or the other condition had to be abandoned in order to obtain a unique solution in the instance of the schoolchildren sample. Thurstone's decision was to retain simple structure and to permit the axes to be oblique. This decision necessitated the assumption of higher order factors, with the obliqueness of the primary factors determining the position of the higher order factors. Nearly all psychometricians have followed Thurstone's lead, with only Guilford (1967a) making the opposite decision. Guilford retained orthogonality and gave up simple structure. This decision led to several important developments that will be discussed later.

Vernon (1950) also proposed a hierarchical model cf intelligence with g at the top. Two major group factors—verbal-educational abilities ($v{:}ed$) and spatial-perceptual-practical abilities ($k{:}m$)—are placed at the second level. The $v{:}ed$ category refers to the abilities measured by traditional tests of scholastic aptitude, whereas the $k{:}m$ classification refers to the abilities measured by spatial and mechanical tests. With more detailed testing, these major abilities can be further divided into the more specialized abilities such as fluency (f), number (n), induction (i), and perceptual speed (p), or further subdivided into numerous minor group factors that are also placed at the third level. Vernon suggested that these latter abilities are not very influential, as these tests do not generate a great deal of additional information. At the bottom of the hierarchy are the specific factors (Spearman's s factors) that underlie high or low performance on a particular test, but yield no information about any other ability. In summary, Vernon's model has a total of four levels in his hierarchy, two of which (the top and bottom level) are consistent if not identical with Spearman's original formulation.

Cattell (1963) provided major extensions to the theories of Spearman (1927), Thurstone (1938), and Vernon (1950). Cattell is probably best known for his distinction between *fluid* and *crystallized* intelligence, which have their underpinnings in Thorndike's (1927) distinction between width and altitude of intellect. "Being able to do harder things than someone else can do" (p.23) is the informal definition of altitude; it focuses on the difficulty scaling of problems. "Knowing more things than someone else, and being able to do more things than someone else" (p. 23) is the informal definition of width; it focuses on the application of mental abilities that are now crystallized into knowledge or a skill. Thorndike (1927) stated,

> Consequently what we may call the level or height or altitude of intellect and what we may call its extent or range or area at the same level are correlated and either one is an indicator of the other. It will be best, however, to keep them separate in our thinking. (p.24)

Thorndike originally assumed that altitude would more likely be determined by nature, whereas width would be by nurture. He wrote:

> According to the orthodox views of what original nature is likely to contribute and what the environment is likely to contribute, it would be reasonable to choose the altitude of intellect and the width. . . as the two extremes, the area . . .being intermediate in its causation. (p. 58)

Cattell's (1963) formulation linked the factorial work of Spearman and Thurstone with a plausible theory of heredity and environment similar to Thorndike's (1927) position. Cattell (1963) suggested that emerging from most studies of the correlations between cognitive tests was a prominent general factor consisting of two components— fluid intelligence or (g_f) and crystallized intelligence or (g_c). Cattell defined fluid intelligence (g_f) as the total linkage or blended accumulation of the brain (i.e., the physiologically determined aspect of intellectual functioning that makes possible the solution of new problems and the comprehension of new relationships). In contrast, crystallized intelligence was defined in terms of the concepts, strategies, and skills acquired through cultural and educational influences. Cattell refined Thorndike's (1927) "axiom" that hereditary is more important than environment in the prediction of intellectual accomplishments when he said, "for any same-age group the nature-nurture variance ratio will be much higher for g_f than g_c on the hypothesis that gf is directly physiologically determined whereas g_c is a product of environmentally varying, experimentally determined investments of g_f" (p. 4).

The concept of fluid intelligence is predicated on the absence of specifically learned skills and knowledge (beyond universally acquired abilities such as holding a pen or making marks on paper) and is entangled with the concept of *culture-fair intelligence tests*. Of course, the distinction between these tests and the more traditional achievement tests is not absolute, just as the distinction between fluid and crystallized intelligence is not absolute. Both gf and gc are usually involved, in varying degrees, in any intellectual functioning; hence, the difficulty is in assessing their distinct contributions. Cattell (1963) maintained that his culture-fair (nonverbal) tests primarily measure g_f and that traditional verbal tests of intelligence and achievement depend much more on g_c.

THE STRUCTURE OF INTELLECT MODEL

The structure-of-intellect model (SOI) was first presented in 1959 by Guilford. Not being hierarchical in nature, it completely denies the existence of general intelligence such as Spearman's g. Instead, it is a morphological model with a cross-classification of abilities in three dimensions. Each dimension intersects the other two to determine different types of intellectual abilities.

The first of these dimensions refers to the type of mental operation involved in the ability. Operations are processes and they define what the organism is able to do with the raw materials of information, in which information is defined as that which the organism discriminates (Guilford, Merrifield, Christensen, & Frick, 1960). The five types of operations (with their letter symbols) and their definitions are:

Cognition (C)—to know, comprehend, have certain items of information in one's possession
Memory (M)—to put items of information into memory storage to prevail beyond the time of stimulation
Divergent Production (D)—to generate from memory storage alternative items to satisfy specified broad requirements
Convergent Production (N)—to retrieve from memory storage clearly specified items
Evaluation (E)—to decide whether or how well an item meets specifications or criteria such as identity, suitability, usability, or other requirements

Each operation category includes 30 different abilities that are parallel to those in every operation category.

The second dimension of the classification relates to the content or area of information in which the operations are performed. In its widely researched second version, the model contains five kinds of contents (Guilford, 1977). The contents are:

Visual (V)—to perceive or image items in the retinal stimulation
Auditory (A)—to perceive or image items in the realm of sounds

Symbolic (S)—an item that is often used to substitute for other items
Semantic (M)—verbal meanings
Behavioral (B)—mental states including feelings, moods, thoughts, intentions

Within each kind of content there is a set of 30 abilities that are parallel with those in each of the other four content categories. Guilford (1979) noted that this second version of the SOI differs from the first one in that the figural category was divided into visual and auditory areas, and that other sensory areas may have to be added after further investigation.

The third dimension is concerned with the form of informational product that results from a particular type of operation applied to a particular kind of content. The six forms of products distinguished in the SOI model are:

Units (U)—items having a thing-like character or composites of attributes
Classes (C)—the conception that underlies groups of items that share at least one attribute
Relations (R)—the meaningful connection between pairs of items
Systems (S)—the organization of sets of three or more items
Transformations (T)—the change in any kind of items, a change including substitutions
Implications (I)—items suggested by given items, including consequences, predictions, conditional responses; analogous to the concept of association

By putting all three dimensions of the SOI theory together into one cross-classification, Guilford obtained a cube-like representation of the model. With five types of operations, five kinds of contents, and six forms of products, there are 150 cells in the model, each representing a unique kind of ability corresponding to what is hypothesized to be a first-order ability.

Each cell in the model, which represents a given type of operation processing a specified kind of content to yield a particular form of product, is known by its three-letter symbol or trigram. The three letters are specified in the order of operation, content, and product. Thus, cognition of semantic relations is denoted CMR. A multiple-choice verbal analogies test is an example of CMR. In this test, success of an examinee depends on seeing (cognizing) what relation exists between the first two words and demonstrating that he or she grasped the relation by completing the second pair of words so as to utilize the same relation. A multiple-choice vocabulary test would reflect the CMU ability. In this instance, the informational product is units. These two types of tests portray two different abilities. Although they may involve both CMR and CMU abilities, each one can be expected to represent one ability more than the other. To change each of these two tests to measure convergent production would be to give the item in a completion format. Here the examinee must produce the response. An example of the ability NMR asks is: BOAT is to WATER as TRAIN is to [RAIL].

It should be mentioned at this point—perhaps somewhat parenthetically—that the last paper Guilford wrote set forth a third version of the SOI model. This paper was submitted for publication only three weeks before his death on Thanksgiving Day in 1987. In this third formulation Guilford (1988) split the operation of memory into two components of *memory recording* and *memory retention* that essentially represent short-term or long-term memory, respectively. Hence, the latest rendition of the SOI model with six forms of product serves to generate 6 x 5 x 6, or 180 cells hypothesized to describe 180 different first-order abilities. This model is presented in Figure 7.1. To the knowledge of the writers, no empirical research has been carried out to validate the new constructs proposed in this SOI model.

Intelligence, from the SOI point of view, consists of an organized set of functions or abilities that are used to process different forms of information in different ways. Guilford's premise was that diligent factor-analytic studies on batteries of experimental tests (including some anchor tests with already established factorial validity) had demonstrated or would demonstrate the existence of each factor as indicated by each cell of the cube (Guilford, 1967a, 1967b; Guilford & Hoepfner, 1971). Guilford and Hoepfner (1971) stated that of all the different factors that were then hypothesized to exist, 98 had been identified.

One common misconception of the SOI theory has been that abilities are orthogonal or independent. This interpretation probably arose because of the rectangular representation of the model and Guilford's insistence on orthogonal rotation. Guilford (1981) stated that he used orthogonal rotations because he believed that oblique rotations gave biased results because of the small number of tests employed in the analysis. In other words, the estimates of the correlations between the factors would be unreliable. In his later search for higher order factors, he preferred to find the most representative tests of a factor and to use the correlations between the factor representatives (Guilford, 1981). Furthermore, if higher order factors, which are to be defined subsequently, do exist, they lie along the major dimensions of the SOI model.

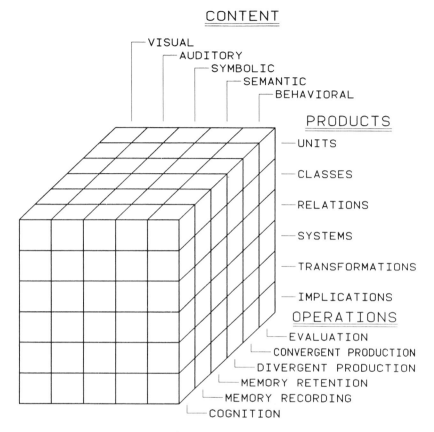

CONTENT

— VISUAL
  — AUDITORY
    — SYMBOLIC
      — SEMANTIC
        — BEHAVIORAL

PRODUCTS
— UNITS
— CLASSES
— RELATIONS
— SYSTEMS
— TRANSFORMATIONS
— IMPLICATIONS

OPERATIONS
— EVALUATION
— CONVERGENT PRODUCTION
— DIVERGENT PRODUCTION
— MEMORY RETENTION
— MEMORY RECORDING
— COGNITION

Figure 7.1. Revised structure-of-intellect model. From J.P. Guilford, "Some Changes in the Structure of Intellect Model," *Educational and Psychological Measurement, 48*(1), 3. © 1988. Reprinted with permission

However, he has denied the existence of g, which would be a fourth-order factor: "Because no all-embracing ability seems to be evident, no single apex seems to be called for . . . any one of them (the 16 broad abilities) could conceivably be placed at the apex of one of a number of hierarchies" (Guilford, 1981, pp. 430-431).

In order for g to exist, Guilford and Hoepfner (1971) argued that there could not be any true zero correlations between tests—"any genuine zero correlations between pairs of intellectual tests is sufficient to disprove the existence of a universal factor like g" (Guilford, 1967b, p. 56). However, 8,674 of 48,140 coefficients found in his analyses were within the interval from -.10 to +.10, and 24% of the correlations were within the 95% confidence interval surrounding zero. Thus, he argued that no single pervasive general factor of intelligence existed.

The SOI model, as a frame of reference for intellectual abilities, has served the heuristic function of generating hypotheses about new factors of intellect as well as numerous doctoral dissertations. Guilford (1967b) stated that it should not be assumed that the entire range of intellectual variables is covered in the set of hypothesized abilities in the SOI model. Additionally, it must not be assumed that the abilities operate in isolation of the intellectual activities of an individual, even when the abilities, which are separate and logically distinct, can be separated by factor analysis (Guilford, 1967b). The fact that abilities routinely operate together is demonstrated by the fact that two or more abilities are ordinarily involved in solving a given problem. The variety of mixtures of abilities present in regular mental functioning causes difficulty in recognizing each ability by direct observation or by laboratory procedures.

Methods of Analysis Used in SOI Research

In the early analyses on the SOI models, Zimmerman's (1946) method of orthogonal graphic rotation of axes was used. In these analyses the axes were aimed at the hypothesized SOI factors. In 1971, Guilford and Hoepfner reanalyzed the data from 31 earlier studies on the SOI model. In these analyses they utilized Cliff's (1966) method of rotating toward hypothesized factor targets. This procedure belongs in a family of methods that has come to be known as *Procrustes solutions*. The targets in these analyses have been the expected SOI factors and have resulted in a confirmation of 98 SOI abilities. As such Procrustean procedures are obviously subjective in nature, they have resulted in much criticism. These critiques are discussed in a later section of this chapter.

In Guilford's years of research on the SOI model, factor axes were nearly always rotated orthogonally. This procedure was followed not because he believed that all the first-order factors were uncorrelated, but rather, as mentioned earlier, because he questioned the validity of oblique rotations (Guilford, 1980). Oblique rotations, he indicated, are likely to give biased results because the locations of the axes are too dependent on the particular combinations of the small number of tests used in the analysis. When two factors correlate nonzero it may be a reflection of faulty test construction. Faulty tests are those that inadvertently contain contributions from another factor. Therefore, one cannot place much confidence in the estimate of the correlations between factors (Guilford & Hoepfner, 1971).

Guilford also rejected the notion of rotating factors according to Thurstone's principles of simple structure. He found that such rotations fail to give an acceptable degree of factor invariance (that is, replicability across studies) and often lack psychological meaningfulness. However, when he rotated factors to give psychological meaning and invariance he often obtained simple structure (Guilford & Hoepfner, 1971).

The searching procedure of factor analysis, viewed by Guilford (1967b), seemed to be sensitive enough to tease out these mental functions. The construction of special tests aimed at assessing each particular ability while controlling for individual differences in other abilities is probably the only clear-cut method through which to demonstrate the separateness of an ability from another. Guilford (1967b) suggested that factor analysis often indicated an ability before a unique test may be constructed.

Following this brief overview of factor theories and models of intelligence, in the next section the similarities among the theories are discussed.

RELATIONS AMONG FACTOR THEORIES OF INTELLIGENCE

In part because of the controversial nature of Guilford's SOI model, similarities among models are often overlooked. Guilford (1967a) stressed that the SOI model is compatible with some of the features of other models and other factor theories. The *fundaments* of Spearman (1927) are SOI units; Spearman's *relations* are SOI relations. The concept of *eduction of relations* as developed by Spearman is equivalent to Guilford's cognition of relations. Although Spearman indicated that this concept was one of two major operations most characteristic of *g*, the SOI model describes four distinct abilities for educting or cognizing relations, one for each of the figural, symbolic, semantic, and behavior content types. Also, Spearman acknowledged several different types of relations among the lines of various kinds of information, including "psychological relation," which is close to the SOI concept equivalent to behavioral relations. Spearman's notion of *eduction of correlates* aligns with the SOI category of convergent production of relations. Finally, the test for the convergent production of relations category fits Spearman's paradigm for *eduction of correlates*.

Vernon's (1950) original major split between the *v:ed* and *k:m* group factors parallels Guilford's (1967b) semantic and figural category distinctions. Vernon's *k:m* factor, which includes space abilities, mechanical information, and psychomotor abilities, is broader than the SOI figural category. The further *v:ed* division between verbal and numerical parallels the semantic and symbolic SOI distinction. Vernon did not mention a category suggestive of behavioral information. Operations or products are only cited incidentally in his further breakdowns. Actually, most SOI factors would probably be considered by Vernon as on the level of specific factors that, in his estimation, are of little consequence. It is reasonable, as Vernon stressed, that content and operations should partially determine the efficacy with which g works on the variety of types of cognitive materials. Currently, stronger evidence would be needed to convince Vernon of the existence of products.

Thurstone's (1938) primary mental abilities are also closely related to Guilford's (1967b) SOI abilities. Reasoning seems to be the operations of cognition and convergent production, with CMS (convergent production of semantic systems) most closely aligned with general reasoning. Number reflects SOI abilities NSI (cognition of symbolic implications) and MSI (memory of symbolic implications). Verbal comprehension is CMU (convergent production of semantic units). Space represents CFS (convergent production of figural systems) and CFT (convergent production of figural transformations). Word fluency is DMT (divergent production of semantic transformations). Perceptual speed is CFI (convergent production of figural implications). Finally, Thurstone's (1938) memory is, of course, the SOI operation of memory.

All of the theorists discussed in this chapter, with the exception of Guilford, tended to agree that something akin to Spearman's g underlies intelligence. Cattell's (1963) distinction between crystallized and fluid intelligence seems to be very closely aligned with Vernon's $v{:}ed$ and $k{:}m$, as both g_c and $v{:}ed$ are characterized by verbal intelligence, whereas g_f and $k{:}m$ are both referred to as nonverbal intelligence. Cattell (1963) argued that inasmuch as Thurstone's (1938) primary mental abilities are essentially cognitive in nature and learned, they are similar to his crystallized intelligence, with only spatial ability loading on his factor of fluid intelligence.

To summarize briefly, although there are similarities between Guilford's theory and the factor theories presented, there remain three major points of disagreement. First, Guilford (1967b) did not incorporate a general factor akin to Spearman's g. Second, Guilford advocated the use of orthogonal rotations and thus implied that abilities are uncorrelated. Third, the major theorists put strong emphasis on the existence of higher order factors, whereas Guilford did not, at least prior to 1981.

CRITICISMS OF THE STRUCTURE OF THE INTELLECT MODEL

Although Guilford's SOI model has dominated discussions of the relationships between intelligence and creativity, the SOI model has been criticized on both conceptual and technical grounds (Butcher, 1973; Carroll, 1968, 1972; Cronbach, 1970; Harris & Harris, 1971; Haynes, 1970; Horn, 1970, 1972, 1977; Horn & Knapp, 1973, 1974; Undheim & Horn,

1977; Vernon, 1979). Critics have objected to the subjectivity of the rotational procedures, to Guilford's insistence on orthogonal as opposed to oblique factors, to the narrowness of the SOI abilities, to the psychological superficiality of the product category, and to the SOI model's implication that the actual intellectual operations are mutually exclusive and comparable. Additionally, critics have asserted that factor-analytic results do not provide convincing support for the SOI model because they are predicated on methods that allow very little opportunity to reject hypotheses.

The SOI theory has been criticized primarily on grounds that the methods of verification used in supportive research have been overly subjective (Carroll, 1972; Harris & Harris, 1971; Horn & Knapp, 1973, 1974). In this case, subjectivity refers to overfactoring to insure the desired number of factors and to the targeted rotational procedures used to insure maximal agreement between results and the desired factor pattern (Undheim & Horn, 1977).

Horn and Knapp (1973, 1974) argued convincingly against the sole use of the Procrustes method of factor analysis that Guilford and his colleagues had been employing. To demonstrate, they generated fully random target matrixes that were not based on any coherent theory, previous results, or rational thinking about substantive issues. They then counted the number of significant (i.e., greater than .30) factor loadings that were in agreement with their theory (so-called hits), the number of times a significant loading was not found when it was hypothesized (misses), and the number of significant loadings when a zero loading was hypothesized (extras). The average hit rate over three studies was 84% for the random model and 87% for the model based on the SOI theory. They interpreted their results as indicating that support for the SOI theory was not compelling because the level of support was not appreciably better than that for the theories generated at random. According to Horn and Knapp (1973), this lack of support had occurred because in Procrustes procedures (Schonemann, 1966) the terminal solutions have been forced to comply with the investigator's hypothesis. Methods of this kind have been used to generate most of the evidence in support of SOI theory. If investigators begin with different hypotheses about a given data set and specify target matrixes based on these hypotheses, then the same Procrustes procedure can produce dramatically different results. Consequently, the Procrustes procedure is viewed as an inadequate methodology to establish the viability of a theory.

In his reply to criticisms by Horn and Knapp (1973), Guilford (1974) noted that they found fault, not with the SOI model, but with the factor-analytic rotation procedures used to demonstrate empirical support for the model. Additionally, he pointed out that Horn and Knapp

(1973) chose only 3 out of the more than 30 matrixes generated by the University of Southern California (USC) Aptitudes Research Project to illustrate that the methods used were inadequate to support the theory. Guilford (1974) recomputed the "batting average" of Horn and Knapp's (1973) goodness-of-fit to the data for random models. Guilford's computations were 93% hits versus 32% errors in contrast to Horn and Knapp's (1974) 84% hits versus 56% errors. More important than quibbling over percentage points, especially in the hit range, Guilford (1974) made the point that some errors are expected in the best of analyses. Some errors were expected in his analysis, as tests were not univocal (one-factor). Of special significance to this debate, he observed that errors would reveal that the factor-analytic methods he used, which were criticized for forcing data to a targeted solution, did not constrict solutions to conform to his hypothesized factor structure.

Proponents of SOI theory have admitted that the methods used in their research are subjective:

> Any subjectivity in decisions on where to rotate is undesirable . . . the facts of life in factor analysis procedures are such that it is often necessary; otherwise strict adherence to the rules of best simple structure may lead one astray psychologically. (Guilford, 1967b, p. 55)

> . . . with rotations of axes guided by theoretical considerations, identifications of hypothesized abilities were forthcoming in 93 percent of the attempts to demonstrate them. This compares with a "batting average" of only 32 percent when selection of measures was just as favorable but rotations were made toward a mathematically described criterion of simple structure. (Guilford & Hoepfner, 1971, p. 41)

The position represented in these quotations implies that a method that supports hypotheses in a high percentage of cases is superior to a method that yields support only in a small percentage of cases. It is not obvious that such an assumption is either warranted or desirable when one is dealing with issues so complex as the dimension of intellectual ability. Methods used should have sufficient power to reject false hypotheses (Horn & Knapp, 1973).

Horn and Knapp (1973,1974) argued convincingly against the sole use of Procrustes factor-analytic methods to provide the evidence in support of the SOI theory because of the inability of the method to reject false hypotheses, and because of the only slightly less favorable support for randomly based hypotheses than that for the SOI hypotheses. They interpreted their results as indicative of the less than compelling evidence offered by Guilford and his colleagues in support of the SOI model. Horn and Knapp (1973, 1974) correctly pointed out that their results did not disconfirm the SOI theory, and, in fact, they had twice as many misses and extras for the random model as compared with the number of misses and extras for the SOI-based model. What they did argue was that if factor-analytic evidence is to be used to support the theory, then better methods need to be employed.

Randomly configured models were also used by Bachelor (1989). She employed confirmatory factor analysis to obtain empirical evidence of the viability of the construct validity of 25 ability factors in the SOI model. The factors were hypothesized to account for the intercorrelations among 73 tests involving cognition, convergent production, and divergent production. Correlational data were taken from 89 tests used by Hoepfner and Guilford (1965) and Guilford et al. (1960). The construct validity of the 9 and 16 intellectual ability factors models as hypothesized by Guilford et al. were evaluated by Jöreskog's confirmatory factor-analysis procedure (Jöreskog & Sörbom, 1984, 1986). The models were obliquely and orthogonally specified, and each was contrasted to three substantive models. The models used as contrasts included a null model (which provided no substantive structure, with each test being perceived as a factor), a general or one-factor model, and a random model. The random models were identical in form to those models hypothesized by Guilford, except that the tests were selected at random to load on the factors (i.e., each factor of the random model had the same number of tests loading on it as in the SOI model), and the models were obliquely specified. The nine factors investigated using the first data set were CSU, CSS, CSC, CSR, CSI, NST, NSU, NSS, and NMS. The second data set contained the 16 factors of DFU, DFC, DFS, DFT, DFI, DMU, DMC, DMR, DMS, DMT, DMI, DSU, DSC, DSR, DSS, and DSI.

Results of confirmatory maximum likelihood factor analyses by Bachelor (1989) were less than supportive of the SOI models investigated because of high factor intercorrelations, occasional low estimated factor loadings, and overall fit indices for substantive models that were not appreciably superior to those for the randomly configured models. The likelihood of orthogonality was sufficiently refuted with respect to the models investigated. On the basis of her findings, Bachelor concluded that neither the high dimensionality of the SOI models nor the simplistic general or single-factor models were able to provide a plausible representation of the correlational data.

Another frequently cited criticism of the Guilford-Hoepfner position is that the results of alternative data-analytic procedures have not been consistent with SOI model predictions. This fact was acknowledged by Guilford and Hoepfner (1971). For example, Harris and Harris (1971) performed both orthogonal and oblique rotations in a reanalysis of nine of Guilford's matrixes and using more traditional factor analysis procedures. The resulting "common comparable factors" they obtained in two of the matrixes did not support the SOI model in detail. In particular, Guilford's cognition operation tended to mix with tests of the convergent production operation. Bachelor and Bachelor (1989) also found a blending of these two operations. They reported a .98 correlation between tests of cognition and convergent production.

Similarly, Haynes (1970) selected the two best (in his estimation) tests of 17 SOI factors and administered these tests to 200 college students. The resulting correlation matrix was analyzed by Wherry's (1959) hierarchical factoring method. Haynes obtained 12 group factors (some roughly corresponding to SOI factors). The distinction among Guilford's specific forms of products, contents, and operations was blurred.

Cronbach's (1970) criticism of the SOI model was based on the fact that a factor analysis that tends to substantiate a theory does not necessarily refute a counter hypothesis. To illustrate, Cronbach pointed to the raw correlations between the tests of the model as a weakness in the SOI model. That is, the number of correlations greater than .40 was counted for each divergent test in the Hoepfner and Guilford (1965) study for the following four groups:

CP   Same content, same product
CX   Same content, different product
XP   Different content, same product
XX   Different content, different product

The rationale for this procedure was that tests on the same content or product should be more highly intercorrelated than are tests on different contents and products. Three relationships were verified: CP > XP, CP > XX, and CX > XX; whereas CP > CX and XP > XX were disconfirmed. Cronbach interpreted these results as lending support to classifying divergent tests with respect to content, but the additional classification with respect to product would seem to add little or nothing.

Guilford's factor distinctions, according to Cronbach (1970), represented only very subtle distinctions between tasks. In Cronbach's opinion, these fine subdivisions add very little predictive or explanatory power. Rather, the broad factors tend to overshadow these *cell factors*. Thus, in Cronbach's estimation, the extraction of fine-grained factors revealed only unimportant details that obscure the essence of the total picture when one looks so closely at the small details. Hence, Guilford's set of elements should be approached, according to Cronbach, as tests of the row or group slices of the cube across all products. In other words, higher order factors are primary in explanatory capabilities.

Cronbach (1970) also pointed out that this criticism was not a definitive one of the SOI theory, and that many more reanalyses would be required to determine which of the cell classifications are important to retain. Cronbach's strategy seemed to be more conducive to determining whether or not higher order factors exist and less indicative of an actual criticism of the SOI model. This interpretation appears to be accurate because he was investigating whether or not the specification of fewer facets of the model would result in correlations as high as or higher than those associated with specifying more facets.

Guilford (1972) challenged conclusions regarding the lack of empirical evidence for SOI factors that were based on procedures involving the averaging of correlation coefficients. He used an example to demonstrate that SOI abilities cannot be generated from averages of intercorrelation coefficients. In particular, large and unexpected correlations can be obtained between factors, as tests designed to assess SOI factors were, for the most part, not univocal. Additionally, Guilford never maintained that divergent production factors are mutually independent or uncorrelated in the population. SOI factors that have the operation, content, or product in common will most likely be correlated. That is, all divergent production factors have an operation in common, and those SOI divergent production factors operating on the same content would have two factors in common and show a commensurate increase in covariation.

The SOI model received some support from the work of Delaney and Maguire (1974). They administered 12 tests of divergent production to 46 adolescents whose full scale IQ on the WISC averaged 69.5 and to 48 adolescents whose full scale IQ on the WISC averaged 104.5. Six of the divergent production factors as hypothesized within the SOI model were reflected among these tests. Six factors were extracted from the correlational data for each group. Results among the group of 46 revealed a clear representation of four of the six hypothesized factors. A fifth factor was reproduced quite fairly. Results among the group of 48 were not so clear-cut as were those for the sample of 46 adolescents. There was some mixing shown among DSU, DMC, and DMU. In five of the factors, tests hypothesized to load on each factor demonstrated the two highest loadings—an outcome that is indicative of an adequate reproduction of the covariation in tests by these factors. These results are noteworthy, as there were only two tests per factor and as the analyses were performed on two small groups.

In rebuttal to Harris and Harris (1971), Haynes (1970), and Cronbach (1970), two points must be made. First, all the critics did find some evidence supporting the SOI model. Second, each of the critics apparently assumed that higher order factors, not first-order factors, were the critical elements of Guilford's SOI model. As Guilford did not make clear his perceptions about higher order factors until the 1981, these criticisms were premature. Furthermore, in that Guilford generally relied on orthogonal methods of rotation in test development, it is quite possible that few higher order factors actually exist.

Favero, Dombrower, Michael, and Richards (1975) administered 76 tests designed to measure 76 different SOI abilities along with the Lorge-Thorndike Intelligence Tests to a sample of 34 nine-year-old children. They found that the median correlation within the five categories of operations (i.e., same type of operation with different kinds of contents and forms of products) was .18, whereas the median correlation between the pairings of operations was .13. Of particular interest was the finding that the median correlation between cognition and convergent production was higher than the median correlation within convergent production (i.e., .25 and .18, respectively). Although this difference is obviously not statistically significantly different, it points to the same conclusion of Harris and Harris (1971) and Bachelor and Bachelor (1989) that these two types of tests tend to become mixed together. The median correlation for within and between kinds of content was .15 and .15, respectively, and for kinds of products was .12 and .14. The findings with respect to products are similar to those of Cronbach (1970): x x p was not greater than x x x. Overall, the high correlations found across the three dimensions of the model have indicated an oblique structure.

In what can be considered a partial criticism of the SOI model, Kelderman, Mellenbergh, and Elshout (1981) tested orthogonal versus oblique models by using LISREL III in seven data sets from previous SOI research. They found that in all cases the oblique model provided a superior fit. They also attempted to test an alternative model that specified one facet instead of three. In six out of seven data sets the computing procedure did not terminate for the alternative model. For the one data set that the program did terminate, the SOI three-facet model gave a better fit. They therefore concluded that in all cases the SOI model was superior to an alternative model. To conclude that the SOI model is superior to an alternative because the program did not terminate in the latter case seems questionable.

Eysenck and Fulker (1979) criticized Guilford's argument that Spearman's g does not exist because 24% of the correlations between SOI tests fell within the 95% confidence interval of zero. They argued that the subjects in Guilford's work were highly selected for intelligence and that such a restriction in the range of ability would reduce the correlations. Also, many of the SOI tests have low reliabilities, with some below .50. Consequently, much of the total variance is error variance and therefore, the tests cannot correlate highly with each other. Finally, Eysenck and Fulker indicated that tests that measure divergent production or behavioral content are more closely related to personality than to intelligence, and that personality tests are not expected to be related to intelligence. Their argument, then, was that the SOI model is oblique, and that higher order factors exist.

GUILFORD'S SEARCH FOR HIGHER-ORDER FACTORS

Guilford (1981, 1982, 1983, 1984, 1985) presented an analytic method for estimating correlations between higher order SOI factors. This method represented a marked shift in emphasis. Guilford (1982) also remarked about the orthogonal representation of the SOI model by stating that the cubical representation of the SOI model was not meant to imply orthogonality of SOI abilities. The use of the cube was for heuristic value. Guilford (1982) stated: "We now see that the factor pattern is indeed oblique, with higher-order abilities or functions indicated" (p. 58).

As may be recalled, a first-order ability was portrayed as a single cell within the geometric representation of the SOI model. Guilford (1982, 1985) provided definitions of second-order and third-order factors within the framework of his SOI model. A second-order factor was defined as one in which one element in each of two of the three dimensions of the SOI model (operations, contents, and products) would be fixed while two or more elements in a third dimension would be free to vary. For example, in the divergent production of only semantic content yielding products of systems, transformations, and implications the factor would be called divergent production of semantic content comprising products of systems, transformations, and implications. Such a second-order factor could be designated as DM.

A third-order factor was defined as one in which a single element in one of the three SOI dimensions is held constant while two or more elements in each of the other two dimensions are free to vary. For example, in the instance of divergent production as a single element in the operations dimension both semantic and symbolic contents might be present in tests along with four forms of products such as units, classes, relations, and systems. Such a third-order factor would be called divergent production of semantic and symbolic content involving four products of units, classes, relations, and systems and would be given the acronym of simply D.

A fourth-order factor, or a general factor, would be one in which at least two elements in each of the three SOI dimensions would be free to vary. Such a general factor could be given the familiar label of g.

Guilford (1982) stated that the 150 first-order SOI factor model suggests 85 second-order factors and 16 third-order factors. Higher order analyses have demonstrated empirical support for more than half of the second-order factors and 15 of the 16 third-order factors (Guilford, 1982).

Because correlations among the third-order factors were not available from the orthogonal rotations, Guilford (1982) combined tests to provide a representative for each basic factor. For example, he selected three tests each to represent the factors DVS and DVI. He then found the mean loading of the representatives on the factors of DVU, DVC, DVS, DVT, and DVI. To find the correlation between DVS and DVI he took the sum of the cross-products of the mean loadings. In this example, he obtained a correlation of .18 between factors DVS and DVI and interpreted this value as suggesting higher order factors: a second-order factor DV with products free to vary and third-order factors—D with both contents and products free to vary and V with both operations and products free to vary.

In another analysis Guilford (1981) selected two different types of operations (memory and divergent production), with content (semantic) held constant but with form of product varying across six elements. He then took the factor representatives of the 12 factors (i.e., MMU, MMC, MMR, MMS, MMT, MMI, DMU, DMR, DMS, DMT, and DMI) and rotated them obliquely. Next, he put an axis through the centroid of the two most extreme vectors on either side of the first centroid axis. He found that the angle separating these two vectors was 60 degrees, indicating a correlation of .50. The second-order factors of DM and MM were identified, and what they had in common was most likely a third-order factor M. He pointed out that the estimates "are not to be regarded as highly accurate, but they are somewhat informative" (p. 419). In general, Guilford found with this methodology that the higher order factors of operations were the most distinguishable and products were the least. This finding was parallel with those results obtained by Cronbach (1970) and Bachelor (1986-1987).

Paralleling Guilford's application of exploratory factor analysis to reveal the existence of higher order constructs in the SOI model were researchers who utilized maximum likelihood confirmatory factor analysis (Jöreskog & Sörbom, 1984, 1986) to reanalyze correlation matrixes originally presented in the reports of the USC Aptitudes Research Project. Of central focus in these reanalyses were tests of alternative hypotheses regarding the tentability of higher order factors and the capability of these factor models to reproduce accurately the covariation among variables as represented by the correlation matrix.

Bachelor and Bachelor (1989) investigated the existence of higher order factors within the convergent production and cognition operations and products dimensions. They used original data presented by Guilford et al. (1960) on a sample of 240 aviation officer candidates and naval air cadets. Reanalyses, using the LISREL method of maximum likelihood confirmatory factor analysis, were performed on an intercorrelation matrix of the 24 tests designed to measure symbolic factors of cognition and convergent production. Results indicated that among tests of symbolic content with varying products, the distinction between higher order cognition and convergent production factors was not compelling. In tests of symbolic cognition, models including the product factors afforded a superior fit over models without this inclusion. However, high intercorrelations among the product factors suggested that only two higher order product factors were involved—a units factor and a nonunits factor. Strong evidence for a third-order symbolic factor was also obtained.

Bachelor (1986-1987) reanalyzed the same correlation matrix of 48 divergent thinking tests (Hoepfner & Guilford, 1965) as did Cronbach (1970). By using confirmatory factor analysis a more objective test of alternate hypotheses regarding the dimensionality of correlation matrixes was possible. Bachelor found substantial support for the existence of three conceptually distinguishable, higher order symbolic, semantic, and figural content factors. Very limited support was found for the existence of higher order product factors. Of the six hypothesized product factors the only suggestion of separation within the matrix of factor intercorrelations was between the units and transformations product factors. Support was clear for the higher order operation of divergent production.

A correlation matrix of 27 tests designed to measure divergent thinking tests was used by Michael and Bachelor (1990) in an investigation to determine the tenability of several alternative hypotheses regarding the presence of higher order factors. Eleven models were tested with maximum likelihood confirmatory factor analysis. Results revealed that obliquely specified models afforded a superior fit to that of corresponding orthogonally specified models. This finding was consistent with previous work by Bachelor (1989), Bachelor and Bachelor (1989), and Khattab, Michael, and Hocevar (1982). Also, this work paralleled the study of Bachelor (1986-1987) in that a general one-factor model accounted for a substantial proportion of covariance among test variables. Tests of several alternate models to assess which most nearly accurately reproduced the correlation matrix revealed that two higher order oblique models consisting of three kinds of content and six forms of products demonstrated goodness-of-fit indices nearly as good as those produced by an oblique nine first-order factors model. This finding led to the conclusion that divergent thinking tests designed to capture creativity can be conceptualized parsimoniously within a higher order factor structure.

However, although Bachelor (1986-1987) observed that the contents model yielded a substantially closer fit than the products model, Michael and Bachelor (1990) found that the opposite was true in their reanalysis of a database designed to measure creativity in tests of divergent thinking.

Following in this vein, Bachelor and Michael (1991) reported that higher order oblique (in contrast with higher order orthogonal) factor models consistently yielded a superior fit to reproducing the covariation among the test variables designed to measure creative thinking. Support was found for higher order operations factor models as well as for higher order contents factors. The products model did not reveal a clear distinction among all of the six hypothesized factors. Units and transformations were somewhat more clearly defined than the other products. These results were not unlike those of Bachelor and Bachelor (1989) and Khattab et al. (1982). The latter found support for the existence of a higher order product factor of transformation that dealt with the contents of symbolic and semantic nature. Bachelor and Michael (1991) used a mixed model that included both first-order and higher order factors. This model provided a slightly better fit over that of the higher order factor models. This finding lent support to the conclusion that creativity may involve some form of hierarchical ordering of both first-order and higher order abilities. Intercorrelations among operations factors of convergent production, cognition, and evaluation suggest the presence of an underlying psychological process that unifies these activities and blurs their conceptual distinction. Results revealed not only that divergent production is a key to a creative activity, but also that the higher order factors of convergent production operations on semantic and symbolic content requiring transformations are essential in creative problem solving in mathematics, science, and engineering (Michael, 1977).

In a study of 590 third graders, van den Bergh (1990) reported that 16 semantic SOI factors accounted for 62% of the true variance in tests of reading comprehension. The SOI factors did not prove to be related differentially to either multiple-choice or open-ended items.

Ulosevich, Michael, and Bachelor (1991) reanalyzed a correlation matrix of 21 SOI tests designed to measure aptitudes required in military leadership. The correlational data were originally presented by Marks, Guilford, and Merrifield (1959) and were from a sample of 204 Marine Officers. Results indicated only a modest correspondence between exploratory analyses obtained by Marks et al. and those identified by Ulosevich et al. (1991). An evaluation of selected alternative models comprising first-order and higher order factors revealed that a two-factor oblique model that separated semantic and figural contents provided the highest degree of reproducibility of the covariation among the 21 tests. A higher order oblique factor that differentiated among the three operations of cognition, divergent production, and evaluation was next in its ability to reproduce the original correlation matrix. Consequently, the covariation among the aptitude tests could be conceptualized meaningfully within the higher order factor structure.

In the most recent of the reanalyses of a database that was originally used by Merrifield, Guilford, and Gershon (1963), Michael and Bachelor (1992) identified both first-order and higher order creative ability factors in a battery of 23 SOI tests and 9 other measures that had been administered to 403 sixth-grade pupils in a suburban middle-class community. Exploratory factor analysis employing both orthogonal (varimax) and oblique (promax) solutions lent support to three of Guilford's hypothesized creativity factors of ideational fluency, sensitivity to problems, and expressional fluency. Confirmatory maximum likelihood factor analyses revealed that a general factor explained a large proportion of the covariation among tests. Higher order oblique factors models involving two kinds of content (semantic and figural), three types of operations (divergent production, evaluation, and cognition), and six forms of products (units, classes, relations, systems, transformations, and implications) accounted for highly comparable proportions of covariation among the test variables, although the products model held a very slight edge over the others. Michael and Bachelor concluded that Guilford and his coworkers tended both to extract and to rotate too many factors, and that the factor structure of creativity measures could be given a more parsimonious interpretation than that provided by Guilford.

In 1983, Guilford discussed that importance of the product of transformations was crucial to tasks involving creative problem solving. He emphasized the role of tranformations within all five SOI operations within that report with particular focus on mathematical and scientific type tasks. Subotnik (1988) also found clear evidence that convergent production of semantic transformations, convergent production of semantic implications, and evaluation of semantic implications were relevant to problem-oriented tasks in mathematics and science for gifted adolescents. Thus, within the framework of the SOI models, creativity extends beyond the operation of divergent production.

OVERVIEW

The dimensionality of mental abilities and intellectual functioning has engaged researchers and psychologists for over 50 years. The SOI model presented by Guilford grew out of those efforts and is currently at the forefront of the discussion on human intellectual ability and its dimensionality. Despite the prominence of the SOI model, it has been criticized on conceptual as well as methodological grounds, both detailed in this review. Even the severest critics have commended the model for contributing to the debate about the nature of human intellectual functioning, for serving to stimulate creative test construction, and for generating innovative statistical methods. Furthermore, the SOI model has heuristic value, and nothing has yet decisively refuted the model.

It is noteworthy that the most cited criticisms of the model stem from problems inherent in the methods used to demonstrate empirical support for the model. A key issue is that Procrustean factor-analytic methods, which are viewed as subjective, cannot test hypotheses in a valid manner. For this reason researchers in the 1980s and 1990s applied maximum likelihood confirmatory factor analysis (Jöreskog & Sörbom, 1986) to data sets from the USC Aptitude Research Project. In this manner, one may more objectively test competing alternative hypotheses regarding the factor structure that underlies correlations among variables. Results of these reanalyses have revealed three major conclusions. First, the search for higher order factors, which was called for by Cronbach (1970) and others, was joined by Guilford (1981). This inquiry was warranted and fruitful, and many of the hypothesized factors were uncovered. Second, the orthogonality of the SOI model was successfully refuted by researchers. Guilford concurred in 1981. Third, creativity within the SOI model extends beyond the operation of divergent production. Research in this area has demonstrated that the creative process necessitates a multidimensional perspective as it is an interaction of mental abilities within an hierarchical order.

Tests designed to measure abilities key to the creative process have been produced in the course of research on the development and nature of creativity. Three major series in this effort are the Torrance Tests of Creative Thinking, the tests developed in the Aptitudes Research Project headed by Guilford, and Wallach and Kogan's creativity tests. The tests developed in the Aptitudes Research Project were designed to facilitate research on the SOI and were a result of the factor-analytic inquiry into the nature of intellectual functioning as well as the creative process. Tests designed to assess creative functioning were generally found within the operation of divergent production. These tests as well as the Torrance tests were typically open-ended with limited data on reliability and validity. Although Torrance tests were generated in another long-term research program, this inquiry focused on education and classroom experiences that promote and encourage creative activities (Torrance, 1962, 1963, 1965). Some Torrance tests were adapted from measures used in the Aptitudes Research Project. In addition, the Torrance test battery scored such qualities as fluency, flexibility, originality, and elaboration, which were factors identified as aspects of creative ability in SOI research. However, Torrance did not attempt to create factorially pure tests as did Guilford; rather, Torrance endeavored to construct situations that would resemble the naturally occurring complexity of creative activity. Each test was consequently scored on some or all of the aforementioned factors.

Wallach and Kogan's (1965) associative creative thinking tests also utilized some SOI tests that were modified for their purposes. In contrast to the test development of Guilford and his colleagues at the Aptitudes Research Project, Wallach and Kogan sought to measure and define creative abilities separate as from intelligence. Wallach and Kogan tests are also scored on the SOI factors of fluency and originality. Psychometric contrasts between the Wallach and Kogan tests and the SOI battery can be found in Richards (1976).

Tests of creative abilities have thus evolved out of research investigations into human mental functioning. The development and construction of each of the sets of tests mentioned earlier have considerable overlap, and yet important distinctions that stem from the theoretical bent of its primary investigator and the setting in which creative activity was assessed.

To conclude, Guilford and his colleagues' efforts have produced a model that not only encompasses intellectual functioning, but creativity as well. The SOI conceptualization of mental abilities has been—and will continue to be—a rich source of research inquiry.

REFERENCES

Bachelor, P.A. (1986-1987). Higher-order factors in Guilford's SOI model: Divergent production. *Educational Research Quarterly, 11,* 29-40.

Bachelor, P.A. (1989) Maximum likelihood confirmatory factor- analytic investigation of factors within Guilford's structure of intellect model. *Journal of Applied Psychology, 5,* 797-804.

Bachelor, P.A., & Bachelor, B.G. (1989). An investigation of the higher-order symbolic factors of cognition and convergent production within the structure-of-intellect model. *Educational and Psychological Measurement, 49,* 537-548.

Bachelor, P., & Michael, W.B. (1991). Higher-order factors of Creativity within Guilford's structure-of-intellect model: A re-analysis of a fifty-three variable data base. *Creativity Research Journal, 4,* 157-175.

Burt, C.L. (1955). The evidence for the concept of intelligence. *British Journal of Educational Psychology, 25,* 158-177.

Butcher, H.J. (1973). Intelligence and creativity. In P. Kline (Ed.), *New approaches in psychological measurement* (pp. 43-64). New York: Wiley.

Carroll, J.B. (1968). Review of the nature of human intelligence by J.P. Guilford. *American Educational Research Journal, 5,* 249-256.

Carroll, J.B. (1972). Stalking the wayward factors. *Contemporary Psychology, 17,* 321-324.

Cattell, R.B. (1963). Theory of fluid and crystallized intelligence: A critical experiment. *Journal of Educational Psychology, 54,* 1-22.

Cliff, N. (1966) Orthogonal rotation to congruity. *Psychometrika, 31,* 33-42.

Cronbach, L.J. (1970). Test validation. In R.L. Thorndike (Ed.), *Educational measurement* (pp. 443-507). Washington, DC: American Council on Education.

Delaney, J.O., & Maguire, T.O. (1974). A comparison between the structures of divergent production abilities of children at levels of intellectual functioning. *Multivariate Behavioral Research, 9,* 37-45.

Eysenck, H.J., & Fulker, D.W. (1979). *The structure and measurement of intelligence.* Berlin: Springer-Verlag.

Favero, J., Dombrower, J., Michael, W.B., & Richards, L. (1975). Interrelationships among 76 individually-administered tests intended to represent 76 different structure-of-intellect abilities and a standardized general intelligence test in a sample of 34 nine-year children. *Educational and Psychological Measurement, 35,* 933-104.

Guilford, J.P. (1959). Three faces of intellect. *American Psychologist, 14,* 469-479.

Guilford, J.P. (1967a). Creativity: Yesterday, today, and tomorrow. *Journal of Creative Behavior, 1,* 3-21.

Guilford, J.P. (1967b). *The nature of human intelligence.* New York: McGraw-Hill.

Guilford, J.P. (1972). Some misconceptions about factors. *Psychological Bulletin, 77,* 392-396.

Guilford, J.P. (1974). Rotation problems in factor analysis. *Psychological Bulletin, 81,* 498-501.

Guilford, J.P. (1977). *Way beyond the IQ: Guide to improving intelligence and creativity.* Buffalo: Creative Education Foundation.

Guilford, J.P. (1979). *Cognitive psychology with a frame of reference.* San Diego: EDITS.

Guilford, J.P. (1980). Fluid and crystallized intelligences: Two fanciful concepts. *Psychological Bulletin, 88,* 406-412.

Guilford, J.P. (1981). Higher-order structure-of-intellect abilities. *Multivariate Behavioral Research, 16,* 411-435.

Guilford, J. P. (1982). Cognitive psychology's ambiguities: Some suggested remedies. *Psychological Review, 89,* 48-59.

Guilford, J.P. (1983). Transformation abilities or functions. *Journal of Creative Behavior, 17,* 75-83.

Guilford, J.P. (1984). Varieties of divergent production. *Journal of Creative Behavior, 18,* 1-10.

Guilford, J.P. (1985). The structure-of-intellect model. In B.B. Wolman (Ed.), *Handbook of intelligence* (pp. 225-266). New York: Wiley.

Guilford, J.P. (1988). Some changes in the structure-of-intellect model. *Educational and Psychological Measurement, 48,* 1-4.

Guilford, J.P., & Hoefner, R. (1971). *The analysis of intelligence.* New York: McGraw-Hill.

Guilford, J.P., Merrifield, P.R., Christensen, P.R., & Frick, J.W. (1960). An investigation of symbolic factors of cognition and convergent production. *Reports from the Psychological Laboratory* (No. 23). Los Angeles: University of Southern California.

Harris, M.L., & Harris, C.W. (1971). A factor analytic interpretation strategy. *Educational and Psychological Measurement, 31,* 589-606.

Haynes, J.R. (1970). Hierarchical analysis of factors in cognition. *American Educational Research Journal, 7,* 55-68.

Hoepfner, R., & Guilford, J.P. (1965). Figural, symbolic, and semantic factor of creative potential in ninth-grade students. *Reports from the Psychological Laboratory* (No. 35). Los Angeles: University of Southern California.

Horn, J.L. (1970). Review of J.P. Guilford's the nature of human intelligence. *Psychometrika, 35,* 273-277.

Horn, J.L. (1972). Structure of intellect: Primary abilities. In R.M. Dreger (Ed.), *Multivariate personality research* (pp. 451-511). New Orleans: Claitor.

Horn, J.L. (1977). Personality and ability theory. In R.B. Cattell & R.M. Dreger (Eds.), *Handbook of modern personality theory* (pp. 139-165). Washington: Hemisphere.

Horn, J.L., & Knapp, J.R. (1973). On the subjective character of the empirical base of Guilford's structure-of-intellect model. *Psychological Bulletin, 80,* 33-43.

Horn, J.L., & Knapp, J.R. (1974). Thirty wrongs do not make a right: Reply to Guilford. *Psychological Bulletin, 81,* 502-504.

Jöreskog, K., & Sörbom, D. (1984). *LISREL VI: Analysis of linear structural relationships by maximum likelihood, instrumental variables, and least squares.* Mooresville, IN: Scientific Software, Inc.

Jöreskog, K., & Sörbom, D. (1986). *LISREL VI: Analysis of linear structural relationships by maximum likelihood, instrumental variables, and least squares methods: User's guide* (4th ed.). Uppsala, Sweden: University of Uppsala.

Kelderman, H., Mellenbergh, G.J., & Elshout, J.J. (1981). Guilford's facet theory of intelligence: An empirical comparison of models. *Multivariate Behavioral Research, 16,* 37-61.

Khattab, A.M., Michael, W.B., & Hocevar, D. (1982) The construct validity of higher-order structure-of-intellect abilities in a battery of test emphasizing the product of transformation: A confirmatory maximum likelihood factor analysis. *Educational and Psychological Measurement, 42,* 1090-1105.

Marks, A., Guilford, J.P., & Merrifield, P.R. (1959). A study of military leadership in relation to selected intellectual factors. *Reports from the Psychological Laboratory* (No. 21). Los Angeles: University of Southern California.

Merrifield, P., Guilford, J.P. & Gershon, A. (1963). The differentiation of divergent production abilities at the sixth-grade level. *Reports from the Psychological Laboratory* (No. 27). Los Angeles: University of Southern California.

Michael, W.B. (1977). Cognitive and affective components of creativity in mathematics and the physical sciences. In J.C. Stanley, W.C. George, & C.H. Solano (Eds.), *The gifted and the creative: A 50-year perspective* (pp. 141-172). Baltimore: The Johns Hopkins University Press.

Michael, W.B., & Bachelor, P. (1990). Higher-order structure- of-intellect creativity factors in divergent production tests. *Creativity Research Journal, 3,* 58-74.

Michael, W.B., & Bachelor, P. (1992). First-order and higher-order creative ability factors in structure-of-intellect measures administered to sixth-grade children. *Educational and Psychological Measurement, 52,* 261-273.

Richards, R.L. (1976). A comparison of selected Guilford and Wallach-Kogan creative thinking tests in conjunction with measures of intelligence. *Journal of Creative Behavior, 10,* 151-164.

Ryle, G. (1949). *The concept of mind.* London: Hutchison.

Schonemann, P.H. (1966). A generalized solution of the orthogonal procrustes problem. *Psychometrika, 31,* 1-10.

Spearman, C. (1927). *The abilities of man.* New York: Macmillan.

Subotnik, R.F. (1988). Factors from the structure-of-intellect model associated with gifted adolescents' problem finding in science: Research with Westinghouse science talent search winners. *Journal of Creative Behavior, 22,* 42-54.

Thorndike, E.L. (1927). *The measurement of intelligence.* New York: Teacher's College, Columbia University.

Thurstone, L.L. (1938). *Primary mental abilities.* Chicago: Chicago University Press.

Thurstone, L.L., & Thurstone, T.E. (1941). Factorial studies of intelligence. *Psychometrics Monographs,* No. 2.

Torrance, E.P. (1962). *Guiding creative talent.* Englewood Cliffs, NJ: Prentice-Hall.

Torrance, E.P. (1963). *Education and the creative potential.* Minneapolis: University of Minnesota.

Torrance, E.P. (1965). *Rewarding creative behavior.* Englewood Cliffs, NJ: Prentice-Hall.

Ulosevich, S., Michael, W.B., & Bachelor, P. (1991). Higher-order factors in structure-of-intellect (SOI) aptitude tests hypothesized to portray constructs of military leadership: A re-analysis of an SOI data base. *Educational and Psychological Measurement, 51,* 15-37.

Undheim, J., & Horn, J.L. (1977). Critical evaluation of Guilford's structure-of-intelligent theory. *Intelligence, 1,* 65-81.

van den Bergh, H. (1990). On the construct validity of multiple-choice items for reading comprehension. *Applied Psychological Measurement, 14,* 1-12.

Vernon, P.E. (1950). *The structure of human abilities*. New York: Wiley.

Vernon, P.E. (1979). *Intelligence: Heredity and environment*. San Francisco: Freeman.

Wallach, M.A., & Kogan, N. (1965). *Modes of thinking in young children: A study of the creativity-intelligence distinction*. New York: Holt, Rinehart & Winston.

Wherry, R.J. (1959). Hierarchical factor solutions without rotation. *Psychometrika, 24,* 45-51.

Zimmerman, W. S. (1946). A simple graphical method of rotation of axes. *Psychometrika, 11,* 51-56.

8 Mental Imagery and Visual Creativity

Ronald A. Finke

Texas A & M University

In the past 20 years, the field of mental imagery has been transformed into one of the dominant areas of research within cognitive psychology. This has resulted largely from the development of novel experimental methods that enable one to study mental images under controlled laboratory conditions (Finke, 1986a, 1989; Kosslyn, 1980; Paivio, 1979; Pinker, 1984; Shepard & Cooper, 1982). Although much of this research has focused on the nature of imagery itself and its functions in traditional perceptual and cognitive tasks, this work also has important implications for the role that imagery plays in visual creativity. In addition, some recent studies have begun to explore the specific ways in which imagery contributes to creative invention and discovery (Finke, 1990; Finke, Ward, & Smith, 1992). Taken together, these studies reveal various properties of images that facilitate creative thinking in general; these properties are reviewed in the present chapter.

Having a scientific basis for investigating the creative aspects of imagery represents a considerable advance over reliance on informal and anecdotal accounts (e.g., Miller, 1986; Shepard, 1978, 1988). It also provides an attractive alternative to so-called "New Age" approaches to creative visualization and related topics. This in turn has led to deeper understandings of the fundamental cognitive processes underlying both imagery and creativity.

VISUAL AND SPATIAL PROPERTIES

A number of studies have shown that mental images exhibit many of the same kinds of properties that are important in the perception of visual shapes, movements, and spatial relations (Farah, 1988, 1989; Finke, 1980, 1989; Finke & Shepard, 1986; Podgorny & Shepard, 1978; Shepard, 1981, 1984). These properties facilitate the exploration and anticipation of perceptual features that are often useful in solving problems or planning actions.

Representing Complex Relationships

One of the advantages of being able to imagine the structure of an object and its parts is that it enables one to represent complex relations simultaneously. For example, when given descriptions of a problem, experts typically form images or construct visual diagrams in which the various features of the problem are depicted all at once (e.g., Beveridge & Parkins, 1987; Clement, 1988; Larkin & Simon, 1987; Simon & Barenfeld, 1969). This makes it easier to recognize key relations that provide insights into the solutions.

Constructing Spatial Analogies

Related work has shown that images are often useful in constructing spatial analogies for solving problems involving ordered relations. For example, Huttenlocher (1968) found that when given problems such as "If A is larger than B, and C is smaller than B, is A larger than C?" subjects construct images that depict the relative sizes simultaneously, thereby making it easier to judge these relations. Imagery is especially helpful in such tasks when category labels indicating relative differences in size are not provided (Kosslyn, Murphy, Bemesderfer, & Feinstein, 1977).

Cognitive Maps

Studies of cognitive "maps" have established that the images people form often reflect the actual spatial relations among the features in their environment (Baird, 1979; Evans, 1980; Kosslyn, Pick, & Fariello, 1974). This is particularly useful when trying to discover novel shortcuts. For example, Levine, Jankovic, and Palij (1982) found that when blindfolded subjects were moved from place to place along a particular route, they could discover shortcuts connecting the various places by imagining the entire spatial layout. Sometimes, however, these cognitive maps are distorted by the presence of salient landmarks, boundaries, and superordinant relations (e.g., Lynch, 1960; McNamara, 1986; Stevens & Coupe, 1978; Tversky, 1981; Tversky & Schiano, 1989).

Mental Image Acuity

Mental images can exhibit many of the distinctive visual characteristics of perceived objects and events. Like perception, imagery has a limited "field" of vision within which the details of an object can be depicted (Kosslyn, 1978). Acuity for visual detail in an image is reduced as an object is imagined at a smaller size or at increasingly more peripheral locations in the visual field (e.g., Finke & Kurtzman, 1981; Kosslyn, 1975). These properties enable one to anticipate the actual visual appearance of an object as it would be seen from a certain distance or location. They also suggest that imagery cannot be explained solely in terms of symbolic representations, as suggested by propositional models (e.g., Kosslyn & Pomerantz, 1977; Pylyshyn, 1973, 1981).

Image Priming and Interference

Forming a mental image can sometimes facilitate ongoing perceptual processes. Farah (1985) found that letters of the alphabet could be detected more easily when one first imagines the letters, and Freyd and Finke (1984a) reported that people could detect small differences in patterns more easily by imagining a visual context that highlighted those differences. Such findings suggest that imagery could be used to improve perceptual skills in creative ways. For example, one could make an unfamiliar form easier to recognize by imagining its unusual or distinctive features, or by mentally creating a helpful context. There is evidence, however, that imagery can sometimes interfere with perception, especially when the imagined form is incompatible with a form that is actually presented (Finke, 1986b; Segal & Fusella, 1970).

Image Adaptation and Aftereffects

Some studies have suggested that forming an image can lead to aftereffects corresponding to those that result when an object or pattern is observed (e.g., Finke & Schmidt, 1977). These imagery aftereffects appear to result not from fatigue or adaptation in the visual system (Rhodes & O'Leary, 1985), but from associations that are formed between the imagined and observed features (Finke, 1989). Changes in visual-motor coordination can also result when one imagines making errors of movement; these changes resemble the visual-motor aftereffects that follow prism adaptation (Finke, 1979). Such findings suggest that imagery could be used to explore the consequences of making novel types of movements.

IMPLICIT ENCODING

The features of an image often consist of details that were not explicitly encoded when an object was initially seen. For example, when asked questions such as "Did Thomas Jefferson have a beard?", most people report that they have to form an image of Thomas Jefferson (Finke, 1989; Kosslyn, 1980). Imagery may thus be useful for recalling details that may not have been important initially. This may help to explain why creative insights sometimes result when a person forms an image and then notices certain features that were previously overlooked.

Incidental Recall

There are a number of demonstrations of the importance of imagery in recalling information that was not explicitly or intentionally memorized. Brooks (1968), for example, found that certain properties of letters, such as the shapes of their corners, could be recalled by imagining and then mentally inspecting the letters, even though one would not have intentionally committed such information to memory. He also showed that, when visualization is disrupted, performance on such tasks is markedly impaired. Shepard (1966) provided a particularly striking example of this use of imagery, asking people to try to recall the number of windows in their house. They reported imagining that they went through their house and counted the windows. Such studies suggest that imagery could be used in creative ways to recover information from memory that would otherwise be unavailable.

Imagery Mnemonics

One of the most effective ways to remember a set of items is to imagine the items interacting in meaningful ways (e.g., Bower, 1970). These meaningful interactions need not be based on purposeful memorization; rather, their effectiveness stems from the creation of novel and distinctive associations among the features of the items, which makes them easier to recall (McDaniel & Einstein, 1986). This forms the basis for many popular mnemonic techniques (e.g., Lorayne & Lucas, 1974; Yates, 1966). Thus, another way to improve one's memory is by trying to imagine creative associations.

Mental Comparisons

Sometimes it is necessary to compare items in memory that have never been explicitly compared before. In such cases, imagery can be considerably useful. For example, in the *symbolic distance* effect, a person is given the names of a pair of items and is asked to compare them along some dimension such as size (as in, "Which is larger, a beaver or a raccoon?"). Most people report that they answer such questions by imagining the items next to each other and then mentally comparing them; this becomes easier as the items become more dissimilar in size (Moyer, 1973). It would therefore be possible to use imagery in this manner to make a variety of novel, creative comparisons.

IMAGE SCANNING

How does one recover information contained in an image, once the image is formed? Many studies have shown that images can be scanned, in a manner similar to scanning an actual picture or map, to retrieve this information. Image scanning can also be used to discover novel spatial relations among the imagined items.

Imagined Scanning of Pictures and Maps

Kosslyn (1973) found that the time it takes to scan between features on imagined pictures of common objects increases as the distance between the features increases. In a subsequent study, Kosslyn, Ball, and Reiser (1978) found that image-scanning times are proportional both to the actual distance between the features and to the number of items that appear along the scan path. More recently, Reed, Hock, and Lockhead (1983) found that image scanning is slowed if the scan path is curved or bent. Thus, scanning distance, the shape of the scan path, and the number of intervening items all influence the time it takes to retrieve information from an image.

Scanning in Three Dimensions

Pinker (1980) reported an effect of distance on image-scanning time for the imagined scanning of three-dimensional configurations of objects. Depending on the instructions, subjects were able to imagine scanning the array of objects in depth, independently of vantage point, or along flat, two-dimensional projections of the objects as they would be seen from particular vantage points. Both types of scanning could be accomplished even after the subjects imagined rotating the array of objects to novel positions (Pinker & Finke, 1980).

Spontaneous Image Scanning

Image scanning can also be used to verify spatial relations that were never explicitly encoded. In an investigation by Finke and Pinker (1982, 1983), subjects were shown simple dot patterns, which were replaced by an arrow pointing in some direction. Their task was to say whether the arrow was pointing at any of the previously seen dots. The subjects reported spontaneously scanning an image of the pattern along the direction indicated by the arrow to see whether the scan path would intersect any of the dots. Their response times displayed the same dependence on scanning distance as had been found in previous image-scanning studies. Moreover, image scanning occurred only when the correct directions could not be anticipated in advance. Image scanning can therefore be used not only to retrieve information, but also to explore novel directions and spatial relations.

MENTAL TRANSFORMATION

Much of the current imagery literature has addressed the topic of mental transformations, particularly the imagined rotation of an object or pattern. Mental transformations enable one to anticipate how something will look when seen from different perspectives or points of view. This facilitates creative exploration and manipulation.

Mental Rotation

Shepard and Metzler (1971) presented subjects with pairs of perspective line drawings of three-dimensional forms, depicting rotational separations either in the picture place or in depth. They found that the time it took to verify that the forms were identical in shape increased in proportion to the size of these rotations, and they concluded that the task was performed by mentally rotating one of the forms into alignment with the other. Using two-dimensional patterns, Cooper (1976) found that the rates of mental rotation were approximately continuous, whereas Cooper (1975) found that the rates were independent of the complexity of the patterns, suggesting that mental rotations are performed on whole, intact representations of patterns. These findings are generally true, however, only after the patterns become sufficiently familiar (Bethell-Fox & Shepard, 1988).

Judging New Directions and Appearances

In addition to anticipating how a particular object will look after being rotated, mental rotation can help one to anticipate changes in the appearance of entire configurations of objects. Huttenlocher and Presson (1973), for example, found that mental rotation can be used to determine the relative positions of landmarks in an environment as they would appear from rotated vantage points. People can also use mental rotation to determine directions of objects relative to themselves following imagined changes in body orientation (Hintzman, O'Dell, & Arndt, 1981), as well as to distinguish right and left turns (Shepard & Hurwitz, 1984). Such skills are of considerable value in orienting oneself within a transformed environment.

Mental Normalization

More abstract types of mental transformations have also been explored. These include the imagined transformation of the size of an object (Bundesen & Larsen, 1975), its shape (Shepard & Feng, 1972), and its color (Dixon & Just, 1978). In general, mental transformations can eliminate differences along stimulus dimensions that are irrelevant to a particular comparison or judgment. For example, mental rotation compensates for irrelevant differences in orientation, so that one can more easily compare the objects according to their shape. This ability to use imagery to mentally normalize irrelevant differences can also result in creative types of mental comparisons.

Representational Momentum

Mental transformations can acquire intertial properties that are analogous to those of physically moving objects. In their study of *representa-*

tional momentum, Freyd and Finke (1984b) found that when people are shown a series of displays depicting an object undergoing smooth motion, they remember having last seen the object in a position that is shifted ahead in time with respect to the actual final position. These shifts in remembered position increase with increasing implied velocity of the displays (Freyd & Finke, 1985) and with increasing retention interval (Freyd & Johnson, 1987). Representational momentum can help one to keep track of actions that momentarily pass out of view, and can also be useful in carrying out mental simulations of imagined events.

MENTAL SYNTHESIS

Another useful property of mental imagery is that it can assist the mental construction of objects and patterns from individual parts to see how the completed form would actually look. This makes it possible to recognize something that one has never actually seen before.

Recognizing Mentally Synthesized Patterns

Thompson and Klatzky (1978) showed that when subjects are given the fragmented pieces of a pattern, they can recognize the pattern by imagining that they are assembling the pieces. When the parts form a coherent, whole pattern, the time it takes to recognize the pattern is independent of the number of parts, which implies that the imagined synthesis is complete. Mental synthesis can also be achieved when the parts are merely described, in which case the recognition times are independent of both the number of parts and the manner in which the parts are described, as long as sufficient time is allowed for completing the synthesis (Glushko & Cooper, 1978). Similar findings have been reported for the recognition of faces when given descriptions of facial features (Intons-Peterson, 1981). Thus, a person can use imagery to recognize patterns and faces that are merely described or shown only in a piecemeal fashion.

Mental Synthesis for Three-Dimensional Objects

These findings have been extended to the mental synthesis of three-dimensional objects. Cooper (1990) presented engineering students with two orthographic views of an object, their task being to verify whether or not a third orthographic view was compatible with the first two. They were then given a surprise recognition test for isometric drawings of the objects; their successful performance on this test suggested that they had constructed three-dimensional representations of the depicted objects in the orthographic verification task. In addition, Klopfer (1985) found that the three-dimensional forms used in the Shepard and Metzler (1971) study on mental rotation could be mentally synthesized when the forms were presented one section at a time.

Image Generation

There are a number of factors that determine the time it takes to mentally synthesize the parts of an object or pattern in an image. Kosslyn, Reiser, Farah, and Fliegel (1983) found that the time required to generate an imagined pattern depends on both the number of parts that the image contains as well as the manner in which the parts are organized. As a general rule, the more complex the imagined form, the longer it takes to generate the image (Glushko & Cooper, 1978; Klopfer, 1985; Kosslyn, Cave, Provost, & von Gierke, 1988). This is apparently true for the generation of three-dimensional images as well (Roth & Kosslyn, 1988).

IMAGE REINTERPRETATION

Once an image is generated, it is often possible to reinterpret the image in unexpected and creative ways. This can result from structural ambiguities and emergent features in the imagined form.

Emergent Patterns in Mental Rotation

Pinker and Finke (1980) investigated the emergence of unexpected patterns following mental rotation. Subjects first learned the locations of objects suspended in a cylinder, which was then rotated to an unexpected position after the objects had been removed, with instructions to mentally rotate the objects. The subjects' task was to then identify the pattern that would be formed by the objects as seen from this new position, in the same way that stars often appear to form recognizable patterns in constellations. After completing their mental rotations, the subjects were able to correctly recognize a parallelogram, although none had been able to guess that this particular pattern would emerge.

Imagined Visual Constructions

Finke, Pinker, and Farah (1989) explored the recognition of patterns that emerge in an image following a sequence of mental constructions and transformations. For each task, a starting pattern was described, which consisted of a simple geometric form or alphanumeric character. This was followed by instructions to alter the pattern in specified ways, for example, by rotating the pattern, combining it with other patterns, or deleting some of its parts. The task was then to try to recognize the final pattern at the end of the transformation sequence. The subjects were able to do this successfully, even though they were rarely able to guess in advance what the final pattern would be. It is therefore possible to discover familiar patterns in an image, even when the patterns cannot be anticipated at the time the image is originally formed.

Constraints on Image Reinterpretation

There are certain constraints on the extent to which an image will yield new discoveries or interpretations. Reed (1974) and Palmer (1977) reported that it was much easier to detect structurally "good" parts in an image, that is, those parts that would normally be included in a simple description of the pattern. More recently, Chambers and Reisberg (1985) found that certain types of classic ambiguous figures, such as the Necker cube, could rarely be reversed in imagination. These findings call attention to cases in which images cannot be reinterpreted as easily as visually perceived patterns.

COMBINATIONAL PLAY

Image discoveries of a highly creative nature can often be achieved when one explores novel combinations of features in mental synthesis. The resulting discoveries are then more likely to be both unexpected and original.

Creative Mental Synthesis

Finke and Slayton (1988) developed an experimental paradigm in which one has the opportunity to engage in creative mental synthesis and discovery. The subjects were given three parts chosen at random from a set of 15 basic geometric forms and alphanumeric characters, and they were instructed to imagine combining the parts to make a recognizable pattern. The procedure yielded a large number of patterns that were judged to be both recognizable and creative. The creative patterns, moreover, could rarely be predicted in advance, either by the experimenters or the subjects, which helped to rule out the possibility of experimenter effects and demand characteristics (Intons-Peterson, 1983).

Creative Invention

The methods of Finke and Slayton (1988) were extended in a series of experiments by Finke (1990) to explore the use of mental synthesis in discovering creative inventions. The parts now consisted of three-dimensional shapes, such as a sphere and a cube, and simple object parts, such as a hook or a wire. Three parts were used for each mental synthesis, and the subjects were instructed to try to construct a practical object or device within various object categories (e.g., furniture, tools, scientific instruments). The subjects were surprisingly successful in using this technique to generate creative inventions, which were judged according to both their practicality and originality. The number of creative inventions increased when both the parts and the object category were specified randomly at the beginning of each trial. These findings provide experimental demonstrations of how creative mental synthesis can be used to generate new ideas for inventions.

Preinventive Forms

Finke (1990) also conducted experiments in which subjects were instructed to generate an imagined form using the given parts, without initially knowing the particular kind of object that the form was supposed to represent. Rather, they were told that these "preinventive forms" were to be interesting and potentially meaningful in a general sense. After completing their preinventive forms, the subjects were given an object category, chosen at random, and were instructed to interpret their forms as a practical object or device within that category. This condition resulted in the greatest number of creative inventions, compared with those in which the subjects had known the category in advance. In addition, more creative inventions were discovered when the subjects used preinventive forms that they themselves had generated. The preinventive form studies suggest that when trying to come up with a creative invention, it might be better to imagine interesting shapes and structures before considering possible functions and applications.

GLOBAL IMAGINATION

In addition to helping one conceive of new ideas for inventions, structures generated in imagination can have more global implications, such as facilitating the discovery of new concepts, the development of mental models, and the generation of novel category exemplars.

Creative Concepts

Finke (1990) reported that the same types of preinventive forms that were useful in discovering creative inventions could also be used as visual metaphors for making conceptual discoveries. Subjects were given subject categories, such as *medicine, psychology,* and *architecture,* and their task was to interpret their preinventive forms as representing a new idea or concept that pertained to that category. Many of these interpretations were judged to be creative concepts, based on the sensibility and originality of the ideas. As with creative inventions, more creative concepts were obtained when the interpretive categories were specified randomly. Thus, preinventive forms generated in imagination can also serve as catalysts for more abstract kinds of creative discoveries.

Mental Models

Imagery can also play an important role in the formation and testing of large-scale mental models (e.g., Gentner & Stevens, 1983; Johnson-Laird, 1983). These models can be used to represent entire conceptual systems. For example, one might generate a mental model to represent how the solar system was formed or how a car engine works. Mental models are inherently dynamic and complex and can be mentally tested and modified by imagining their consequences.

Structured Imagination

When people generate exemplars of novel categories, their exemplars often have much in common with the members of familiar categories. For example, Ward (1991) found that when asked to generate examples of alien creatures that might actually live on another planet, even one markedly different from earth, subjects would generate creatures that exhibited many of the features of familiar earth creatures (e.g., possessing arms and legs, eyes and ears, and bilateral symmetry). Such findings demonstrate that creative imagination can be highly structured with respect to preexisting categories. Related studies on design fixation have shown that the exact form that an invention or idea will take is often influenced by the particular examples a person is shown prior to engaging in creative imagination (Jansson & Smith, 1991).

INVOLVEMENT, MODULARITY, AND NEUROLOGICAL CONNECTIONS

This section considers some additional topics that bear on the creative aspects of mental imagery.

Imaginative Involvement

To adequately explore creative possibilities in one's imagination, it is necessary to be able to explore images deeply and without interruption. Some people experience this kind of deep involvement with their imagery to the extent that they momentarily forget about their surroundings or ongoing activities (E.R. Hilgard, 1977; J.R. Hilgard, 1970; Spanos & McPeake, 1975; Tellegen & Atkinson, 1974). For example, when reading a book, a person may become so absorbed in imagining the story that he or she may not realize having actually read the pages. Or, when driving a car, a person might become so involved in imaginative thinking that he or she does not remember what the road or scenery looked like. Imaginative involvement can facilitate creative exploration and discovery by allowing one to escape momentarily from everyday distractions.

Modularity

Imagery is not a unitary phenomenon; there are many components that make up imagery skills. For example, one can distinguish among the processes of retrieving information to be included in an image, putting the information together in forming the image, scanning the image to recover the information, transforming the image, and regenerating parts of the image that fade (Kosslyn, 1980; Kosslyn, Brunn, Cave, & Wallach, 1984). In addition, one can distinguish between categorical and spatial processes in imagery (e.g., Kosslyn, 1987) and between identifying and localizing features in an image (Farah, Hammond, Levine, & Calvanio, 1988; Levine, Warach, & Farah, 1985). These distinctions are in the spirit of recent componential approaches to both creativity (Finke, Ward, & Smith, 1992; Sternberg & Lubart, 1991) and visual recognition (Biederman, 1987; Marr & Nishihara, 1978; Pinker, 1984).

Neurological Connections

Contrary to the popular notion that creative thinking is essentially a "right-hemisphere" process (e.g., Springer & Deutsch, 1981), some recent evidence suggests that the left cerebral hemisphere plays an important role in generating and assembling a mental image. Damage to posterior regions of the left hemisphere, for example, can affect image generation while leaving other types of visual skills intact (Farah, 1984, 1988). Electrophysiological studies have shown increased activity in the left hemisphere during image generation (Farah, Peronnet, Gonon, & Giard, 1988). Studies using split-brain patients have found that the left hemisphere is superior to the right hemisphere for many types of imagery tasks, particularly those involving the generation of highly detailed visual images (Kosslyn, Holtzman, Farah, & Gazzaniga, 1985) and the use of spatial versus categorical information (Kosslyn et al., 1989). However, there are also reported failures to find some of these differences (e.g., Sergent, 1991), suggesting that creative imagery probably involves interactions between both cerebral hemispheres (see Katz, this volume).

THEORETICAL AND PRACTICAL IMPLICATIONS

The various studies reviewed in this chapter have a number of implications for basic research on imagery in particular and creative cognitive processes in general. They indicate, first of all, that it is possible to explore creative imagery using the experimental methods of cognitive psychology and cognitive science. Traditional studies on imagery have resulted in findings that suggest new ways to study the creative aspects of imagery, whereas studies specifically designed to explore creative visualization have revealed some of the important cognitive processes that underlie creative exploration and discovery.

Second, these findings indicate that images have many properties that can contribute to creative thinking. These include the capacity for an image to be mentally scanned, transformed, and reinterpreted. In addition, the visual and spatial characteristics of an image allow one to consider complex relations and to anticipate the possible consequences of actions.

Third, these findings suggest new ways in which one might go about trying to think more creatively. For example, if one were trying to design a new invention or come up with a creative concept, one might generate an image (such as a preinventive form) and then explore its possible uses and interpretations. This could be accomplished by imagining various transformations of the form, changing the context in which the form might appear, and searching for emergent features in the form.

Finke et al. (1992) have proposed a general model of these and other creative cognitive processes, called the *Geneplore* model. The model distinguishes those processes used in the generation of preinventive forms (such as mental synthesis and transformation) and those used in the exploration and interpretation of the forms (such as attribute finding and functional inference). The Geneplore model also attempts to identify the specific properties of preinventive forms that contribute to creative discovery, such as novelty, ambiguity, incongruity, and the emergence of unexpected features. The model can account for many of the findings on creative imagery and is general enough to apply to other aspects of creativity as well.

REFERENCES

Baird, J.C. (1979). Studies of the cognitive representation of spatial relations. *Journal of Experimental Psychology: General, 108,* 90-106.

Bethell-Fox, C.E., & Shepard, R.N. (1988). Mental rotation: Effects of stimulus complexity and familiarity. *Journal of Experimental Psychology: Human Perception and Performance, 14,* 12-23.

Beveridge, M., & Parkins, E. (1987). Visual representation in analogue problem solving. *Memory & Cognition, 15,* 230-237.

Biederman, I. (1987). Recognition-by-components: A theory of human image understanding. *Psychological Review, 94,* 115- 147.

Bower, G.H. (1970). Imagery as a relational organizer in associative learning. *Journal of Verbal Learning and Verbal Behavior, 9,* 529-533.

Brooks, L.R. (1968). Spatial and verbal components of the act of recall. *Canadian Journal of Psychology, 22,* 349-368.

Bundesen, C., & Larsen, A. (1975). Visual transformation of size. *Journal of Experimental Psychology: Human Perception and Performance, 1,* 214-220.

Chambers, D., & Reisberg, D. (1985). Can mental images be ambiguous? *Journal of Experimental Psychology: Human Perception and Performance, 11,* 317-328.

Clement, J. (1988). Observed methods for generating analogies in scientific problem solving. *Cognitive Science, 12,* 563-586.

Cooper, L.A. (1975). Mental rotation of random two-dimensional shapes. *Cognitive Psychology, 7,* 20-43.

Cooper, L.A. (1976). Demonstration of a mental analog of an external rotation. *Perception & Psychophysics, 19,* 296-302.

Cooper, L.A. (1990). Mental representation of three-dimensional objects in visual problem solving and recognition. *Journal of Experimental Psychology: Learning, Memory, and Cognition, 16,* 1097-1106.

Dixon, P., & Just, M.A. (1978). Normalization of irrelevant dimensions in stimulus comparisons. *Journal of Experimental Psychology: Human Perception and Performance, 4,* 36-46.

Evans, G.W. (1980). Environmental cognition. *Psychological Bulletin, 88,* 259-287.

Farah, M.J. (1984). The neurological basis of mental imagery: A componential analysis. *Cognition, 18,* 245-272.

Farah, M.J. (1985). Psychophysical evidence for a shared representational medium for mental images and percepts. *Journal of Experimental Psychology: General, 114,* 91-103.

Farah, M.J. (1988). Is visual imagery really visual? Overlooked evidence from neuropsychology. *Psychological Review, 95,* 307-317.

Farah, M.J. (1989). Mechanisms of imagery-perceptual interaction. *Journal of Experimental Psychology: Human Perception and Performance, 15,* 203-211.

Farah, M.J., Hammond, K.M., Levine, D.N., & Calvanio, R. (1988). Visual and spatial mental imagery: Dissociable systems of representation. *Cognitive Psychology, 20,* 439- 462.

Farah, M.J., Peronnet, F., Gonon, M.A., & Giard, M.H. (1988). Electrophysiological evidence for a shared representational medium for visual images and visual percepts. *Journal of Experimental Psychology: General, 117,* 248-257.

Finke, R.A. (1979). The functional equivalence of mental images and errors of movement. *Cognitive Psychology, 11,* 235-264.

Finke, R.A. (1980). Levels of equivalence in imagery and perception. *Psychological Review, 87,* 113-132.

Finke, R.A. (1986a). Mental imagery and the visual system. *Scientific American, 254,* 88-95.

Finke, R.A. (1986b). Some consequences of visualization in pattern identification and detection. *American Journal of Psychology, 99,* 257-274.

Finke, R.A. (1989). *Principles of mental imagery.* Cambridge, MA: MIT Press.

Finke, R.A. (1990). *Creative imagery: Discoveries and inventions in visualization.* Hillsdale, NJ: Erlbaum.

Finke, R.A., & Kurtzman, H.S. (1981). Mapping the visual field in mental imagery. *Journal of Experimental Psychology: General, 110,* 501-517.

Finke, R.A., & Pinker, S. (1982). Spontaneous imagery scanning in mental extrapolation. *Journal of Experimental Psychology: Learning, Memory, and Cognition, 8,* 142-147.

Finke, R.A., & Pinker, S. (1983). Directional scanning of remembered visual patterns. *Journal of Experimental Psychology: Learning, Memory, and Cognition, 9,* 398-410.

Finke, R.A., Pinker, S., & Farah, M.J. (1989). Reinterpreting visual patterns in mental imagery. *Cognitive Science, 13,* 51-78.

Finke, R.A., & Schmidt, M.J. (1977). Orientation-specific color aftereffects following imagination. *Journal of Experimental Psychology: Human Perception and Performance, 3,* 599-606.

Finke, R.A., & Shepard, R.N. (1986). Visual functions of mental imagery. In K.R. Boff, L. Kaufman, & J. Thomas (Eds.), *Handbook of perception and human performance* (Vol. 2, pp. 1-66). New York: Wiley-Interscience.

Finke, R.A., & Slayton, K. (1988). Explorations of creative visual synthesis in mental imagery. *Memory & Cognition, 16,* 252-257.

Finke, R.A., Ward, T.B., & Smith, S.M. (1992). *Creative cognition: Theory, research, and applications.* Cambridge, MA: MIT Press.

Freyd, J.J., & Finke, R.A. (1984a). Facilitation of length discrimination using real and imagined context frames. *American Journal of Psychology, 97*, 323-341.

Freyd, J.J., & Finke, R.A. (1984b). Representational momentum. *Journal of Experimental Psychology: Learning, Memory, and Cognition, 10*, 126-132.

Freyd, J.J., & Finke, R.A. (1985). A velocity effect for representational momentum. *Bulletin of the Psychonomic Society, 23*, 443-446.

Freyd, J.J., & Johnson, J.Q. (1987). Probing the time course of representational momentum. *Journal of Experimental Psychology: Learning, Memory, and Cognition, 13*, 259-268.

Gentner, D., & Stevens, A.L. (1983). *Mental models*. Hillsdale, NJ: Erlbaum.

Glushko, R.J., & Cooper, L.A. (1978). Spatial comprehension and comparison processes in verification tasks. *Cognitive Psychology, 10*, 391-421.

Hilgard, E.R. (1977). *Divided consciousness: Multiple controls in human thought and action*. New York: Wiley-Interscience.

Hilgard, J.R. (1970). *Personality and hypnosis: A study of imaginative involvement*. Chicago: University of Chicago Press.

Hintzman, D.L., O'Dell, C.S., & Arndt, D.R. (1981). Orientation in cognitive maps. *Cognitive Psychology, 13*, 149-206.

Huttenlocher, J. (1968). Constructing spatial images: A strategy in reasoning. *Psychological Review, 4*, 277-299.

Huttenlocher, J., & Presson, C. (1973). Mental rotation and the perspective problem. *Cognitive Psychology, 4*, 277-299.

Intons-Peterson, M.J. (1981). Constructing and using unusual and common images. *Journal of Experimental Psychology: Human Learning and Memory, 7*, 133-144.

Intons-Peterson, M.J. (1983). Imagery paradigms: How vulnerable are they to experimenters' expectations? *Journal of Experimental Psychology: Human Perception and Performance, 9*, 394-412.

Jannson, D.G., & Smith, S.M. (1991). Design fixation. *Design Studies, 12*, 3-11.

Johnson-Laird, P.N. (1983). *Mental models: Towards a cognitive science of language, inference, and consciousness*. Cambridge: Cambridge University Press.

Klopfer, D.S. (1985). Constructing mental representations of objects from successive views. *Journal of Experimental Psychology: Human Perception and Performance, 11*, 566-582.

Kosslyn, S.M. (1973). Scanning visual images: Some structural implications. *Perception & Psychophysics, 14*, 90-94.

Kosslyn, S.M. (1975). Information representation in visual images. *Cognitive Psychology, 7*, 341-370.

Kosslyn, S.M. (1978). Measuring the visual angle of the mind's eye. *Cognitive Psychology, 10*, 356-389.

Kosslyn, S.M. (1980). *Image and mind*. Cambridge, MA: Harvard University Press.

Kosslyn, S.M. (1987). Seeing and imagining in the cerebral hemispheres: A computational approach. *Psychological Review, 94*, 148-175.

Kosslyn, S.M., Ball, T., & Reiser, B.J. (1978). Visual images preserve metric spatial information: Evidence from studies of image scanning. *Journal of Experimental Psychology: Human Perception and Performance, 4*, 47-60.

Kosslyn, S.M., Brunn, J.L., Cave, C.B., & Wallach, R.W. (1984). Individual differences in mental imagery ability: A computational analysis. *Cognition, 18*, 195-244.

Kosslyn, S.M., Cave, C.B., Provost, D.A., & von Gierke, S.M. (1988). Sequential processes in image generation. *Cognitive Psychology, 20*, 319-343.

Kosslyn, S.M., Holtzman, J.D., Farah, M.J., & Gazzaniga, M.S. (1985). A computational analysis of mental image generation: Evidence from functional dissociations in split-brain patients. *Journal of Experimental Psychology: General, 114*, 311-341.

Kosslyn, S.M., Koenig, O., Barrett, A., Cave, C.B., Tang, J., & Gabrieli, J. D.E. (1989). Evidence for two types of spatial representations: Hemispheric specialization for categorical and coordinate relations. *Journal of Experimental Psychology: Human Perception and Performance, 15*, 723-735.

Kosslyn, S.M., Murphy, G.L., Bemesderfer, M.E., & Feinstein, K.J. (1977). Category and continuum in mental comparisons. *Journal of Experimental Psychology: General, 106*, 341-375.

Kosslyn, S.M., Pick, H.L., & Fariello, G.R. (1974). Cognitive maps in children and men. *Child Development, 45*, 707-716.

Kosslyn, S.M., & Pomerantz, J.R. (1977). Imagery, propositions, and the form of internal representations. *Cognitive Psychology, 9*, 52-76.

Kosslyn, S.M., Reiser, B.J., Farah, M.J., & Fliegel, S.L. (1983). Generating visual images: Units and relations. *Journal of Experimental Psychology: General, 112*, 278-303.

Larkin, J.H., & Simon, H.A. (1987). Why a diagram is (sometimes) worth ten thousand words. *Cognitive Science, 11*, 65-99.

Levine, D.N., Warach, J., & Farah, M. (1985). Two visual systems in mental imagery: Dissociation of "what" and "where" in imagery disorders due to bilateral posterior cerebral lesions. *Neurology, 35*, 1010-1018.

Levine, M., Janokovic, I.N., & Palij, M. (1982). Principles of spatial problem solving. *Journal of Experimental Psychology: General, 111*, 157-175.

Lorayne, H., & Lucas, J. (1974). *The memory book.* New York: Ballantine.

Lynch, K. (1960). *The image of the city.* Cambridge, MA: MIT Press.

Marr, D., & Nishihara, H.K. (1978). Representation and recognition of the spatial organization of three-dimensional shapes. *Proceedings of the Royal Society of London, 200*, 269-294.

McDaniel, M.A., & Einstein, G.O. (1986). Bizarre imagery as an effective memory aid: The importance of distinctiveness. *Journal of Experimental Psychology: Learning, Memory, and Cognition, 12*, 54-65.

McNamara, T.P. (1986). Mental representations of spatial relations. *Cognitive Psychology, 18*, 87-121.

Miller, A. I. (1986). *Imagery in scientific thought*. Cambridge, MA: MIT Press.

Moyer, R.S. (1973). Comparing objects in memory: Evidence suggesting an internal psychophysics. *Perception & Psychophysics, 13*, 180-184.

Paivio, A. (1979). *Imagery and verbal processes*. Hillsdale, NJ: Erlbaum.

Palmer, S.E. (1977). Hierarchical structure in perceptual representation. *Cognitive Psychology, 9*, 441-474.

Pinker, S. (1980). Mental imagery and the third dimension. *Journal of Experimental Psychology: General, 109*, 354-371.

Pinker, S. (1984). Visual cognition: An introduction. *Cognition, 18*, 1-63.

Pinker, S., & Finke, R.A. (1980). Emergent two-dimensional patterns in images rotated in depth. *Journal of Experimental Psychology: Human Perception and Performance, 6*, 244-264.

Podgorny, P., & Shepard, R.N. (1978). Functional representations common to visual perception and imagination. *Journal of Experimental Psychology: Human Perception and Performance, 4*, 21-35.

Pylyshyn, Z.W. (1973). What the mind's eye tells the mind's brain: A critique of mental imagery. *Psychological Bulletin, 80*, 1-24.

Pylyshyn, Z.W. (1981). The imagery debate: Analogue media versus tacit knowledge. *Psychological Review, 88*, 16-45.

Reed, S.K. (1974). Structural descriptions and the limitations of visual images. *Memory & Cognition, 2*, 329-336.

Reed, S. K., Hock, H.S., & Lockhead, G.R. (1983). Tacit knowledge and the effect of pattern configuration on mental scanning. *Memory & Cognition, 11*, 137-143.

Rhodes, G., & O'Leary, A. (1985). Imagery effects on early visual processing. *Perception & Psychophysics, 37*, 382-388.

Roth, J.D., & Kosslyn, S.M. (1988). Construction of the third dimension in mental imagery. *Cognitive Psychology, 20*, 344-361.

Segal, S.J., & Fusella, V. (1970). Influences of imaged pictures and sounds on detection of visual and auditory signals. *Journal of Experimental Psychology, 83*, 458-464.

Sergent, J. (1991). Judgments of relative position and distance on representations of spatial relations. *Journal of Experimental Psychology: Human Perception and Performance, 91*, 762-780.

Shepard, R.N. (1966). Learning and recall as organization and search. *Journal of Verbal Learning and Verbal Behavior, 5*, 201-204.

Shepard, R.N. (1978). Externalization of mental images and the act of creation. In B. S. Randhawa & W. E. Coffman (Eds.), *Visual learning, thinking, and communication* (pp. 133-189). New York: Academic Press.

Shepard, R.N. (1981). Psychophysical complementarity. In M. Kubovy & J. R. Pomerantz (Eds.), *Perceptual organization* (pp. 279-341). Hillsdale, NJ: Erlbaum.

Shepard, R.N. (1984). Ecological constraints on internal representation: Resonant kinematics of perceiving, imagining, thinking, and dreaming. *Psychological Review, 91*, 417-447.

Shepard, R.N. (1988). The imagination of the scientist. In K. Egan & D. Nadaner (Eds.), *Imagination and education* (pp. 153-185). New York: Teachers College Press.

Shepard, R.N., & Cooper, L.A. (1982). *Mental images and their transformations.* Cambridge, MA: MIT Press.

Shepard, R.N., & Feng, C. (1972). A chronometric study of mental paper folding. *Cognitive Psychology, 3,* 228-243.

Shepard, R.N., & Hurwitz, S. (1984). Upward direction, mental rotation, and discrimination of left and right turns in maps. *Cognition, 18,* 161-193.

Shepard, R.N., & Metzler, J. (1971). Mental rotation of three-dimensional objects. *Science, 171,* 701-703.

Simon, H.A., & Barenfeld, M. (1969). Information processing analysis of perceptual processes in problem solving. *Psychological Review, 76,* 473-483.

Spanos, N.P., & McPeake, J.D. (1975). Involvement in everyday imaginative activities, attitudes toward hypnosis, and hypnotic susceptibility. *Journal of Personality and Social Psychology, 31,* 594-598.

Springer, S.P., & Deutsch, G. (1981). *Left brain, right brain.* San Francisco: Freeman.

Sternberg, R.J., & Lubart, T.I. (1991). An investment theory of creativity and its development. *Human Development, 34,* 1-31.

Stevens, A., & Coupe, P. (1978). Distortions in judged spatial relations. *Cognitive Psychology, 10,* 422-437.

Tellegen, A., & Atkinson, G. (1974). Openness to absorbing and self-altering experiences ("absorption"), a trait related to hypnotic susceptibility. *Journal of Abnormal Psychology, 83,* 268-277.

Thompson, A.L., & Klatzky, R.L. (1978). Studies of visual synthesis: Integration of fragments into forms. *Journal of Experimental Psychology: Human Perception and Performance, 4,* 244-263.

Tversky, B. (1981). Distortions in memory for maps. *Cognitive Psychology, 13,* 407-433.

Tversky, B., & Schiano, D.J. (1989). Perceptual and cognitive factors in distortions in memory for graphs and maps. *Journal of Experimental Psychology: General, 118,* 387-398.

Ward, T.B. (1991, November). *Structured imagination: The role of conceptual structure in exemplar generation.* Paper presented at the meeting of the Psychonomic Society, San Francisco, CA.

Yates, F.A. (1966). *The art of memory.* Chicago: University of Chicago Press.

9 Creativity and the Cerebral Hemispheres*

Albert N. Katz

University of Western Ontario

The introspective reports of highly creative individuals suggest that the creative product is the result of a set of distinct cognitive processes (see Bogen & Bogen, 1988; Ghiselin, 1952; Krueger, 1976; Lee, 1950; Wallas, 1926). Wallas, for example, argued that such processes are articulated within a four-stage model involving: (a) preparation (acquiring a rich, integrated knowledge base), (b) incubation (unconscious mental work), (c) illumination (a sudden reorganization of knowledge resulting in insight), and (d) verification (a deliberate check and refinement of the insight). Later work has emphasized the distinctiveness and interplay of the processes that are involved, and not the implied serial, self-terminating aspect of Wallas's model (e.g., Vinacke, 1974, pp. 356-361).

Of most immediate interest is the speculation by many that Wallas's (1926) stages represent the interaction of two cognitive components: one of which is characterized by fluid, primary process thinking, and the other by more directed, reality-based secondary thinking. These components can be mapped onto the creative act. In the inspirational phase of creativity (analogous to the incubation and illumination phas-

---

*The preparation of this chapter was supported by a grant (Grant GP0007040) to the author from the Natural Sciences and Engineering Research Council of Canada.

es), a problem on which the creator has been working is suddenly perceived in a new way; old ideas are rearranged, and a novel synthesis recognized. The elaboration phase (analogous to verification) involves a conscious, systematic evaluation of the implications of the insight.

The partition of the creative act into separable components involving different cognitive processes may appear to parallel the separation of the qualitatively different cognitive processes subserved by the left and right cerebral hemispheres. The left hemisphere has been described as subserving cognitive functions that are verbal, sequential, logical, and analytical (e.g., Bogen, 1969; whereas the right cerebral hemisphere has been described as subserving cognitive functions that emphasize pattern perception, synthesis, and the holistic rearrangement of cognitive elements (e.g., Bogen, 1969; Levy-Agresti & Sperry, 1968). A factor analysis of tasks presumably sensitive to these differences produced the expected two-factor solution, indicating the functional separation of verbal-sequential (or *propositional*) from visuospatial (or *appositional*) cognitive functions (Gordon, 1986). Bogen, DeZure, TenHouten, and Marsh (1972) argued that differences in such tasks reflect the predominance of one hemisphere over another. They coined the term *hemisphericity* to capture their belief in the cerebral basis for these cognitive differences.

The parallel between the stages in the creative act and the duality of cognitive functions associated with different hemispheres of the brain has led to the argument that the creative act might be coordinated with cognitive activity subserved by the two hemispheres and with the interaction of the these activities (Bogen & Bogen, 1969; Hoppe, 1977). The early literature on this parallelism was marked by a noticeable lack of empirical data, a tendency to treat the functions of the cerebral hemispheres in an overly simplified fashion without recognizing that, even with a highly lateralized function such as language, one can find evidence that both hemispheres are engaged at some level, and finally, with the simplistic argument that the essential aspect of creativity resides in the right hemisphere. The claim that creativity is located "in" the right hemisphere (Edwards, 1979; Hendren, 1989) should be dispelled with at once. As Hines (1991, p. 223) pointed out, such a position would lead to the foolish argument that "Beethoven would have been as great a composer and Titian just as great a painter had their left hemispheres been removed." Creativity, like other complex activities, draws on many cognitive processes, some of which may be executed better by the left and some by the right hemisphere. To the extent that specific creative activities require more of the processes subserved by one of the hemispheres, the participation of that hemisphere will result in greater impairment in performance (if participation is reduced by damage) or greater facilitation (if aroused).

In this chapter the *empirical* evidence for the link between creativity and hemisphericity is examined. It is organized conjointly around issues in the measurement of hemispheric specialization and of creativity. With respect to creativity, there is a longstanding question in identifying what constitutes creativity (Katz & Thompson, 1993). At one level we can study the performance of people chosen for their acknowledged creative giftedness in real-life work situations (see Simonton [1984] for archival analyses and MacKinnon [1975] for a study of eminent people nominated by peers). At the second level we can study people chosen as creative on the basis of performance on psychometric instruments constructed to measure components assumed to be involved in creativity (Brown, 1989). Finally, we can study people chosen because they express cognitive functions that we associate with creativity, such as the use of fantasy, or are involved in activities deemed as being creative, such as music, art, or science.

The three levels of creativity can be crossed with three levels of hemispheric-related research: research on direct measures of hemispheric activity (such as with indices of brain activity or through people with specific brain lesions), research on more indirect indices of cerebral functioning (such as through performance on propositional-appositional cognitive tests), and research on correlated functions (e.g., by showing that changes in creativity are correlated with changes in procedures that can be shown to influence the hemispheres in different ways). Each of the three approaches to studying hemisphere activity is examined for each of the three approaches to creativity.

CREATIVITY: GIFTED PEOPLE

Direct Measures of Hemisphericity

To my knowledge there is no well-controlled study in which hemisphericity has been assessed in real-life creators. There are, however, a few suggestive case studies of creative people who have suffered brain damage of one sort or another. Reviews by Hines (1991) and Gardner (1982) indicate that: (a) both hemispheres of the brain are involved in high-level creative performance, (b) different creative activities demand different cognitive skills, and (c) such skills may call on the two hemispheres differently. For instance, damage to either the left or right hemisphere has a negative effect on painters, although the type of effect appears to depend on the location of the damage. Artists who suffered unilateral right hemispheric damage still produce art, but tend to create paintings that are radically different than those seen before the brain injury. According to Gardner (1982, p. 323), "the paintings become more directly expressive, more raw and sensuous; it is as if an inhibitory mechanism has been released and the patients can now give freer vent to their most primitive, least disguised feelings."

Similar conclusions regarding the distribution and coordination of cognitive resources can be drawn from the study of gifted children. O'Boyle, Alexander, and Benbow (1991) measured the brain activity of mathematically precocious and average math ability children during the performance of neutral tasks or tasks aimed at tapping either right (RH) or left hemisphere (LH) processes. In the neutral baseline condition, EEG alpha was significantly greater over the right hemisphere in the math gifted group, indicating enhanced activation of the left hemisphere during the ostensibly neutral cognitive state. While performing a task aimed at tapping right hemisphere functioning, the gifted participants exhibited a significant reduction of alpha in the right hemisphere, but no alpha suppression was found with the participants of average ability. For the verbal left hemisphere task, differential alpha suppression was not evident. O'Boyle et al. (1991) took these data to suggest "that enhanced RH involvement during cognitive processing may be a correlate of mathematical precocity. Moreover the pattern of activation across tasks suggests that the ability to effectively coordinate LH and RH processing resources at an early age may be linked to intellectual giftedness" (p.138).

Indirect Measures of Hemisphericity

Indirect measures that are relevant involve correlates of cerebral asymmetry, such as handedness and specific task performance related to left hemisphere/propositional thinking (P) or right hemisphere/appositional thinking (A). Based on the contralateral anatomical structure of humans, one can deduce that a bias toward left-side processing indicates the arousal of right hemisphere-supported mechanisms and a bias toward the right as a special arousal of left hemisphere mechanisms.

Handedness. There is anecdotal speculation that more well-known creative geniuses have been left-handed than would be expected by chance alone. For instance, it has been noted that Leonardo da Vinci, Michelangelo, and other artistic geniuses were left-handed (Springer & Deutch, 1989). Because cerebral hemisphere asymmetry can be reduced in left-handers, such an observation would be consistent with the hypothesis of greater right hemisphere involvement in task performance for such people (Benbow, 1986). Unfortunately, the comprehensive archival study of creative genius has yet to be done, and the data from talented individuals in specific domains are variable (O'Boyle & Benbow, 1990a).

Dichotic Listening and Visual Field Task Performance. In the standard dichotic listening procedure, two different items are presented simultaneously, one to each ear. The participants' task is to remember as many items as possible. One can interpret the data as indicating greater left hemisphere involvement if more items that had been presented to the right ear are remembered; a left ear advantage indicates right hemisphere processing (Kimura, 1964). In the visual field task, items are randomly presented to the right or left visual field and participants are directed to identify the item presented on each trial. A right field advantage indicates greater left hemisphere processing, whereas a left field advantage is taken as support for right hemisphere processing superiority (Kimura, 1966).

There are no published papers in which these procedures have been employed with eminent creators. There is some evidence from the study of precocious youths. O'Boyle and Benbow (1990b) presented gifted children and average ability matched controls with a verbal dichotic listening task known to produce a robust right-ear/left-hemisphere advantage for normal right-handed participants. Compared to the average group of children, the gifted showed an attenuated right-ear advantage due to the uncharacteristically high level of performance achieved for stimuli presented to the left ear/right hemisphere. In a second study, O'Boyle and Benbow employed a visual field task known to produce a reliable left-field/right-hemisphere advantage. Although both the average ability and gifted children demonstrated a leftside bias, the bias was greater for the gifted. To quote O'Boyle and Benbow:

> These results suggests that during cognition, the RH of the intellectually precocious may be at a higher state of arousal as compared to average ability youths. By way of speculation, this enhanced RH involvement may provide additional processing resources that are unavailable to those of more moderate ability. (p. 215)

Hemisphericity. The relative dominance of one hemisphere over the other has typically been studied through one of two methods. In one, the shift in gaze to the right or left that occurs when people engage in reflective thinking has been taken as an index of hemisphericity, with conjugate lateral eye movements (CLEMs) to the right indicative of left hemisphere dominance and those to the left indicative of right hemisphere dominance (Kinsbourne, 1974; Zenhausern & Kraemer, 1991). Although popular, this technique has not been employed with unambiguously creative samples.

The second approach is to present participants with cognitive tasks that are known to show right and left hemisphere dominance. From these performance tests the relative performance of the two hemispheres can be approximated by the ratio of performance on right hemisphere (appositional) to left hemisphere (propositional) tasks (the A/P ratio; Bogen et al., 1972). Katz (1986) computed an A/P ratio from the archival data on eminent creative architects, scientists, and mathematicians studied at the Institute of Personality Assessment and Research, University of California at Berkeley. Hemisphericity was found to be related to indices of creativity, especially to objective indices (such as the number of patents held by the creator or the number of articles written about the person) and subjective indices (such as ratings given by an expert panel of peers), but not to tests that purport to measure creative abilities. The various indices of creativity were not predicted by a measure of general intelligence constructed for use with the gifted. Moreover, the direction of the relationship between hemisphericity and creativity was incompatible with the view that right hemisphere dominance would be simplistically related to creativity. Rather, creativity was related to left hemisphere dominance for architects and right hemisphere dominance for mathematicians and scientists. Katz (1986) suggested that

> Creativity depends on the cognitive functions supported by both hemispheres: different professions demand a specific cognitive mode for efficient performance; creative performance is reflected in those who can access and are efficient in using the cognitive mode supported by the complementary cerebral hemisphere. (p. 97)

Correlates of Creativity and Hemisphericity

Two types of data are reviewed in this section. The first reflect conditions known to differentially influence one of the cerebral hemispheres and creative output. Hypnotic induction and marijuana intoxication are the prototype examples. The second is based on studies of the relationship between creativity and paper-and-pencil tests presumed to tap right or left hemisphere "styles" of thought.

With respect to the first source of data, there is evidence that both hypnotic induction and marijuana intoxication are associated with the relative predominance of right hemisphere functioning. Here again there are no known controlled studies in which these techniques have been applied to real-life creators, although anecdotal evidence suggests that the link should exist (Krippner, 1968). There is some evidence for the link, at least with less gifted populations. These data are reviewed later.

With respect to the second source of data, Masten (1989) observed that gifted adolescents who were classified as having a right hemispheric learning style (see Torrance, Reynolds, Riegel, & Ball, 1977) produced more original responses on a standardized creativity test than those with left hemisphere preferences. Similar preference for right hemisphere-supported activities, or for integrating right and left hemisphere styles, were reported for the gifted by Torrance and Mourad (1979) and Kershner and Ledger (1985).

Discussion

Although the data are very incomplete, the general pattern that emerges from the literature on people who exhibit creative performance in real-life activities is one in which the cognitive processes for which the right hemisphere is most specialized may play some privileged role in creativity. However, this role (whatever it may be) is integrated and coordinated with cognitive activities subserved by the left hemisphere. Moreover, the emergence of either a left or right hemispheric dominance may depend on the type of creative activity being performed.

CREATIVITY AS DEFINED BY TEST SCORES

In this section creativity is defined by performance on tasks constructed to measure some presumed attribute of creative performance, such as divergent thinking.

Direct Measures of Hemisphericity

Federico (1984) recorded brain activity over a set of sites in the right and left hemispheres through event-related potentials (ERPs) initiated to visual, auditory, or bimodal stimuli. The participants also performed a set of cognitive tasks, some of which have been correlated with creative abilities (including Field Dependence-Independence, Tolerance of Ambiguity, Category Width, and Cognitive Complexity). Although the data are complex, the results of most immediate interest are the findings that both hemispheres are associated with the facilitation and inhibition of different cognitive functions. Activity in the parietal and temporal regions of the right hemisphere is associated with increased activity for performing field-independence tasks, but reduced activity for reading comprehension. Although Federico (1984) did not relate his study to creativity as such, the results are consistent with the notion that creativity involves bilateral hemispheric activity and the inhibition of cognitive functions of one hemisphere while the other hemisphere is active in doing a creative-relevant task (see Bogen & Bogen, 1969).

The most detailed work on the relationship between creativity and hemispheric activity has come from a series of studies in which Martindale and his colleagues have examined the EEGs of people who scored high or low on tests of creative ability. The general finding has been of greater right hemisphere activity for the high creative test scorers; these effects were often observed while the participants were actually solving the creativity tasks (Martindale & Hasenfus, 1978, Martindale & Hines, 1975; see also Martindale, 1977-1978, for a review). The most extensive investigation in this series was reported by Martindale, Hines, Mitchell, and Covello (1984). In three studies, Martindale et al. attempted to test the generalizability of the earlier results by (a) examining whether the hemispheric asymmetry would be observed in both the inspirational and elaborative phases of creative performance, and (b) demonstrating that the hemispheric asymmetry was specific to creativity and would not emerge with a noncreative task. In all cases greater RH activation was found, for both analogues of the inspirational (operationalized by asking participants to generate random speech, or to think of plots for fantasy stories) and the elaborative phase (generating a story orally, writing story). As Martindale et al. (1984) reported:

> There is a relationship between creativity and hemispheric asymmetry during creative activity. Creative Ss tend to show high levels of right-hemisphere activity (as compared to left-hemisphere activity) during creative production . . . this difference between more- and less-creative Ss is found during creative production but not during basal recordings or during a reading task. (pp. 84-85)

They speculated that, because greater right-hemisphere activation is found for both the inspirational and elaborative phases, "creative production involves an alternation back and forth" between the two phases.

Indirect Measures of Hemisphericity

Handedness. Several studies have shown a small effect favoring left-handers on some measures of divergent thinking for figural (but not verbal) tests on some measures of divergent thinking (e.g., Burke, Chrisler, & Devlin, 1989). In general, however, studies that have examined handedness and creative test performance have tended to show little in the way of a relationship. Katz (1980) reported correlations of virtually zero, ranging from $r = .010$ (for the Remote Associate Test) to a "high" of $r = .098$ for the Revised Art Scale. Correlations with divergent thinking tests fell between these extremes. Similarly convincing null effects were reported by Hattie and Fitzgerald (1983).

Dichotic Listening and Visual Field Tasks. Over the last decade several studies have appeared that have employed dichotic or visual field tasks as a means of assessing individual differences in laterality of function, and then relating these difference scores to scores obtained on creativity tests. Unfortunately, in many of these studies sample sizes were too small for the statistical analyses performed, the reliability of the hemispheric indices not considered, and the effects not shown to be specific to creativity per se. For instance, Poreh and Whitman (1991) obtained 12 measures pertaining to creativity from a sample of 47 students and performed a factor analysis on this dataset. They also obtained scores on a verbal dichotic listening task, from which one would expect to find a right ear/left hemisphere advantage. Individual differences in hemisphericity were only related to performance on a factor described by the Remote Associate Test (RAT) and a verbal closure test; as the right ear/left hemisphere advantage increased, participants did increasingly better on the two cognitive tests. Although a relationship between creative test performance and hemisphericity was obtained, it is difficult to know whether these data reflect verbal superiority or a relationship between left hemisphericity and the elaborative phase of creativity. Moreover, because the RAT correlates so highly with verbal intelligence, it is not clear that these results are specific to creative activities and do not tap noncreative intellectual factors. Other studies, with the same weaknesses, can be found in the literature, although sometimes evidence can be found for left ear/right hemisphere superiority on some (but not all) indices of creativity (e.g., Tegano, Fu, & Moran, 1983).

Katz (1983) described the one relatively large-scale study ($N = 100$) in which hemisphericity was measured by dichotic and visual field tasks that favored both right and left hemisphere. In addition, control cognitive tasks and a wide range of creativity test measures were employed. In general, the number of creativity-hemisphericity relationships was low. Nonetheless, when intelligence and verbal reasoning were controlled, Katz found several relationships between hemisphericity and creativity (defined by scoring above the median on at least three very different types of creativity tests). Knowing *only* the scores obtained on a measure of conjugate lateral eye movements (CLEMs) and three lateralized function tests, one could correctly classify around 75% of the sample as high or low creativity. (The lateralized function test effects will be discussed here, and the CLEM data in the next section.) As Katz described it, the creative and less creative samples differed with a *"pattern* of lateralized brain functions—i.e., greater left-hemisphere lateralization of verbal processes and bilateral (not right-hemisphere lateralized) processing of nonverbal, melodic processing" (p. 13; emphasis in original). Thus one can speculate from these data that the highly creative individual may be better able to both recruit and use the right hemispheric processes often associated with inspirational aspects of creativity and be more efficient at accessing the left hemispheric processes required for elaboration.

Hemisphericity. Katz (1983) also measured conjugate lateral eye movements (CLEMs) and found strong evidence that the highly creative individual tended to look leftward while engaged in reflective thinking. This indicates a preference by highly creative individuals to habitually use right hemisphere-supported processing in thinking. Although the effects are often weak, similar observation of right hemisphericity in high creative scorers have been reported by Harnad (1972) and Falcone and Loder (1984). In support of right hemisphere mediation, Hines and Martindale (1974) reported a tendency for participants to perform better on tests of creativity when forced by means of specially constructed goggles to look leftward (relative to the rightward-looking condition) while taking the tests.

Harpaz (1990) described a large sample (N = 184) study in which a set of "right" and "left" hemisphere-supported tasks were given to participants. A variant of the A/P ratio was computed and correlated with the performance measures of Torrance's Test of Creative Thinking. As Harpaz (p. 167) noted, "It is evident that some creativity tests have relatively high correlations with the . . . measures of hemisphere dominance. Four out of eight creativity tests utilized were fully or partially correlated with the right hemisphere dominance tests while only one test showed a significant correlation with left hemisphere dominance." The correlations were often impressively high (e.g., r = .59, between right hemisphere dominance and figurative fluency). It should also be noted that the one left hemisphere relationship was with a verbal test of creativity, and that most (but not all) of the observed right hemisphere effects were with figural tests of creativity.

Correlates of Hemisphericity and Creativity

As noted earlier there is evidence that hypnotic induction and marijuana intoxication both arouse the right hemisphere to a greater extent than they do the left hemisphere. With respect to hypnotic induction, Bakan (1969) reported that people who habitually exhibit left CLEMs were more hypnotizable than those who exhibit right CLEMs. Gur and Gur (1974) and Gur and Reyher (1973) confirmed and extended Bakan's results by demonstrating that hypnotizability is particularly related to right hemisphere functioning for people who are strongly right handed. Using the EEG as a measure of lateralized performance Morgan, MacDonald, and Hilgard (1974) and Morgan, MacDonald and MacDonald (1971) indicated that hypnotic responsivity is associated with the relative predominance of right hemispheric functioning. The evidence with marijuana intoxication is not as strong, but it is nonetheless suggestive. Tart (1971) found that, with marijuana intoxication, participants report impairment on left hemisphere (propositional) marker activities, such as those requiring verbalization and temporal or sequential integration, whereas right hemisphere (appositional) activities (such as those involving the synthesis of perceptual patterns) were reported as being facilitated. Harshman, Crawford, and Hecht (1976) gave participants a battery of tasks when nonintoxicated and when marijuana intoxicated. Consistent with the self-reports obtained by Tart, participants when intoxicated performed worse on verbal-analytic tasks but better on nonverbal holistic tasks. Harshman et al. (1976) provided evidence that this performance shift is related to hemisphericity by collecting dichotic listening scores from their participants; enhancement on the nonverbal holistic tests was limited to those participants with larger ear difference scores (i.e., those for whom the right and left hemisphere functions were most highly differentiated).

The hemispheric explanation for hypnotic induction and marijuana intoxication might imply that these procedures could be used to examine the hemispheric-creativity link in an experimental manner and not, as in most of the evidence reviewed earlier, in merely a correlational fashion (see Crawford [1982] for a review, and Katz [1978] for explication of the required experimental design). In the experimental design, one would wish to show that people who are under hypnosis (or are intoxicated) demonstrate heightened creativity compared to their nonhypnotized (or nonintoxicated) baselines. Although experimental manipulations are possible, most of the available evidence is correlational.

The correlational evidence is that people who are highly susceptible to hypnotic induction tend to perform better than do poor inductors on standardized tests of creativity (Ashton & McDonald, 1985; K. Bowers, 1968, 1971; K. Bowers & van der Meulen, 1970; P. Bowers, 1967; Perry, Wilder, & Appignanesi, 1973). The experimental evidence is much weaker. P. Bowers (1967), K. Bowers and van der Meulen (1970), and Jackson and Gorassini (1990) all reported data that can be taken as weak support for the hypothesis: In all these studies the hypnotized participants scored higher than nonhypnotized controls, but only on some of the measures of creativity that were employed. In other studies no support was found (e.g., Ashton & McDonald, 1985). The strongest evidence was provided by Gur and Rayner (1976) who, employing only highly hypnotizable participants, observed higher scores on Torrances's figural (but not verbal) tests of creativity when participants were under hypnotic induction compared to when nonhypnotized.

The evidence for a link between marijuana intoxication, creativity, and right hemisphere mediation is even more elusive. Most of the evidence is anecdotal (DiCyan, 1971; Krippner, 1968). There is supportive correlational evidence of a positive association between marijuana use and creativity (Victor, Grossman, & Eisenman, 1973). More direct experimental evidence can be extracted from Weckowitz et al. (1975). In this study a battery of tests was administered to groups of participants who differed in the amount of marijuana they had ingested. The data indicated that relative task enhancements and impairments differed as a function of the amount of marijuana ingested. Consistent with the hypothesis, they observed better performance on some divergent (creativity) test for participants given low levels of the drug, relative to no drug controls.

Discussion

Taken together the data seem to support the following conclusions. First, evidence of hemisphericity, when it does arise, indicates a privileged role for right hemispheric-mediated processes. Most of the studies reviewed here either indicate that creativity (as defined by performance on tests that purport to measure aspects of creative processing) is related to right hemisphere mediation or that no relationship exists; few of the studies have reported a relationship between left hemispheric-mediated tasks and creativity. Second, when the right hemisphere/creativity link is observed, it appears to emerge with nonverbal tests and is less likely to be found with verbal tests of creativity. Third, in many of the studies a battery of creativity tests was given, and hemisphericity relationships, when are they are seen, are usually found with only a few of these tests. The failure to find effects more generalizable to the battery may speak to the current underdeveloped state of creativity measurement. However, it is equally likely that the failure reflects complexities in hemisphericity itself and the conditions under which asymmetries of cerebral functions will emerge in complex activities. There is evidence that successful creative activity involves the coordination of resources from both hemispheres (e.g., Katz, 1983; Martindale et al., 1984), although the evidence for this conclusion is more indirect than the similar conclusion made earlier for gifted populations.

CREATIVITY IN EVERYDAY CONDITIONS

In this section creativity is defined by a set of functions that are tacitly assumed to be intrinsic to creative activities. Such functions include the use of imagination and fantasy in everyday activity. Moreover, people are more likely to call on those functions if they employ them habitually, as would be the case with artists (compared to nonartist controls).

Direct Measures of Hemisphericity

Animal Analogue Studies. Bogen and Bogen (1988) described an experiment in which experimental rats were trained in an escape procedure while the right hemisphere was rendered inactive by drugs. The same rats were then trained in an alternate escape procedure while the left hemisphere was inactive. In the critical test, successful escape depended on combining the two procedures. Control rats trained on the two procedures in succession (and with no chemical depression of hemispheres) performed no better on the task then rats that had no previous training at all. In contrast, the experimental rats learned the successful answer very quickly. Arguing by analogy, Bogen and Bogen suggested that laterality of cognition function in humans, and the incompleteness of interhemispheric communication, provide one mechanism for adaptive responding in novel or complex situations. Hoppe and Kyle (1990) went further and postulated that, in humans, creativity in particular may depend in part on the intercallosal process by which the "presentational symbolization and imagery in the right hemisphere are available to the left hemisphere via the corpus callosum" (p.153).

Commissurotomy Patients. There are patients who have had operations severing the major neural pathways joining the two cerebral hemispheres. Several of these patients have been studied in depth with regard to creative functioning by Hoppe (1988; Hoppe & Kyle, 1990) and TenHouten (1994). Hoppe (1988) compared the performance of eight commissurotomized patients with eight normal controls (matched for age, sex, handedness, and ethnic and linguistic background) on a task in which the participants were, over several showings, required to describe their reactions to an evocative film. EEG recordings, from a variety of sites, were taken throughout. Compared to the normal controls, the commissurotomized patients used fewer affect-laden words and few adjectives, spoken in a manner indicative of a passive and indirect presentation of self, and in general they revealed a speech "that was dull, uninvolved, flat and lacking in colour and expressiveness.

Commissurotomy patients tended not to fantasize about, imagine or interpret the symbols, and they also tended to describe the circumstances surrounding events, as opposed to describing their feelings about these events" (Hoppe & Kyle, 1990, p. 151). Hoppe and Kyle went on to state: "If one cannot fantasize about, imagine, or interpret symbols, so richly presented in the film, and if one is only describing the circumstances surrounding events but not one's own feelings about events, then one lacks creativity, as commissurotomy patients do" (p. 152).

Seven of the eight patients suffered from what has been called *alexithymia*, a cognitive-affective disturbance in which one has difficulty in identifying one's feelings or describing them to others. The EEG data indicated that the alexithmic participants differed from the expressive ones by showing less activation in the right temporal area and in language areas of the left hemisphere. Hoppe and Kyle suggested that these data reflect a right hemispheric-based inability to grasp imagery and symbolism and a left hemispheric-based inhibition in conducting inner speech between the two language areas.

TenHouten (1994) analyzed the handwriting of the same subjects in sentences they wrote about the film used in the experiment. Employing a quantitative method for measuring and interpreting handwriting, a professional graphologist scored the sentences, without knowledge of status as a member of the commissurotomy or control group. The graphological features studied differed markedly between the two groups such that "commissurotomy patients, in contrast to precision-matched controls, show deficits in Creative Aspirations, Creative Organization, Goal Direction, Libidinal Energy, Expression of Feelings, and Control." TenHouten described these differences as indications of deficits in intentionality (i.e., a lack in the patients regarding their cares about the state of future affairs and their inability to develop a program and to carry this program through, overcoming distractions and obstacles). TenHouten speculated further that the lack of creativity of the patients was due to both a failure of callosal communication (as described by Hoppe) and a failure of will power and intentionality.

Task Manipulations. There is evidence that direct measures of brain functioning can be related to on-the-job performance, often predicting better than paper-and-pencil tests (e.g., Lewis, 1983). Clare and Suter (1983) found that the predominate effect for both a drawing and a writing task was suppression of EEG alpha in both the left and right hemispheres. Such effects are interpreted as reflecting bilateral cortical activation and "the integration of function between the left and right hemispheres in normal humans" (p. 22). An EEG asymmetry was noted inasmuch as the writing task produced evidence of greater left than right hemisphere activity; enhanced right hemisphere activity was not found for the drawing task, suggesting that drawing should not be construed as an exclusively right hemisphere task. Similarly, the generalized effects of the writing task indicate that the right hemisphere plays a role in writing. Clare and Suter concluded: "The present results are consistent with the general position that while the left hemisphere can write with some difficulty and the right hemisphere can draw with some difficulty, fully competent performance of either of these tasks requires the integrated activity of both hemispheres" (p. 25).

Others have also noted the interactive effects of the two hemispheres in intact brains in intellectual tasks of the sort associated with creative output (e.g., Galin, Johnstone, & Herron, 1978). Sergent, Zuck, Terriah, and MacDonald (1992), employing positron emission tomography (PET) imaging and magnetic resonance imaging (MRI) techniques, asked a sample of musicians to complete a set of tasks relevant to different domains of music performance (reading, listening, and playing). They concluded "that sight-reading and piano performance entail processing demands that are realised by a cerebral network distributed over the four cortical lobes and the cerebellum" (p. 108). It should be noted as well that for each task activation is found in both left and right hemispheres, supporting the earlier conclusion of interactive effects.

Occupational Manipulation. Dumas and Morgan (1975) tested for asymmetry of EEG asymmetry with a sample of artists and of engineers on tasks chosen to differentially engage the left or right hemisphere. Task-specific asymmetries were observed, but the artists and engineers did *not* differ from one another. The authors suggested "that when a person has a dominant cognitive style, he does not necessarily use one hemisphere for the tasks appropriate to the other hemisphere, but rather has differential aptitudes in lateralized functions and perhaps seek out environments in which the more developed mode is utilized more" (p. 227).

Indirect Measures of Hemisphericity

Handedness. Peterson and Lansky (1974) reported that 29% of the faculty in architecture schools were left-handed, a frequency of observation much higher than expected by chance. In a follow-up study, they reported that a more than expected number of left-handers enter undergraduate studies in architecture and are more successful in completing the program than are right-handers (Peterson & Lansky, 1977). Byrne (1974) reported a greater number of mixed handers in a sample of musicians compared to a control group of nonmusicians. A similar advantage to left-handers has been reported in mathematics students and mathematics professors by Annett and Kilshaw (1983). However, other studies have either failed to replicate these effects or have postulated some moderating variable as the causal link and, as O'Boyle and Benbow (1990b) pointed out in a comprehensive review, "Needless to say, the variability of these findings speaks to the likelihood of a Type I error" (p. 364).

Dichotic Listening Data. Hassler (1990) asked musical composers, instrumentalists, and painters to complete a battery of hemispheric reference tasks. The results showed effects moderated by sex of participant, handedness, and level of talent. Overall, however, musicians demonstrated superior spatial performance relative to a nonmusician control group; spatial performance is usually taken as a right hemisphere-mediated task. Moreover, based on dichotic listening data, Hassler concluded: "Our results seem to support the assumption that left-hemisphere and right-hemisphere functions contributing to processes associated with verbal processing are more effectively integrated in musicians than in non-musicians" (p. 13). Thus, these data, as with others reported in this chapter, suggest a special role for right hemisphere-mediated processes and more efficient bilateral integration of processes in the skilled or more expert practitioner.

Hemisphericity. Harpaz (1990), employing a variant of the A/P ratio, found that economics and accounting students scored consistently higher on left hemisphere marker tests, whereas creative arts students tended to perform better on right hemisphere tests. The relationship between hemisphericity and work-related activities has also been studied through various other techniques. As mentioned earlier, recent work has confirmed that the directions of lateral eye movements (CLEMs) is a reliable individual difference measure and has been taken by some to be an index of the habitual use of the right (leftward CLEMs) or left (rightward CLEMs) hemisphere in information processing (see Zenhausern & Kraemer, 1991). Bakan (1969) found that people who exhibit rightward CLEMs tend to report having less vivid visual imagery and tend to major in "hard" disciplines, such as mathematics, in college. Harnad (1972) examined mathematics professors and graduate students from Princeton. Those who habitually employed leftward CLEMs reported using more imagery, indulging in more outside artistic activities, and tended to have a more evaluative reaction to prose than did right movers. Taken together these data are consistent with Dumas and Morgan's (1975) conclusion that people with a dominant cognitive style seek out suitable environments in which to express themselves. Interestingly, Albert (1983) made a parallel point with respect to creativity in general:

It is evident that different general fields have different cognitive and personality requirements for success in them and draw their more successful recruits from different types of early backgrounds and temperaments. The better the match between requirements of a particular field and an interested person with high intelligence, the more likely eminence will occur in that career. (p. 31)

Discussion

A complex picture emerges in which people who perform different occupations may habitually call on different cognitive resources, with right hemispheric-supported processes being associated more with artistic activities and left hemispheric-supported processes being associated with mathematics and other "hard" sciences. However, this hemisphericity cannot be taken as evidence that the mental operations that are required to perform artistic or mathematic tasks are performed in one or the other cerebral hemispheres; the evidence is, even for seemingly lateralized tasks such as drawing or writing, that integration and coordination of the resources from both hemispheres is needed for effective performance. This picture that emerges from EEG and other less direct indices of brain activity is strongly reinforced by the commissurotomy data. Such patients show a deficit in the everyday tendencies that we associate with creative activity, such as an inability to integrate fantasy with logical discourse. This lack of creativity may stem from either (or both) an inability to perform the natural interactive communication between the hemispheres or a failure to construct an intentional program that would support integrated, elaborated activities.

CONCLUSIONS AND CAVEATS

The following conclusions arise from the empirical literature. First, creative activity cannot be localized as a special function unique to one of the cerebral hemispheres. Rather, productive thought involves the integration and coordination of processes subserved by both hemispheres. This conclusion is based on case studies of eminent creators who have suffered unilateral brain damage or precociously gifted youth, analysis of archival data using indirect indices of hemisphericity, EEG analyses and indirect measures of people who score high on tests of creativity, and, finally, the examination of patients who have had the hemispheres surgically disconnected with resulting loss of fantasy and other normal functions associated with creative activity.

Second, there appears to be some privileged role in creativity to the cognitive functions associated with the right hemisphere. This conclusion is based on a narrower database, specifically the performance of gifted youth, EEG recordings while participants are taking tasks that purportedly measure creativity, and indirect measures such as conjugate lateral eye movement data. Although based on a narrower set of converging operations than that on which the first conclusion rests, it should be emphasized that a right hemisphere superiority is found in the majority of cases in which cerebral hemisphere asymmetries arise; rarely does one find evidence for left hemisphere superiority.

Third, there is some evidence that different creative tasks may differentially call on cognitive resources for which the two hemispheres are specialized. That is, the cognitive processes (and hence the hemispheres subserved by these processes) necessary to be creative as an artist appear to be different than those required for mathematics. It may well be that highly creative individuals are better able to make use of the cognitive resources of the hemisphere that is nondominant for the creative task at hand (Katz, 1986; O'Boyle & Benbow, 1990b).

Finally, there is some evidence that creativity-related hemisphere asymmetries can be found both online (as the person performs a task) and as a consequence of habitual patterns of behavior. EEG, ERP, and PET readings, for instance, reflect brain activity during the act of performing a given task (relative to a neutral task baseline), and A/P ratios or CLEM measures reflect an habitual tendency to employ cognitive processes associated with right or left hemisphere dominance. It should be noted that hemisphericity effects are associated with both types of indices, perhaps suggesting that hemispheric asymmetries are related both to a "creative style," as well as to specific task-related mental operations.

The conclusions listed earlier were based on converging operations for hemisphericity; nonetheless, they must be tempered by some warnings. With respect to hemispheric asymmetry, virtually every measure of hemisphericity described earlier has been questioned, albeit on different grounds. An examination of patients with commissurotomy or with unilateral brain damage reflect performance disturbed in ways other than that just caused by the cerebral damage or in whom the damage may have changed normal cerebral functioning. One can question whether the effects observed would generalize to nonpatient populations. There are individuals who are born without the callosum, and, in principle, some of these questions can be answered by testing such people for creative functioning. EEG and ERP data can be artifactual, influenced by motor movements and other noise factors, although skillful technicians should be sensitive to such factors. Conjugate eye movement data can be readily affected by changing the type of question asked or the experimental situation, and, even though CLEMs are a reliable individual difference measure, the relationship with hemispheric asymmetries is not certain. Similar arguments can be made for the cognitive variables that are entered into the A/P ratio. Indeed, Zenhausern and Kraemer (1991) with a discussion of CLEMs, and Gordon (1986) with a discussion of appropositional and propositional variables, independently made the point that the measures may more appropriately be thought of as functional asymmetries that may (or may not) be associated with different cerebral hemispheres. Finally, the claim that hypnotism and marijuana intoxication differentially arouse each hemisphere is still controversial, and, at least with hypnotism, the argument has been made that the hypnotism-creativity link is due to factors unrelated to hemispheric asymmetries (Jackson & Gorassini, 1990).

Creativity was examined as a function of performance that has led to recognition in real life, of test score performance and of everyday cognitive functions. The aim was to use a broad approach to the measurement of creativity. Nonetheless, the identification of behaviors that uniquely can be labeled as *creative* is a problem that has not yet been satisfactorily solved. For instance, one can argue that the phenomena associated with eminent creators are due to self-esteem or other noncognitive factors related to social recognition and not to creativity per se. Consequently integrated hemispheric activity may reflect this correlate of eminence and would be found in noncreative samples that possessed the same correlate. Similarly, the tests employed as measures of creativity most often identify people who will, to use Nicholls (1972) apt phrase, "never produce anything original or useful." These individuals score high on tests that meet a folk, but not necessarily a scientific, definition of creativity. Even assuming that the tests do capture a portion of the variance that we would like to attribute to creative thought, the separation of these tests into verbal and figural components suggests that the observed relationships with hemisphericity are to some extent based on method variance. Analogous arguments can be made for identification of fantasy or imagery as the central motif of creative thought.

In conclusion, the caveats notwithstanding, the convergence of empirical evidence from such a broad array of techniques and measures give credence to speculations linking creative behavior to specialized hemispheric-supported cognitive functions. The convergence is nonetheless based on a relatively small number of studies. In many of the categories employed to organize this chapter, only one, or even no, studies are available. For instance, there are no studies of which I am aware in which eminent people have had EEG readings taken while solving problems from their domain of interest and from unrelated domains.

Similarly, there are no studies examining the eminent or gifted person on a battery of right and left hemisphere marker cognitive tasks, no examination of the archival evidence for handedness in eminent creators, nor any studies examining the comparative performance of artists versus nonartists (or scientist vs. nonscientists) on direct or most indirect measures of hemisphericity. In fact, there are no studies in which EEG readings are taken of everyday people involved in solving insight problems. Clearly more research is required in each of the categories employed here.

REFERENCES

Albert, R.S. (1983). Exceptional creativity and achievement. In R.S. Albert (Ed.), *Genius and eminence* (pp. 19-35). Oxford: Pergamon Press.

Annett, M., & Kilshaw, D. (1983). Mathematical ability and lateral asymmetry. *Cortex, 18*, 547-568.

Ashton, M., & McDonald, R. (1985). Effects of hypnosis on verbal and non-verbal creativity. *International Journal of Clinical and Experimental Hypnosis, 33*, 12-26.

Bakan, P. (1969). Hypnotizability, laterality of eye-movements and functional brain asymmetry. *Perceptual and Motor Skills, 28*, 927-932.

Benbow, C. (1986). Physiological correlates of extreme intellectual precocity. *Neuropsychologia, 24*, 719-725.

Bogen, J. (1969). The other side of the brain II: An appositional mind. *Bulletin of the Los Angeles Neurological Society, 34*, 135-162.

Bogen, J., & Bogen, G. (1969). The other side of the brain III: The corpus callosum and creativity. *Bulletin of the Los Angeles Neurological Society, 34*, 191-220.

Bogen, J., & Bogen, G. (1988). Creativity and the corpus callosum. In K. Hoppe (Ed.), *Hemispheric specialization* (pp. 293-301). Philadelphia: Saunders.

Bogen, J., DeZure, R., TenHouten, W., & Marsh, J. (1972). The other side of the brain IV: The A/P ratio. *Bulletin of the Los Angeles Neurological Society, 37*, 49-59.

Bowers, K. (1968). Hypnosis and creativity: A preliminary investigation. International *Journal of Clinical and Experimental Hypnosis, 16*, 38-52.

Bowers, K. (1971). Sex and susceptibility as moderator variables in the relationship of creativity and hypnotic susceptibility. *Journal of Abnormal Psychology, 78*, 93-100.

Bowers, K., & van der Meulen, S. (1970). Effect of hypnotic susceptibility on creativity test performance. *Journal of Personality and Social Psychology, 14*, 247-256.

Bowers, P. (1967). Effect of hypnosis and suggestions of reduced defensiveness on creativity test performance. *Journal of Personality, 35*, 311-332.

Brown, R. (1989). Creativity: What are we to measure? In J. Glover, R. Ronning, & C. Reynolds (Eds.), *Handbook of creativity* (pp. 3-32). New York: Plenum.

Burke, B., Chrisler, J., & Devlin, A. (1989). The creative thinking, environmental frustration, and self-concept of left- and right-handers. *Creativity Research Journal, 2*, 279-285.

Byrne, B. (1974). Handedness and musical ability. *British Journal of Psychology, 65*, 279-281

Clare, S., & Suter, S. (1983). Drawing and the cerebral hemispheres: Bilateral EEG alpha. *Biological Psychology, 16*, 15-27.

Crawford, H. (1982). Cognitive processing during hypnosis: Much unfinished business. *Research Communications in Psychology, Psychiatry and Behavior, 7*, 169-179.

DiCyan, E. (1971). Poetry and creativeness: With notes on the role of psychedelic agents. *Perspectives in Biology and Medicine, 14*, 639-650.

Dumas, R., & Morgan, A. (1975). EEG asymmetry as a function of occupation, task, and task difficulty. *Neuropsychologia, 13*, 219-228.

Edwards, B. (1979). *Drawing on the right side of the brain*. Los Angeles: Tarcher.

Falcone, D., & Loder, K. (1984). A modified lateral eye movement measure, the right hemisphere and creativity. *Perceptual and Motor Skills, 58*, 823-830.

Federico, P-A. (1984). Event-related-potential (ERP) correlates of cognitive styles, abilities and aptitudes. *Personality and Individual Differences, 5*, 575-585.

Galin, D., Johnstone, J., & Herron, J. (1978). Effects of task difficulty on EEG measures of cerebral engagement. *Neuropsychologia, 16*, 461-472.

Gardner, H. (1982). *Art, mind, and brain*. New York: Basic Books

Ghiselin, B. (1952). *The creative process*. New York: Mentor Books.

Gordon, H. (1986). The cognitive laterality battery: Tests of specialized cognitive function. *International Journal of Neuroscience, 29*, 223-244.

Gur, R.C., & Gur, R.E. (1974). Handedness, sex, and eyedness as moderating variables in the relationship between hypnotic susceptibility and functional brain asymmetry. *Journal of Abnormal Psychology, 83*, 635-643.

Gur, R.C., & Rayner, J. (1976). Enhancement of creativity via free-imagery and hypnosis. *The American Journal of Clinical Hypnosis, 18*, 237-249.

Gur, R.E., & Reyher, J. (1973). Relationship between style of hypnotic induction and direction of lateral eye movements. *Journal of Abnormal Psychology, 82*, 499-505.

Harnad, S. (1972). Creativity, lateral saccades and the nondominant hemisphere. *Perceptual and Motor Skills, 34*, 653-654.

Harpaz, I. (1990). Asymmetry of hemispheric functions and creativity: An empirical examination. *Journal of Creative Behavior, 24*, 161-170.

Harshman, R., Crawford, H., & Hecht, E. (1976). Marijuana, cognitive style and lateralized hemispheric functions. In S. Cohen & R. Stillman (Eds.), *The therapeutic potential of marijuana* (pp. 205-254). New York: Plenum Medical Book Company.

Hassler, M. (1990). Functional cerebral asymmetries and cognitive abilities in musicians, painters, and controls. *Brain and Cognition, 13,* 1-7.

Hattie, J., & Fitzgerald, D. (1983). Do left-handers tend to be more creative? *Journal of Creative Behavior, 17,* 269.

Hendren, G. (1989). Using sign language to access right brain communication: A tool for teachers. *Journal of Creative Behavior, 23,* 116-120.

Hines, D., & Martindale, C. (1974). Induced lateral eye-movements and creative and intellectual performance. *Perceptual and Motor Skills, 39,* 153-154.

Hines, T. (1991). The myth of right hemisphere creativity. *Journal of Creative Behavior, 25,* 223-227.

Hoppe, K. (1977). Split brains and psychoanalysis. *Psychoanalytic Quarterly, 46,* 220-224.

Hoppe, K. (1988). Hemispheric specialization and creativity. In K. Hoppe (Ed.), *Hemispheric specialization* (pp. 303-315). Philadelphia: Saunders.

Hoppe K., & Kyle, N. (1990). Dual brain, creativity, and health. *Creativity Research Journal, 3,* 150-157.

Jackson, L., & Gorassini, D. (1990). Artifact in the hypnosis-creativity relationship. *Journal of General Psychology, 116,* 333-334.

Katz, A. (1978). Creativity and the right cerebral hemisphere: Towards a physiologically based theory of creativity. *Journal of Creative Behavior, 12,* 253-264.

Katz, A. (1980). Do left-handers tend to be more creative? *Journal of Creative Behavior, 14,* 271.

Katz, A. (1983). Creativity and individual differences in asymmetric hemispheric functioning. *Empirical Studies of the Arts, 1,* 3-16.

Katz, A. (1986). The relationship between creativity and cerebral hemisphericity for creative architects, scientists, and mathematicians. *Empirical Studies of the Arts, 4,* 97-108.

Katz, A., & Thompson, M. (1993). On judging creativity: By one's acts shall ye be known (and vice-versa). *Creativity Research Journal, 6,* 345-364.

Kershner, J., & Ledger, G. (1985). Effect of sex, intelligence, and style of thinking on creativity: A comparison of gifted and average IQ children. *Journal of Personality and Social Psychology, 48,* 1033-1040.

Kimura, D. (1964). Left-right differences in the perception of melodies. *Quarterly Journal of Experimental Psychology, 16,* 355-358.

Kimura, D. (1966). Dual functional asymmetry of the brain in visual perception. *Neuropsychologia, 4,* 275-285.

Kinsbourne, M. (1974). Direction of gaze and distribution of cerebral thought processes. *Neuropsychologica, 12,* 279-281.

Krippner, S. (1968). The psychedelic state, the hypnotic trance and the creative act. *Journal of Humanistic Psychology, 8*, 49-67.

Krueger, T. (1976). *Visual imagery in problem solving and scientific creativity.* Derby, CT: Seal Press.

Lee, D. (1950). Lineal and nonlineal codefications of reality. *Psychosomatic Medicine, 12*, 89-97.

Levy-Agresti, J., & Sperry, R. (1968). Differential perceptual capacities in major and minor hemispheres. *Proceedings of the National Academy of Science, 61*, 1151.

Lewis, G. (1983). Event related brain electrical and magnetic activity: Toward predicting on-job performance. *International Journal of Neuroscience, 18*, 159-182.

MacKinnon, D. (1975). IPAR's contribution to the conceptualization and study of creativity. In I. Taylor & J. Getzels (Eds.), *Perspectives in creativity* (pp. 60-89). Chicago: Aldine.

Martindale, C. (1977-1978). Creativity, consciousness, and cortical arousal. *Journal of the Altered States of Consciousness, 3*, 69-87.

Martindale, C., & Hasenfus, N. (1978). EEG differences as a function of creativity, stage of the creative process and effort to be original. *Biological Psychology, 6*, 157-167.

Martindale, C., & Hines, D. (1975). Creativity and cortical activation during creative, intellectual and EEG feedback tasks. *Biological Psychology, 3*, 91-100.

Martindale, C., Hines, D., Mitchell, L., & Covello, E. (1984). EEG alpha asymmetry and creativity. *Personality and Individual Differences, 5*, 77-86.

Masten, W. (1989). Learning style, repeated stimuli, and originality in intellectually gifted adolescents. *Psychological Reports, 65*, 751-754.

Morgan, A., MacDonald, H., & Hilgard, E. (1974). EEG alpha: lateral asymmetry related to task and hypnotizability. *Psychophysiology, 11*, 275-282.

Morgan, A., McDonald, P., & MacDonald, H. (1971). Differences in bilateral alpha activity as a function of experimental task with a note on lateral eye movements and hypnotizability. *Neuropsychologia, 9*, 459-469.

Nicholls, J. (1972). Creativity in the person who will never produce anything original and useful: The concept of creativity as a normally distributed trait. *American Psychologist, 27*, 717-727.

O'Boyle, M., Alexander, J., & Benbow, C. (1991). Enhanced right hemisphere activation in the mathematically precocious: A preliminary EEG investigation. *Brain and Cognition, 17*, 138-153.

O'Boyle, M., & Benbow, C. (1990a). Enhanced right hemisphere involvement during cognitive processing may relate to intellectual precocity. *Neuropsychologica, 28*, 211-216.

O'Boyle, M., & Benbow, C. (1990b). Handedness and its relationships to ability and talent. In S. Coren (Ed.), *Left-handedness: Behavioral implications and anomalies* (Vol. 67, pp. 343-372). Amsterdam: North-Holland.

Perry, C., Wilder, S., & Appignanesi, A. (1973). Hypnotic susceptibility and performance on a battery of creativity measures. *The American Journal of Clinical Hypnosis, 15*, 170-180.

Peterson, J., & Lansky, L. (1974). Left-handedness among architects: Some facts and some speculations. *Perceptual and Motor Skills, 38*, 547-550.

Peterson, J., & Lansky, L. (1977). Left-handedness among architects: Partial replication and some new data. *Perceptual and Motor Skills, 45*, 1216-1218.

Poreh, A., & Whitman, R. (1991) Creative cognitive processes and hemispheric specialization. *Journal of Creative Behavior, 25*, 169-179.

Sergent, J., Zuck, E., Terriah, S., & MacDonald, B. (1992). Distributed neural network underlying musical sight-reading and keyboard performance. *Science, 257*, 106-109.

Simonton, D. (1984). *Genius, creativity and leadership*. Cambridge MA: Harvard University Press.

Springer, S., & Deutsch, G. (1989). *Left brain, right brain* (3rd ed.). New York: Freeman.

Tart, C. (1971). *On being stoned: A psychological study of marijuana intoxication*. Palo Alto, CA: Science and Behavior Books.

Tegano, D., Fu, V., & Moran, J. (1983). Divergent thinking and hemispheric dominance for language function among preschool children. *Perceptual and Motor Skills, 56*, 691-698.

TenHouten, W. (1994) Creativity, intentionality, and alexithymia: A graphological analysis of split-brained patients and normal controls. In M.P. Shaw & M.A. Runco (Eds.), *Creativity and affect* (pp. 225-250). Norwood, NJ: Ablex.

Torrance, E., & Mourad, S. (1979). Role of hemisphericity in performance on selected measures of creativity. *Gifted Child Quarterly, 23*, 44-55.

Torrance, E., Reynolds, C., Riegel, T., & Ball, O. (1977). Your style of learning and thinking, forms A and B. *Gifted Child Quarterly, 21*, 97-106.

Victor, H., Grossman, J., & Eisenman, R. (1973). Openness to experience and marijuana use in high school students. *Journal of Consulting and Clinical Psychology, 41*, 38-45.

Vinacke, W.E. (1974). *The psychology of thinking* (2nd ed.). New York: McGraw-Hill.

Wallas, G. (1926). *The art of thought*. New York: Harcourt and Brace.

Weckowitz, T., Fedora, O., Mason, J., Radstaak, D., Bay, K., & Yonge, K. (1975). Effect of marijuana on divergent and convergent production cognitive tests. *Journal of Abnormal Psychology, 84*, 386-398.

Zenhausern, R., & Kraemer, M. (1991). The dual nature of lateral eye movements. *International Journal of Neuroscience, 56*, 169-175.

10 Humor and Creativity: A Review of the Empirical Literature

Karen O'Quin

SUNY College at Buffalo

Peter Derks

College of William and Mary

The jester takes a place alongside the scientist and the artist in Koestler's (1964) triptych of the creative. Koestler noted that the logical pattern was the same in all three cases, namely, "the discovery of hidden similarities" (p. 27). Perhaps it was necessary for an individual to be outside the behaviorist stream of psychology to recognize the parallels between humor and creativity. For whatever reason, Koestler's ideas about humor had little immediate impact on creativity research, and perhaps even less impact on humor research. One of the few experiments of that time to use humor as a creative activity failed to mention him (Johnson, Parrott, & Stratton, 1968), and one of the earliest empirical studies of the relationship between humor and creativity failed in the same regard (Treadwell, 1970). A book edited by Goldstein and McGhee (1972) supplied much of the momentum for more recent humor research, and it cited Koestler as a humor theorist, but contained no chapter specifically on humor and creativity.

Since that time there has been a great deal of research on the humor-creativity link (e.g., McGhee [1979] reviewed humor and creativity in children). The purpose of the present chapter is to review the empirical literature on the relationship between humor and creativity, with the focus on published studies. A recent review of the theoretical literature on creativity and humor (Murdock & Ganim, 1993) included little in the way of empirical research. We feel the time has come to concentrate on research, first, because so many studies of many age groups exist, and these can help to clarify the humor-creativity relationship, and second, because some authors have assumed that humor is simply a type of creativity (e.g., Johnson et al., 1968) without examining the basis for that assumption.

DEFINITION

The parallels between humor and creativity are readily evident. Originality and surprisingness are typically considered to be defining characteristics of creativity, both by creativity experts (e.g., Besemer & Treffinger, 1981; Torrance, 1988) and by psychotherapists and others who may dabble in the field (e.g., Rogers, 1961). Originality and surprisingness are also often suggested as characteristics of humor (e.g., Keith-Spiegel, 1972). The jester must say or do something that is not obvious. The success of this original, unexpected act is most often measured by how funny it is. Wicker, Thorelli, Baron, and Ponder (1981) found that funniness correlated significantly with surprise. Being funny may be a problem to be solved with novelty and ingenuity. The banal or the bizarre will not do. Instead, there must be a balance governed by a departure from one idea with the introduction of another, different but salient one. Wicker et al. (1981) also found that resolution made a significant contribution to funniness,[1] and Pollio and Mers (1974) reported that the funnier jokes in comedy routines were those with punchlines that were, after the fact, more predictable.

---

[1]Interestingly, *resolution* was the term used by Besemer and her colleagues (Besemer & Treffinger, 1981; Besemer & O'Quin, 1986; O'Quin & Besemer, 1989) to refer to the second dimension in a three-dimensional theory of the general attributes of creative products. The other two dimensions were *novelty* (of which surprisingness is a subscale) and a "style" dimension called *elaboration and synthesis*. Wicker et al. (1981) measured resolution with the question, "After you got over your surprise, how much did the unexpected thing in the joke MAKE SENSE?" (p. 361). The bipolar adjective "makes sense-senseless" is part of the *resolution* dimension on Besemer and O'Quin's Creative Product Semantic Scale (CPSS; O'Quin & Besemer, 1989). Besemer and O'Quin (1986), in developing the CPSS, included a "humorous" item, believing it would be related to surprisingness, but in their study, it did not correlate with other items in the scale; however, an early form of the CPSS was used to evaluate cartoons (Besemer & O'Quin, 1987).

DeBono (1992) wrote "Humor occurs when we are taken from the main track and deposited at the end of a side-track. From there we can see our way back to the starting point. Creativity occurs in exactly the same way" (p. 146). Although DeBono presented no data in support of his assertion, the railroad train-of-thought metaphor has long been popular (Eastman, 1936). Humor, as well as creativity, can be characterized by divergence followed by convergence. The familiar is made strange, then the strange is made familiar (Gordon, 1961).

Cognitive Processes

The discussion of humor and creativity should focus first on the cognitive processes involved. In the humor literature, Keith-Spiegel (1972) reviewed the classic incongruity theories in which humor arises from "disjointed, ill-suited pairings of ideas or situations or presentations of ideas or situations that are divergent from habitual customs" (p. 7). Morreall (1987) further examined the classic theories. Suls (1972, 1983) presented a more explicit information-processing model of humor that focused on the resolution of incongruities. In tying together humor and creativity, Koestler coined the term *bisociation* to describe the mixing of ideas involved in abruptly perceiving as similar two habitually incompatible contexts. Such linking has also been labeled *remote association* (Mednick, 1962), *contrary recognition* (Perkins, 1981), and *selection of variation* or *incongruous juxtaposition* (Martindale, 1990). Escarpit (1969) noted that the key both to humor and scientific inventiveness was a "sudden change of the angle of vision on reality" (p. 255). Rouff (1975) suggested that humor comprehension and creativity should be similar because both require the ability to link disparities.

Wallach (1970) proposed that ideational fluency is the essence of creativity. Because humor often depends on unexpected or unusual associations, a person's ability to generate and understand humor would seem to depend, at least partly, on ideational fluency (Couturier, Mansfield, & Gallagher, 1981).

Many humor tests present collections of jokes or cartoons for individuals to judge on some scale of funniness (e.g., Eysenck & Wilson, 1976; Mindess, Miller, Turek, Bender, & Corbin, 1985; Tollefson & Cattell, 1966). These tests are intended to categorize subjects on certain personality or motivational variables. Their relationship to cognitive processes is, therefore, only tangential. The rationale is that certain topics such as sex or aggression can become salient in a permissible way (Freud, 1905/1960). On a list of jokes, an individual can react in a socially acceptable way to topics that might otherwise be avoided or inhibited. For example, Davis and Farina (1970) found that male subjects seemed to use funniness ratings as a way of communicating their sexual interest in an attractive female experimenter.

On the other hand, Colell and Domino (1980) reported that highly creative subjects preferred incongruity humor to either sexual or aggressive humor. One humor appreciation test that measures factors that are more cognitive in nature is the "sense of humor inventory" (3-WD) developed by Ruch and Hehl (Ruch, 1992). These researchers found that incongruity resolution and its irreverent counterpart, nonsense, appeal to two different kinds of information processors. Incongruity resolution, for all its apparent problem-solving character, is preferred by more conservative individuals. Conservatism was measured by the Wilson (1973) scale and related to political conservatism and more generally to an aversion to novelty and change. Conservative thinking, then, seems to be convergent.

Nonsense receives high ratings from sensation seekers (as operationalized by Zuckerman, 1979). People who prefer adventure and uncertainty also seem to like their incongruity unresolved. These may be the divergent thinkers. In this formulation, problem solving is only partly relevant. In understanding jokes, the individual perceives not only a salient subject, but a salient style as well (Derks & Arora, 1993). Thus, in humor appreciation individuals are reacting like experts in a problem-solving task (Bedard & Chi, 1992). The style of humor is recognized and appreciated as a match to the style of the individual. Nonsense (i.e., incongruity without resolution) should be appreciated by the more creative sensation seeker.

A different interpretation of the resolution of an incongruity is that it is indeed a problem-solving task, which requires some cognitive effort. This formulation predicts that funniness will be related to effort or "comprehension difficulty" by the classic inverted U (Berlyne, 1960, 1972; Wyer & Collins, 1992). A joke that is too easy or too hard to "get" will not be amusing. Some experiments support this prediction (Wyer & Collins, 1992; Zigler, Levine, & Gould, 1967), but other experiments did not find any relation between difficulty and funniness (Wicker et al., 1981). In any case, whether the process is perceptual and automatic or more cognitive and effortful the more creative the incongruity resolution, the less entertaining it will be. That is, for the conservative thinker who prefers incongruity resolution, the resolution should be of intermediate, rather than great, difficulty. The sensation seeker, on the other hand, would rather react to nonsense and would not be likely to appreciate the creative resolution supplied by the joke. Therefore, the really creative joke attempt should not appeal to either the conservative or the sensation-seeking mind.

A methodologically sophisticated approach to the study of cognitive factors in humor (and, tangentially, in the humor-creativity relationship) was employed by Feingold and Mazzella (1991). They administered multiple measures of humor information, humor reasoning, joke knowledge, general verbal ability, and so on. In one sample, they also administered Mednick's Remote Associates Test (RAT). They found that the RAT correlated highly with humor reasoning ability (the ability to select or deduce the correct punchline).

Social Processes

The jester may need to utilize more information than the scientist or the artist for the product to be successful. Not only must the incongruity be recognized, but the immediate interests and the intellect of the audience must be considered. Interestingly, although few have noted it (Neve, 1988), Freud (1905/1960) himself took successful joking to be a process involving the audience. He noted that "a joke . . . is the most social of all the mental functions that aim at a yield of pleasure. It often calls for three persons and its completion requires the participation of someone else in the mental process it starts" (p. 179). Since the time of Freud, many theorists and researchers in the field of humor have noted the importance of considering the audience in understanding the phenomenon of humor (e.g., Deren, 1989; Sherman, 1988). Social factors do not seem to impinge on the scientist or the artist to such a great extent, although "acceptance finding," which implicitly involves a social persuasion dimension, is considered by some to be part of the creative problem-solving process (e.g., Parnes, 1981).

Social and group factors in humor were also addressed by Goodchilds (1972) in her analysis and review of the literature on wittiness. Wittiness has typically been measured by the Observer Wit Tally, in which observers credit a subject with a successful witticism when two other group members laugh. Smith and White (1965) reported a low but significant relationship between a wit measure and a measure of creativity. Goodchilds (1972) asked whether the "puzzling trio—creating, creating humor, and creating humorously" (p. 187) were similar. She suggested that persons who are spontaneously humorous are also spontaneously creative. Obviously, we believe they are.

More generally, social factors in humor have been discussed by many researchers (e.g., Kane, Suls, & Tedeschi, 1977). It is outside the scope of the present chapter to discuss all of them, but, to cite a few, Chapman has done extensive work with humor and social interaction in children (e.g., Chapman, 1983), sociologists and anthropologists have carefully described the social implications of humor (e.g., Apte, 1983;

Fine, 1983), and social psychologists have studied humor in small groups (White & Camarena, 1989) and in dyadic bargaining situations (O'Quin & Aronoff, 1981).

HUMOR AS A FORM OF CREATIVITY

One of the reasons that this chapter seemed necessary is that some authors have assumed that humor is simply a form of creativity (e.g., Johnson et al., 1968) without examining the basis for that assumption. Sense of humor has been included in several measures that attempted to assess creative personality or creative potential (e.g., Davis & Subkoviak, 1975; Leland, 1986). In addition, the production of story titles or cartoon captions has a long history in the measurement of creativity. Guilford (1967) discussed what he called "cleverness tests" to measure originality, which he considered to be part of the concept of divergent thinking. The most commonly used was Plot Titles, in which subjects were asked to make up titles for a short (one-paragraph) story, and the responses were judged for cleverness. Cartoons from magazines were also used, and subjects were supposed to write punchlines for each one. The Riddles task called for two solutions to each riddle, one of which was supposed to be clever. Guilford (1967) noted that puns were quite common when responses were supposed to be clever: "A pun is an example of a transformation: a sudden shift of meaning occurs" (p. 156).

In the same vein, several experiments have used the production of captions for a drawing or picture as a creative task. In one of the earliest studies (before Koestler's, 1964, book), Ziller, Behringer, and Goodchilds (1962) used quantity and quality of cartoon captions as their only measure of group creativity. Appropriately, they found that "open" groups with changing membership did better on both measures than "closed" groups that worked at the task with the same people contributing. New ideas from outside not only increased the number but also the funniness of captions suggested for a *Saturday Evening Post* cartoon.

Johnson et al. (1968) used cartoon captions as one of five problem-solving tasks to evaluate the effects of instructions and training. The other four tasks were making up plot titles, titling a table, drawing conclusions, and constructing a sentence using four specific words. The captions were given to the last of four successive panels. Although these tasks varied in divergence and did not correlate among themselves, the general results were consistent. When only one solution was requested in the instructions, the average quality (funniness for the cartoon caption) was better than if many solutions were required. The best captions, however, occurred when many were produced. Apparently the creators were able to select their better captions, but they still generated good alternatives. In fact, the captions selected by the participants as their best also received high ratings from two judges. Training subjects in the tasks by giving them examples of good and poor solutions reduced the number of captions and further increased the quality. Of course, the quality of the examples and the quality of the responses were evaluated by the same judges. These results suggest that critical selection reduces the number of poor responses and may favor the generation of an occasional superior product.

In order to make the captions creation task more divergent, college students were asked to make up funny captions for still photographs from old movies (Derks, 1987; Derks & Hervas, 1988). These stimuli did not imply one correct answer. The responses were judged by other students who demonstrated range and sensitivity in judging a variety of cartoons. This evaluation procedure is similar to that used and recommended in the field of creativity by Amabile (1990), Finke, Ward, and Smith (1992), and especially Ziv (1989). Unlike the results of Johnson et al. (1968), there was evidence that the best captions for people instructed to give quantity and not to be critical were slightly better than for those aiming for quality. There was also an indication of improved quality of the captions as the participants continued to make them up. The best captions of a series occurred after the worst, on over 60% of the trials, a difference that was consistent and significant across several experiments.

Even more divergent, whether the caption production was guided by a goal of quantity or quality, the participants showed no evidence of running out of ideas. Latency between the captions increased for the first few, then stabilized so that people were producing captions at the same rate to the end of the 10-minute task. Furthermore, there was very little overlap among the ideas. In one study, only 15 of 1,909 captions (0.8%) were duplicates (Derks, 1987).

Turner (1980) asked people to create cartoon captions, but he also used what we consider to be a very creative measure of humor production. Subjects were asked to perform a "witty monologue" (with 30 seconds to prepare!) using a box of interesting items to spark their imaginations. Turner found that the high self-monitors performed the best. High self-monitoring has also been found to correlate with extraversion (Gabrenya & Arkin, 1980), and Ziv and Gadish (1990) reported significant correlations between extraversion and self-reported humor. Ruch (1992) found extraversion to be a consistent personality correlate of self-reported sense of humor. In another vein, Lefcourt, Antrobus, and Hogg (1974) reported that those with an internal locus of control were more witty than externals on a humor production measure. Cloyd (1964) isolated various patterns of behavior in informal interactions by letting the participants describe the activities of group members. An individual who "jokes and makes humorous remarks" also challenges opinions, gets off the subject, interrupts others, is egotistical and cynical, and is (worst of all) liberal! This pattern was labeled C and could have been called *class clown*.

The occurrence of ideas in a humor production task seems to model the style of creativity in general. The content of those ideas, however, is usually fairly mundane. Nevo and Nevo (1983) asked 12th-grade males in Israel to respond normally and then humorously to pictures modeled after the Rosenzweig Picture Frustration Test (Rosenzweig, Clark, & Helen, 1946). When the boys made their humorous responses "they used Freud's techniques as if they had read his writings" (p. 188). Faced with a frustrating situation, they significantly increased the intensity of their aggressive response. Their humor was most often attempted through "presentation by the opposite" or fantasy. A salient topic presented incongruously was their solution to the problem of being funny.

Research on the personality of professional comedians indicates a related pattern (Fisher & Fisher, 1981). In their responses to inkblots, professional comedians seem to emphasize the "small" (parts of the figures were called small or little) and "down" (elements were indicated to be down, below, or underneath the overall pattern) items. The investigators argued that the comedians' diminished perspective served as a springboard for incongruous comparisons. The viewpoint of the comedians seemed to have been engendered by a childhood of "conflict and stylistic contradiction" that produced the ability to create contrast between good and evil, comic and tragic (Salameh, 1982). One nice thing is that when asked about the rewards of their careers, *enjoyable* and *fun* were at the top, with *personal enrichment* and *self-actualization* close behind (Stebbins, 1990). As far as humor defined as a creative act is concerned, stand-up comics and their improvisations should be a good source of original and successful ideas (Fry & Allen, 1975; Janus, 1975; Mintz, 1985; Olson, 1988; Stebbins, 1990).

The studies reported here may be slightly premature in assuming that humor is a type of creativity without necessarily examining the basis for that assumption. They may be forgiven, however, because classical theorists in the field of creativity have mentioned humor as being a characteristic of creativity or creative persons. Guilford (1987), for example, reviewed 25 years of his own work in creativity and noted that the transformations task in his Structure-of-Intellect model involved making up clever titles for a short story, and that one way to be clever is to use puns (p. 49). Torrance (1962) noted that the work of creative children was characterized by humor and playfulness (p. 78). His scoring instructions for the Torrance Tests of Creative Thinking include assigning a point to humor in assessing the Originality and Interest scores. More recently, Urban (1991) described the evaluation criteria for children's drawings on the Test for Creative Thinking-Drawing Production (TCT-DP), which asks the examinees to complete a drawing on the basis of six given figural fragments. Humor was 1 of 11 criteria and was defined as "any drawing which elicits a humorous response" (p. 181) on the part of the evaluator. The points for each of the 11 scores were summed to yield a total score that Urban saw as an index of creative potential.

HUMOR AS A PREDICTOR OF CREATIVITY

Many researchers have recognized the multifaceted nature of both humor and creativity. Therefore, attempts to predict creativity from humor (or vice versa) have often employed tests of both constructs. A comprehensive meta-analysis of the empirical literature in which measures of both humor and creativity were used was conducted by O'Quin (1992). Meta-analysis is the application of statistical procedures to the empirical findings from individual studies to combine and summarize them (Rosenthal & Rosnow, 1991; Wolf, 1986). The effect size index O'Quin (1992) chose was the correlation coefficient. Results of the meta-analysis showed an uncorrected average correlation between humor and creativity measures of .34. The standard deviation was small enough to conclude that the relationship between humor and creativity across many studies was indeed higher than zero.

In an early study, Treadwell (1970) found that self-reports of humor appreciation and humor use were correlated fairly highly with each other ($r = .50$), but had lower correlations with caption production ($.19 < rs < .29$). She found that caption production correlated modestly with the RAT, Gestalt transformations, novelty of production, and desire for novelty. The self-report measures of humor, on the other hand, did not.

Babad (1974) distinguished more directly between humor appreciation and humor production with subjects appreciating 36 humor items and actively generating humor for 15 cartoons. He also administered verbal and nonverbal tests of creativity. Babad differentiated between the simple number of productions of humor and the number of productions judged to be funny. Interestingly, humor appreciation was significantly correlated with the number of productions but *not* the number of funny productions. With regard to the creativity tests, the number of productions was significantly related to fluency and flexibility; however, the number of *funny* productions was not related to either fluency or flexibility. Originality did not correlate better than chance with any of the humor measures.

Ward and Cox (1974) had judges assess both the creativity and the humorousness of products created by entrants in a radio station contest; listeners had been asked to send in "humorous and original little green things" (p. 202). High correlations were found between originality and humor. This study is one of the few in the literature that used a product-oriented definition of humor.

Wicker et al. (1981) found a very high correlation (.74) between ratings of funniness of jokes and ratings of originality/creativity (actually, their phrasing was "How ORIGINAL or creative is the person who wrote the joke?"). This correlation decreased to .63 when resolution was partialled out and to .46 when surprise was partialled out (both of which were still significant). However, when both surprise and resolution were partialled out, the correlation decreased to .18, which was not significant. In fact, the pattern of correlations suggested that originality/creativity related to other variables measured in the study as if it approximated a conjunctive function of surprise and resolution. Wicker et al. (1981) noted a strong parallel between these results and a popular operational definition of creativity: that the creative product is both unusual and appropriate.

Ziv has produced several studies supporting the humor-creativity link. Ziv (1980, Study 1) used a 16-item self-report measure of humor and a Humor Creativity Test which involved writing cartoon captions; the captions produced were judged for funniness. The creativity measures were two verbal subtests of the TTCT. Positive correlations between humor and creativity measures were found (.48 < rs < .62). Ziv (1980, Study 2) used peer nominations of a "good sense of humor"; 13 boys and 12 girls were identified as humorists. The creativity measures were the same TTCT subtests. Humorists of both sexes were found to score significantly higher on the TTCT subtests.

Ziv and Gadish (1990, Study 2) used a 14-item self-report sense of humor test and their creativity measure was the originality subtest of the Hebrew version of the Comprehensive Aptitude Test Battery. They found that both male and female adolescents who scored in the upper third of the humor distribution had significantly higher originality scores than those in the lower third.

Weisberg and Springer (1961) interviewed 32 high-IQ fourth-grade children. They reported a significant difference in humor (as rated by the interviewer on a 6-point scale) between children judged high and low in creativity (as measured by the TTCT). In fact, humor was one of the three variables most highly related to creativity; the other two were strength of self-image and ease of early recall.

McGhee and Panoutsopoulou (1990) measured divergent thinking and both humor appreciation (funniness of cartoons and jokes) and humor comprehension (ability to explain *why* jokes or cartoons were funny). Divergent thinking was not correlated with either humor comprehension or humor appreciation in either 7-year-olds or 13-year-olds. At age 10, divergent thinking was significantly correlated with cartoon comprehension, but not joke comprehension or humor appreciation. However, each age group was fairly small (22 < *ns* < 26).

A negative correlation between multiple humor tests and a divergent task that should test originality was reported by Couturier et al. (1981). The Barron-Welsh Revised Art Scale (BWAS), which finds the selection of off-balance, complex figures to correlate with various creativity measures and is independent of intelligence, was negatively correlated to recognizing humorous definitions (*r* = -.15) and completing jokes (*r* = -.23). The RAT correlated positively (*r* = .08 and .37, respectively) with these humor tasks and negatively with the art test (*r* = -.29). The consistently negative pattern of correlations in this study for the BWAS (it also correlated negatively with two measures of intelligence) is quite puzzling.

More recently, Fabrizi and Pollio (1987) and Feingold and Mazzella (1991) used a variety of humor tests that had high reliabilities for the two studies. The creativity tests used by Fabrizi and Pollio (1987) were the TTCT and teachers' ratings for "producing unique and creative ideas." There were several humor measures: Teachers rated the children on how often they produced humor in the classroom, peers nominated the "funniest in the class," and observers rated humorous events. The general pattern of results suggested no correlation between humor and creativity for 7th graders and modest positive correlations for 11th graders. Feingold and Mazzella (1991) used a short form of the RAT as their measure of creativity and, as discussed earlier, numerous measures of humor. They found significant positive correlations between the RAT and all their humor measures (*r* = .31 to .56, average = .46). The most interesting difference between the two studies, however, was the age range of the subjects. Fabrizi and Pollio (1987) tested 7th and 11th graders, whereas Feingold and Mazzella (1991) examined college students. The average correlations between humor and creativity show a progressive rise from .01 for the 7th graders to .45 for the college students. Of course, differences in the measures of both humor and creativity between the two studies preclude firm conclusions about age differences. But Fabrizi and Pollio (1987) suggested that for early adolescents, being funny connotes silliness and acting out or relatively low self-esteem, whereas for late adolescents, being funny connotes creative originality and a fairly secure sense of self.

The most frequent humor measure used, whether alone or in conjunction with additional tests, was nomination by others for being funny. This nomination was very often made by teachers, and the students were frequently around preschool age (Barnett & Kleiber, 1982; Durrett & Huffman, 1968; Lieberman, 1965; McGhee, 1980; Singer & Rummo, 1973; Truhon, 1983; Weisberg & Springer, 1961). Although the creative measures were usually some version of unusual uses, the correlations were quite variable, although positive. When sex differences were reported, as by Barnett and Kleiber (1982), females showed higher correlations between humor and creativity than males. Perhaps the female advantage occurs because they are more often verbal and better liked by the teachers. The rowdy class clown may have been ignored. It is interesting to note that teacher ratings of humor frequency correlated consistently lower with observer ratings of laughter production (the focal child produced an event at which someone else laughed) than did peer nominations of the funniest in the class (Fabrizi & Pollio, 1987)

In an older population (college freshmen), humor and creativity were unrelated (Schoel & Busse, 1971). Teacher nominations were used for their humor variable, and an unusual uses test and the RAT measured creativity. Hauck and Thomas (1972), however, let peers in the fourth, fifth, and sixth grades do the nominating and found a correlation of .89 with the Torrance tests. Singer and Berkowitz (1972) let Duke fraternity brothers nominate wits and clowns. The wits did well on unusual uses. The clowns did not.

The most mature nominated group was the sample of Vaillant and Vaillant (1990). Their subjects were chosen from Terman's study of gifted children that was conducted in the 1920s; subjects were in their late 70s at the time of Vaillant and Vaillant's study. The interviewer rating of "altruism, humor or sublimation as a major defense" correlated .70 with lifetime creative productivity. Here, however, the question of causality is especially difficult, and the measure of humor especially nonspecific.

Measures of Humor Production

As for studies assessing the production of humor, the correlations with creativity are not always better, even though they tend to sample young adults. Compared with the convergent RAT, correlations were modest (.29) when student nurses enrolled in an introductory psychology class were asked to make up humorous captions for TAT cards (Day & Langevin, 1969). Brodzinsky and Rubien (1976) chose upper and lower quartile subjects based on the RAT; high scorers produced significantly funnier cartoon captions than low scorers. Treadwell (1970) reported a correlation of .24 between the RAT and cartoon caption production. For college students on the Make-A-Joke Test, the correlations with the RAT were even higher (r = .47; Feingold & Mazzella, 1991).

Lindgren and Lindgren (1965) used the number of captions produced for three cartoons as a humor production measure (the captions were not judged for funniness). Their measure of creativity was the Asymmetrical Preference Test (APT); the rationale was that "creative people tend to prefer art forms that are characterized by complexity and imbalance" (p. 578). Note that the logic for this test parallels that for the Barron-Welsh Revised Art Scale mentioned earlier (Couturier et al., 1981). Lindgren and Lindgren found no significant relationship between number of captions and APT scores for either male or female undergraduates. Babad (1974) also failed to find a significant relationship between number of *funny* productions and any of his creativity measures.

Comparisons with divergent tasks, such as unusual uses, have not been much higher. Clabby (1980) found that a wit score based on the funniness of slogans produced by college students was positively correlated with uncommon uses and verbal fluency, but not as highly ($r = .33$) as might be expected given the apparent similarity of the tasks. Clabby (1979) used humorous words as *reinforcers*; his rationale was that previous work suggested that the opportunity to experience novel word associations had positively rewarding properties for highly creative students. Clabby (1979) found, however, that high and low creative subjects (as measured by the RAT) did not differ significantly in their choice of words that were rewarded by humor.

Ziv (1980, Study 1) combined funniness of cartoon captions produced and a self-report humor measure into a single humor score. He found solid correlations ($.48 < rs < .56$) between the humor scores and the Torrance tests of unusual uses and "just suppose," but it is unclear what portion of the variance in the humor scores was due to humor production and what portion to self-reports.

McGhee (1980) had observers and teachers rate the verbal and behavioral attempts at humor production in young children. The creativity measure was observers' ratings of overall amount of creativity. Results showed that creativity ratings were significantly positively related to humor initiation after the age of 6 (but not before).

Humor Appreciation

As might be expected, humor appreciation, with all its mysteries, has been used fairly rarely to assess creativity. Treadwell (1970) found no significant correlations between a self-report measure of humor appreciation and either the RAT or a Gestalt transformations measure. However, Babad (1974) reported a significant correlation between humor appreciation and fluency, and Rouff (1975) found a significant correlation with the comprehension of 20 cartoons and the RAT. Ziv (1980, Study 2) found that humorists of both sexes (as identified by a sociometric nomination for having a good sense of humor) had significantly higher creativity scores (on the same Torrance tests) than nonhumorists. Although the term *humorist* may imply production of humor, "have a good sense of humor" (p. 165) seems to suggest humor appreciation more than humor production.

Verma (1981) found that highly creative subjects (on the Wallach-Kogan Tests) had higher humor appreciation scores than low creative subjects. When sex differences are reported, adolescent females continue to show higher correlations than the males. As humor appreciation tests become more cognitively sophisticated, there may be more justification for using them to study creativity.

On the other hand, it may be that one should not expect humor appreciation to correlate highly with creativity, or certainly not to correlate as highly as humor production. The latter is conceptually much closer to the concept of creativity. The relationship between humor appreciation and creativity may come about more indirectly, perhaps through humor's facilitation of a relaxing "game-like" atmosphere (e.g., Wallach & Kogan, 1965) or a positive affect (Isen, Johnson, Mertz, & Robinson, 1985; Isen, Daubman, & Nowicki, 1987).

Another indirect connection is suggested by a set of tests that has shown power in demonstrating a relation between humor and health (e.g., Lefcourt & Martin, 1986). It could be argued that using humor to cope with adversity should be a very creative way to live. As yet the correlations of these tests with creativity tests have not been reported. Martin, Kuiper, Olinger, and Dance (1993) documented the positive relation between the use of humor to cope, self-satisfaction, and control of stress. Rotton (1992), however, reported that comedians do not live any longer than anyone else. As noted earlier (Stebbins, 1990), they do enjoy their lives.

HUMOR AS A PRODUCER OF CREATIVITY

Traditionally and theoretically, humor should have two related effects on thinking that would facilitate creativity. The cheerful mood associated with humor (e.g., Isen et al., 1987) should reduce tension and anxiety. In a state of relaxation, individuals would show less fixation and rigidity in their responses to situations.

Beyond the reduced rigidity there should also be a wider range of options that could be considered. The cognitive network could be expanded thanks to priming by the incongruous. There is evidence that both these factors can contribute to a relation between humor and creativity. Six research reports in the humor/creativity literature actually manipulated humor as an independent variable.

Isen et al. (1987) reported three studies of humor and creativity, although the word *humor* never appeared in the article. Their purpose was to study the effects of positive affect on creativity, and one of their manipulations of positive affect was a comedy film. The dependent variable in two of their studies was creative problem solving, using a classic candle, tacks, and matchbox task. Such a task could be considered a measure of insight; however, the relationship between insight and creativity is usually considered to be close. For example, Guilford (1967, p. 321) saw insight as a step in creative production, and Sternberg (1985, p. 125) noted that in the componential view, creativity is due largely to the insightful use of knowledge-acquisition components. In two studies, Isen et al. (1987) manipulated humor by using a 5-minute clip of a comedy bloopers film entitled *Gag Reel*. In the neutral condition, subjects saw a 5-minute segment of a math film. Results in the first two studies showed that subjects in the humor condition were significantly more likely to produce correct solutions to the problem-solving task than subjects in the neutral film condition. Isen et al.'s last study used a 7-item short form of the RAT as the measure of creativity, and they compared the same comedy film with no manipulation; results showed that comedy film subjects gave significantly more remote associates on the RAT.

Isen et al. (1985, Study 2) used the same experimental and control films as Isen et al. (1987), but included an additional manipulation of affect (subjects were exposed to words of positive, neutral, or negative valence after viewing the films). Their creativity measure was production of unusual first associates to neutral words. The neutral valence condition probably provides the best test of the humor-creativity relationship in this study; humor film subjects gave more unusual first associates ($M = 5.41$) than did control film subjects ($M = 3.80$). Isen et al. (1985) did not directly test this difference; however, our secondary analysis of their data showed that the mean difference between these two conditions was significant ($t(30) = 2.54$, two-tailed $p < .02$). The mean difference between comedy and neutral films was not significant in either the positive or negative valence word conditions (our secondary analysis showed $p > .24$).

Ziv also conducted several studies with humor as an independent variable. Ziv (1976), for example, had several classrooms of adolescents listen to a comedy record; others did not. After the humor experience, there was an increase in creative performance on the Torrance tests of unusual uses and just suppose. The increase was most marked for originality. These results were replicated with teacher-training students in a second study (Ziv, 1980, Study 3). A "double humor" manipulation was used in yet another study (Ziv, 1983, Study 1); experimental subjects received both comedy film clips and a cartoon caption task. The

Torrance tests were again used as the measure of creativity, and humor groups had significantly higher scores. Finally, a different manipulation was used by Ziv (1983, Study 2): Experimental subjects were instructed to give humorous answers on the Torrance Tests; control subjects were told to continue as before. Experimental subjects had significantly higher creativity scores than control subjects.

Kline, Greene, and Noice (1990) compared subjects who had viewed a humorous Candid Camera videotape with those who had viewed a neutral video or a violent, bloody videotape. The creativity measure was word atypicality. Humor and neutral subjects did not differ, but both generated more atypical words than did the violent videotape subjects.

Like Isen et al. (1987), Trice (1985) examined actual problem solving following exposure to humor. Trice induced a negative mood by giving his subjects a failing experience on unsolvable anagrams. Following cartoon viewing, people could discover the answers to solvable anagrams, whereas those without humor experience remained "helpless" and fixated on failure.

Another question for humor as a producer of creativity is the duration of the effect. All the tests reported here were immediate; a humor experience is followed right away by creative tasks or problems. Certainly workshops that evoke humor to enhance creativity would be an ideal testing ground for a longer lasting effect (Goodman, 1983). Such conferences are enormously popular (J. Goodman, personal communication, February 8, 1993; J. Morreall, personal communication, February 17, 1993). They are probably at least as effective as creativity workshops in general (Stein, 1974).

GROUP RESEARCH

If a humorous atmosphere aids individual originality by increasing freedom and breaking boundaries (e.g., Ziv, 1976), then it should also be helpful to groups. Firestien and McCowan (1988) found that groups trained in creative problem solving did indeed produce more ideas while showing more signs of humor. However, inferring causality is once again a problem because of selection bias (Campbell & Stanley, 1963). Students who choose to take creative studies courses may be more humorous to begin with than those who choose business or home economics.

Pollio and Bainum (1983) tried to perform a causal manipulation by composing groups of individuals who were more or less witty in earlier problem-solving tasks. Although the groups that laughed more produced more words from a string of letters, the effect of witty participants was not consistent. Furthermore, the number of witty remarks did not correlate with word production, and nothing correlated with performance on a NASA survival task (a convergent group problem-solving task).

Production and divergence seem to contribute to a jovial group, but not necessarily to convergent problem solving. For groups, then, the value of humor is not as clear as for the individual. Production may increase, but flexibility may require the introduction of new members (Ziller et al., 1962). For the individual, however, Isen et al. (1987) said it best: "Good feelings increase the tendency to combine materials in new ways" (p. 1130).

PLAY AND CREATIVITY

There is a substantial literature that examines the relationship between play and creativity. It is outside the scope of this chapter to thoroughly discuss this literature. However, the connection between play and humor is not necessarily as obvious as it seems.

Singer (1973) suggested that it is possible to see the early precursors of creativity in children's make-believe play. Getzels and Jackson (1962) noted that creative children tend to be more playful and tend to rank the importance of a sense of humor more highly than less creative children. In his review of the literature on the relationship between humor and creativity in children, McGhee (1979) suggested that children use the production of humorous fantasies, incongruities, and absurdities in their play to maintain an optimally varied and interesting environment.

Lieberman (1965, 1967, 1977) is probably the researcher most closely associated with studying the relationship between play and creativity; her playfulness scale includes five subscales, including spontaneity, manifest joy, and sense of humor. Thus, Lieberman explicitly considers humor to be a part of children's play.

Christie and Johnsen (1983) reviewed both the correlational and experimental literature on the role of play in social and intellectual development. They noted that play and creativity have much in common. In particular, play often involves symbolic transformations in which objects and actions are used in new or unusual ways, similar to the novel, imaginative combinations of ideas involved in creative thinking. Pellegrini's (1984-85) review of the experimental literature on play and creativity generally concurred with Christie and Johnsen (1983), although Pelligrini pointed out that exploration had been confounded with play in several studies. Pelligrini emphasized that guided exploration using questions from adults seemed to relate more closely to creativity in children rather than free play per se. A similar cautionary note about experimenter expectancy effects was sounded by Smith and Whitney (1987).

Berretta and Privette (1990) found that fourth graders who participated in flexible play experiences (emphasizing children's ideas rather than rules or adult suggestions) scored higher on the TTCT than those who participated in structured play (which emphasized following instructions). Similarly, Pellegrini (1992) found that the flexibility dimension of rough-and-tumble play correlated with prosocial problem-solving flexibility.

METHODOLOGICAL ISSUES

A problem for the comparison of creativity and humor and an indication of their relevance to each other is the recurrent inclusion of humor or funniness as an element in the scoring of creativity tasks (e.g., Guilford, 1967; Torrance, 1962; Urban, 1991). Ziv (1983, Study 2) found that instructions to "be funny" did, in fact, improve performance and originality on tests of unusual uses. More generally a game-like rather than a test-like atmosphere has been recommended for measuring creativity (Wallach & Kogan, 1965).

It is possible that the "funny" unusual uses are not only incongruous but aggressive as well (Nevo & Nevo, 1983). As an example, Hudson (1968) asked his adolescent students to role play when doing unusual uses. The roles were a stuffy, cautious computer engineer named Higgins and a wild, free-wheeling artist named McMice. Both roles increased the freedom of responses and "almost everyone benefitted: the effect was to increase fluency all around" (p. 69). The possible uses for milk bottles, pound notes, car tires, and the like were too sexual and violent to repeat. Such responses were quite original, quite aggressive, and probably quite funny to the adolescents.

Validity

A second important methodological issue for both the humor and creativity literatures concerns validity of measurement. Wallach and Kogan (1965) issued a damning critique of creativity measurement more than 25 years ago, concluding that creativity measures of the time lacked convergent validity. They noted that, in numerous studies, creativity measures correlated more highly with measures of other constructs (e.g., intelligence) than they did with each other. The TTCT, one of the tests Wallach and Kogan included in their critique, remained the most widely used measure of creativity in the 1980s (Lissitz & Willhoft, 1985).

Hocevar (1981) echoed Wallach and Kogan's concerns in a thorough review of the literature on creativity measurement, and Brown (1989) has found no less reason to complain. Treffinger (1987) was more optimistic, but he also noted that construct validity is lacking in many investigations of creativity. Of course, more recent work in the measurement of creativity addresses validity concerns (e.g., Zarnegar, Hocevar, & Michael, 1988), but these new measures have not yet reached the humor-creativity literature.

Other validity issues have also been raised in the creativity literature (Heausler & Thompson, 1988). For example, Lissitz and Willhoft (1985) found that scores on the TTCT were highly sensitive to a brief experimenter manipulation, and Ziv (1989) pointed out that children and adolescents identified as creative by many creativity tests do not necessarily produce creative products.

The state of affairs with regard to validity in the humor literature is somewhat better; at least criteria such as laughter and smiling are relatively objective (Frank & Ekman, 1993; LaFrance, 1983). As Ziv (1989) noted, "Humor creation is judged by the simple and obvious criteria of creating something judged by others to be humorous" (p. 102). However, the choice of humor measures by researchers reviewed in this chapter reveals that there is little agreement as to exactly what constitutes humor production, a sense of humor, and humor appreciation.

SUMMARY AND CONCLUSIONS

A creative product is not always (or even usually) funny, and a funny idea is creative only in a very special way, involving originality and a resolution that takes social, human factors into account. We believe that Koestler (1964) was not exactly right. Granted, there are similar cognitive and emotional processes involved that give the two parallel psychological implications. Creativity requires flexible examination of the connections among ideas, and humor depends on the selection and evaluation of different associations at different levels of analysis. Still, an original idea that does not solve a problem is usually not considered creative. A joke that leaves the incongruity unresolved is nonsense, but might still be funny. The production of ideas is necessary, and the evaluation of those ideas is critical for both. Creativity and humor do require similar mental processes. The specific applications are, however, different.

Several empirical questions are prompted by our review of the literature. First, are the effects of humor simply explained by positive affect (e.g., Isen et al., 1985; Isen et al., 1987)? Optimism and positive thinking have been shown to be related to a number of beneficial physical and psychological outcomes (e.g., Scheier & Carver, 1985, 1992, 1993), and it seems a short cognitive leap from optimism to good mood and humor (e.g., McGhee, 1991). Is humor simply a stronger laboratory manipulation of positive affect than most laboratory manipulations, or does humor make a unique contribution?

Creativity does seem best fostered in a relaxed, positive mood (e.g., Wallach & Kogan, 1965; Ziv, 1983, Study 2). Humor and laughter can certainly lead to such a relaxed, positive state (e.g., Isen et al., 1987). However, further work is needed to examine the environmental circumstances, or task contexts, that foster both humor and creativity. For example, Ziller et al. (1962) gave some groups of male college students a failure experience; these groups evaluated their cartoon-captioning performance as significantly less adequate than success-experience groups. Creating humor was easier for these subjects in a free, flexible, happy environment. Wallach and Kogan (1965) strongly supported the notion that a "game-like" atmosphere is necessary for optimal creative performance (cf. Wallach, 1970). The roles played by positive affect and general optimism in the humor-creativity relationship seem to be important, and deserve greater consideration in future research.

Second, is humor use or appreciation different from humor production? There is some evidence that this is true. O'Connell (1969), for example, found a correlation between humor appreciation and humor production of .02. Similarly, O'Quin (1992) performed a secondary analysis of the data reported by Treadwell (1970), and the new factor analysis showed that self-reports of humor use and appreciation were factorially distinct from a cartoon caption creation variable. As noted earlier, Babad (1974) found humor appreciation to be significantly related to the number of productions, but not to the number of funny productions. Logically, humor production should be more closely related to creativity than humor appreciation, but again, more work in this area is clearly needed.

What, then, is the theoretical relationship between humor appreciation and humor production? It seems that one can certainly be an appreciator of humor without also being a producer, but the reverse does not seem at all likely. It is hard to imagine a humor producer who is not also capable of humor appreciation. Still, Fabrizi and Pollio (1987) found that students who produced many humor events that other people laughed and smiled at did not necessarily respond when such events were produced by others. However, we suggest that humor appreciation can exist without production, but humor production is less likely to exist without appreciation.

A similar examination of the relationship between humor and creativity might be fruitful. It is conceivable that humor is a special case of creativity. Indeed, one of Murdock and Ganim's (1993) conclusions was that humor was "sufficiently integrated to be considered a subset of creativity" (p. 66). We disagree with this conclusion; our review of the empirical literature suggests that there is insufficient evidence for that conclusion. Rather, they seem to be two interdisciplinary areas that overlap most clearly in the area of humor production. Although one may argue that humor appreciation itself requires a modicum of creativity, humor production is probably more directly and strongly related to creativity. We concur with McGhee (1980), "As with all great discoveries, then, a higher level of creativity should be required to create a joke, cartoon, or other humour situation, than simply to understand the same event when it is initiated by another person" (p. 122).

It is also possible that humor and creativity are related because of their mutual correlation with another construct, such as intelligence. It is beyond the scope of this chapter to fully consider the literature relating humor and creativity to intelligence. However, the intelligence-creativity correlation is well established across a full range of intelligence scores (e.g., Hocevar, 1981); the threshold theory, which suggests that measures of intelligence and creativity are related only up to a moderate level of intelligence, has not been all that well supported (cf. Runco & Albert, 1986). Some measures of humor, especially humor comprehension (e.g., Ziv & Gadish, 1990) and humor cognition (Feingold & Mazzella, 1991), have been linked to intelligence.

As discussed earlier, a major problem in investigating the humor-creativity link is the lack of clarity of the two constructs. Humor is sometimes considered to be a form of creativity. Creativity measures assign points for humor or include tasks that involve humor. Such confounds must be removed before the true nature of the relationship between the two constructs can be thoroughly examined.

At least theory construction is becoming more rigorous in both fields (Ganim, 1992). The work of Attardo and Raskin (1991), Ruch (1992), and Wyer and Collins (1992) for humor, and Finke et al. (1992) for creativity, are recent examples. However, there still remain problems with basic definitions. For example, years ago, Treffinger, Renzulli and Feldhusen (1971) noted the lack of a single and widely accepted theory of creativity to focus the research. More recently, Tefft (1990) noted that, despite a tremendous surge in creativity research between the mid-1960s and the mid-1980s, no consensus relating to a definition of creativity had been reached. An edited volume on creativity theories also made it clear that no overarching theory of creativity has yet been achieved (Runco & Albert, in press). Piirto (1992) briefly summarized major theories of creativity and their proponents, as she said, "to provide an overview of the deep morass one surveys when beginning to study creativity" (p. 318).

In addition, there still remain problems with the interface between the fields of humor and creativity. For example, Murdock and Ganim (1993) noted limitations on the way the concept of humor has been treated by creativity researchers, and they suggested a broader examination of the humor literature by creativity researchers. We strongly concur with this conclusion. Ultimately, a general unified theory of cognition must encompass the phenomena of humor and creativity (Newell, 1990). When it does, the propositions will be closely related, and the researchers in both fields will have no trouble communicating.

REFERENCES

Amabile, T.M. (1990). Within you, without you: The social psychology of creativity and beyond. In M.A. Runco & R.S. Albert (Eds.), *Theories of creativity* (pp. 61-91). Newbury Park, CA: Sage.

Apte, M.L. (1983). Humor research, methodology, and theory in anthropology. In P.E. McGhee & J.H. Goldstein (Eds.), *Handbook of humor research: Vol. 1: Basic issues* (pp. 183- 212). New York: Springer-Verlag.

Attardo, S., & Raskin, V. (1991). Script theory revis(it)ed: Joke similarity and joke representation model. *Humor: International Journal of Humor Research, 4*, 293-347.

Babad, E.Y. (1974). A multi-method approach to the assessment of humor: A critical look at humor tests. *Journal of Personality, 22*, 618-631.

Barnett, L.A., & Kleiber, D.A. (1982). Concomitants of playfulness in early childhood: Cognitive abilities and gender. *Journal of Genetic Psychology, 141*(1), 115-127.

Bedard, J., & Chi, M.T.H. (1992). Expertise. *Current Directions in Psychological Science, 1*, 135-139.

Berlyne, D.E. (1960). *Conflict, arousal, and curiosity.* New York: McGraw Hill.

Berlyne, D.E. (1972). Humor and its kin. In J.H. Goldstein & P.E. McGhee (Eds.), *The psychology of humor: Theoretical perspectives and empirical issues* (pp. 43-60). New York: Academic Press.

Berretta, S., & Privette, G. (1990). Influence of play on creative thinking. *Perceptual and Motor Skills, 71*(2), 659-666.

Besemer, S.P., & O'Quin, K. (1986). Analyzing creative products: Refinement and test of a judging instrument. *Journal of Creative Behavior, 20*, 115-126.

Besemer, S.P., & O'Quin, K. (1987). Creative product analysis: Testing a model by developing a judging instrument. In S.G. Isaksen (Ed.), *Frontiers of creativity research* (pp. 341-357). Buffalo, NY: Bearly Limited.

Besemer, S.P., & Treffinger, D.J. (1981). Analysis of creative products: Review and synthesis. *Journal of Creative Behavior, 15*, 158-178.

Brodzinsky, D.M., & Rubien, J. (1976). Humor production as a function of sex of subject, creativity, and cartoon content. *Journal of Consulting and Clinical Psychology, 44*(4), 597-600.

Brown, R.T. (1989). Creativity: What are we to measure? In J.A. Glover, R.R. Ronning, & C.R. Reynolds (Eds.), *Handbook of creativity* (pp. 3-32). New York: Plenum Press.

Campbell, D.T., & Stanley, J.C. (1963). *Experimental and quasi-experimental designs for research.* Chicago: Rand McNally.

Chapman, A.J. (1983). Humor and laughter in social interaction and some implications for humor research. In P.E. McGhee, & J.H. Goldstein (Eds.), *Handbook of humor research: Vol. 1 Basic issues* (pp. 135-158). New York: Springer-Verlag.

Christie, J.F., & Johnsen, E.P. (1983). The role of play in social-intellectual development. *Review of Educational Research, 53*(1), 93-115.

Clabby, J.F. (1979). Humor as a preferred activity of the creative and humor as a facilitator of learning. *Psychology: A Quarterly Journal of Human Behavior, 16*(1), 5-12.

Clabby, J.F. (1980). The wit: A personality analysis. *Journal of Personality Assessment, 44*(3), 307-310.

Cloyd, J.S. (1964). Patterns of behavior in informal interaction. *Sociometry, 27,* 161-173.

Colell, C.A., & Domino, G. (1980). Humor preferences and creativity. *Journal of Creative Behavior, 14,* 215,221.

Couturier, L.C., Mansfield, R.S., & Gallagher, J.M. (1981). Relationships between humor, formal operational ability, and creativity in eighth graders. *Journal of Genetic Psychology, 139,* 221-226.

Davis, G.A., & Subkoviak, M.J. (1975). Multidimensional analysis of a personality-based test of creative potential. *Journal of Educational Measurement, 12,* 37-43.

Davis, J.M., & Farina, A. (1970). Humor appreciation as social communication. *Journal of Personality and Social Psychology, 15,* 175-178.

Day, H.I., & Langevin, R. (1969). Curiosity and intelligence: Two necessary conditions for a high level of creativity. *Journal of Special Education, 3,* 263-268.

DeBono, E. (1992). *Serious creativity.* New York: Harper Business.

Deren, V. (1989). Funny to some, not to others: An analysis of some adolescent responses to Australian humor literature. *Humor: International Journal of Humor Research, 2,* 55-72.

Derks, P.L. (1987). Humor production: An examination of three models of creativity. *Journal of Creative Behavior, 21,* 325-326.

Derks, P., & Arora, S. (1993). Sex and salience in the appreciation of cartoon humor. *Humor: International Journal of Humor Research, 6,* 57-69.

Derks, P., & Hervas, D. (1988). Creativity in humor production: Quantity and quality in divergent thinking. *Bulletin of the Psychonomic Society, 26*(1), 37-39.

Durrett, M.E., & Huffman, W. (1968). Playfulness and divergent thinking among Mexican-American children. *Journal of Home Economics, 60*(5), 355-358.

Eastman, M. (1936). *Enjoyment of laughter*. New York: Simon and Schuster.

Escarpit, R. (1969). Humorous attitude and scientific inventivity. *Impact of Science on Society, 19*, 253-258.

Eysenck, H.J., & Wilson, G.D. (1976). *Know your own personality*. New York: Barnes & Noble.

Fabrizi, M.S., & Pollio, H.R. (1987). Are funny teenagers creative? *Psychological Reports, 61*, 751-761.

Feingold, A., & Mazzella, R. (1991). Psychometric intelligence and verbal humor ability. *Personality and Individual Differences, 12*, 427-435.

Fine, G.A. (1983). Sociological approaches to the study of humor. In P.E. McGhee & J.H. Goldstein (Eds.), *Handbook of humor research; Vol. 1 Basic issues* (pp. 159-182). New York: Springer-Verlag.

Finke, R.A., Ward, T.B., & Smith, S.M. (1992). *Creative cognition: Theory, research, and applications*. Cambridge, MA: MIT Press.

Firestien, R.L., & McCowan R.J. (1988). Creative problem solving and communication behavior in small groups. *Creativity Research Journal, 1*, 106-114.

Fisher, S,. & Fisher, R. (1981). *Pretend the world is funny and forever: A psychological analysis of comedians, clowns and actors*. Hillsdale, NJ: Erlbaum.

Frank, M.G., & Ekman, P. (1993). Not all smiles are created equal: The difference between enjoyment and nonenjoyment smiles. *Humor: International Journal of Humor Research, 6*, 9-26.

Freud, S. (1960). *Jokes and their relation to the unconscious* (J. Strachey, Ed. and Trans.). New York: W. W. Norton. (Original work published 1905)

Fry, W.F., Jr., & Allen, M. (1975). *Make 'em laugh: Life studies of comedy writers*. Palo Alto, CA: Science and Behavior Books.

Gabrenya, W.K., & Arkin, R.M. (1980). Self-monitoring scale: Factor structure and correlates. *Personality and Social Psychology Bulletin, 6*, 13-22.

Ganim, R.M. (1992). *An examination of the relationship between creativity and humor*. Unpublished master's thesis, State University College, Buffalo, NY.

Getzels, J.W., & Jackson, P.W. (1962). *Creativity and intelligence: Explorations with gifted students*. London: Wiley.

Goldstein, J.H., & McGhee, P.E. (1972). *The psychology of humor: Theoretical perspectives and empirical issues*. New York: Academic Press.

Goodchilds, J. (1972). On being witty: Causes, correlates and consequences. In J.H. Goldstein & P.E. McGhee (Eds.), *The psychology of humor: Theoretical perspectives and empirical issues* (pp. 173-194). New York: Academic Press.

Goodman, J. (1983). How to get more smileage out of your life: Making sense of humor, then serving it. In P.E. McGhee & J.H. Goldstein (Eds.), *Handbook of humor research* (Vol. II, pp. 1-21). New York: Springer-Verlag.

Gordon, W. (1961). *Synectics: The development of creative capacity*. New York: Harper & Row.

Guilford, J.P. (1967). *The nature of human intelligence*. New York: McGraw-Hill.

Guilford, J.P. (1987). Creativity research: Past, present and future. In S.G. Isaksen (Ed.), *Frontiers of creativity research: Beyond the basics* (pp. 33-65). Buffalo: Bearly Limited.

Hauck, W.E., & Thomas, J.W. (1972). The relationship of humor to intelligence, creativity, and intentional and incidental learning. *Journal of Experimental Education, 40*(4), 52-55.

Heausler, N.L., & Thompson, B. (1988). Structure of the Torrance Tests of Creative Thinking. *Educational and Psychological Measurement, 48*, 463-468.

Hocevar, D. (1981). Measurement of creativity: Review and critique. *Journal of Personality Assessment, 45*, 450-460.

Hudson, L. (1968). *Frames of mind: Ability, perception and self-perception in the arts and sciences*. London: Methuen.

Isen, A.M., Daubman, K.A., & Nowicki, G.P. (1987). Positive affect facilitates creative problem solving. *Journal of Personality and Social Psychology, 52*, 1122-1131.

Isen, A.M., Johnson, M.M.S., Mertz, E., & Robinson, G.F. (1985). The influence of positive affect on the unusualness of word associations. *Journal of Personality and Social Psychology, 48*(6), 1413-1426.

Janus, S. (1975). The great comedians: Personality and other factors. *American Journal of Psychoanalysis, 35*, 169-174.

Johnson, D.M., Parrott, G.L., & Stratton, R.P. (1968). Production and judgement of solutions to five problems. *Journal of Educational Psychology Monograph Supplement, 59*(6, pt. 2).

Kane, T.R., Suls, J., & Tedeschi, J.T. (1977). Humour as a tool of social interaction. In A.J. Chapman & H.C. Foot (Eds.), *It's a funny thing, humour* (pp. 13-16). Oxford: Pergamon.

Keith-Spiegel, P. (1972). Early conceptions of humor: Varieties and issues. In J.H. Goldstein & P.E. McGhee (Eds.), *The psychology of humor: Theoretical perspectives and empirical issues* (pp. 3-39). New York: Academic Press.

Kline, L.M., Greene, T.R., & Noice, H. (1990). The influence of violent video material on cognitive task performance. *Psychology in the Schools, 27*(3), 228-232.

Koestler, A. (1964). *The act of creation*. New York: Dell.

LaFrance, M. (1983). Felt versus feigned funniness: Issues in coding smiling and laughing. In P.E. McGhee & J.H. Goldstein (Eds.), *Handbook of humor research: Vol. I: Basic issues* (pp. 1-12). New York: Springer-Verlag.

Lefcourt, H.M., Antrobus, P., & Hogg, E. (1974). Humor response and humor production as a function of locus of control, field dependence and type of reinforcements. *Journal of Personality, 42*(4), 632-651.

Lefcourt, H.M., & Martin, R.A. (1986). *Humor and life stress: Antidote to adversity.* New York: Springer-Verlag.

Leland, T.W. (1986). *Construction and validation of a multidimensional inventory of creative personality.* Unpublished doctoral dissertation, Auburn University, Auburn, AL.

Lieberman, J.N. (1965). Playfulness and divergent thinking: An investigation of their relationship at the kindergarten level. *Journal of Genetic Psychology, 107*(2), 219-224.

Lieberman, J.N. (1967). A developmental analysis of playfulness as a clue to cognitive style. *Journal of Creative Behavior, 1*(4), 391-397.

Lieberman, J.N. (1977). *Playfulness: Its relationship to imagination and creativity.* New York: Academic Press.

Lindgren, H.C., & Lindgren, F. (1965). Brainstorming and orneriness as facilitators of creativity. *Psychological Reports, 16*, 577-583.

Lissitz, R.W., & Willhoft, J.L. (1985). A methodological study of the Torrance Tests of Creativity. *Journal of Educational Measurement, 22*, 1-11.

Martin, R.A., Kuiper, N.A., Olinger, L.J., & Dance, K.A. (1993). Humor, coping with stress, self-concept, and psychological well-being. *Humor: International Journal of Humor Research, 6*, 89-104.

Martindale, C. (1990). *The clockwork muse: The predictability of artistic change.* New York: Basic Books.

McGhee, P.E. (1979). *Humor: Its origin and development.* San Francisco: Freeman.

McGhee, P.E. (1980). Development of the creative aspects of humor. In P.E. McGhee & A.J. Chapman (Eds.), *Children's humour* (pp. 119-139). Chichester, England: Wiley.

McGhee, P.E. (1991). *The laughter remedy: Health, healing and the amuse system.* Randolph, NJ: The Laughter Remedy.

McGhee, P.E., & Panoutsopoulou, T. (1990). The role of cognitive factors in children's metaphor and humor comprehension. *Humor: International Journal of Humor Research, 3*(4), 379-402.

Mednick, S.A. (1962). The associative basis of the creative process. *Psychological Review, 69*, 220-232.

Mindess, H., Miller, C., Turek, J., Bender, A., & Corbin, S. (1985). *The Antioch Humor Test: Making sense of humor.* New York: Avon Books.

Mintz, L.E. (1985). Standup comedy as social and cultural mediation. *American Quarterly, 37*, 71-80.

Morreall, J. (Ed.). (1987). *The philosophy of laughter and humor.* Albany: State University of New York Press.

Murdock, M.C., & Ganim, R.M. (1993). Creativity and humor: Integration and incongruity. *Journal of Creative Behavior, 27*, 57-70.

Neve, M. (1988). Freud's theory of humour, wit and jokes. In J. Durant & J. Miller (Eds.), *Laughing matters: A serious look at humour* (pp. 35-43). New York: John Wiley and Sons.

Nevo, O., & Nevo, B. (1983). What do you do when asked to answer humorously? *Journal of Personality and Social Psychology, 44*,188-194.

Newell, A. (1990). *Unified theories of cognition.* Cambridge, MA: Harvard University Press.

O'Connell, W.E. (1969). Creativity in humor. *Journal of Social Psychology, 78*(2), 237-241.

Olson, S.K. (1988). Standup comedy. In L.E. Mintz (Ed.), *Humor in America: A research guide to genres and topics* (pp. 109-136). New York: Greenwood.

O'Quin, K. (1992, July 6-9). *Humor and creativity: A meta-analysis.* Paper presented at the 10th International Conference on Humor and Laughter, Paris, France.

O'Quin, K., & Aronoff, J. (1981). Humor as a technique of social influence. *Social Psychology Quarterly, 44*, 349-357.

O'Quin, K., & Besemer, S.P. (1989). The development, reliability and validity of the Revised Creative Product Semantic Scale. *Creativity Research Journal, 2*, 268-279.

Parnes, S.J. (1981). *The magic of your mind.* Buffalo: Bearly Limited.

Pellegrini, A.D. (1984-85). The effects of exploration and play on young children's associative fluency. *Imagination, Cognition and Personality, 4*(1), 29-40.

Pellegrini, A.D. (1992). Rough-and-tumble play and social problem solving flexibility. *Creativity Research Journal, 5*, 13-26.

Perkins, D.N. (1981). *The mind's best work.* Cambridge, MA: Harvard University Press.

Piirto, J. (1992). *Understanding those who create.* Dayton: Ohio Psychological Press.

Pollio, H.R., & Bainum, C.K. (1983). Are funny groups good at solving problems?: A methodological evaluation and some preliminary results. *Small Group Behavior, 14*(4), 379-404.

Pollio, H.R., & Mers, R.W. (1974). Predictability and the appreciation of comedy. *The Bulletin of the Psychonomic Society, 4*, 229-232.

Rogers, C. (1961). *On becoming a person.* Boston: Houghton Mifflin.

Rosenthal, R., & Rosnow, R.L. (1991). *Essentials of behavioral research: Methods and data analysis.* New York: McGraw-Hill.

Rosenzweig, S., Clark, L., & Helen, J. (1946). Scoring samples for the Rosenzweig Picture Frustration Study. *Journal of Psychology, 21*, 45-72.

Rotton, J. (1992). Trait humor and longevity: Do comics have the last laugh? *Health Psychology, 11*, 262-266.

Rouff, L.L. (1975). Creativity and sense of humor. *Psychological Reports, 37*(3, pt. 1), 1022.

Ruch, W. (1992). Assessment or appreciation of humor: Studies with 3 WD humor test. In C.D. Spielberger & J.N. Butcher (Eds.), *Advances in personality assessment* (Vol. 9, pp. 27-75). Hillsdale, NJ: Erlbaum.

Runco, M.A., & Albert, R.S. (1986). The threshold theory regarding creativity and intelligence: An empirical test with gifted and nongifted children. *Creative Child and Adult Quarterly, 11*, 212-218.

Runco, M.A., & Albert, R.S. (in press). *Theories of creativity* (rev. ed.). Cresskill, NJ: Hampton Press.

Salameh, W.A. (1982). From constrictive childhood to creative adulthood: The making of standup comedians. In L.E. Mintz (Ed.), *Third International Conference on Humor: Conference abstracts* (pp. 19-20). Washington, DC: Workshop Library on World Humor.

Scheier, M.F., & Carver, C.S. (1985). Optimism, coping and health: Assessment and implications of generalized outcome expectancies. *Health Psychology, 4,* 219-247.

Scheier, M.F., & Carver, C.S. (1992). Effects of optimism on psychological and physical well-being: Theoretical overview and empirical update. *Cognitive Therapy and Research, 16,* 201-228.

Scheier, M.F., & Carver, C.S. (1993). On the power of positive thinking: The benefits of being optimistic. *Current Directions in Psychological Science, 2,* 26-30.

Schoel, D.R., & Busse, T.V. (1971). Humor and creative abilities. *Psychological Reports, 29*(1), 34.

Sherman, L.W. (1988). Humor and social distance in elementary school children. *Humor: International Journal of Humor Research, 1,* 389-404.

Singer, D.L., & Berkowitz, L. (1972). Differing "creativities" in the wit and the clown. *Perceptual and Motor Skills, 35,* 3-6.

Singer, D.L., & Rummo, J. (1973). Ideational creativity and behavioral style in kindergarten-age children. *Developmental Psychology, 8*(2), 154-161.

Singer, J.L. (1973). *The child's world of make-believe.* New York: Academic Press.

Smith, E.E., & White, H.L. (1965). Wit, creativity and sarcasm. *Journal of Applied Psychology, 49*(2), 131-134.

Smith, P.K., & Whitney, S. (1987). Play and associative fluency: Experimenter effects may be responsible for previous positive findings. *Developmental Psychology, 23*(1), 49-53.

Stebbins, R.A. (1990). *The laugh-makers: Stand-up comedy as art, business, and life-style.* Montreal: McGill-Queen's University Press.

Stein, M.I. (1974). *Stimulating creativity* (Vol. 1). New York: Academic Press.

Sternberg, R.J. (1985). *Beyond IQ: A triarchic theory of human intelligence.* Cambridge, England: Cambridge University Press.

Suls, J.M. (1972). A two-stage model for the appreciation of jokes and cartoons: An information-processing analysis. In J.H. Goldstein & P.E. McGhee (Eds.), *The psychology of humor: Theoretical perspectives and empirical issues* (pp. 81-100). New York: Academic Press.

Suls, J.M. (1983). Cognitive processes in humor appreciation. In P.E. McGhee & J.H. Goldstein (Eds.), *Handbook of humor research: Vol. I: Basic issues* (pp. 39-58). New York: Springer-Verlag.

Tefft, M.E. (1990). *A factor analysis of the TTCT, MBTI and KAI: The creative level-style issue re-examined.* Unpublished master's thesis, State University of New York College at Buffalo, Buffalo, NY.

Tollefson, D.L., & Cattell, R.B. (1966). *The IPAT Humor Test*. Champaign, IL: Institute for Personality and Ability Testing.

Torrance, E.P. (1962). *Guiding creative talent*. Englewood Cliffs, NJ: Prentice-Hall.

Torrance, E.P. (1988). The nature of creativity as manifest in its testing. In R.J. Sternberg (Ed.), *The nature of creativity: Contemporary psychological perspectives* (pp. 43-75). Cambridge: Cambridge University Press.

Treadwell, Y. (1970). Humor and creativity. *Psychological Reports, 26*, 55-58.

Treffinger, D.J. (1987). Research on creativity assessment. In S.G. Isaksen (Ed.), *Frontiers of creativity research: Beyond the basics* (pp. 103-119). Buffalo: Bearly Limited, .

Treffinger, D.J., Renzulli, J.S., & Feldhusen, J.F. (1971). Problems in the assessment of creative thinking. *Journal of Creative Behavior, 5*, 104-112.

Trice, A.D. (1985). Alleviation of helpless responding by a humorous experience. *Psychological Reports, 57*, 474.

Truhon, S.A. (1983). Playfulness, play, and creativity: A path analytic model. *Journal of Genetic Psychology, 143*(1), 19-28.

Turner, R.G. (1980). Self-monitoring and humor production. *Journal of Personality, 48*, 163-172.

Urban, K.K. (1991). On the development of creativity in children. *Creativity Research Journal, 4*(2), 177-191.

Vaillant, G.E., & Vaillant, C.O. (1990). Determinants and consequences of creativity in a cohort of gifted women. *Psychology of Women Quarterly, 14*(4), 607-616.

Verma, L.K. (1981). Humour differences among creative and non-creative high school students from various academic streams. *Indian Psychological Review, 20*(2), 1-6.

Wallach, M.A. (1970). Creativity. In P.H. Mussen (Ed.), *Carmichael's manual of child psychology* (Vol. 1, pp. 1211-1272). New York: Wiley.

Wallach, M.A., & Kogan, N. (1965). *Modes of thinking in young children: A study of the creativity-intelligence distinction*. New York: Holt, Rinehart & Winston.

Ward, W.C., & Cox, P. (1974). A field study of nonverbal creativity. *Journal of Personality, 42*, 202-219.

Weisberg, P.S., & Springer, K.J. (1961). Environmental factors in creative function. *Archives of General Psychiatry, 5*, 554-564.

White, S., & Camarena, P. (1989). Laughter as a stress reducer in small groups. *Humor: International Journal of Humor Research, 2*, 73-79.

Wicker, F.W., Thorelli, I.M., Baron, W.L., III, & Ponder, M.R. (1981). Relationships among affective and cognitive factors in humor. *Journal of Research in Personality, 15*, 359-370.

Wilson, G.D. (1973). A dynamic theory of conservatism. In G.D. Wilson (Ed.), *The psychology of conservatism* (pp. 257-266). London: Academic Press.

Wolf, F.M. (1986). *Meta-analysis: Quantitative methods for research synthesis.* Beverly Hills, CA: Sage.

Wyer, R.S., Jr., & Collins, J.E., II. (1992). A theory of humor elicitation. *Psychological Review, 99,* 663-688.

Zarnegar, Z., Hocevar, D., & Michael, W.B. (1988). Components of original thinking in gifted children. *Educational and Psychological Measurement, 48,* 5-16.

Zigler, E., Levine, J., & Gould, L. (1967). Cognitive challenge as a factor in children's humor appreciation. *Journal of Personality and Social Psychology, 6,* 332-336.

Ziller, R.C., Behringer, R.D., & Goodchilds, J.D. (1962). Group creativity under conditions of success or failure and variations in group stability. *Journal of Applied Psychology, 46,* 43-49.

Ziv, A. (1976). Facilitating effects of humor on creativity. *Journal of Educational Psychology, 68*(3), 318-322.

Ziv, A. (1980). Humor and creativity. *Creative Child and Adult Quarterly, 5*(3), 159-170.

Ziv, A. (1983). The influence of humorous atmosphere on divergent thinking. *Contemporary Educational Psychology, 8*(1), 68-75.

Ziv, A. (1989). Using humor to develop creative thinking. *Journal of Children in Contemporary Society, 20*(1-2), 99-116.

Ziv, A., & Gadish, O. (1990). Humor and giftedness. *Journal for the Education of the Gifted, 13*(4), 332-345.

Zuckerman, M. (1979). *Sensation seeking: Beyond the optimal level of arousal.* Hillsdale, NJ: Erlbaum.

11 Problem Finding: The Search for Mechanism*

Eileen S. Jay
David N. Perkins
Harvard University

PROBLEM FINDING: AN EMERGING FIELD OF STUDY

The act of finding and formulating a problem is a key aspect of creative thinking and creative performance in many fields, an act that is distinct from and perhaps more important than problem solving. Einstein asserted that:

> The formulation of a problem is often more essential than its solution, which may be merely a matter of mathematical or experimental skill. To raise new questions, new possibilities, to regard old questions from a new angle, requires creative imagination and marks real advance in science. (Einstein & Infeld, 1938, p. 92)

Wertheimer (1945) generalized the point to all thinking as follows: "The function of thinking is not just solving an actual problem but discover-

*Correspondence may be sent to Eileen Jay or David Perkins, Project Zero, Harvard Graduate School of Education, Longfellow Hall, Appian Way, Cambridge, MA 02138.

ing, envisaging, going into deeper questions . . . Envisaging, putting the productive question is often a more important, often a greater achievement than the solution of a set question" (p. 123). Numerous other references attest to the importance of problem-finding activity for creative thinking in various fields, such as philosophy, mathematics, technical invention, history, and scientific investigation (Bunge, 1967; Fischer, 1970; Osborn, 1963; Polya, 1965; Rossman, 1931).

In spite of its acknowledged importance, problem finding has received little attention in the mainstream cognitive literature, whereas rich theories, minute analyses, and elaborate teaching programs on the subject of problem solving appear in great abundance. The vast literature on problem solving mostly consists of analyses of the cognitive processes involved when a problem is given or after the problem has already been defined. Although numerous theories propose stages of problem solving or thinking that include problem definition as the initial step (Dewey, 1910; Newell & Simon, 1972; Sternberg, 1988; Wallas, 1926), there has been surprisingly little theoretical or empirical work specifically examining the nature of problem finding and its relationship to problem solving.

Nevertheless, over the past 20 years, problem finding has been emerging as a topic of study. Today it occupies a secure niche within the field of creativity research. The first widely cited empirical connection between problem finding and creativity was made by Getzels and Csikszentmihalyi (1976) in their seminal work involving a study of student artists. Getzels and Csikszentmihalyi found a correlation between the degree of problem-finding behavior artists exhibited while preparing for and drawing a still life and the rated creativity of the final products. Problem-finding behavior in this task was also correlated with artists' success in the field 7 and 18 years later (Csikszentmihalyi, 1990).

Since the original Getzels and Csikszentmihalyi research, there has been a growing interest in studying and writing about problem finding. Work has included differentiation of distinct types of problem situations, theoretical analyses associating problem finding with various cognitive processes, and empirical studies relating problem finding and creative activity in a variety of disciplines (see Dillon, 1982; Subotnik & Moore, 1988 for reviews). Articles on problem finding have appeared in several journals on creativity, including *The Journal of Creative Behavior* and the *Creativity Research Journal*. A recent edited volume entitled *Problem Finding, Problem Solving, and Creativity* (Runco, 1994c) lends weight to the importance problem finding deserves along with problem solving in understanding creativity.

The present review surveys the problem-finding literature and examines how the various views and approaches contribute to an overall understanding of why and how problem finding occurs. Because the body of literature specifically on problem finding is limited, it will also prove useful to draw on concepts and findings from the cognitive literature at large.

DEFINING PROBLEM FINDING

The term *problem finding* is of somewhat obscure origin. The sociologist Merton (1945) used the term to describe the unique contributions of scientists whose questions brought about major shifts in thinking within their disciplines. In speaking on originality, Macworth (1965) stated that "problem solving is a choice between existing programs . . . whereas problem finding is the detection of the need for a new program based on a choice between existing and expected programs" (p. 57). More recent use of and interest in the term began with the work of Getzels and Csikszentmihalyi (1976); they defined *problem finding* as "the way problems are envisaged, posed, formulated, created" (p. 5).

Fundamentally, problem finding refers to behavior, attitudes, and thought processes directed toward the envisionment, posing, formulation, and creation of problems, as opposed to the processes involved in solving them. Although not falling directly under the rubric of problem finding, numerous other related terms have been used to describe this aspect of thinking, such as problem formulation, problem posing, problemizing, creative problem discovery, problem sensing, problem identification, problem expression, problem construction, and problem definition (Allender, 1969; Brown & Walter, 1983; Bunge, 1967; Dudek & Cote, 1994; Mumford, Reiter-Palmon, & Redmond, 1994; Runco, 1994a; Runco & Okuda, 1988; Taylor, 1972).

It is useful to break the term *problem finding* down into its component parts. What constitutes a *problem*? Getzels (1982) contrasted a common-usage sense of the word *problem*, meaning an undesired situation, difficulty, or obstacle that one wishes to avoid or mitigate, with a sense of problem as "a question raised or to be raised for inquiry." Here, problem refers to a desirable situation that one strives to find or create. Thus, the act of problem finding is not just one of detecting a difficulty. It also includes envisioning and creating new, deeper questions and fresh avenues for inquiry.

Why use the term *finding*? Problems in the obstacle sense usually require no finding because they often present themselves, as when one's car breaks down on the highway. However, problems in the inquiry sense must be found because typically "dilemmas do not present themselves automatically as *problems* capable of resolution or even of sensible contemplation. They must be posed and formulated in fruitful and often radical ways if they are to be moved toward solution" (Getzels, 1975, p. 12).

Runco (1994a) suggested that, like creativity, problem finding is not unidimensional, but rather is a highly interactive complex or family of behaviors, skills, and tendencies. This view has gained support from the many aspects of problem finding featured in different writings. Authors talk about the importance of envisaging (Wertheimer, 1945) and being sensitive to gaps (Henle, 1974) to emphasize the element of seeing and conceiving problem-forming possibilities in a situation. Then there are the processes involved in actually defining and formulating the question or problem statement (Hoover & Feldhusen, 1990; Runco & Okuda, 1988). Runco and Chand (1994) emphasized the typically over-looked evaluative component of problem finding, acknowledging that ideally an individual evaluates at each step of the process to assess the originality of his or her inquiry, to insure that the problem is workable, that ideas are relevant, and so on. Finally, Michael (1977) claimed that problem finding takes place not only at the beginning of the process, but may occur continuously as problem reformulation at numerous points in the creative process.

Hence, a comprehensive definition of problem finding would encompass, at the very least: (a) conceiving and envisaging problems or question-forming possibilities in a situation, (b) defining and formulat-ing the actual problem statement, (c) periodically assessing the quality of the problem formulation and its solution options, and (d) problem refor-mulation from time to time.

THE SEARCH FOR MECHANISM: UNDERSTANDING WHY AND HOW

In efforts to understand cognitive processes, progress requires going beyond definitions to gain insight into mechanism. Broadly speaking, the quest for mechanism involves developing causal models for the phe-nomenon in question. Searching for mechanism typically includes trying to understand *why* and *how* people exhibit particular patterns of behav-ior or thought.

When investigating problem finding, the "why" question is par-ticularly important, as can be seen from the contrast case with problem solving. The onset of problem solving is clear; it occurs when a person encounters a task or problem. In the case of problem finding, however, no well-defined task has been established. Indeed, the point of problem finding is to generate a task, goal, or challenge. A problem-solving task establishes a context that may draw one into the solving process, but problem finding inherently lacks this support. Most often, the impetus for problem finding must come from the individual. It can involve active initiation of a new problem by the individual or can involve recognition of inconsistencies or other aspects of the situation that prompt the individual to form questions. Considering the effort required, a central question for understanding the mechanism of problem finding is this: "Why do people problem find?" or more specifically, "What contributes to an individual's impetus to problem find?"

The question "*How* do people problem find?" is a more typical one aimed at understanding the process. A number of authors have touched on the process of problem finding. Several address the issue of whether problem finding acts as a separate phase or as an integrated process with problem solving in the thinking enterprise (Dudek & Cote, 1994; Kay, 1994; Michael, 1977). Others propose specific strategic mechanisms for how the problem definition and construction process itself occurs (Mumford et al., 1994; Langley, Simon, Bradshaw, & Zytgow, 1987). These and other process models are reviewed later.

The two guiding questions (a) "Why do people problem find?" and (b) "How do people problem find?" provide a framework for the following review. The framework aids in discerning how the various theoretical views and empirical findings contribute toward an overall understanding of problem finding. For additional organization, the research on problem finding is sorted into four categories: (a) context, (b) cognitive abilities, (c) cognitive processes, and (d) dispositions. Although some theories and findings straddle categories, they are discussed according to their primary themes.

In the process of reviewing each category, we examine whether each factor is a characteristic *enabling* problem finding or a characteristic *promoting* problem finding (cf. Perkins, 1988a). An enabling characteristic equips a person for doing problem finding without particularly pressing the person to do so, much as being tall equips a person to play basketball better without otherwise encouraging the person to play basketball. A promoting characteristic, in contrast, yields such a press. For example, practice would directly promote better basketball playing. This distinction is important because a very different picture of problem finding emerges, depending on exactly how a characteristic that fosters problem finding does so. A characteristic that merely enables problem finding has more limited explanatory power than one that specifically promotes it.

At the end of the review, we revisit the why and how questions in terms of enabling or promoting roles in order to assess how each of the factors contributes toward building a comprehensive model of problem finding.

CONTEXTS

This section examines the role context plays in problem finding using three different senses of the term *context*. First, we look at context in terms of the type of problem situation. Second, because the domain in which problem finding takes place is an important part of the context, we review problem-finding research within specific disciplines. Third is a brief recognition that problem finding by individuals (or groups) occurs in a social context, an element that needs to be acknowledged in problem-finding research.

Types of Problem Situations

Taking into account the type of problem situation is tremendously important because it affects what we mean by problem finding and, consequently, affects how we interpret the processes. Differences in context may in fact call for different kinds of problem finding. So whenever we speak of problem finding, evaluate models, or interpret research, it is important to identify what kind of problem finding is meant.

In some cases, problem situations are highly structured, whereas in others they are fairly open and unstructured, the latter requiring more initiation and formulation. Many cognitive scientists distinguish between well-structured and ill-structured problems (Frederiksen, 1984) or well-defined and ill-defined problem spaces (Sternberg, 1982), and several authors have addressed this dimension specifically with regard to problem finding.

Getzels (1982) introduced a classification of problem situations into three types: presented, discovered, and created. In *presented* problem situations, the problem is given to the problem solver by another person, as for example when a teacher presents a math problem for students to solve, and usually has a known method of solution that the solver must figure out. In *discovered* problem situations, the problem exists, but the problem solver discovers it, often through detection of an obstacle or inexplicable occurrence, as when a scientist detects an anomaly in findings or data. In *created* problem situations, the problem does not exist until someone invents or creates it, such as when an inventor decides to design a new gadget. Dillon (1982) presented a similar taxonomy consisting of existent, emergent, and potential problems that demand different levels of problem-finding activity, namely, recognizing, discovering, and inventing a problem respectively.

Two multidimensional frameworks of problem situations were recently offered. Wakefield (1989) placed the dimensions of problems and their solutions along two orthogonally arranged continua from open to closed. He considered problem finding to be characterized by two types of situations: insight problems (open problem, closed solution) and creative problems (open problem, open solution). Rostan (in press) presented a three-dimensional model that relates problem formulation, method formulation, and solution formulation with continua varying in the degree to which the formulation is well defined.

Highly structured, well-defined contexts, such as Getzels's (1982) presented problems described earlier, leave little room for problem finding because the problem is given. The key problem-finding feature of initiation is not invoked here; however, there can be some role for problem finding in these contexts. It could be argued that problem-finding processes are involved whenever there is creative representation or reframing of the problem. Nevertheless, a model of problem finding that concentrates only on rather structured problem settings would yield a rather limited conception of problem finding centered on certain skills but neglecting the demands of initiation.

Moderately structured contexts occur often in the real world, such as when there is a well-recognized problem in the field or when problems arise from other problems. In these discovered or emergent problems, to use Getzels's (1982) and Dillon's (1982) terms, the overall goals may be evident, but the problem (or subproblem) is implicit and must be found and formulated by the individual. This kind of problem finding draws on an array of creative skills and attitudes, such as sensitivity to problem situations, keen observation of discrepant events, a questioning attitude, imaginative formulation of the problem, and so on.

The most paradigmatic and demanding problem-finding situation is the created or potential problem in which the problem space is ill defined and the impetus arises entirely from the individual. Problem-finding activities become more important as the degree of a priori structure decreases, and individuals must structure and direct their problem-solving activities using their own resources (Mumford et al., 1994). The challenge of problem finding in ill-defined situations is that it entails initiation in the form of a true creative impulse to explore new possibilities and connections. According to Sternberg (1985), it requires first the discovery of a problem area or topic, and later the structuring of the problem into a workable springboard for solution generation. Given that most problems in the real world are ill structured and that constructing problems in open-task situations is what is typically meant by creative problem finding, we should evaluate theoretical models of problem finding by the extent to which they explain why and how people pose problems in real-world, ill-defined contexts.

Problem context has implications for research methodology as well. Moore and Murdock (1991) cautioned that although many studies purport to investigate real-world problem finding, often the experimenters predetermine the task, the tables, and the objects used in the problem context. For example, in many studies, subjects are shown examples of visual/verbal ideational tasks, puzzle-like games, or real-world problems and are asked to design one of their own as the problem-finding exercise. These empirical studies can be useful in identifying component problem-finding skills and abilities. However, they represent rather structured problem contexts because the experimenters, not the subjects, instigate problem-finding activity and because subjects do not have total freedom to provide their own constraints. These studies do not approach the real crux of problem finding, which is how people come to sense gaps and form their own problems in ill-structured contexts. In evaluating research, it is important to look at the nature of the problem-finding task because what is meant by problem finding is not the same in structured and ill-defined contexts.

Moore and Murdock (1991) raised the need for observational studies of problem finders in real-world settings, in which problem initiation must originate from the individual. In calling for more research situated in the natural environment, Runco (1994a) acknowledged that problems encountered in the natural environment may differ from experimental problems designed to be realistic in the degree of motivation, interest, and payoffs, at the very least. Interestingly, problem-finding research has not turned toward the more real-world biographical case studies, observational techniques, or in-depth protocols characteristic of creativity research.

Recall from an earlier section in this chapter that we wish to assess whether or not particular factors play enabling or promoting roles in explaining why and how people problem find. Context can promote problem finding indirectly by providing an external stimulus or situation that provokes people to generate questions or problems. For example, a person who discovers an anomaly or unexplained occurrence may be stimulated to pose problems. Yet the way in which context promotes problem finding is indirect because unless the person (or group) notices the problem potential and initiates question asking, problem finding will not occur. Moreover, the more ill defined the problem situation is, the more there is a requisite for active initiation by the inquirer. Therefore, context may at times indirectly promote problem finding, but cannot in itself explain why it happens.

Problem Finding in Specific Disciplines

Art. In Getzels and Csikszentmihalyi's (1976) longitudinal study of male art students, subjects were given the task of drawing a still life of their own choosing from a set of objects. The investigators divided the process into the problem-formulation stage during which a student arranged the objects in preparation for drawing, and the problem solving stage which began when the student actually started drawing the still life. During the problem-formulation stage, patterns of behavior indicative of good problem finding included exploring and manipulating more objects, choosing more unusual objects, and allowing the problem to emerge rather than drawing on preconceived ideas. During the problem-solving stage, Getzels and Csikszentmihalyi used as criteria of problem finding a continued openness to reformulation of the problem, a willingness to switch directions when a new approach suggested itself, and a tendency to refrain from viewing the work as absolutely finished. The final products were independently judged for the artistic creativity of the drawing. Getzels and Csikszentmihalyi found a strong correlation between the degree of problem finding and the rated creativity of the student artists' drawings. Those students rated high in problem-finding attributes were also found to achieve a high degree of professional success even 18 years later (see Csikszentmihalyi, 1990).

Kay (1991) found interesting differences in problem-finding performance on a spatial task among professional artists, semiprofessional artists, and nonartists. Although expecting the most problem-finding behavior from the professional group, Kay found that it was the semiprofessional group who exhibited the discovery-oriented behavior most similar to Getzels and Csikszentmihalyi's art students. Kay hypothesized that professional artists develop a personal aesthetic bias that serves as an organizing principle and thereby mitigates the need for problem defining anew with each problem situation.

Rostan (in press) compared problem-finding and problem-solving performance in groups of artists and scientists who were critically acclaimed professional producers in their fields with those who were considered professionally competent but less productive. The problem-finding tasks were verbal/numerical and puzzle-type games in which subjects were instructed to discover or construct a problem. The critically acclaimed professional producers, compared to the professionally competent, allocated a greater proportion of time and discovery-oriented behavior to the finding of a problem.

In his study of high school seniors, Wakefield (1989) found significant correlations between arts orientation (i.e., interest in art) and thinking in logical, divergent, and creative problem situations.

According to Wakefield, because creative problem situations involve open problems and open solutions, they require problem finding. Creative and divergent thinking were also highly correlated with activities and achievements in art (as well as literature and science) measured by the Creative Behaviors Inventory.

In a small-scale replication of Getzels and Csikszentmihalyi's (1976) study, Dudek and Cote (1994) found no correlation between exploratory behavior in the preparatory phase and the rated quality or originality of collages, a finding contrary to that of Getzels and Csikszentmihalyi. Behavioral acts in the solution phase were, however, correlated to quality and originality. In their interpretation, Dudek and Cote deemphasized the importance of finding a new, original problem in the preparatory phase of each work; rather, they said, "problems" reside in the head of the artist over time and are basically neither original nor resolvable. Often there is no new problem to find. Instead, creation is driven by an ongoing emotional involvement of the artist to find solutions that involve personal expression through symbolic means. In contrast with science in which the concept of finding problems and asking questions is appropriate, Dudek and Cote contended that the purpose of art is not to offer answers to problems but rather to reflect emotional realities. We note that the notion that art is inevitably or principally about "emotional realities" has been questioned (Gombrich, 1961; Goodman, 1976).

Reading and writing. Moore (1985) replicated Getzels and Csikszentmihalyi's (1976) study of artists with student writers, using the same procedures and the same kind of potential problem situation. As with the study of artists, results indicated a relationship between problem finding and the originality of the product, in this case, a written essay. Creative student writers displayed discovery-oriented behavior resembling that of the art students—exploring more in the problem formulation phase and exhibiting a high tolerance for change in their products in the solution phase.

Two experiments conducted by Glover (1979) examined the kinds of questions asked by college students identified as relatively creative or relatively noncreative using the Torrance Thinking Creatively with Words Test (Torrance, 1974). In one experiment, creative students asked significantly more application-, synthesis-, and evaluation-level questions in interview settings, whereas less creative students asked significantly more knowledge- and comprehension-level questions. In a second experiment, creative students wrote greater numbers of higher order questions in the margins of reading materials than less creative students who wrote more factual level questions.

Science. In a review of literature on scientific creativity, Mansfield and Busse (1981) noted that sensitivity in the selection of research problems had great promise for differentiating the truly creative scientist from the less creative one. The field of science contains notable examples of discoveries that hinged on an insightful formulation of a problem, including Einstein's theory of relativity or Kepler's theory of elliptical planetary orbits. The contention that finding and formulating problems is crucial to creative work in science has long been acknowledged by many prominent scientists (Beveridge, 1957; Bunge, 1967; Einstein & Infeld, 1938). However, systematic study of the relationship between scientific creativity and problem finding is only beginning to emerge.

In a survey of winners of the Westinghouse Science Talent Search, Subotnik (1984) concluded that, for adolescents talented in science, the choice of research question was motivated by curiosity and desire to make a contribution. A follow-up study of these adolescents while in graduate school years indicated that subjects who were classified as problem finders were more likely to be involved in research with a mentor relationship and had better chance for academic success in their fields (Subotnik & Steiner, 1994).

Hoover and Feldhusen (1990) studied gifted ninth-grade students' scientific problem-finding ability, which was assessed by asking students to generate questions or hypotheses in realistic, ill-defined situations. The hypothesis formulation ability was not highly related to intelligence, aptitudes, attitude toward science, attitude toward problem solving, or tolerance for ambiguity. Surprisingly, a follow-up study showed that the hypothesis generating abilities were not correlated with supposed measures of creativity, including fluency, flexibility, originality, and tolerance for ambiguity.

A teaching experiment conducted by Yager (1989) compared the Science-Technology-Society (STS) curriculum, which is centered around exploring, questioning, and explanation, with a traditional approach. In a posttest of student-generated questions to a presented event, students in the STS classes showed greater growth in the number and uniqueness of questions, causes, and consequences generated.

Jay (1996) assessed ninth-grade students' problem-finding behavior in a naturalistic setting while they engaged in open-ended science inquiry. A problem-finding scaffolding intervention significantly increased the number of problems generated, altered the type of problems, and induced articulation of more open-ended questions, compared to students' spontaneous problem-finding behavior. Problem finding was not highly related to interest in science, prior knowledge, understanding of science processes, creative activities, or measures of creative tendency. However, two aspects of intrinsic motivation—curiosity and independent mastery—were significant predictors of problem-finding performance.

In the related discipline of mathematics, Brown and Walter (1983) offered excellent practical definitions and examples of creative problem posing in mathematics. Brown and Walter's work, which was based on educational practice rather than research, presented a wealth of classroom strategies for learning the art of conceiving and formulating mathematical problems.

Real-world contexts. In early studies, two investigators used simulated in-baskets containing various documents, memos, and letters to study inquiry styles, including sensitivity to problems. Shulman (1965) gave a teacher's basket to 21 teacher trainees, and Allender (1969) gave a mayor's basket to 51 children in grades 4 through 6. Shulman found that subjects with a dialectical or "seeking" style, as determined by various creativity tests, rated significantly higher on inquiry time, problem sensitivity, and general inquiry scores than didactic-style subjects. Problem sensitivity was defined as the number of embedded potentially problematic elements to which a subject reacted in the inquiry situation. Similarly, Allender (1969) found that subjects with higher inquiry time sensed more problems and asked more questions, which in turn generated more information search behavior.

Two more recent studies (Chand & Runco, 1992; Okuda, Runco, & Berger, 1991) investigated problem finding by having subjects generate real-world problems concerning home, work, or school life. Results indicated that problem-finding measures were more predictive of creative activities than traditional divergent thinking measures, and that use of real-world tasks added significantly to predictive power (Okuda et al., 1991). The investigators further found that scores elicited by explicit instructions to seek original problems and solutions were significantly correlated with creative activities and accomplishments (Chand & Runco, 1992). Another study of school problems generated by students examined the quality of the problems posed (Getzels & Smilansky, 1983). The problems students formulated were predominantly *egocentric*, perceiving the problematic situation from their own point of view, rather than *socially sensitive*, considering the motives and needs of all those involved. The tendency to pose quality (i.e., more socially sensitive) problems was related to specific intellectual characteristics, including intelligence, academic aptitude (especially in mathematics), and divergent thinking, measured by standardized tests and the Torrance Tests of Creative Thinking.

Experienced teachers and teacher trainees were the subjects for a replication of Getzels and Csikszentmihalyi's (1976) study as applied to teacher problem finding in the classroom (Moore, 1990). Although novices and student teachers tended to pose more problems, experienced teachers asked higher level questions than student teachers.

It is worth mentioning again here that Runco (1994a) noted the difference between real-world problems and realistic problems. Real-world problems, like those described in the earlier experiments, are designed to resemble problems that might be found in the natural environment. Runco noted that research is now emphasizing realistic problems that occur in a more relevant context, and he recommended additional moves toward research situated in the natural environment.

Taken together, the studies of problem finding in the various disciplines reviewed here suggest that the domain context may make a difference in why and how problem finding occurs. This raises many domain-related questions, such as: Do various disciplines call for different kinds of problem finding? To what extent is creative problem finding in individuals a general characteristic versus a domain-specific one? More research on problem finding in various disciplines is needed to understand the effect domain context has on problem finding.

Social Context and the Field

The study of cognition and of creativity overwhelmingly emphasizes skills and attributes of the individual. Existing research on problem finding also shows this trend. Csikszentmihalyi (1990) cautioned that personal characteristics such as personality, values, or discovery orientation are at best only correlates of creativity, conditions that facilitate its occurrence. He advocated a systems perspective that goes beyond the person and takes into account the social context of creative actions (Csikszentmihalyi, 1988b). Creativity is determined at least as much by the domain of endeavor and by the *field*, which is comprised of people who decide whether the individual's actions depart from the usual and make enough of a contribution to be deemed creative. Likewise, the degree of innovation of a new problem formulation is determined by the domain and the field. Accordingly, a comprehensive approach to the study of problem finding would go beyond the person and encompass the domain and social contexts as well. This is not to say that studying the processes and attributes of the individual should be neglected, but rather that research should take a broad view of the context in which problem finding occurs.

COGNITIVE ABILITIES

This section reviews work on the relationship between problem finding and particular cognitive competencies or abilities. Research investigates the extent to which there are cognitive prerequisites for problem finding as well as correlations between problem finding and cognitive abilities associated with creativity.

Postformal Abstract Thought

Adopting a Piagetian perspective, Arlin (1975, 1984) claimed that problem finding is a postformal operation, that formal reasoning in the Piagetian sense is a necessary but not sufficient condition for effective problem finding. In fact, Arlin proposed problem finding as a distinct fifth stage of cognitive development. Postformal thinking, the ability to take propositions as its objects of analysis, is considered metasystemic in that it is one level of reflection removed from formal-operational thinking (see Commons, Richards, & Armon, 1984).

The rationale for problem finding as postformal is this: An abstract mental coordination of multiple sources and systems of reference is required in order for thinkers to conceive generative questions of themselves and of phenomena that surround them. Problem definition is thought to involve abstract formulation and definition of the problem before resolving it, a process requiring mental coordination of several possibilities as well as evaluative judgment (Arlin, 1984; Pitt, 1976). Thus, Arlin contended that problem finding requires the presence of special kinds of reflective mental abilities.

Because Arlin refers only to the discovery of abstract overarching, self-referential questions, Arlin focused on a particular type of problem finding that one might consider rather "high-end." Indeed, for this type of problem finding, the higher order cognitive ability to reflect on propositions as objects of analysis does seem necessary. However, not all problem finding yields high-level abstract, self-referential questions, so the definition of problem finding on which Arlin based her theory may be overly restrictive. Arlin's theory lacks coverage because a theoretical account of problem finding must be able to credit creative and inventive question generation at all levels of cognitive capability, not just at abstract levels. The kind of high-level problem finding that Arlin described is evident more frequently in those with a high degree of expertise and experience in a field. So although Arlin's theory is not applicable to problem finding overall, perhaps a within-domain version of Arlin's thesis can be preserved.

With its somewhat limited applicability, the cognitive competence of postformal abstract thought does not contribute much explanatory power to the search for mechanisms of why and how in problem finding mentioned earlier. Because postformal thought is not a prerequisite ability for problem finding, it can be neither an enabling nor promoting factor for problem finding overall. In certain cases of high-end abstract problem finding, though, it may help to enable, but not to promote, problem finding.

Divergent Thinking

A widely used approach in the early study of creativity centered on the measurement of divergent thinking abilities, employing batteries of divergent thinking tests developed by Guilford (1967), Torrance (1966), and Wallach and Kogan (1965). Divergent, as opposed to convergent, thinking is needed when there are many diverse possible answers or solutions to a problem. For example, one type of problem found on many divergent thinking tests requires a person to think of many different and unusual uses for a common item, such as a tin can or a brick.

Wakefield (1985) studied the relationship between problem finding and divergent thinking by asking fifth-grade children to list all things a line figure could represent (a typical visual divergent thinking task) followed by a request to construct their own figure and to provide lists of what it could represent (a task used to estimate problem finding). Wakefield's findings indicated that problem finding scores were significantly correlated with creative tendency, the latter measured by the Group Inventory for Finding Creative Talent (Rimm & Davis, 1976), but not to measures of intelligence (WISC-R). Just the opposite was true for responses to presented drawings.

Similarly, in a study of the problem finding of adolescents, Runco and Okuda (1988) administered verbal divergent thinking tasks consisting of three presented problems and one discovered problem, in which subjects think of a problem and then provide the solution. Like Wakefield, they found that discovered problems were more highly correlated with creativity scores (the Creative Activities Check List; Runco, 1987) than presented problems were. In fact, discovered problems, which presumably reflect some problem-finding skills, significantly contributed to the prediction of creative activity, even when controlling for the presented problem situation.

These and related studies play an important role in helping to further establish a connection between problem finding and creativity. However, there is controversy over how indicative divergent thinking tests are of actual creative performance, with many critics dismissing any meaningful relationship. Although the research discussed earlier suggests some predictive validity of divergent thinking for concurrent creative activity in children, there is no evidence at present to suggest that children who are gifted divergent thinkers will grow up to be creative or productive (Kay, 1994). Some authors (Nicholls, 1972; Wallach, 1983) have expressed concerns about whether or not divergent thinking tasks demonstrate anything about real-world adult creativity. In reviewing the relationship of performance on various tests of creativity and demonstrated creative achievement by scientists, Mansfield and Busse (1981) determined that assessments using unusual uses tests displayed hardly any relation to professional creativity in scientists. If divergent thinking tasks are an insufficient predictor of real-world creative performance for adults, it may be necessary as well to turn to other predictors and factors in trying to understand problem finding.

Other Cognitive Competencies

In the literature on creativity, a number of cognitive competencies have been suggested as the basis of creativity, among them remote associates, bisociation, and Janusian thinking (see Perkins, 1981, 1988a, for reviews). In general, the evidence reveals that the case for specific competencies underlying creative ability is not strong (Mansfield & Busse, 1981; Nickerson, Perkins, & Smith, 1985; Perkins, 1988a). A distinction can be drawn between competencies that contribute to general cognition and those that specifically promote creativity. The aforementioned cognitive competencies may make one more creative in that they enhance cognitive functioning in general, but may not promote creativity in particular. It is reasonable to think that the same logic would apply to problem finding. In the terms we used earlier, the evidence would suggest that these cognitive competencies would at best enable, but not promote, problem finding. They would explain problem finding only to the extent that they explain general cognitive functioning.

COGNITIVE PROCESSES

This section covers perspectives that help in understanding the problem finding process itself. First are some views on the sequence of problem finding. Second, although there is no direct research on problem finding from a knowledge perspective, here we review the general literature on knowledge and relate it to issues concerning problem finding. Finally, specific strategies and perspectives on problem finding are examined and the conceptual controversy over strategies views is discussed.

Problem Finding Processes: Stage-like or Interactive

The problem finding process and its placement vis-à-vis problem solving have been described in two rather distinct ways. One view stems from traditional models of problem solving that propose sequenced steps in the problem-solving process. These models all cite problem finding or problem definition as the initial step followed by steps aimed at solving the problem. Terms for the problem definition stage include: observation of need and problem formulation (Rossman, 1931), preparation (Wallas, 1926), felt need and problem defined (Dewey, 1910), and understanding the problem (Polya, 1957). These stage-like views imply that the problem definition step is completed before advancing to subsequent steps for solving the problem.

More recent theorists attending to the role of problem finding in the process describe a more interactive and iterative process than the linear, invariant problem-solving steps of previous models. A more dynamic view allows for problem-finding activity throughout the process, both initially *and* during problem solving (Dudek & Cote, 1994). Problem finding takes place not only at the beginning of the creative process, but may also occur at such evaluation points as choosing a solution or in problem reformulation (Michael, 1977). Runco and Chand (1994) distinguished between problem discovery that occurs early in the process and problem definition that occurs at various points during the framing or reframing of a problem. However, throughout the process, they claim, there are continuous interactions among problem finding, evaluations, and strategies. Getzels and Csikszentmihalyi (1976) found an openness to reformulation of the problem (which they viewed as a kind of problem-finding behavior), even during the so-called problem-solving stage in the most creative artists.

The interactive view suggests a new, broader interpretation of problem finding. Stage-like models imply that problem finding primarily entails statement of the original problem, so that problem finding ends when the problem statement is completed, after which problem-solving mechanisms take over. Interactive views, on the other hand, suggest that problem finding is not a discrete stage, but a process and attitude that continues throughout the endeavor. One continues to look for new problems and subproblems, to reconceptualize and reframe the original problem, and to evaluate the current formulation of the problem all along the way.

Knowledge

Expertise and the organization of knowledge. There can be little question that content knowledge plays at least an enabling role in problem finding. It would be difficult to conceive a problem without drawing on one's existing knowledge. Beyond such simple logic, though, consideration of the role of knowledge in problem finding raises a more provocative question: Does an individual's problem-finding competence vary directly with content mastery in a domain?

A body of contemporary research on expertise in solving problems in areas as diverse as chess (Chase & Simon, 1973), physics (Chi, Glaser, & Rees, 1982; Larkin, 1983), mathematics (Schoenfeld & Herrmann, 1982), and computer programming (Soloway & Ehrlich, 1984) argues for the importance of an extensive content-specific repertoire of knowledge for skilled performance of any sort within the domain. This research has revealed that expertise depends on an extensive and highly organized knowledge base of schemata specific to the domain in question (Chase & Simon, 1973; Glaser, 1984; Newell & Simon, 1972). According to this theory of expertise, one might predict that problem-finding ability would be a function of the *amount* of knowledge individuals have at their disposal and the ways in which the information is *organized*. By this logic, experts in a domain should be better problem finders than novices.

Are experts, by virtue of their higher level of knowledge in a domain, necessarily better problem finders than novices? Examining the amount of knowledge per se between experts and novices merely leads to differences in the level of sophistication of problems. Certainly, the expert can formulate more sophisticated questions. However, the fact that an expert can pose the question, "Is the observed reflectivity of a metal dependent on its electrical properties?", shows no particular superiority in problem-finding ability over the child who asks, "Why is metal shiny?" Both are working at the edges of their competence and are posing questions that draw appropriately on their respective states of knowledge. Having a greater amount of knowledge per se does not necessarily result in better problem-finding ability relative to one's level of knowledge.

According to the research on expertise, what characterizes expertise is not merely an extensive bank of content knowledge, but also a highly organized set of knowledge structures or schemata that allow for rapid recognition-like orientation to the "deep structure" of a problem. Studies show that experts in physics organize their problem representations around principles and abstractions, whereas novices organize theirs around dominant objects and domain concepts (Chi, Feltovich, & Glaser, 1981). Performance protocols of experts in chess (Chase & Simon, 1973; deGroot, 1965) and computer programming (Soloway & Ehrlich, 1984) have documented a skill for quick, recognition-like orientation to the deep structure of a problem.

What would these differences in knowledge organization mean for an understanding of the mechanism of problem finding? From the earlier discussion of research on art, recall Kay's (1991) findings that showed no difference in problem finding between professional artists and nonartists. One possible explanation is that professional artists, by their intense experience, know what will fail, eliminating the need for extensive explorations. On the other hand, in a study of radiologists, expert radiologists used their specialized schemata to impose structure on a noisy x-ray, whereas novices were misled by the noise (Lesgold, Feltovich, Glaser, & Wang, 1981).

Experts' more specialized schemata may help clear away noise as well as suggest avenues of inquiry. Perhaps the ability to impose structure on a confusing situation aids in problem finding. Conversely, it is possible that imposition of highly organized schemata might work against problem finding in that it forms a mental set that could restrict consideration of alternative frameworks and approaches. As expertise is accumulated, more and more knowledge becomes compiled into highly context-specific automatized forms that consequently resist scrutiny and challenge (Anderson, 1983). Given that creativity in problem finding is often a matter of breaking a mental set, it could be said that the novice by virtue of fewer structured schemata is actually more open to new questions and alternative perspectives on the situation.

Although their questions may be more field appropriate and more sophisticated, experts' ideas may not be any more original relative to their state of knowledge than those of novices. In fact, sophisticated knowledge structures may actually be an inhibiting factor for problem finding. At present, we do not really know whether knowledge structures play an enabling or inhibiting role. In any case, the knowledge aspect of expertise is not a promoting factor because it does not itself guarantee or even encourage a person to problem find. When problem-finding competence is displayed by experts, it may be other attributes they possess, such as strategies or dispositions, that play a role in promoting problem finding.

Conceptual frameworks. One type of problem finding, especially in theory-rich domains such as science, occurs when the inquirer discovers an anomaly, an occurrence that cannot be explained by the inquirer's current ideas or concepts, or even contradicts them. Detection of an anomaly can be an impetus for problem finding and can motivate rich and profitable question posing. Research in the area of conceptual change indicates that both willingness to acknowledge anomalies and subsequent problem posing are likely to depend on the degree of commitment to a conceptual framework, called *paradigms* by Kuhn (1962). "Paradigms determine what questions are asked, what hypotheses entertained, what data are relevant, indeed, even what data are seen" (Carey, 1985, p. 499). When operating within a paradigm, having a conceptual framework aids problem finding by helping in the construction of problems that are sensible and appropriate to the paradigm. However, problem finding that breaks outside of a paradigm is a far more puzzling and difficult process.

Paradigm-breaking problem finding is often instigated by an anomaly that violates paradigm-based expectations and cannot be resolved by the usual methods and explanations. In historic examples of paradigm shift—Einstein's theory of relativity, Darwin's theory of evolution, or Newtonian theories of motion—the theory change involved truly creative divergence from accepted theory. Paradigm-breaking problem finding is hard to achieve because it requires the novel framing of a problem in the face of strongly held beliefs. Hence, a paradox occurs in the causal relationship between conceptual frameworks and problem finding. Frameworks are, at the same time, barriers and launching pads for problem finding. They inhibit problem finding by locking one into the paradigm; yet at the same time it is necessary to have some conceptual frameworks in order to launch the generation of problems.

Lack of awareness of an anomaly may be the explanation for some instances in which people remain inactive as problem finders. Unexploited opportunities for problem posing may occur because of: (a) failure to notice inconsistencies between evidence and one's intuitive mental models, and (b) limited appreciation for standards that call for reconciliation of inconsistencies. Researchers examining the shifts in paradigm required when learning about scientific domains found that students' robust intuitive models often override their concern for internal coherence (diSessa, 1983; Posner, Strike, Hewson, & Gertzog, 1982). The degree to which individuals are driven to overcome the obstacles of existing conceptual frameworks in order to engage in problem finding may depend on dispositional factors, such as sensitivity to anomalies, values for consistency and coherence, and intrinsic motivation. These dispositional factors are discussed later in this chapter.

Strategies and Heuristics

Within the field of cognitive science that predominantly investigates strategies and heuristics for problem solving, a few researchers have applied similar techniques and models to the topic of problem finding or problem construction. They all acknowledge that the challenge in deciphering the process of problem finding lies in understanding how people produce novel ideas and problems when the problem space is, by nature, ill defined.

Problem construction operations. Mumford et al. (in press) proposed a model of operational steps for problem construction that, in their view, is concerned with defining the goals, objectives, parameters, and structure of the problem-solving effort. According to Mumford et al., problem construction requires the flexible use of problem representation (i.e., screening and reorganizing available representations in order to formulate new and alternative understandings of the problem situation). Their model consists of the following operations for problem construction: (a) *attention and perception* (i.e., sensitivity to environmental events, cues, and discrepancies), (b) *activation of representations* (i.e., recall of representations from analogous problem situations), (c) *screening strategy selection* (i.e., selection of representations for retention or discard), (d) *element selection strategy* (i.e., selection of the particular elements, such as goals, constraints, and strategies, that are salient to the problem situation; and (e) *element reorganization* (i.e., reorganization of the salient elements into a coherent representational system). The outcome of this reorganizing operation provides a plan for problem solving that serves to structure an ill-defined domain and direct the individual's attempt to generate a novel problem solution.

An empirical study derived from this model showed that active processing toward problem construction, resulting from the experimenter's request for multiple problem restatement, led to significantly higher ratings of both solution quality and solution originality in a marketing problem (Redmond, Mumford, & Teach, in press). According to Mumford et al., people often *satisfice*, applying the first available or most strongly activated representation to structure ill-defined problems. However, when people put effort into more conscious problem construction, they more systematically search for representations, reorganize elements, and consider a broader range of possibilities, all of which lead to more alternative understandings of the problem.

Goal transformation. Bereiter (1988) claimed that the process of generating a creative problem is one of goal transformation. In particular, it involves transforming situations in which creativity is a separate goal to ones in which creativity is entailed. More specifically, the initial goal (Goal1 = Accomplish task + Achieve creative result) is transformed to a goal (Goal2 = Solve problem) in which the problem is of sufficient importance and difficulty that any solution will necessarily be creative. Using the example of developing a thesis topic, one's initial goal is to accomplish the task of coming up with a research problem, hopefully achieving a creative result in the process. Goal transformation occurs when one frames the problem in such a way that merely solving it guarantees a creative result. The most critical and difficult part of problem formulation is the transformation because once Goal2 is established, it can be achieved by normal problem solving.

Computational model. Based on their existing computational models (BACON, GLAUBER, STAHL, and DALTON) of problem solving in diverse domains, Langley et al. (1987) envisioned the possibility of devising a computational problem generator that applies problem-solving heuristics to the creation of new problems. The proposed computer problem generator would employ the general problem-solving tactic of generation and selection: Generative rules allow for the construction of candidate problems, whereas evaluative rules filter options according to established criteria. An example of a generative heuristic that Langley and his colleagues proposed is recursive problem generation—if causes or effects are found for a phenomenon, the problem can then be posed of finding *their* causes and effects. Although Langley et al. were vague about the filtering processes in problem formulation, the possibility of creating evaluative criterion with an aesthetic in a computer program has already been illustrated in the AM program developed by Lenat (1983), which evaluates according to criteria for the "interestingness" of a concept.

In Langley et al.'s proposal we see some promise for the suggestion that generation and selection may serve as a feasible mechanism for problem finding. Problem finding would occur through repeated generation of options and filtering of those options using appropriate criteria. If a computer problem generator, such as the one proposed by Langley et al., could be constructed, it could support the idea of generation and selection strategies as components for a problem-finding mechanism.

Controversy over the strategies view. Controversy has arisen over the question of whether problem finding is explainable in terms of strategic and heuristic steps or whether a special kind of creative thinking is involved. Langley et al. (1987) took a strong position on this issue, and in his 1985 American Psychology Association address entitled "The Psychology of Scientific Discovery," Simon explicitly argued that creativity involves nothing more than normal problem solving processes. Simon (1988) and Langley et al. (1987) refuted the view often expressed by scientists, philosophers, and psychologists that problem finding is a more creative aspect of scientific discovery than problem solving. Rather, they argued that problem-finding strategies are no different from strategies used for problem solving. In fact, they claimed that problem-finding processes are simply a particular variety of problem-solving processes—that problem finding *is* problem solving. They maintained that the kind of heuristics and strategies that characterize problem solving in general can be applied to the formulation of a problem, and that no special explanation of problem finding as a creative ability is necessary.

In sharp opposition to the Langley et al. view, Csikszentmihalyi (1988a) considered problem finding to be the hallmark of creativity. According to him, creative thinking lies in the ability to discover new problems never before formulated, a facility deemed quite independent of the rational problem-solving capacity. His main criticism of Langley et al. raises doubts about the capability of computer simulations of scientific discoveries to engage in the creative achievement of discovering and exploring new problem areas (Csikszentmihalyi, 1988b). He claimed that although programs such as BACON may replicate a previous creative achievement when fed the right data, they cannot be credited with creativity for they are not truly producing novel approaches within a historical context. To be considered creative, according to Csikszentmihalyi, a work must introduce some variations or innovations in the domain at a time in history when the variations are novel and can be instrumental in revising and enlarging the domain. Csikszentmihalyi (1988a) further argued that the computational model at best accounts for the rational side of creativity while neglecting important affective and motivational aspects of creative thinking.

In order to make sense of the controversy between these viewpoints, we return to the two issues that are at stake. One issue asks: Can the mechanism of problem finding be explained in terms of strategies and heuristics, or is a special kind of creative thinking involved? The debate between Langley et al. and Csikszentmihalyi notwithstanding, the proper response to this question is that it need not be either/or. It is reasonable to assume that people may use problem-solving strategies as they formulate problems, yet it is also plausible that creative problem finding calls for special kinds of strategizing as well as drawing on affective, nonrational elements.

The second issue asks: Is problem finding just a form of problem solving? Yes, problem finding is problem solving of a sort, but not a very typical sort. One obvious difference is that problem solving is often a process of converging in the effort to reach a solution, whereas problem finding is a process of expanding to entertain a wide range of alternatives. Another difference lies in the way creativity is exhibited. Although solving a problem certainly can involve creativity, a crucial characteristic of creative problem finding is the invention of new problems that push against existing boundaries. A distinctive feature of human invention is the ability to consciously break boundaries (Perkins, 1988b). Although the generating heuristics used by the computer such as Langley et al.'s model can systematically generate plausible research problems, it falls short in explaining *why* people problem find and how they conceive problems with a creative twist or problems that break boundaries. For these issues, our account of problem finding must turn to matters of context, individual style, and disposition.

DISPOSITIONS

Although the study of cognition in general has been mostly dominated by abilities, knowledge, and strategies perspectives, there is interest in exploring the role of disposition in thinking (Baron, 1985; Ennis, 1987; Perkins, Jay, & Tishman, 1993) and in creativity (Barron & Harrington, 1981; Perkins, 1981). Dispositions are abiding behavioral tendencies in an individual produced by attitudes, values, interests, long-term motives, and like characteristics. Disposition contrasts with abilities in that disposition concerns what a person is *disposed* to do, rather than what the person is *able* to do. For thinking and creative behavior to occur spontaneously, merely having the ability is not enough; a person must have the disposition to do the behavior as well.

As with cognition in general, the dispositional aspects of problem finding deserve more attention than they have received, relative to the abilities and process perspectives outlined in the previous sections. To the extent problem finding remains defined as a matter of generating options, the abilities and processes accounts will dominate over considerations of style or disposition, and the assumption that the most capable problem finders are people of high ability will be perpetuated (Moore & Murdock, 1991). A dispositional account, on the other hand, would suggest that the most capable problem finders possess not only ability and skill, but also attitudes, values, interests, and other dispositions that lead toward a tendency to seek out and form new problems.

Although several authors acknowledge the importance of dispositions and related constructs such as cognitive style in problem finding (Hoover, 1990; Hoover & Feldhusen, 1994; Moore & Murdock, 1991), there is little direct research on problem-finding dispositions. We review here the existing work on problem-finding dispositions and consider writings on the dispositional character of creativity in general to help illuminate the case of problem finding.

Dispositions for Problem Finding

The concern for problem finding. Getzels and Csikszentmihalyi (1976) attributed high levels of problem finding to a creative tendency that is evident more in some persons than in others. Getzels and Csikszentmihalyi considered problem finding to be more than a set of behaviors, but rather a mental attitude or dispositional trait. They called it the "concern for problem finding." In their study, art students given the task of drawing a still life were rated on attributes and patterns of behavior considered to be indicative of attention to problem finding. At the problem definition stage, students with greater concern for problem finding spent more time and attention exploring alternative approaches to a work before settling on one—manipulating more objects, exploring the objects more thoroughly, and choosing more unusual objects. They tended not to use objects to reflect preconceived ideas or principles, but rather to let the arrangement emerge out of the process of interacting with the objects. During the actual drawing phase or the problem-solving stage, they displayed sustained attention to problem finding in the form of a continued openness to reformulation of the problem, a willingness to switch directions when a new approach suggested itself, and a tendency to refrain from viewing the work as fixed or finished.

Getzels and Csikszentmihalyi's (1976) portrait of problem finding consists of distinct patterns of behavior that one might consider an individual style or disposition. The principal attributes of this disposition are attention to formulation of the problem throughout the process and fending off closure even during the solving stage. The problem finder explores extensively before committing to a direction, remains open to new directions, and resists viewing the work as finished. A personal style that favors attention to problem finding is a characteristic that not only enables problem finding, but promotes it directly.

Csikszentmihalyi (1988a) added theoretical structure to the dispositional side of problem finding through his energistic view of creativity. To be moved to find new problems and expand the boundaries in a domain, the creative person must have an acute interest in the domain, the perseverance to maintain psychic energy necessary for the discovery process, and a dissatisfaction with the state of knowledge along with the motivation to search for alternatives.

Personality characteristics. Mumford, Costanza, Threlfall, Baughman, and Reiter-Palmon (in press) conducted an exploratory study that examined the relationship between personality characteristics and problem construction activities. Subjects were assessed on personality variables thought to be promoters of problem construction (e.g., category flexibility, problem anticipation) and those thought to be inhibitors (e.g., anxiety, judgmentalism). The problem construction task required subjects to solve matrix-analogy problems and then generate new problems of their own making that were later judged on quality and originality.

The results indicated that people who produced original, high-quality problem constructions were self-initiated discoverers—internally controlled and self-confident, yet open and flexible in their orientation toward creative problems. At the same time, they scored low in competitiveness and meeting external requirements, indicating guidance by internal rather than external demands. Interestingly, those who produced original but low-quality problems were similarly free from external demands, yet lacked the self-initiated discovery orientation. Meanwhile, the people who produced high-quality problems but with little originality were motivated mostly by external engagement and competition. Mumford et al. suggested that the self-initiated discovery orientation, similar to Getzels and Csikszentmihalyi's (1976) concern for problem finding, may facilitate conscious application of the cognitive operations underlying problem construction, thereby contributing to the consistent production of original, high-quality problems.

The explanatory role of dispositions. The two research efforts just described, as well as work on dispositions in other areas, suggest that there is great explanatory potential in uncovering the dispositional aspects of problem finding. What explanatory power does the dispositional component contribute to the story thus far built from the context, abilities, knowledge, and strategies factors reviewed in previous sections of this chapter?

Before addressing that question, it is important to verify the distinctness of dispositions from other elements. Recall from the introduction of this section that dispositions were defined in contrast to abilities: They describe what a person is *disposed* to do, rather than what a person is *able* to do. Although Getzels and Csikszentmihalyi (1976) clearly had in mind a dispositional perspective on problem finding, it is important to note that their methodology did not really give distinctive evidence for a dispositional, in contrast to an abilities, account. That is, Getzels and Csikszentmihalyi assumed that the student artists who did not engage in as much problem finding could well have done so had they been so disposed; there was no shortfall of problem-finding abilities or processes. But their methodology did not demonstrate this.

The first author conducted a study of high school science students that directly examined the contrast between dispositions and abilities in problem finding (Jay, 1996). In open-ended exploration of physical science materials, students generally displayed modest levels of spontaneous problem-finding behavior, yet they improved significantly in the number and type of problems posed when problem-finding scaffolding was introduced. This reveals an ability to do problem finding when prompted, but a lack of disposition to problem find spontaneously. The fact that problem finding does not spontaneously occur very much, even though the ability exists, means that inclination, motivation, or other dispositional elements are probably necessary to activate the behavior. The study also found that particular facets of instrinsic motivation, specifically curiosity and desire for independent mastery, played a significant role in predicting problem-finding behavior. Together, these findings suggest the possibility of a strong dispositional compo-nent to problem finding.

We return to the question of how a dispositional perspective con-tributes toward completing our understanding of problem finding. The dis-position for problem finding is perhaps the strongest explanatory factor in our quest for understanding *why* people problem find. Ability, knowledge, or strategy perspectives alone are insufficient for explaining the why of problem finding because they fail to account for the impetus that activates the behavior. Having the disposition to problem find, on the other hand, means that one not only has the capabilities and tools for problem finding, but is inclined to actively seek out and generate problems. Being disposed to actively search for problems is central to problem finding. These disposi-tions not only enable problem finding, but promote it directly.

A sharper conception of dispositions would contribute toward our understanding of how, as well as why, creative problem finding occurs. Tendencies such as openness and flexibility, fending off closure, and internal control begin to illuminate how the problem-finding process works beyond what abilities and strategies can explain. Dispositional mechanisms should be explored further. For example, Perkins et al. (1993) claimed that dispositions consist of sensitivities as well as inclinations. Perhaps sensitivities for noticing anomalies, incon-sistencies, and problem situations along with related inclinations for curiosity, desire for understanding, or simply playfulness are what acti-vates and fuels problem finding. Runco (1994b) acknowledged that some individuals appreciate that tension and disequilibrium can lead to insight and pleasure and anticipate the challenge that comes when rec-ognizing a problem or sensing ambiguity in a situation. This leads cre-ative individuals to seek out and see problem-finding potential where others do not. It is because of dispositions such as these that abilities are invoked and strategies deployed. Clearly, dispositions are complex in their composition and mechanism. More research is necessary to begin to define the concept and distinguish its attributes.

Values

Values associated with creativity. It is logical that values that promote cre-ativity in general would positively contribute to creativity in problem finding. Several broad standards and values are characteristic of creative individuals and are thought to foster creativity in general. Personality studies have shown that creative artists and scientists value originality directly and seek it out, have a desire to push limits and break boundaries, and have a high tolerance for ambiguity, disorganization, and asymmetry (Barron, 1975; MacKinnon, 1965; Mansfield & Busse, 1981; Perkins, 1981).

Perkins (1988a) argued that values are more than merely consequences of creativity: They are causes of creative action. Creativity emerges because the person in question is trying to produce things that satisfy the values he or she embraces. Similarly, values may be causes of problem finding. Indeed, values can *promote* problem finding; for example, the desire to push at the limits of one's understanding and to break boundaries is a strong impetus for initiating problems. These values directly promote problem finding by instigating the process; moreover, they help to explain why people make the effort to problem find. Similarly, individuals who value originality are likely to generate and select problems with a bias toward the criterion of originality, thereby promoting the quality of problem finding. Tolerance of ambiguity enables, though may not directly promote, problem finding by allowing one to remain open to possibilities while fending off closure of the problem. The associated values and drive to make sense of and achieve unity out of ambiguity, however, may serve to promote problem finding directly.

Domain-related values. Although the earlier described values are associated with creativity in general, some values are contextually appropriate for different domains and disciplines. For example, across the sciences, consistency, parsimony, elegance, generality, fundamentality, and predictive power are among the widely accepted values. Within the cultures of specific fields, such as physics or chemistry, there may be even more highly context-specific values (e.g., consistency with certain overriding principles or forces central to the domain). In 20th-century art, creativity has become an explicit and highly valued attribute. To attain renown, an artist cannot simply be a superb craftsperson. The artist must make an original statement.

Domain-related values are important to both the why and how of problem finding. As to the why, domain-related values can directly promote problem finding by serving as an impetus for generating problems. In striving for consistency and parsimony, for instance, scientists are led to pose questions and problems that test for these values. Einstein noticed that, in applying Maxwell's equations to moving bodies, different formulas had to be used depending on the frame of reference. It was his dissatisfaction with the asymmetry in this situation that drove him to pose the problems that eventually led to his theory of relativity. As to the how of problem finding, these values are some of the most important criteria, serving to bias the generation and selective filtering of problems.

Motivation

In our earlier discussions of why people seek problems, we referred to external events that sparked problem-finding activity. Even in the presence of a triggering event, however, there must be an accompanying internal motivation that urges an individual to make the effort to pose problems. We know that problem finding is hard, demanding both effort and perseverance. Motivation is necessary for an individual to engage in problem posing in the first place and to sustain interest and effort throughout the problem formulation process.

Work in the area of social psychology contrasts intrinsic motivation and extrinsic motivation. Individuals are *intrinsically* motivated when they perceive themselves as engaging in an activity primarily out of their own interest in it; they are *extrinsically* motivated if they perceive themselves as engaging in the activity in order to obtain some extrinsic goal, such as a reward (Lepper, Greene, & Nisbett, 1973). Amabile (1983, 1990) offered evidence that the intrinsically motivated state is conducive to creativity, whereas the extrinsically motivated state tends to be detrimental.

What kind of motivation stimulates an individual to problem find in real-world, ill-structured contexts? Of the features Amabile (1983) found contributed to intrinsic motivation, curiosity and playfulness seem most applicable to problem finding. Those individuals with strong curiosity and desire for understanding are apt to be those who are driven to ask questions, ponder over problems, and exhibit sustained effort. Playfulness and delight in posing intriguing questions also appears to be a salient attribute of those individuals who are frequent problem finders. Possibly, a recursive process of motivation is involved in problem finding. Curiosity and playfulness may lead the individual to form a problem, which is interesting, and in turn promotes further curiosity, and so on. Hence, interest in problem finding becomes self-perpetuating.

The typical assumption is that intrinsic motivation is necessary to incite creative performance and therefore precedes the engagement of cognitive skills and effort. Challenging this assumption, Runco (1994b) proposed instead that cognitive appraisals and recognition come before intrinsic motivation. Individuals must recognize that there is a gap or problem worth their time before they invest the emotion involved in becoming motivated. Appraisals are necessary for recognition of a worthwhile problem. It is as a result of finding a potentially rewarding problem that an individual will probably become intrinsically motivated. Thus, in this view, problem finding is first, not intrinsic motivation.

THE SEARCH FOR MECHANISM REVISITED

The previous sections of this chapter examined research and theoretical work on problem finding from the perspectives of context, abilities, processes, and dispositions. We framed this review in terms of the search for mechanism. It makes sense now to return to the benchmarks for understanding problem finding that were established earlier: understanding why and understanding how. To what extent and in what ways to do each of the windows on problem finding—context, abilities, processes, and dispositions—contribute to an understanding of why and how people problem find?

In the effort to explain *why* people problem find, both context and disposition play a role, but abilities and processes (including knowledge and strategies) do not. Cognitive abilities can enable a person to problem find, but they do not promote it because abilities themselves do not offer an impetus for raising questions. Likewise, the possession of relevant processes, knowledge, or strategies per se does not entirely account for why problem finding begins. In some cases, knowledge provides a partial explanation because existing knowledge can suggest the whereabouts of interesting gaps. However, earlier discussion of conceptual frameworks showed that having knowledge does not always yield sufficient push for, and may even inhibit, the detection of anomalies, inconsistencies, and gaps. So, knowledge must be coupled with other explanatory factors to account for the why of problem finding.

In contrast, context can play a role in promoting problem finding or at least in providing the external stimulus that provokes the generation of questions and problems. It can offer a strong push in the form of a presented problem, a moderate stimulus such as an anomaly that needs to be discovered, or an ill-defined situation requiring a high degree of problem-forming initiative. The strongest explanatory factor for why people problem find, however, is certain kinds of dispositions because they can directly promote problem finding. They help explain why some people are prone to initiating problem-finding activities. Characteristics such as a concern for problem finding, commitment to exploratory values, intrinsic motivation, and sensitivity to problem-posing opportunities can yield a strong inclination to engage in self-initiated problem generation.

The mechanism for *why* people problem find can be summarized as follows: Abilities, knowledge, and strategies enable a person to problem find, and contexts provide the stimulus, but it is dispositions that actually promote the initiation of problem finding. Consequently, research must include deep exploration of the dispositional side of problem finding. So far the topic has barely been scratched. Although inferences can be made from dispositional aspects of creativity, direct study of dispositions in problem finding is imperative if light is to be shed on what contributes to the initiation of problem finding. Similarly, the role of context in promoting problem finding needs exploration, including which elements in a situation trigger problem initiation, the effect of different types of problem situations, and the role of social context and the field.

The factors contribute in varying ways with regard to understanding *how* people problem find. Cognitive abilities play a negligible role in explaining good problem-finding performance; they explain it only to the extent that they contribute to cognitive functioning in general. Context matters because the way in which problem finding occurs may differ depending on the type of problem situation. As to cognitive processing, knowledge and its efficient access possibly plays a role in the how of problem finding; however, as discussed earlier, it is not yet known whether structures of knowledge or conceptual frameworks serve to enhance or inhibit how well a person problem finds. In the same way that strategy and heuristic approaches have illuminated other cognitive processes, strategies accounts may be key to understanding the how of problem finding. Although the work of problem finding may be accomplished by strategies, the deployment of strategies is directed by dispositions. Dispositions can explain how an individual's tendencies, such as openness to new directions, fending off closure, or bias for originality, might influence the way a problem occurs.

In sum, the mechanism of *how* people problem find can be reduced to the following statement: Although context defires the situation and knowledge enables (or at times inhibits) problem-finding competence, the mechanism of problem finding is organized by strategies and directed by the dispositions. All of the factors play a role; therefore, no single account can serve to explain how problem finding occurs. Existing problem-finding models and experiments tend to concentrate on a single component, be it ability, strategy, or disposition. Ideally, investigations of problem finding should become more comprehensive rather than compartmentalized. A complete understanding of how people problem find should reveal how the many facets of cognition involved work together to yield the behavior.

REFERENCES

Allender, J.S. (1969). A study of inquiry activity in elementary school children. *American Educational Research Journal, 6*, 543-558.

Amabile, T.M. (1983). *The social psychology of creativity*. New York: Springer-Verlag.

Amabile, T.M. (1990). Social influences on creativity: Evaluation, coaction, and surveillance. *Creativity Research Journal, 3*, 1, 6-21.

Anderson, J.R. (1983). *The architecture of cognition*. Cambridge, MA: Harvard University Press.

Arlin, P. (1975). Cognitive development in adulthood: A fifth stage? *Developmental Psychology, 11*(5), 602-606.

Arlin, P. (1984). Adolescent and adult thought: A structural interpretation. In M. Commons, F. Richards, & C. Armon (Eds.), *Beyond formal operations: Late adolescent and adult cognitive development* (pp. 258-271). New York: Praeger.

Baron, J. (1985). *Rationality and intelligence.* New York: Cambridge University Press.

Barron, F. (1975). The disposition toward originality. In C. Taylor & F. Barron (Eds.), *Scientific creativity: Its recognition and development* (pp. 139-152). Huntington, NY: Krieger.

Barron, F., & Harrington, D.M. (1981). Creativity, intelligence, and personality. *Annual Review of Psychology, 32,* 439-76.

Bereiter, C. (1988). *Creativity and expertise: Elements of a theory.* Unpublished report, Centre for Applied Cognitive Science, Ontario Institute for Studies in Education, Toronto, Ontario, Canada.

Beveridge, W.I. (1957). *The art of scientific investigation.* New York: Random House.

Brown, S., & Walter, M. (1983). *The art of problem posing.* Philadelphia, PA: Franklin Institute Press.

Bunge, M. (1967). *Scientific research (Vol 1: The search for system).* New York: Springer.

Carey, S. (1985). Are children fundamentally different kinds of thinkers and learners than adults? In S.F. Chipman, J.W. Segal, & R. Glaser (Eds.), *Thinking and learning skills (Vol. 2: Research and open questions,* pp. 485-517). Hillsdale NJ: Erlbaum.

Chand, I., & Runco, M.A. (1992). Problem finding skills as components in the creative process. *Personality and Individual Differences, 14,* 155-162.

Chase, W.C., & Simon, H.A. (1973). Perception in chess. *Cognitive Psychology, 4,* 55-81.

Chi, M., Feltovich, P., & Glaser, R. (1981). Categorization and representation of physics problems by experts and novices. *Cognitive Science, 5,* 121-152.

Chi, M., Glaser, R., & Rees, E. (1982). Expertise in problem solving. In R. Sternberg (Ed.), *Advances in the psychology of human intelligence* (pp. 7-75). Hillsdale, NJ: Erlbaum.

Commons, M., Richards, F., & Armon, C. (Eds.). (1984). *Beyond formal operations: Late adolescent and adult cognitive development.* New York, New York: Praeger.

Csikszentmihalyi, M. (1988a). Motivation and creativity: Toward a synthesis of structural and energistic approaches to cognition. *New Ideas in Psychology, 6*(2), 177-181.

Csikszentmihalyi, M. (1988b). Society, culture, and person: A systems view of creativity. In R. Sternberg (Ed.), *The nature of creativity: Contemporary psychological perspectives* (pp. 325-339). Cambridge, England: Cambridge University Press.

Csikszentmihalyi, M. (1990). The domain of creativity. In M.A. Runco (Ed.), *Theories of creativity* (pp. 190-212). Newbury Park, CA: Sage.

deGroot, A.D. (1965). *Thought and choice in chess.* The Hague: Mouton.

Dewey, J. (1910). *How we think*. Boston: Heath.

Dillon, J.T. (1982). Problem finding and solving. *Journal of Creative Behavior, 16*(2), 97-111.

diSessa, A. (1983). Phenomenology and the evolution of intuition. In D. Gentner & A. Stevens (Eds.), *Mental models* (pp. 15-33). Hillsdale, NJ: Erlbaum.

Dudek, S.Z., & Cote, R. (1994). Problem finding revisited. In M.A. Runco (Ed.), *Problem finding, problem solving, and creativity* (pp. 130-133). Norwood, NJ: Ablex.

Einstein, A., & Infeld, L. (1938). *The evolution of physics*. New York: Simon & Schuster.

Ennis, R.H. (1987). A taxonomy of critical thinking dispositions and abilities. In J.B. Baron & R.S. Sternberg (Eds.). *Teaching thinking skills: Theory and practice* (pp. 9-26). New York: W.H. Freeman.

Fischer, D.H. (1970). *Historians' fallacies: Toward a logic of historical thought*. New York: Harper & Row.

Frederiksen, M. (1984). Implications of cognitive theory for instruction in problem solving. *Review of Educational Research, 54*, 363-407.

Getzels, J.W. (1975). Problem-finding and the inventiveness of solutions. *Journal of Creative Behavior, 9*(1), 12-18.

Getzels, J.W. (1982). The problem of the problem. In R. Hogarth (Ed.), *New directions for methodology of social and behavioral science: Question framing and response consistency* (No. 11). San Francisco: Jossey-Bass.

Getzels, J.W., & Csikszentmihalyi, M. (1976). *The creative vision: A longitudinal study of problem finding in art*. New York: Wiley.

Getzels, J.W., & Smilansky, J. (1983). Individual differences in pupil perceptions of school problems. *British Journal of Educational Psychology, 53*, 307-316.

Glaser, R. (1984). Education and thinking: The role of knowledge. *American Psychologist, 39*, 93-104.

Glover, J.A. (1979). Levels of questions asked in interview and reading sessions by creative and relatively noncreative college students. *Journal of Genetic Psychology, 135*, 103-108.

Gombrich, E.H. (1961). *Art and illusion: A study in the psychology of pictorial representation*. Princeton, NJ: Princeton University Press.

Goodman, N.A. (1976). *Languages of art*. Indianapolis: Hackett.

Guilford, J.P. (1967). *The nature of human intelligence*. New York: McGraw-Hill.

Henle, M. (1974). The snail beneath the shell. In S. Rosner & L.E. Alit (Eds.), *Essays in creativity*. Croton-on-Hudson, NY: North Riner Press.

Hoover, S.M. (1990). Problem finding\solving in science: Moving toward theory. *Creativity Research Journal, 3*(4), 330-332.

Hoover, S.M., & Feldhusen, J.F. (1990). The scientific hypothesis formulation ability of gifted ninth-grade students. *Journal of Educational Psychology, 82*(4), 838-848.

Hoover, S.M., & Feldhusen, J.F. (1994). Scientific problem solving and problem finding: A theoretical model. In M.A. Runco (Ed.), *Problem finding, problem solving, and creativity* (pp. 201-219). Norwood, NJ: Ablex.

Jay, E.S. (1996). *The nature of problem finding in students' scientific inquiry.* Unpublished doctoral dissertation, Harvard University, Graduate School of Education, Cambridge, MA.

Kay, S. (1991). The figural problem solving and problem finding of professional and semiprofessional artists and nonartists. *Creativity Research Journal, 4*(3), 233-252.

Kay, S. (1994). A method for investigating the creative thought process. In M.A. Runco (Ed.), *Problem finding, problem solving, and creativity* (pp. 116-129). Norwood, NJ: Ablex.

Kuhn, T.S. (1962). *The structure of scientific revolutions.* Chicago: University of Chicago Press.

Langley, P., Simon, H.A., Bradshaw, G.L., & Zytkow, J. (1987). *Scientific discovery: Computational explorations of the creative process.* Cambridge, MA: MIT Press.

Larkin, J. (1983). The role of problem representation in physics. In D. Gentner & A. Stevens (Eds.), *Mental models* (pp. 75-98). Hillsdale, NJ: Erlbaum.

Lenat, D. (1983). Toward a theory of heuristics. In R. Groner, M. Groner, & W.F. Bischof (Eds.), *Methods of heuristics* (pp. 351-404). Hillsdale, NJ: Lawrence Erlbaum.

Lepper, M., Greene, D., & Nisbett, R. (1973). Undermining children's intrinsic interest with extrinsic rewards: A test of the "overjustification" hypothesis. *Journal of Personality and Social Psychology, 28,* 129-137.

Lesgold, A.M., Feltovich, P., Glaser, R., & Wang, Y. (1981). *The acquisition of perceptual diagnostic skill in radiology* (Tech. Rep. PDS-1). Pittsburgh, PA: University of Pittsburgh, Learning Research and Development Center.

MacKinnon, D.W. (1965). Personality and the realization of creative potential. *American Psychologist, 20,* 273-281.

Macworth, N.H. (1965). *Originality.* American Psychologist, 20, 51-66.

Mansfield, R., & Busse, T. (1981). *The psychology of creativity and discovery: Scientists and their work.* Chicago: Nelson-Hall.

Merton, R.S. (1945). Sociology of knowledge. In G. Gurvitch & W.E. Moore (Eds.), *Twentieth century sociology.* New York: Philosophical Library.

Michael, W.B. (1977). Cognitive and affective components of creativity in mathematics and the physical sciences. In J.C. Stanley, W.C. Solano, & C.H. George (Eds.), *The gifted and the creative: A Fifty-year perspective* (pp. 141-172). Baltimore, MD: Johns Hopkins University Press.

Moore, M.T. (1985). The relationship between the originality of essays and variables in the problem-discovery process: A study of creative and noncreative middle school students. *Research in the Teaching of English, 19*(1), 84-95.

Moore, M.T. (1990). Problem finding and teacher experience. *Journal of Creative Behavior, 24*(1), 39-58.

Moore, M.T., & Murdock, M.C. (1991). On problems in problem-finding research. *Creativity Research Journal, 4*(3), 290-293.

Mumford, M.D., Costanza, D.P., Threlfall, K.V., Baughman, W.A., & Reiter-Palmon, R. (in press). Personality variables and problem construction activities: An exploratory investigation. *Creativity Research Journal.*

Mumford, M.D., Reiter-Palmon, R., & Redmond, M.R. (1994). Problem construction and cognition: Applying problem representations in ill-defined domains. In M.A. Runco (Ed.), *Problem finding, problem solving, and creativity* (pp. 1-39). Norwood, NJ: Ablex.

Newell, A., & Simon, H. (1972). *Human problem solving*. Englewood Cliffs, NJ: Prentice-Hall.

Nicholls, J.G. (1972). Creativity in the person who will never produce anything original or useful. *American Psychologist, 27,* 717-727.

Nickerson, R., Perkins, D.N., & Smith, E. (1985). *The teaching of thinking*. Hillsdale, NJ: Erlbaum.

Okuda, S.M., Runco, M.A., & Berger, D.E. (1991). Creativity and the finding and solving of real-world problems. *Journal of Psychoeducational Assessment, 9,* 45-53.

Osborn, A.F. (1963). *Applied imagination* (3rd ed.). New York: Charles Scribner's Sons.

Perkins, D.N. (1981). *The mind's best work*. Cambridge, MA: Harvard University Press.

Perkins, D.N. (1988a). Creativity and the quest for mechanism. In R.S. Sternberg & E. Smith (Eds.), *The psychology of human thought* (pp. 309-336). Cambridge, England: Cambridge University Press.

Perkins, D.N. (1988b). The possibility of invention. In R. Sternberg (Ed.), *The nature of creativity* (pp. 362-385). Cambridge, England: Cambridge University Press.

Perkins, D.N., Jay, E., & Tishman, S. (1993). Beyond abilities: A dispositional theory of thinking. *Merrill-Palmer Quarterly, 39*(1) 1-21.

Pitt, R.B. (1976). *Toward a comprehensive model of problem solving*. Unpublished doctoral dissertation, University of California, San Diego.

Polya, G. (1957). *How to solve it: A new aspect of mathematical method* (2nd ed.). Princeton, NJ: Princeton University Press.

Polya, G. (1965). *Mathematical discovery: On understanding, learning, and teaching problem solving* (Vol. 2). New York: Wiley.

Posner, G., Strike, K., Hewson, P., & Gertzog, W. (1982). Accommodation of a scientific conception: Toward a theory of conceptual change. *Science Education, 66*(2), 211-227.

Redmond, M.R., Mumford, M.D., & Teach, R. (in press). Putting creativity to work: Effects of leader behavior on subordinate creativity. *Organizational Behavior and Human Decision Processes.*

Rimm, S.B., & Davis, G.A. (1976). GIFT: An instrument for the identification of creativity. *Journal of Creative Behavior, 10,* 178-182.

Rossman, J. (1931). *The psychology of the inventor: A study of the patented* (2nd ed.). Washington, DC: Inventors Publishing.

Rostan, S. (in press). Problem finding, problem solving, and cognitive controls: An empirical investigation of critically acclaimed professional productivity. *Creativity Research Journal*.

Runco, M.A. (1987). The generality of creativity in gifted and nongifted children. *Gifted Child Quarterly, 31*, 121-125.

Runco, M.A. (1994a). Conclusions concerning problem finding, problem solving, and creativity. In M.A. Runco (Ed.), *Problem finding, problem solving, and creativity* (pp. 270-290). Norwood, NJ: Ablex.

Runco, M.A. (1994b). Creativity and its discontents. In M.P. Shaw & M.A. Runco (Eds.), *Creativity and affect*. Norwood, NJ: Ablex.

Runco, M.A. (Ed.). (1994c). *Problem finding, problem solving, and creativity*. Norwood, NJ: Ablex.

Runco, M.A., & Chand, I. (1994). Problem finding, evaluative thinking, and creativity. In M.A. Runco (Ed.), *Problem finding, problem solving, and creativity* (pp. 40-76). Norwood, NJ: Ablex.

Runco, M.A., & Okuda, S.M. (1988). Problem discovery, divergent thinking, and the creative process. *Journal of Youth and Adolescence, 17*(3), 211-220.

Schoenfeld, A., & Herrmann, D.J. (1982). Problem perception and knowledge structure in expert and novice mathematical problem solvers. *Journal of Experimental Psychology: Learning, Memory, and Cognition, 8*, 484-494.

Shulman, L. (1965). Seeking styles and individual differences in patterns of inquiry. *School Review, 73*, 258-266.

Simon, H. (1988). Creativity and motivation: A response to Csikszentmihalyi. *New Ideas in Psychology, 6*(2), 177-181.

Soloway, E., & Ehrlich, K. (1984). Empirical studies of programming knowledge. *IEEE Transactions on Software Engineering, SE-10*, 595-609.

Sternberg, R.J. (1982). *Handbook of human intelligence*. New York: Cambridge University Press.

Sternberg, R.J. (1985). *Beyond IQ: A triachic theory of human intelligence*. New York: Cambridge University Press.

Sternberg, R.J. (1988). *The nature of creativity*. New York: Cambridge University Press.

Subotnik, R.F. (1984). Factors from the structure of intellect model associated with gifted adolescents' problem finding in science: Research with Westinghouse Science Talent Search winners. *Journal of Creative Behavior, 22*, 42-54.

Subotnik, R.F., & Moore, M.T. (1988). Literature on problem finding. *Questioning Exchange, 2*(2), 87-93.

Subotnik, R.F., & Steiner, C.L. (1994). Problem identification in academic research: A longitudinal case study from adolescence to young adulthood. In M.A. Runco (Ed.), *Problem finding, problem solving, and creativity* (pp. 188-200). Norwood, NJ: Ablex.

Taylor, I.A. (1972). *A theory of creative transactualization: a systematic approach to creativity with implications for creative leadership* (Occasional Paper, No. 8). Buffalo, NY: Creative Education Foundation.

Torrance, E. (1966). *Torrance Tests of Creative Thinking.* Lexington, MA: Personnel Press.

Torrance, E. (1974). *Torrance Tests of Creative Thinking.* Lexington, MA: Personnel Press.

Wakefield, J.F. (1985). Towards creativity: Problem finding in a divergent-thinking exercise. *Child Study Journal, 15*(4), 265-270.

Wakefield, J.F. (1989). Creativity and cognition: Some implications for arts education. *Creativity Research Journal, 2,* 51-63.

Wallach, M.A. (1983). What do tests tell us about talent? In R.S. Albert (Ed.), *Genius and eminence* (pp. 113-123). Oxford, England: Pergamon Press.

Wallach, M.A., & Kogan, N. (1965). *Modes of thinking in young children.* New York: Holt, Rinehart & Winston.

Wallas, G. (1926). *The art of thought.* New York: Harcourt, Brace.

Wertheimer, M. (1945). *Productive thinking.* Westport, CT: Greenwood Press.

Yager, R.E. (1989). Development of student creative skills: A quest for successful science education. *Creativity Research Journal, 2,* 196-203.

12   Mental Illness, Deviance, and Creativity*

Russell Eisenman

McNeese State University

The belief that creativity and mental illness are related has a long history. Lombroso (1891) was one of the earliest scholars to say that creativity and mental illness go hand in hand, and many others have suggested the same (Bower, 1989; Grinder, 1985; Wallace, 1985; Zigler & Farber, 1985) This belief has often been based less on empirical and scientific findings than on folk wisdom. In essence, this has been a folk wisdom case history approach because people seem to be well aware of creative people who have shown signs of mental illness, such as Van Gogh cutting off his ear and giving it to a prostitute. If I mention to people that I am writing about creativity and mental illness they often say something like "Oh, yes, madness and creativity are linked." This seems to be a popular stereotype.

Several years ago, Eisenman (1969b) found that students believed that mental illness and creativity are related, even though they had been informed by me that such was not the case (which is what I believed at that time). Their willingness to put on their test an answer that contradict-

Correspondence may be sent to Russell Eisenman, Department of Psychology, McNeese State University, Lake Charles, LA 70609-1895

ed the teacher shows how strong this belief is because students are usually quite willing to throw back to the teacher what the teacher has said in order to get a good grade. At the time, I thought that the alleged link of creativity and mental illness was nonsense. I had worked with the mentally ill, and they seemed the farthermost thing from creative. They seemed lost in their own tragic worlds, with distorted perceptions of reality, not in a creative fashion. Rothenberg (1990) suggested that mental illness does not facilitate creativity, but interferes with it. And Terman's sample of intellectually gifted children grew up and had less mental illness than the general population (Terman & Oden, 1959).

In this chapter I discuss the alleged relationship between creativity and mental illness. The concept of regression in the service of the ego is important for understanding the creativity/mental illness link, and is also discussed; however, although it derives from psychoanalysis (there are many important psychoanalytic writings) I critique psychoanalysis as a theory of dubious value. Evidence is presented showing that the creativity/mental illness link is most notable with hypomania. I point out the importance of the brain, genetics, and biochemistry for understanding behavior. Finally, I discuss the concept of deviance, which helps bring together much data in a way many are not accustomed to, but which aids our understanding.

One can also look at creativity as related to personality, and not just in relation to mental illness. For information on personality approaches to creativity, the reader is referred to the chapter by Eysenck in this volume. Additional clinical psychology issues, not obviously related to creativity, can be found in Mindell (1993). An excellent source for the mental disorders in general, including psychoses, is Carson and Butcher (1992).

THE CREATIVITY/MENTAL ILLNESS RELATIONSHIP

Since I wrote that paper on the beliefs of students, I have been convinced that, in some instances, there can be a relationship between creativity and mental illness, although I would not expect there to always be such a link. Perhaps it exists in certain limited instances, such as among highly talented people who also have hypomania, an early and only moderate kind of manic depression. In the hypomanic state the person would have a rush of energy that might allow him or her to think of many things, including some unusual things that do not seem to fit. However, the energy could allow the individual to work on putting ideas together, and he or she could come up with creative ideas and creative work (Richards, 1990; Richards & Kinney, 1990).

If the hypomania advanced to full-blown mania, I would be more skeptical that the manic person could be productive, although he or she would have many unusual thoughts. It may be, however, that some full-blown manic depressives (technically, bipolar disorder) can be creative even in the throes of their mania.

Depression would definitely seem to mitigate against creativity. Have you ever seen depressed people or been very depressed yourself? Depression does not seem conducive to doing much of anything except sitting around and feeling sorry for oneself. Hershman and Lieb (1988) believed that depression could also foster creativity. They argued that most creativity springs from manic depression, which is a rather radical idea. Further, they suggested that the manic state could be conducive to creative production, and that the depressive state may allow for a critical sorting out of what works and what does not. Thus, in their view, the depressive part of the manic depression can aid in creativity by putting a critical eye on the ideas produced during the manic stage. Of course, this is speculation on their part. They do not defend their position with scientific research, but instead point to case histories that they say support their viewpoint. Case histories have their place (Eisenman, 1993b, Wallace, 1989). However, it is almost impossible to get a case history published in American Psychological Association journals, which want only scientific studies or theory based on such studies. Unfortunately, case histories can be used to prove anything one wants, hence their bad reputation in this scientifically oriented age. This is what Hershman and Lieb (1988) may have done in saying that case histories show that both mania and depression foster creativity. They may have selected case histories that fit their belief, or selectively viewed the case histories to find evidence supporting their position. Still, they may be partially correct. It is possible that, in some instances, people have been creative in part because of mania or depression.

In addition, the art of the mentally ill often shows creativity (Gedo, 1990b; Prinzhorn, 1984), and this may be a kind of creativity that most people can never attain. Also, as the person is recovering from chronic psychosis, or at least is stabilized and not in an acute psychosis, their art work may show creativity (Gedo, 1990b). This would be more likely for painting and less likely for a field that demands a great deal of coherence, such as writing. In the beginning of the acute phase of psychosis, the person may be so disorganized that little creativity is possible, although this may be countered by the fact that his or her mind would be most open, receiving all kinds of bizarre impressions. If these impressions can be expressed in any form, this expression might well be a highly original, creative one, effectively utilizing fantasy and risk taking that most people would avoid (Davis, 1992; Eisenman 1969a, 1982, 1987a).

One could argue that the unusual communications of psychotic people is always creative, only others cannot usually understand it. On the few occasions when one does understand the bizarre psychotic communications, it is apparent that all kinds of symbolization is being employed, such as a lamp representing evil, the sun standing for good, words used to mean different things than they normally mean, and so on.

On the other hand, creativity often involves high-level thinking, which seems like it would be impeded by any kind of mental disturbance. In fact, much of creativity seems to involve superior thinking, not distorted thinking (Boden, 1990; Runco, 1991). In my study of prisoners, the most creative were the conduct disorders, not the psychotics (Eisenman, 1992). In a study of the effects of mental illness and physical illness on creativity, both had negative, not positive effects (Eisenman, 1990). From my work with schizophrenics, I found that they prefer simple polygons, like noncreative people do (Eisenman, 1991a), so it was surprising that Livesay (1984) predicted that schizophrenics would be higher in cognitive complexity than people without thought disorder. It was not surprising that he found that his schizophrenics were significantly less cognitively complex than the nonschizophrenics. *Mental illness* is a vague concept, usually referring to the most serious of the mental disorders: schizophrenia, bipolar disorder (manic depression), or psychotic depression. Other mental disorders, such as obsessive-compulsive disorder or anxiety disorder, are probably sometimes considered to be a mental illness, but usually are not. They, too, however, would seem to have a harmful effect on the clear, original thinking that is demanded for creativity.

REGRESSION IN THE SERVICE OF THE EGO: A PSYCHOANALYTIC PERSPECTIVE

A concept that might help tie together some of the conflicting findings regarding creativity and mental illness is that of regression in the service of the ego (Kris, 1952). Writing from a psychoanalytic perspective, Kris said that creative work may occur when the person regresses, but in the service of the ego, not the id. Regression in the service of the id (defined as the instinctual drives, such as sex and aggression) would be a totally irrational process and akin to psychosis or psychotic-like behavior. Any kind of regression has something in common with the nonnormal nature of psychosis, but if the regression were truly in the service of the ego, it would be a regression in which there was both some loss of control and some subsequent control. Thus, insights gained during the regression, which here would likely refer to wild, primary process thinking (as opposed to the normal, everyday, rational, secondary process thinking), could be utilized during the more rational postregression stage. Or perhaps, even during regression, if it were in the service of the ego, the person could utilize the irrational thinking in some useful fashion and come up with a more creative outlook or invent an original and useful product (Dudek & Verrault, 1989; Kris, 1952; Rothenberg, 1990; Simonton, 1990).

PROBLEMS WITH PSYCHOANALYTIC THEORY

Psychoanalytic language is very abstract, which is one of my objections to this theory. There really is nothing that is the id or the ego, or even the superego, nor are there any concrete things that could be designated a primary or secondary process. All these things are abstractions, and if they help in understanding things better then they are useful. But psychoanalysis often misleads because one thinks we understand things when using their abstract terms, when it might be better to study the overt behavior of humans, their brain functioning, and other things that are more objective. Some people follow Freud and psychoanalysis with great enthusiasm, utilizing the terms and thinking of everything in those terms. At times the psychoanalytic insights are good; however, they often need to be translated into more operational terms if they are to have scientific usefulness.

These criticisms seem particularly true for psychoanalysis and its highly abstract language system, but they can be made for all fields, which tend to have their own parochial way of looking at things. For example, behaviorism has been just as dogmatic as psychoanalysis, although the value of behaviorism is that in attempting to tie things down to observable behavior, it allows for a more objective, scientific understanding, in which hypotheses can be tested and supported or rejected. Theories can be assessed via scientific investigations involving the collection of data and these theories can then be supported or falsified (Bernard, 1990; Kuhn, 1970; Popper, 1968). Imagine trying to falsify the id, or the psychoanalytic concept of the mind as composed of the id, ego, and superego, with the id and the superego as warriors fighting each other, and the ego as a conscious executive mediator. These concepts are so abstract it would be almost impossible to operationalize them for testing, and if one did succeed in operationalizing them, psychoanalysts might say, "That is not what we mean by our concepts."

At least Kris's (1952) conception of regression in the service of the ego is an advance over Freud's idea that creativity is entirely unconscious, based on motives about which the creative person has no clue (Freud, 1916/1964). Freud's view seems to neglect conscious thinking and in-control behaviors. Creative people often know what they are doing and have some high degree of conscious control (as well as being influenced by things they are not aware of). But, both views appeal to concepts difficult to test, unless operationalized in a way that most psychoanalysts would say destroys their integrity. Yet ironically, these same psychoanalysts will often insist that psychoanalysis is a science. It is certainly not a science in the sense of what most who do research think a science is: testing hypotheses, testing theories, operationalizing concepts, supporting or falsifying theories, and so on. At best, psychoanalysis, if a science at all, is a science in its most primitive stage, has remained so for many years, and most of its practitioners show little or no desire to advance beyond the abstract concepts that rule it. This is not to say that psychoanalysis cannot have interesting ideas or useful insights for psychotherapy. It is to say that it remains mired in itself and will make limited contributions to advancing knowledge about creativity or anything else because it will always be limited by its metaphors and terminology (Eisenman, 1987b). Again, this is true in general of any theory or school, but seems particularly a problem for psychoanalysis.

This is not to say that psychoanalysis is entirely incapable of contributing to an understanding of creativity. There *have* been some interesting psychoanalytic writings about creativity (Arieti, 1976; Gedo, 1990a, 1990b, 1991; Millett, 1991; Rosner & Abt, 1974; Rothenberg, 1979, 1990). One of the most interesting is Gedo's (1990a) report on his psychoanalysis of creative people. He found that for some clients, psychological conflicts hamper creativity, for some creativity helps bolster their self-esteem and prevent a dangerous collapse, whereas for others their creativity drives them into psychological illness. Thus, the creativity/mental illness relationship can have many different bases.

While trying to defend psychoanalysis, Kernberg (1993) admitted that the number of people wanting to become psychoanalysts has declined, and that psychoanalytic research has made limited contributions. This may be due, at least in part, to what one psychoanalyst called the resistance of the field to new ideas (Gillette, 1992). Two obvious facets of current-day thinking, which may be resisted by those clinging to Freud's intrapsychic approach, are (a) the great strides made in understanding humans as biological entities, and (b) the emphasis on social factors, in addition to personality. Failure to see individuals as biological and social beings and overemphasizing personality (or failing to see how it interacts with these other facets) leads to a limited approach. In fact, failing to see social and biological bases can lead to blaming the victim, instead of seeing how complex causation really is.

Psychoanalysis is really at least three things: a theory, which is what I have been discussing; a kind of psychotherapy; and a method of investigation, such as using free association to uncover what the subject thinks. This use of psychoanalysis as a method—free association or interpretation of dreams, to take two examples—could be an important contribution to creativity research. Psychoanalysts, following Freud, typically do not gather quantifiable data to test ideas about their theory. But, someone could avoid psychoanalytic concepts and simply use some of the methods as an aid in understanding. Psychoanalytic methods have a great deal of utility for research, but they have been underutilized. Incidentally, for stinging critiques of psychoanalysis, far more negative than my position, see Eysenck (1992) and Masson (1984, 1990).

MENTAL ILLNESS AND CREATIVITY

In the beginning of this chapter, I suggested that (a) hypomania rather than the full-blown manic-depressive disorder may be most associated with creativity, and (b) that already talented people may be the most likely to increase their creativity via hypomania. Richards and Kinney (1990) found support for the first of these propositions in that the milder mood swings were tied more closely to the enhancement of creativity than more extreme mood swings. However, for the second proposition they found that mild mood swings can enhance the creativity not only of eminent people but for what they call everyday creativity (Cropley, 1990; Richards, 1990; Richards & Kinney, 1990; Richards, Kinney, Benet, & Merzel, 1988; Richards, Kinney, Lunde, Benet, & Merzel, 1988). Thus, Richards and Kinney (1990) extended the findings of Andreasen (1987) with unipolar depressed writers and of Jamison (1989) with British artists and writers. Both Andreasen and Jamison showed the importance of mood alteration for enhancing creativity, even when the alteration would be considered a mood disorder (Andreasen & Glick, 1988; Jamison, Gerner, Hammen, & Padesky, 1980). It should be noted that the writers in Andreasen (1987) were not eminent writers, but those in a workshop. Perhaps they were more would-be writers than truly successful writers.

Subclinical "Disorder"

Schuldberg (1990) suggested that instead of thinking of creativity or psychopathology as representing categories in which one either has it or not, it is better to conceptualize both as a continua. Thus, he was able to show that having schizotypal as well as hypomanic traits can enhance creativity. *Schizotypal traits* are those that have much in common with schizophrenia, but are not full-blown schizophrenia. My objection to linking schizophrenia with creativity has been that the true schizophrenic is unable to control thinking or affect, and I do not see how this could be associated with creativity. Schuldberg (1990) suggested that having schizotypal traits might enhance creativity, and thus subclinical as opposed to a complete schizophrenic disorder would relate positively to creativity.

One of the major deficits of schizophrenics is thought disorder, which is often manifested in the loose associations of schizophrenics. One says one word, or they think of an idea, and that brings about a whole train of associations that seem to cause the schizophrenic to now think of something totally different, and they are unable to follow the original idea. This does not seem like it would relate to creativity because the schizophrenic cannot control his or her associative process. Hence, my skepticism about thinking that schizophrenia could be related to creativity. However, Schuldberg suggested that it is the schizophrenic's flight of ideas and not his or her loose associations that facilitate creativity.

A normal person having a flight of ideas (but not overly loose associations like a schizophrenic) could have a greater chance of being creative. Even loose associations could facilitate creativity if the person had some control over them. If the person had both loose associations but also some control, such as the ego strength as discussed by Barron (1953, 1993) and Frank (1967), the person might be able to utilize his or her "pathology" for productive purposes (Flach, 1990; Rothenberg, 1990; Schuldberg, 1990; Strauss, Rakfeldt, Harding, & Lieberman, 1989).

The Brain

It may be that creativity can be facilitated by brain processes that we usually think of in negative terms, including the production of mental illness. The major mental illnesses may be largely brain disorders, as opposed to the environmental/learning effects that psychologists have tended to favor, even in recent times. Even some of the lesser mental disorders, such as obsessive compulsiveness, may be due to genetic or biochemical processes, more so than to learning.

Part of my education on this matter occurred when a friend of mine called me on the telephone. She was in her late 30s and worked only part time as a writer. Although she was one of the most intellectually perceptive, mentally healthy people I knew, from her words over the telephone I could tell that she was now a manic depressive. The day before she seemed normal, but on the phone she had a bipolar disorder, with lots of manic speech patterns, such as rapidly going from one idea to another, with much of it not making much sense. Besides feeling terrible that this had happened to a friend of mine, I thought about what it meant. One day normal, the next day psychotic: This hardly seems like something that was produced by environmental factors, but was more consistent with a biochemical disorder. Bodies send messages to the brain via chemical and electrical impulses. If things get messed up, all kinds of strange things can happen, including, under certain circumstances, what is called psychosis. A similar thing happened to my niece when she developed diabetes, which is clearly not a learned disorder. One day she was fine, but the next day she needed to drink excessive amounts of water and eat large quantities of food. Her body chemistry had changed. Her eating and drinking reflected the physiological needs that were present in her current pathological condition—diabetes.

There is a happy ending, of sorts, regarding my friend. Although she was violent and required brief hospitalization, she is now under control via lithium, which seems to work wonders in helping manic depressives control their illness. She founded a support group for people with depression or manic depression. In addition to spending time on that she continued her writing and also working with her support group to help people who have suffered like she did. Recently, she got an advanced degree and is now working with the mentally ill in her new job. The only negative side, besides having to take lithium for the rest of her life (and the side effects, such as weight gain, which lithium salt induces), is that she seems to have occasional fears or phobias that seem to be carryovers from her disorder. For example, at times she is too terrified to ride on a train. It may be that one does not totally overcome psychosis, but carries some residual effects.

The Resistance of Psychologists

Psychologists are often resistant to thinking that the psychoses may develop much like any other physical illness. This may be in part because this view tends to give greater power to psychiatrists and other medical doctors, whose training involves a greater understanding of physiology and brain pathology than almost all psychologists. Nonpsychologists may also be taken in by the overemphasis on environmental causes of things, such as learning harmful ideas or behaviors. Although many things can be explained environmentally, there may be many other important human behaviors that are better explained (or at least partially explained) in terms of genetics, physiology, the brain, and so forth. Evidence comes from the finding that relatives of obsessive compulsives often have Tourette's syndrome, a genetic disorder (Pauls, Towbin, Leckman, Zahner, & Cohen, 1986). There may be a genetic disorder that results in some family members becoming obsessive compulsive while, for some unknown reasons, others get Tourette's syndrome.

Similarly, for example, whereas most research seems to link manic depression not schizophrenia to creativity, some findings have shown that relatives of schizophrenics are higher in creativity than people who are not related to a schizophrenic (Heston, 1966; Karlsson, 1968, 1978; McNeil, 1971). One way to explain this is to say that (a) schizophrenia is, at least in part, a genetic disorder, and (b) the relatives of the schizophrenics also inherit something unusual, but in their case instead of inducing a full-blown schizophrenic illness, this inherited something enhances creativity.

Suggested Brain, Biochemical, and Genetic Effects

If the brain and biochemistry play an important role in creativity, what is that role? We do not know, but there have been some suggestions. It may be that changes in the body or brain that cause harmful things, such as mental illness, can also produce helpful things that facilitate creativity. Prentky (1979, 1980, 1989) discussed some of these kinds of things in detail, citing everything from research on humans to work with monkeys. The latter kind of research can show how damage to certain parts of the brain affects the ability of the animal, such as bilateral amygdalectomy causing decreased Galvanic Skin Response (GSR) to both pure and novel tones (Bagshwa, Kimble, & Pribam, 1965), or a hippocampelectomy causing animals to act as if they cannot demonstrate internal inhibition (Kimble, 1968). On the human level, much of the work is speculative because one cannot go around damaging the brains of human subjects to map out what brain area relates to what kind of behavior (although research can be ethically done on people who have suffered a particular kind of brain injury).

Hoppe (1988) suggested that the brain functioning that increases emotionality might also increase creativity. Alternatively, brain pathology could enhance creativity if it leads to mental illness, which in turn results in decreased social inhibitions and increased motivation and imagination (Ludwig, 1989). It may be that certain brain processes that facilitate the occurrence of mental illness also facilitate the occurrence of creativity (Miller, 1988), or that the same gene that produces manic depression or other pathology also produces creativity. If that is the case, it might explain the positive relationship between mental illness and creativity, which recent research supports (Rushton, 1990). Also, some things that are explicable at the brain level are also explicable at the environmental level. Consider the concept of arousability. Although much of brain function is related to arousability, arousability can also be induced environmentally, and it is known to have an effect on creativity and probably intelligence as well (Martindale & Greenough, 1973).

The specifics need to be known, which will only be found by more scientific research. Some hints are that affective disorder, especially bipolar disorder, is related to creativity, but schizophrenia is not (Andreasen, 1987; Soueif & Farag, 1971; although, see the studies mentioned earlier about relatives of schizophrenics: Heston, 1966; Karlsson, 1968, 1978; McNeil, 1971), and that creativity is highest when the bipolar disorder is under good control (Andreasen & Glick, 1988). The creativity and mental illness of many eminent people supports the notion of a link between creativity and madness, at least in some instances (Bower, 1989; Hershman & Lieb, 1988; Holden, 1986). Creativity is, by definition, deviant (Eisenman, 1991a). Perhaps whatever produces the creative deviance also produces, in some instances, mental illness or disorder.

THE CONCEPT OF DEVIANCE

A major advance in understanding many things—including creativity or mental illness—would occur if the concept of deviance is used. As I point out in my deviance book (Eisenman, 1991a), *deviance* is a concept used by some sociologists and almost no psychologists. Psychologists talk about specific things, such as schizophrenia or drug abuse, but seldom bring a deviance perspective to bear on it. On the other hand, sociologists have somewhat of an advantage in that they use the concept of deviance to explain things in a nonobvious fashion. But sociologists almost always use deviance to indicate that something is bad, such as crime, in which most of the deviance research occurs. Deviance can be good as in creativity, independence of judgment, the person in the lynch mob who says "This is wrong," and so on.

For creativity, mental illness, and other concepts, deviance is a useful concept because it focuses on how the person came to be defined as deviant. Deviance is often based on social definition. Jan is defined as a drug abuser and so treated by society and may go to prison, be forced into psychotherapy, kicked out of the apartment by an angry manager, and receive other indignities, whereas Kelly who does the same things with regard to drugs is not so defined and does not suffer the horrible consequences that befall Jan. Kelly's self-esteem is thus higher than Jan's, given what Jan has to go through.

One approach to deviance, the social labeling school, holds that deviance is nothing more than the successful application of the deviance label. Like many theories, this contains some wisdom, but goes too far. The mentally ill are typically disturbed, not simply because someone labels them as mentally ill. Prisoners are usually antisocial people with no remorse for the horrible things they do (Eisenman, 1991a, 1991b,

1993a), again not simply because they have been labeled as criminals. However, the labeling can make things worse, and thus the social labeling approach has some utility. Especially in emotional areas such as with sex or drugs, a person's deviance may be little more than the social label attached to something he or she did that many others, perhaps most, also do (Eisenman, 1991a, 1994).

To be creative is, by definition, to be deviant, with deviance defined as meaning *different*. Creative people will often engage in behavior that others disapprove of. Their creative behavior is already disapproved of by many members of conventional society, and it is easy for creative people, given their disregard for social convention and their risk-taking proclivities, to engage in other conduct that society condemns. This is how I view my research findings in which creativity and illicit drug usage are positively correlated (Eisenman, 1991a; Eisenman, Grossman, & Goldstein, 1980; Grossman, Goldstein, & Eisenman, 1974; Victor, Grossman, & Eisenman, 1973).

An interesting alternative interpretation was provided by Martindale (1989). Although he did not use the concept of deviance, he saw drug usage, including alcohol, as part of the creative process, in that psychopathology and creativity often go hand in hand. My findings are correlational and thus do not show that drug usage causes creativity. But Martindale (1989) seemed to be saying that drug usage can be part of psychopathology, which may be part of the same process as creativity. Although he never came right out and said it, it appears to me that Martindale was suggesting that drug usage may be part of the cause of creative behavior. If Martindale is correct, there are at least two ways in which drugs could cause or facilitate creativity. Drugs could disinhibit ("loosen up") people so that they become less rigid and thus have unusual or low probability associations and thoughts, which should facilitate creativity. Or drugs could be part of a general psychopathology, which is linked to creativity. In this light, drugs would be part of the basis of creativity, although more indirectly than in the disinhibition explanation. Whether cause or correlation, drug usage has been found to be related to creativity, and if our national War on Drugs policy is continued, with its attendant criminal prosecution as well as propaganda against all drug users, some of the most creative people will continue to be locked up and persecuted (Eisenman, 1994).

CONCLUSIONS

There does seem to be a link between creativity and mental illness, but it is most apparent in the case of hypomania, which is sometimes associated with increased creativity. It may be the case that those who profit from hypomania are those already predisposed—by personality, training, or something else—toward being creative. Psychoanalysis has provided some interesting ideas about creativity, especially the concept of regression in the service of the ego. However, psychoanalysis is flawed as an objective science, and its contributions are limited. For understanding such things as psychosis, it is very important to look at the brain and to take into account genetics and biochemistry. Many psychologists are resistant to this kind of approach because their background has probably emphasized learning rather than genetics or biochemistry. Further, admitting the importance of these topics tends to give more power to medical doctors, who are sometimes the enemy of psychologists, as in fights over who can do psychotherapy. But as my experience with my friend indicated, it makes more sense to compare her manic depressiveness to a real medical illness (e.g., diabetes) than to say that she learned to act in this strange, psychotic fashion. The concept of deviance is extremely important, although it has been mostly ignored by psychologists and misused by sociologists, who usually limit it to negative deviance. Yet both creativity and mental illness are deviant, and a theory that deals with such differences can help in better understanding what is happening. To take only one example, it may be that the things that produce psychosis also produce other differences in the person, which thereby facilitates creativity.

REFERENCES

Andreasen, N.C. (1987). Creativity and mental illness: Prevalence rates in writers and their first-degree relatives. *American Journal of Psychiatry, 144*, 1288-1292.

Andreasen, N.C., & Glick, I.D. (1988). Bipolar affective disorder and creativity: Implications and clinical management. *Comprehensive Psychiatry, 29*, 207-217.

Arieti, S. (1976). *Creativity, the magic synthesis.* New York: Basic Books.

Bagshaw, M.H., Kimble, D.P., & Pribram, K.H. (1965). The GSR of monkeys during orienting and habituation and after ablation of the amygdala, hippocampus and infero-temporal cortex. *Neuropsychologia, 3*, 111-119.

Barron, F. (1953). An ego-strength scale which predicts response to psychotherapy. *Journal of Consulting Psychology, 5*, 327-333.

Barron, F. (1995). *No rootless flower: An ecology of creativity.* Cresskill, NJ: Hampton Press.

Bernard, T.J. (1990). Twenty years of testing theories: What have we learned and why? *Journal of Research in Crime and Delinquency, 27*, 325-347.

Boden, M.A. (1990). *The creative mind: Myths and mechanisms*. New York: Basic Books.

Bower, H. (1989). Beethoven's creative illness. *Australian and New Zealand Journal of Psychiatry, 23*, 111-116.

Carson, R.C., & Butcher, J.N. (1992). *Abnormal psychology and modern life* (9th ed.). New York: HarperCollins.

Cropley, A.J. (1990). Creativity and mental health in everyday life. *Creativity Research Journal, 3*, 167-178.

Davis, G.A. (1992). *Creativity is forever* (3rd ed.). Dubuque, IA: Kendall/Hunt.

Dudek, S.Z., & Verrault, R. (1989). The creative thinking and ego functioning of children. *Creativity Research Journal, 2*, 64-86.

Eisenman, R. (1969a). Components of creativity, verbal conditioning, and risk taking. *Perceptual and Motor Skills, 39*, 687-700.

Eisenman, R. (1969b). Creativity and mental illness: A prevalent stereotype. *Perceptual and Motor Skills, 29*, 34.

Eisenman, R. (1982). Sexual behavior as related to sex fantasies and experimental manipulation of authoritarianism and creativity. *Journal of Personality and Social Psychology, 43*, 853-860.

Eisenman, R. (1987a). Creativity, birth order, and risk taking. *Bulletin of the Psychonomic Society, 25*, 87-88.

Eisenman, R. (1987b). Sexual acting out: Diagnostic category or moral judgment? *Bulletin of the Psychonomic Society, 25*, 198-200.

Eisenman, R. (1990). Creativity, preference for complexity, and physical and mental illness. *Creativity Research Journal, 3*, 231-236.

Eisenman, R. (1991a). *From crime to creativity: Psychological and social factors in deviance*. Dubuque, IA: Kendall/Hunt.

Eisenman, R. (1991b). Monitoring and postconfinement treatment of sex offenders: An urgent need. *Psychological Reports, 69*, 1089-1090.

Eisenman, R. (1992). Creativity in prisoners: Conduct disorders and psychotics. *Creativity Research Journal, 5*, 175-181.

Eisenman, R. (1993a). Characteristics of adolescent felons in a prison treatment program. *Adolescence, 28*, 695-699

Eisenman, R. (1993b). Living with a psychopathic personality: Case history of a successful anti-social personality. *Acta Paedopsychiatrica, 55*, 241-243.

Eisenman, R. (1994). Creativity and impulsivity: The deviance perspective. In R. Eisenman, *Contemporary social issues: Drugs, crime, creativity, and education* (pp. 53-66). Ashland, OH: Book Masters.

Eisenman, R., Grossman, J.C., & Goldstein, R. (1980). Undergraduate marijuana use as related to internal sensation novelty seeking and openness to experience. *Journal of Clinical Psychology, 36*, 1013-1019.

Eysenck, H.J. (1992). *The decline and fall of the Freudian empire*. Washington, DC: Scott-Townsend.

Flach, F. (1990). Disorders of the pathways involved in the creative process. *Creativity Research Journal, 3*, 158-165.

Frank, G.H. (1967). A review of research with measures of ego strength derived from the MMPI and the Rorschach. *Journal of General Psychology, 77,* 183-206.

Freud, S. (1964). *Leonardo da Vinci and a memory of his childhood.* New York: Norton. (Original work published 1916).

Gedo, J.E. (1990a). More on creativity and its vicissitudes. In M.A. Runco & R.S. Albert (Eds.), *Theories of creativity* (pp. 35-45). Newbury Park, CA: Sage.

Gedo, J.E. (1990b). More on the healing power of art: The case of John Ensor. *Creativity Research Journal, 3,* 33-57.

Gedo, J.E. (1991). *The biology of clinical encounters: Psychoanalysis as a science of the mind.* Hillsdale, NJ: Analytic Press.

Gillette, E. (1992). Psychoanalysts' resistance to new ideas. *Journal of the American Psychoanalytic Association, 40,* 1232-1235.

Grinder, R.E. (1985). The gifted in our midst: By their divine deeds, neurosis, and mental test scores we have known them. In F.D. Horowitz & M. O'Brien (Eds), *The gifted and talented: Developmental perspectives* (pp. 5-35). Washington, DC: American Psychological Association.

Grossman, J.C., Goldstein, J., & Eisenman, R. (1974). Openness to experience and marijuana use in college students. *Psychiatric Quarterly, 48,* 86-92.

Hershman, D.J., & Lieb, J. (1988). *The key to genius: Manic-depression and the creative life.* Buffalo, NY: Prometheus Books.

Heston, L.L. (1966). Psychiatric disorders in foster home reared children of schizophrenic mothers. *British Journal of Psychiatry, 112,* 819-825.

Holden, C. (1986). Manic depression and creativity. *Science, 233,* 725.

Hoppe, K.D. (1988). Hemispheric specialization and creativity. *Psychiatric Clinics of North America, 11,* 303-315.

Jamison, K.R., (1989). Mood disorders and patterns of creativity in British writers and artists. *Psychiatry, 52,* 125-134.

Jamison, K.R., Gerner, R., Hammen, C., & Padesky, C. (1980). Clouds and silver linings: Positive experiences associated with primary affective disorders. *American Journal of Psychiatry, 137,* 198-202.

Karlsson, J.L. (1968). Genealogical studies of schizophrenia. In D. Rosenthal & S.S. Kety (Eds.), *The transmission of schizophrenia* (pp. 85-94). Oxford, England: Pergamon.

Karlsson, J.L. (1978). *Inheritance of creative intelligence: A study of genetics in relation to giftedness and its implications for future generations.* Chicago: Nelson-Hall.

Kernberg, O.F. (1993). The current status of psychoanalysis. *Journal of the American Psychoanalytic Association, 41,* 45-62.

Kimble, D.P. (1968). The hippocampus and internal inhibition. *Psychological Bulletin, 70,* 285-295.

Kris, E. (1952). *Psychoanalytic explorations in art.* New York: International Universities Press.

Kuhn, T. (1970). *The structure of scientific revolutions.* Chicago: University of Chicago Press.

Livesay, J.R. (1984). Cognitive complexity-simplicity and inconsistent interpersonal judgment in thought-disordered schizophrenia. *Psychological Reports, 54*, 759-768.

Ludwig, A.M. (1989). Reflections on creativity and madness. *American Journal of Psychotherapy, 43*, 4-14.

Martindale, C. (1989). Personality, situation, and creativity. In J.A. Glover, R.R. Ronning, & C.R. Reynolds (Eds.), *Handbook of creativity* (pp. 211-232). New York: Plenum.

Martindale, C., & Greenough, J. (1973). The differential effect of increased arousal on creative and intellectual performance. *Journal of Genetic Psychology, 123*, 329-335.

Masson, J.M. (1984). *The assault on truth: Freud's suppression of the seduction theory.* New York: Farrar, Straus, & Giroux.

Masson, J.M. (1990). *Final analysis: The making and unmaking of a psychoanalyst.* Reading, MA: Addison-Wesley.

McNeil, T.F. (1971). Prebirth and postbirth influences on the relationship between creative ability and recorded mental illness. *Journal of Personality, 39*, 391-406.

Miller, L. (1988). Ego autonomy, creativity, and cognitive style: A neuropsychodynamic approach. *Psychiatric Clinics of North America, 11*, 383-397.

Millett, K. (1991). *The loony-bin trip.* New York: Touchstone (Simon & Schuster).

Mindell, J.A. (1993). *Issues in clinical psychology.* Dubuque, IA: William C. Brown & Benchmark.

Pauls, D.L., Towbin, K.E., Leckman, J.F., Zahner, G.E.P., & Cohen, D.J. (1986). Gilles de la Tourette's syndrome and obsessive-compulsive disorder: Evidence supporting a genetic relationship. *Archives of General Psychiatry, 43*, 1180-1182.

Popper, K. (1968). *The logic of scientific discovery.* New York: Harper & Row.

Prentky, R.A. (1979). Creativity and psychopathology: A neurocognitive perspective. In B.A. Maher (Ed.), *Progress in experimental personality research* (Vol. 9, pp. 1-39). New York: Academic Press.

Prentky, R.A. (1980). *Creativity and psychopathology: A neurocognitive perspective.* New York: Praeger.

Prentky, R.A. (1989). Creativity and psychopathology: Gamboling at the seat of madness. In J.A. Glover, R.R. Ronning, & C.R. Reynolds (Eds.), *Handbook of creativity* (pp. 243-269). New York: Plenum.

Prinzhorn, H. (1984). *Selected work.* Urbana-Champaign: University of Illinois.

Richards, R. (1990). Everyday creativity, eminent creativity, and health: "Afterview" for CRJ issues on creativity and health. *Creativity Research Journal, 3*, 300-326.

Richards, R., & Kinney, D.K. (1990). Mood swings and creativity. *Creativity Research Journal, 3*, 203-218.

Richards, R., Kinney, D.K., Benet, M., & Merzel, A.P.C. (1988). Assessing everyday creativity: Characteristics of The Lifetime Creativity

Scales and validation with three large samples. *Journal of Personality and Social Psychology, 54*, 476-485.

Richards, R., Kinney, D.K., Lunde, I., Benet, M., & Merzel, A.P.C. (1988). Creativity in manic-depressives, cyclothymes, and their normal relatives, and control subjects. *Journal of Abnormal Psychology, 97*, 281-288.

Rosner, S., & Abt, L.E. (1974). *Essays in creativity.* Croton on Hudson, NY: North River Press.

Rothenberg, A. (1979). *The emerging goddess: The creative process in art, science, and other fields.* Chicago: University of Chicago Press.

Rothenberg, A. (1990). Creativity, mental health, and alcoholism. *Creativity Research Journal, 3*, 179-201.

Runco, M.A. (Ed.), (1991). *Divergent thinking.* Norwood, NJ: Ablex.

Rushton, J.P. (1990). Creativity, intelligence, and psychoticism. *Personality and Individual Differences, 11*, 1291-1298.

Schuldberg, D. (1990). Schizotypal and hypomanic traits, creativity, and physical health. *Creativity Research Journal, 3*, 218-230.

Simonton, D.K. (1990). Political psychology and societal creativity. *Creativity Research Journal, 3*, 85-99.

Soueif, M.I., & Farag, S.E. (1971). Creative thinking aptitude in schizophrenia: A factorial study. *Sciences de l'Art, 8*, 51-60.

Strauss, J.S., Rakfeldt, J., Harding, C.M., & Lieberman, P. (1989). Psychological and social aspects of negative symptoms. *British Journal of Psychiatry, 155*(Suppl. 7), 128-132.

Terman, L.M., & Oden, M.H. (1959). *The gifted group at mid-life* (Vol. 5), *Genetic studies of genius.* Stanford, CA: Stanford University Press.

Victor, H.R., Grossman, J.C., & Eisenman, R. (1973).Openness to experience and marijuana use in high school students. *Journal of Consulting and Clinical Psychology, 41*, 78-85.

Wallace, D.B. (1985). Giftedness and the construction of a creative life. In F.D. Horowitz & M. O'Brien (Eds), *The gifted and talented: Developmental perspectives* (pp. 361-385). Washington, DC: American Psychological Association.

Wallace, D.B. (1989). Studying the individual: The case study method and other genres. *Archives de Psychologie, 57*, 69-90.

Zigler, E., & Farber, E.A. (1985). Commonalities between the intellectual extremes: Giftedness and mental retardation. In F.D. Horowitz & M. O'Brien (Eds), *The gifted and talented: Developmental perspectives* (pp. 387-408). Washington, DC: American Psychological Association.

Author Index

Subject Index